SAINT PHILIP NERI

SAINT PHILIP NERI

HIS WORK *and* HIS LEGACY

EDOARDO ALDO CERRATO, C.O.

Translated from the Italian by Clareece G. Godt

CLUNY
Providence, Rhode Island

Cluny Media edition, 2021

Saint Philip Neri: His Work and His Legacy was originally published in Italian by Cooperativa Sociale Il Giovane Artigiano, in March 2002.

For more information regarding this title
or any other Cluny Media publication,
please write to info@clunymedia.com, or to
Cluny Media, P.O. Box 1664, Providence, RI 02901

VISIT US ONLINE AT WWW.CLUNYMEDIA.COM

ISBN: 978-1952826658

NIHIL OBSTAT: GEORGIUS D. SMITH, S.TH.D., PH.D., *censor deputatus*

IMPRIMATUR: JOHANNES BAPTISTA GALLO, C.O.,
Congregationis Oratorii Bugellen, Vicarius
DATUM BUGELLAE, DIE XXX M. JANUARII A. D. 2002,
IN FESTO B. SEBASTIANI VALFRÈ

Cover design by Clarke & Clarke
Cover image: Carlo Dolci, *Saint Philip Neri*,
1645 or 1646, oil on canvas
Courtesy of Wikimedia Commons

CONTENTS

To my Mother and to my Father,
daughter and son of the land of Piedmont
which gave to the Oratory the Blesseds
Giovenale Ancina and Sebastiano Valfré

TRANSLATOR'S ACKNOWLEDGMENTS

by Clareece G. Godt

I would like first of all to thank the author Father, now Bishop, Edoardo Aldo Cerrato, C.O., for having encouraged me to prepare this translation, and to Alberto Bianco, who both patiently reviewed my questions as I began this work. It would never have been finished without the kind help and encouragement of the Pittsburgh Oratorians, particularly Fr. David Abernethy, C.O., Provost of the Oratory of Pittsburgh, Fr. Drew Morgan, C.O., and Fr. Joshua Kibler, C.O., who have answered many questions regarding style and content. I owe a debt of gratitude to Donna Marie Lewis of the National Institute for Newman Studies for her unfailing help in finding papal documents and homilies and talks given at various Oratorian Congresses on the Internet, as well as several writings of Newman, and also to Giulia Marotta, research coordinator at the Institute, who assisted me many times and was generous with her time. Giulia Petrucci has been very generous in helping with numerous translation problems, and similarly Sr. Dolores Dean, O.S.B., for help in editing a number of passages, particularly in Chapter V. Finally, my thanks go to Professor Francesca Savoia of the Department of French and Italian at the University of Pittsburgh for her kind help with names, and to Monika Losagio, Administrator of the Department, for her help in making copies on the department printer. To all of these, I express my deep gratitude.

NOTE TO THE READER

by Edoardo Aldo Cerrato, C.O.

Biographies of St. Philip Neri and significant studies of him and of his work have been plentiful in recent years. The monumental work of Fr. Antonio Cistellini, published in three volumes in 1989, suffices alone to say that this argument has been treated with admirable fullness. And in addition, there have been many other works of a more popularizing nature, but still serious and valuable, for example Hans Tercic's essay which was translated into Italian in the Jubilee Year 2000.

Why, then, this publication?

The occasion is the anniversary of an event significant for the Oratory and therefore in the life of the Church, if the presence of the Oratory, as history suggests, has not been in vain.

Sixty years ago, in April 1942, the new text of the Constitutions and the General Statutes was issued. This resulted from a very long and laborious revision of the Constitutions approved by Paul V in 1612, which had sustained the life of the Congregations that had arisen over the centuries, formed in imitation of the Congregation in Rome. The same General Congress also issued a document entitled *Institutum Oratorii San Philippi Neri*, which established that while the individual communities remained autonomous, the Congregations would be linked by an organic bond of communion.

It is worth recalling on the occasion of this anniversary at least the principal stages of this long and complex history, tied to the work of men who really believed in and worked hard for its realization. Chapter IV presents the documents that serve as the authentic sources for this history. Our intention has been not to offer anything new, but to uncover the nature of the Oratory from the authentic sources, which have been critically evaluated by authors of proven competence. We have also wished to gather into one volume all the bibliographical information that has been found in numerous different publications, and sometimes not previously published.

These pages, therefore, do not presume to be original, being rather the fruit of studies of works punctually cited; nor certainly do they mean to place themselves alongside publications or works circulated pro-manuscripto that present as relevant and prophetic St. Philip Neri and his work.

By examining our history, we have looked for the testimony of our roots, while sharing fully in Victor Hugo's conviction: "Look at an oak tree in the spring: ancient trunk, old roots, old branches: green leaves, fresh and new. The tradition is the newness: the tradition produces the newness, the new is the spring of the tradition."

"Now, dear Father, because the years weigh upon our shoulders and our labors have wearied us, let us think to the perpetuity of our work and to leaving offshoots, so that if we have men we will have all the rest; the mercy of God in the midst of men has done everything that we enjoy today, and we should not fear that people will not succeed as we would like."

(F. M. Tarugi to Fr. Philip, December 28, 1584, in Archives of the Congregation in Naples, 31, 425–27)

CHAPTER 1

Philip Neri: The Roots

WE SCRUTINIZE HIS AMIABLE FACE: PHILIP NERI,

- Florentine and secular priest of the Diocese of Rome;
- Heart overflowing with the Holy Spirit received in the Catacombs of the martyrs and Christians of the earliest age;
- Praying, not through dutiful fidelity and practices, but by a necessity of love that poured forth from every fiber of his being;
- An apostle as simple and humble as he was incomparably effective in this Rome, of which he would say: "whoever does good for Rome, does good for the whole world."

PHILIP NERI,

- Inspired with the inspiration that the Holy Spirit gives to those who give their lives over to Him, an offering that is total and full of trusting abandonment;
- Pervaded with an amiability that is not only the effect of a felicitous human temperament, but charity derived from the encounter with God;
- Joyous with a joy that "is the gift of God welling up from a good conscience, assisted by the disdain for worldly goods, united to the contemplation of celestial things."

PHILIP NERI,

- Layman for thirty-six years and priest for the remaining forty-four of his life, but always "*Christifidelis*," impassioned disciple of that Master of whom Philip would say: "Whoever wants something other than Christ, knows not what he wants; whoever asks for something other than Christ, knows not what he asks; whoever works and not for Christ, knows not what he does" (Cardinal Eduardo Martinez Somalo, in Santa Maria in Vallicella, October, 6, 2000).

BECAUSE OUR INTENTION IS TO RETRACE, WITH SOME SIMPLE reflections, the "path" that Fr. Philip marked out for us, we dedicate this chapter to Philip Neri, Florentine, priest of Rome, the one who began that movement the fascinating idea of which has arrived intact all the way to the beginning of the Third Millenium. It retains a youthfulness in its proposed way of life that four and a half centuries have diminished not at all.

> The spirituality of the Oratory is the spirituality of St. Philip Neri, transmitted, in its simple, fundamental outlines, to the various Oratorian Congregations across the centuries. Thanks to its ductility, it has been adapted to the changes of time and circumstance, in new expressions and new responses, yet it has always remained faithful to the original inspiration. This adaptability within a tradition comes out of St. Philip's own way of acting. He left behind only a few writings, and no treatise on spirituality. Instead he left to his disciples and followers the unforgettable memory of himself, of his wise sayings, and of his way of acting, which was often emblematic and always extremely suggestive.[1]

It is just this "*unforgettable memory*" of Fr. Philip that we wish to offer in these introductory pages: not in the form of biography—there are many of these, both from earlier times and more recent[2]—but through some "asterisks"[3] which reflect certain "rays" of his luminous life.

Before these, we present a chronological compendium[4] of the life and work of Fr. Philip, which also includes notes on certain figures interwoven with his history, and bibliographical references chosen mostly from the field of "Oratorian" literature.

1. CHRONOLOGICAL COMPENDIUM

1515–1521

On July 21, 1515, Philip Neri was born in Florence, in the Oltrarno, in the quarter of San Piero Gattolini, and was baptized Philip Romolo the following day in "bel San Giovanni"[5] by Giovan Battista di Jacopo.[6]

Florence was preparing to receive the visit of the Florentine Leo X (1513–1521) with a welcome worthy of the splendor of this Renaissance Pontiff.[7] In Spain a much more hidden event, but one rich in incomparable fruits, marked the year 1515: St. Teresa of Jesus was born in Ávila on March 28. She would be canonized in 1622 together with St. Philip, and in 1970 would receive the title of "Doctor of the Church," as a teacher of prayer.

Philip was the second child of messer Francesco Neri (whose father was Philip from Castelfranco di Sopra[8]) and Lucrezia[9] (daughter of Antonio da Mosciano and Lena di Giovanni Soldi). The Neri family, whose coat of arms bore three gold stars in an azure field and who had a noble sepulcher in San Michele Bertelde, had been in Florence for four generations. The first rose to the respectable profession of notary, which Francesco also exercised, but unwillingly, since he was greatly attracted to alchemy.

The first child, Caterina, was born in 1513, married Barnaba Trevi and had Lucrezia (who became Sr. M. Anna, Dominican nun of San Pier Martire) and Dianora (who became Sr. M. Vittoria, Dominican nun of Santa Lucia in Via San Gallo). With both of them Fr. Philip maintained a considerable correspondence.[10] Caterina died in 1567.

The third child, Elisabetta, was born in 1518, married Antonio Cioni and was a witness in Florence, May 11 and 12, 1596, at the canonical proceedings for the cause of Philip, providing important memories[11] of Philip's childhood and adolescence. She died in 1602.

In 1520 Antonio was born, but died soon after.

In 1520–1521 the family, which had moved to Costa San Giorgio, lost their mother. Messer Francesco married Alessandra, daughter of Michele Lensi; Alessandra loved Philip tenderly, and suffered greatly when he left Florence.

1522–1530

In 1523 St. Caterina Ricci,[12] with whom Fr. Philip had a spiritual friendship, was born; in 1530 St. Antonio M. Zaccaria[13] founded the Barnabites who had strong ties with Philip and the first Oratorians. Philip completed his first studies, with a certain master Clement, and attended the Convento di San Marco,[14] where, from the time of St. Antonino and of Savonarola,[15] certain members of the community took care of the religious and spiritual formation of children and youth. The memory of this experience would remain indelible in Philip, and years later he said: "what of good I received at the beginning I received from your Fathers of San Marco in Florence."[16]

1531–1532

Philip left Florence,[17] distressed by the events of those years: the Sack of Rome in 1527, marking the fall from temporal power of the Medici Pope Clement VII (1523–1534), brought the toppling of the power of the Medici in Florence, too. For three years the city tasted again a democratic republic, the second, Savonarolian in spirit. The peace made between Clement VII and the Emperor restored Medici power, which was imposed after an assault of sixteen months, until the city surrendered on August 12, 1530. Ferocious repressions ensued; the famine added anguish upon anguish. It is in this situation that Philip departed for San Germano,[18] later named Cassino, where he was to be the guest of a relative, Romolo, a merchant whose business offered good prospects for a prosperous future.[19]

1533–1534

Paul III Farnese (1534–1549) succeeded Pope Clement VII on the Chair of Peter.

Philip arrived in Rome, dressed as a pilgrim, and found hospitality at the house of Galeotto del Caccia, director of the Central Customs Office at Sant'Eustachio, where he spent about three years as tutor of the children, as compensation for lodging and modest meals.[20]

1535–1537

Pope Paul III, by the felicitous naming of cardinals, the "*Consilium de emendanda Ecclesia*" and the announcement of the Council, brought a breath of sincere renewal into the Church.

Philip attended lectures in philosophy and theology at the Augustinian and at the Sapienza,[21] but towards the end of 1537 he sold his books, offered what he got for them to the young Calabrese Guglielmo Sirleto,[22] who had come to Rome to seek his fortune. Philip then gave himself over to an "eremitical"[23] life, characterized by assiduous ascetic exercises and prayer. At the same time, following in the path of the Compagnia del Divino Amore,[24] he went often to the hospital of San Giacomo degli Incurabili[25]: "Philippo Neri da Santo Ludoico [S. Luigi dei Francesi] fiorentino" appears in the register of the members of the company that supported the hospital. He would always preserve a lively memory of his service in San Giacomo, where he met St. Camillo de Lellis, and to which he often returned with his Oratorians, and sent offerings as well.

St. Ignatius Loyola had arrived in Rome a few months before with the first members of the Society of Jesus, among whom was St. Francis Saverio.[26] Philip and Ignatius met most probably in the terrible winter of famine of 1538–1539, when the first Jesuits gathered the sick and the poor in the house of the Frangipane and took them to the various hospitals. Philip might have heard Ignatius' preaching in Santa Maria di Monserrato. He heard the sermons[27] of Ignatius' companions, Lainez and Salmeron, with pleasure in the "little church of Jesus," Santa Maria della Strada.

1543
The Council of Trent began.[28]

1544
In a mystical experience, the secret of which he guarded most deeply, the twenty-nine-year-old Philip prayed to God that he might "*avere spirito*,"[29] and received an extraordinary effusion of the Holy Spirit which invaded his heart, dilating it and inflaming it with love.[30] Tradition holds that this happened just before Pentecost, and in the catacombs of San Sebastiano, which were the only ones accessible: Philip was accustomed to visiting that place[31] and spent hours there in prayer, apparently sometimes the whole night: "that mysterious and solitary place evoked for him a fascinating and suggestive history: the events in the lives of the first generations of Christians, their heroic profession of faith, the long processions of martyrs, the holy Rome of Peter and Paul, empurpled with Christian blood. This remained alive in him, and a source of inspiration."[32]

1548
In 1547, St. Cajetan (Gaetano da Thiene[33]) died in Naples. He was founder of the Theatines Clerics Regular, in whom Philip took some interest, and who played a notable role in the Catholic Reform.

With Persiano Rosa,[34] one of the "spiritual" priests of San Girolamo della Carità, whom Philip chose as his confessor, Philip began the Forty Hours Devotion at the Confraternity of the Most Holy Trinity,[35] which was itself dedicated to the cult of the Most Holy Eucharist. Philip lent the fire of his preaching to the devotion.[36] The Confraternity had been erected by the Vicar of Rome Filippo Archinto, who had entrusted to them the church of San Salvatore in Campo, and it became the promoter of great charitable works, above all in hospitality to pilgrims and then to the poor who were released from the hospitals with nowhere to go.

1550

St. Camillus de Lellis is born.[37] He later became a penitent of Fr. Philip's and founded the Order of the Ministers of the Sick in 1584. A new pope, Julius III (1550–1555), elected with great difficulty in the longest conclave of the century, brought back with him a worldly atmosphere that seemed to have been left behind. He declared a Holy Year, which brought a great number of pilgrims to Rome, upwards of five hundred of whom Philip and the Company of the Trinity assisted daily.

1551

In March, in obedience to his spiritual director [Persiano Rosa] Philip received minor orders and the subdiaconate in San Tommaso in Parione. The diaconate was conferred upon him on Holy Saturday, March 29, in St. John Lateran, and he was ordained priest[38] in San Tommaso in Parione on May 23 by the viceregent of Rome, Giovanni Lunei, titular bishop of Sebaste. Philip moved to San Girolamo della Carità, "*madre dello spirito*" in the Rome of that time.[39] With old and new friends who chose him as confessor and spiritual father, Philip began, in the intimacy of his room, the meetings that would give rise to the Oratory,[40] including the practice of the Visit to the Seven Churches,[41] pilgrimage of meditation and of penance which he himself did in his years of solitary life.

1555

At the death of Pope Julius III, and after the twenty days of the pontificate of Marcellus II, on May 26, Paul IV Carafa (1555–1559) ascended to the Pontificate, and imposed a climate of terrible rigor.

Francesco Maria Tarugi,[42] Costanzo Tassoni,[43] and Alessandro Fedeli,[44] men who would exercise a fundamental role in the development of the work of St. Philip, entered his circle, as they began to frequent the Oratory.

1556–1557

In 1556 St. Ignatius of Loyola died.

The *Avvisi dalle Indie di Portogallo*,[45] diffused in Rome, inflamed the minds of Philip and of his young disciples, and made them fervently disposed to go as missionaries to the infidels and to give their lives for the sake of preaching the Gospel.[46] Philip, who had either encouraged that enthusiasm or had been just caught up in it, was dissuaded from leaving for India by the Florentine Agostino Ghettini, a monk at Tre Fontane. This event marked a decisive turn in the life of Fr. Philip, and may be considered the beginning of an orderly structuring of the work which kept increasing. In this period Philip encountered the first vexations, in the form of people who suspected Philip of gathering young men around him for questionable purposes. Others who were well-known began to come: Cesare Baronio[47] and Antonio Gallonio[48]; somewhat later, Giovan Battista Bordini [*sic*].[49]

1558

Fr. Persiano Rosa, who had been so close to Philip spiritually and temperamentally, died repeating his usual "*Allegramente, allegramente!*" The meetings moved from the little rooms of the Father to the "place for grain storage of the Confraternity of the Carità," above the nave of the church, reorganized into a place of prayer and reflection;[50] it is the "first Oratory" of St. Philip.

1559

In August Paul IV died, and on December 25, Pius IV Medici (1559–1565), maternal uncle of Charles Borromeo, ascended the pontifical Throne.

In April Philip Neri had been questioned by the Cardinal Vicar Virgilio Rosario,[51] "who prohibited him from being part of a group." But on May 22 the Cardinal died unexpectedly, and that was the end of the suspicions of Philip. Paul IV, better informed, sent Philip two candles from Candlemas as a sign of reconciliation. On October 11 Ser Francesco Neri died in Florence, and a year later, Philip renounced his paternal inheritance in favor of his sister Caterina. His relationship with his family was one of affectionate detachment, the same as he had with Florence.

1562

Philip's first serious illness[52] led him to make a will[53] in favor of Costanzo Tassoni.

1563

The Council of Trent closed on December 4. In Naples St. Francesco Caracciolo was born,[54] founder, together with the Ven. Agostino Adorno, of the Congregation of the Minor Clerks Regular, with whom Fr. Philip had a relationship of reciprocal esteem.

During the Visit to the Seven Churches, Philip met Cardinal Charles Borromeo[55] who from that moment was always devoted to the Father and who always looked to him for counsel for the things of greatest importance. Despite their differences of character and of methods, Philip always prized the Cardinal's holiness, and the Cardinal Philip's.[56]

1564

Pope Pius IV died in December.

In obedience to the explicit summons of the Pope, brought about by pressure from the Florentine community in Rome, Philip assumed the pastoral care of the parish of San Giovanni dei Fiorentini. His first disciples were ordained to the priesthood in this year, and he had them undertake this responsibility. In San Giovanni,[57] community life[58] began with Cesare Baronio, ordained priest on May 27, Alessandro Fedeli and Giovan Francesco Bordini, ordained September 1. By the express will of Fr. Philip, an exception was made and two very promising youths were allowed to live with them, Germanico Fedeli,[59] nephew of Alessandro, and Ottavio Parravicino,[60] of whom Baronio was tutor.

1565

In January Pius V (1566–1572)[61] was elected.

Fr. Philip entrusted Tassoni to Cardinal Charles Borromeo who was leaving for Milan and was asking Philip insistently for priests to help begin the reform of the clergy in the diocese.

1566

Bonsignore Cacciaguerra[62] died in San Girolamo. He was a very singular priest and mystic, who had taught his disciples and penitents to follow the practice of daily communion.

S. Giovanni Angelo Velli[63] and Francesco M. Tarugi entered the community; Velli was ordained to the priesthood in November.

1567–1568

By now a good number of Philip's disciples lived at San Girolamo. Among these was Alessandro Borla,[64] who was there from 1568 on. Above all by Tarugi's initiative, but with Philip's support (Philip still lived at San Girolamo but was the Father of the whole community), Borla began to write the draft of the first rules of the common life.[65] Cardinal Charles Borromeo began to insist that Fr. Philip transfer to Milan together with his followers.

1569

Another wave of suspicion hit Fr. Philip, who was denounced to Pius V concerning the orthodoxy of the sermons at the Oratory, "which were given by simple, uneducated persons." The Pope, "having asked privately to be informed about this…was edified and untroubled."[66] He was also familiar with the sphere of the Oratory through Tarugi, whom he asked to be majordomo of the house of his nephew, Cardinal Michele Bonelli (from Alessandria and sometimes known as Cardinal Alessandria), and through the Dominican house at Santa Maria sopra Minerva that Fr. Philip visited often. He became so familiar with that house that they often entrusted their novices to him, and sometimes he even officiated at their clothing.

Given this climate of suspicion, Philip was thinking of accepting Borromeo's proposal[67] that he should come to Milan. However,

Costanzo Tassoni had returned, and he died in October. Antonio Talpa,[68] who would be ordained priest in 1571, entered the Community; with him came two others from the Marches, one of whom, Camillo Severini,[69] left a sad memory behind him.

1571

In June, Fr. Tarugi left with the legation of Cardinal Bonelli[70] to go to Spain, Portugal, and France to bring the Catholic States together in a League against the Turks. On October 17 the battle of Lepanto was fought, and won primarily through prayer. Cesare Baronio dedicated himself to vigils and penances to such a degree that he became seriously ill. His health was restored by a prodigy of prayer of Fr. Philip who demanded, or rather, "laid claim to" his healing.[71]

Tommaso Bozzi,[72] a disciple of the Father's for many years, and Nicolò Gigli[73] entered the community. Several years before, Francesco Soto de Langa[74] had entered the Community. He was the first soprano of the pontifical Chapel and contributed considerably to establishing the Oratorian musical tradition. During this year Giovanni Animuccia[75] died, he who had played a determining role in the music and the Lauds at the Oratory.[76]

In this period the General Superior of the Jesuits, San Francesco Borgia,[77] asked Fr. Philip to undertake the formation of the young aspirants to their Order; the Father had to refuse because of the lack of available Fathers in the Congregation, but the invitation speaks eloquently about the rapport between the Jesuit house and Fr. Philip's.

1572–1573

On May 1, 1572, Pius V died, and Gregory XIII succeeded him (1572–1585).[78] Cardinal Borromeo renewed his request from Milan, but Fr. Philip, although he had not yet decided entirely to refuse, remained evasive.

1574

S. Giovanni Leonardi[79] founded in Lucca the Clerks Regular of the

Mother of God; he moved to Rome in 1583, and enjoyed reciprocal fraternal relationships with Fr. Philip and the Oratorians.

Thanks to the initiative of the Fathers who lived in San Giovanni, the exercises of the Oratory, which were still held in San Girolamo, now much too small, were moved to the new Oratory constructed near the church of the Florentines.

Fabrizio Mezzabarba[80] and Pompeo Pateri[81] entered the Community.

1575

In Rome the Jubilee was celebrated.[82]

In the spring the Fathers Pateri, Mezzabarba, and Alessandro Fedeli were sent to Milan. On July 15 Pope Gregory XIII with the Bull *Copiosus in misericordia Deus*[83] erected the Congregation of the Oratory,[84] entrusting to it the little parish church of Santa Maria in Vallicella,[85]which had been recently restored, but which Fr. Philip and the Congregation began immediately to reconstruct from the foundations up. On September 27, the Archbishop of Florence Alessandro de Medici (the future Leo XI), an extremely affectionate penitent of Fr. Philip's, blessed the cornerstone of the "Chiesa Nuova."[86] He maintained a continuing relationship with Milan, where in October Fathers Gigli and Perracchione[87] went. Francesco Bozzi[88] was accepted into the Community.

1576

In March Fedeli and Mezzabarba return to Rome. Gigli is called back in June.

1577

On February 3 Msgr. Alessandro de' Medici celebrated the first Mass at the Vallicella. On March 15 the first assembly of the Congregation was held. The book of the Decrees records the details. In May Fr. Philip was elected Provost. In April the Oratory is transferred to the Vallicella, being accommodated provisionally in the stables of Alfonso

Visconti,[89] although it continued to meet also in San Giovanni. Pietro Perracchione and Agostino Manni entered the Congregation.[90]

1578

In August the Pope visited the Vallicella and Fr. Tarugi wrote for the occasion a memorandum on the state of the Congregation, a comprehensive list of its members,[91] subdivided in "*sacerdoti de la Congregazione de l'Oratorio da V. Santità eretta*" [priests of the Congregation of the Oratory by Your Holiness erected] (twenty-three, two of whom were absent), and persons "*in minor gradi*" (clerics, laymen and domestics, not easily identifiable).

Others enter the Congregation, Flaminio Ricci,[92] and the brothers G. Giovenale[93] and G. Matteo[94] Ancina.

1579

Cardinal Charles Borromeo, in Rome for a time, visited the Vallicella[95]; it was his last attempt to have men from Fr. Philip for Milan. The House of San Severino and of Fermo[96] asked to be aggregated to the Roman House.

1580

The first elections were held in the Congregation, in which Fr. Tarugi was elected rector of the House of the Vallicella, while the Provost, Fr. Philip, still resided at San Girolamo. New although brief preoccupations beset the Community, when the Cardinal Vicar Giacomo Savelli began an investigation of the Fathers assigned to give sermons and hear confessions. It concluded with full approval and also with the Fathers being assigned as confessors to those detained by the Holy Office.[97]

1581

A new and worrisome illness struck Fr. Philip, who wrote his second will, witnessed October 2.

1582

The Congregation instituted the Collegio Polacco.[98] A first draft of the Constitutions was completed by Tarugi and Talpa.[99]

1583

Bordini was given the task of drawing up in Latin the text of the Constitutions, which would go under the name of *Compendium*.[100] It was reviewed by Fr. Philip. A *Breviatio* or *Summa* was also prepared.[101] On March 16, in the Massimo house, Philip's prayers obtained the prodigious sign of the resurrection of the young prince Paolo[102] for whom he felt great affection. In June Fr. Tarugi went to Naples to evaluate the possibilities of founding a House there, as requested by representatives of the city. On November 22, Fr. Philip, at the urging of the Pope, left his beloved room in San Girolamo and moved to the Vallicella to live with the Fathers of his Congregation.[103]

1584

St. Charles Borromeo died at the age of 46, consumed by his apostolic labors and by his rigorous life of penance.

In May, Gregory XIII died and was succeeded by Sixtus V (1585–1590).[104]

On January 16, a new and grave illness kept Philip in bed for a long time. In March the House of San Severino is incorporated into that of Rome.[105] A papal bull entrusted to the Congregation the Abbey of San Giovanni in Venere[106] with the demanding obligation of the pastoral care of all of its territory. Fr. Talpa, as procurator, took possession of it.

Alessio Figliucci[107] edited the edition of the *Tre libri dell'educazione christiana de' figliuoli* di Silvio Antoniano.[108]

1586

Fr. Fabrizio Mezzabarba died. A new illness of Fr. Philip's increased the worries of the community, which was now rather small because of the departure of those who left to found the House in Naples.[109] The

Congregation decided to close the Collegio Polacco. Baronio, dedicated as always to his study of ecclesiastical history as Fr. Philip had directed him, published the Martyrology,[110] which he had written at the request of the Pope.

1587

The simple and witty San Felice da Cantalice died,[111] friend of Fr. Philip's and with whom he had shared many a moment of spiritual good humor.

In the elections of the Congregation Fr. Angelo Velli became rector of the Roman House. Fr. Giovan Francesco Bordini departed for Poland as part of a legation with Cardinal Ippolito Aldobrandini. Frederic Borromeo,[112] an intimate of Fr. Philip's,[113] and to whom Fr. Philip would open his heart in confidence, is made Cardinal.

1588

The first volume of Baronio's *Annales Ecclestiastici*[114] was published, fruit of thirty years of work. They would never have been published at all if Cardinal Antonio Caraffa, Librarian of Holy Roman Church had not made Fr. Cesare do it, putting at his disposal the Vatican printing office, which he had founded. For the redaction of the indices Baronio had the assistance of various members of the Congregation; the first volume, published between June and July, was presented to Sixtus V and met with immediate and noteworthy approval. Fr. Ricci recalled that each time a volume came out, Fr. Philip would give Baronio the prize of serving thirty Masses; or, making him sit in lowest place, would order someone to deliver a talk finding Baronio blameworthy in himself, in his place of origin, and in all his works. Baronio accepted humbly the prizes that were given to him.

On October 3 Fr. Philip added a Codicil to his will. The Congregation finished the editing of the new text of the *Constitutions*[115] and sent a copy to Naples.

1589

The work in the basement of the apse of the Chiesa Nuova was finished, and the church was rapidly becoming fully ready for use.

1590

Pope Sixtus V died on August 27, and after the extremely brief pontificate of Urban VII, Gregory XIV (1590–1591) succeeded him. Gregory was devoted to Fr. Philip and had every intention of elevating him with the first group of new cardinals.[116]

On February 11, the bodies of the Holy Martyrs Papia and Maurus were transferred to the Vallicella from the Church of San Adriano at the Roman Forum. It was a moment when Fr. Philip could scarcely contain his sense of blessedness, since he had been enamored from his youth by the witness of the martyrs, and he was devoted to the cult of their relics.[117] At the elections in June Fr. Tommaso Bozzi was elected rector. The Father insisted that his resignation as Confessor to the community be accepted; Alessandro Fedeli, the deacon of the Community, was elected to succeed him. Fr. Pietro Consolini[118] entered the Community, one of the last but among the most beloved of Fr. Philip's disciples, who enjoyed a deep intimacy with him.

1591

In October Gregory XIV died, and was succeeded for a pontificate of two months by Pope Innocent IX.

A new infirmity took its toll on Fr. Philip's body, already weakened by age and problems of health. At the same time a terrible famine united to epidemics mowed down the population of Rome, which within one year lost half of its population of a hundred and twenty thousand people, and some of the Oratorians fell victim as well. The Community of San Severino was almost wiped out; in Rome Fr. Niccolò Gigli died, very delicate son of Fr. Philip, whom the Father loved tenderly.[119] A week later, the young Jesuit St. Luigi Gonzaga[120] died, struck down by the epidemic and worn out by his assistance to the poorest of the sick. During the summer of this year Cardinal

Agostino Valier composed the dialogue "*Philippus, sive de Christiana laetitia*."[121]

1592

St. Joseph Calasanzio,[122] founder of the Scuole Pie, arrived in Rome. He would die like Philip in 1595; Baronio was a defender of his work.

In January Cardinal Aldobrandini, an affectionate disciple of Fr. Philip's, was elected Pope and took the name of Clement VIII (1591–1605). It was said, "Philip has ascended the throne of Peter."

Fr. Philip's friendship for the Pontiff was expressed in the few years he had still to live in affectionate letters[123] and demanding missions, such as the reconciliation with Henry IV of France (1595),[124] an event of incalculable weight, one of the most important chapters in the life of the Church at the end of the sixteenth century. The Pope was strongly influenced by Fr. Philip's decision. Baronio served as Fr. Philip's emissary.

The new Pope knew the worth of Fr. Philip's men, and did not hesitate to grieve him by taking away their most prized for the good of the Church: in February Fr. Giovan Francesco Bordini was elected Bishop of Cavaillon, and in October Fr. Francesco M. Tarugi was elected Archbishop of Avignon. In November Fr. Philip was gravely ill again.

1593–1594

Msgr. Tarugi left for his seat. The governance of the Abbey had become onerous for the Roman Congregation, and was entrusted to the House in Naples. In June Fr. Philip resigned from his position as Provost and proposed Cesare Baronio as his successor; at the regular elections in July, Baronio was elected. A copy of the revised Constitutions, with the addition of the General Decrees, was sent to Naples.[125] There was discussion of a visit to all the Houses, to be carried out by Fr. Pateri in 1594.[126] In October, shortly before he became ill, Fr. Philip was received by the Pope who reiterated his intention to name him Cardinal, "and the Father raised his berretta, and looking up to heaven, said: Paradise, paradise."[127]

1595

In April Fr. Philip was "assailed by a great pain in his heart, together with fever"; he recovered once again, but now he was failing. Following Cesare Baronio's suggestion, the Pope elected Cardinal Federico Borromeo Archbishop of Milan, despite Borromeo's attempts to avoid it, even by appealing to Fr. Philip. Another infirmity led the Father to revise his will on May 13. On May 22, Federigo Borromeo was present and administered the Viaticum to him: "A little after I communicated him," the Cardinal attests,[128] "he said, 'I haven't done any good at all, nothing, nothing...' In those words that I said in communicating him: "Domine non sum dignus...' he replied in a strong voice 'Never, never have I been worthy'; and all of this with a strength of spirit incredible in that frail little dying body." Fabrizio Massimo who was present testified that, having received the Sacraments, the Father said: "Vanitas vanitatum: whoever seeks anything but Christ knows not what he wants; whoever seeks other than Christ, knows not what he asks for."[129] One last prodigious recovery: Fr. Philip was able to celebrate Mass on May 23, and the day after, the Solemnity of Corpus Christi: it was his last Mass, which he celebrated "joyfully, like singing."[130] In the evening he received Cardinal Agostino Cusani and other prelates for confession, and he recited the Divine Office with them. In the night between May 25 and 26, toward three in the morning, he slept sweetly in the Lord, after having blessed his Congregation, and assisted by Fr. Baronio and by the whole Community. Standing by the body of the Father, Cesare Baronio opened his breviary to find the appropriate words and read a verse of Psalm 79 which fell under his eye: "respice de caelo et vide et visita vineam istam et protégé quam plantavit dextera tua."[131] On August 2 the canonical process for canonization was opened. In November Baronio was nominated Apostolic Pronotary and Confessor of the Pope. In December the Congregation decreed that no more Houses were to be aggregated.

1596

The Father's room was transformed into a chapel. On May 25 Fr.

Baronio was elected Provost, but on June 4 he was named Cardinal, along with Msgr. Tarugi who returned to Rome. On June 7 Fr. Angelo Velli was elected Provost.

1597

In April the Congregation decided how the Secular Oratory was to be structured. In September Cardinal Tarugi was transferred to the see of Siena. The Congregations of Fermo, Palermo, and the Congregation of Lanciano dedicated to the Abbey of San Giovanni in Venere are erected by papal bulls. The following year the Community in Brescia of the "Fathers of the Peace" is erected as a Congregation.

1599

The examination of Philip's remains was completed. On the fourth anniversary of his death, Cardinal Alessandro de Medici consecrated the Chiesa Nuova. Fr. Velli was reelected Provost. In September the Congregation of Thonon is erected with a Pontifical Brief that named Francis de Sales as Provost.[132]

1600

On July 6, Cardinal Tarugi placed the first stone for the chapel, built by Nero del Nero, to house the incorrupt remains of Fr. Philip. Gallonio's *Vita Beati Patris Philippi Nerii fiorentiini* is published; the following year it would come out in Italian.

1601

In February the Congregation decreed that the House of San Severino would be suppressed; it passed to the Barnabites.

1602

On May 24 in a tribute of incomparable affection and devotion, the Father's remains were solemnly transferred to the new chapel.[133] Fr. Flaminio Ricci was elected Provost.

1604

Msgr. Giovanni Giovenale Ancina died in Saluzzo. His nomination had been announced as bishop of that diocese in Piedmont in the Consistory of August 26, 1602, and he was consecrated at the Chiesa Nuova on September 1 of the following year.

1605

On March 5 Clement VIII died. His successor for a few weeks was Alessandro Cardinal de Medici,[134] who took the name of Leo XI: Fr. Philip had predicted his brief pontificate. In May Pope Paul V Borghese was elected (1605–1621).

Fr. Ricci was reelected Provost.

1607

The Congregation of Aquila is erected. On June 30 the Venerable Cesare Baronio died at the Vallicella, where he had been able to return for some little time to enjoy his "sweet nest," and of which he had always kept the key in his pocket. He was buried under the presbytery of the Chiesa Nuova.[135]

1608

The Venerable Francesco Maria Tarugi followed his fraternal friend into the kingdom of heaven a year later on June 11, and also rests in the humble sepulcher of the Fathers, under the presbytery of the Vallicella, next to Baronio. Fr. Angelo Velli was elected Provost.

1611

Fr. Pietro Consolini was elected Provost. In this year the first six priests who would constitute the Oratory of Bérulle[136] gathered together, recognized canonically by Paul V in 1613.

1612

On February 12 with the Brief *Christifidelium*, Paul V approved the *Instituta Congregationis Oratorii de Urbe*.[137] A brief of March 3 forbids the erection of other Oratorian Congregations except under specified conditions; this would be completed by the Motu Proprio of June 26.[138] The Congregation decided that the Houses of Rome and Naples would be separated.

1615

On May 25, Paul V inscribes Fr. Philip in the list of the Blessed[139]: all of Rome was already devoted to him. The House of Naples accepted the Roman Constitutions, and the aggregation continued.

1622

On March 12 Gregory XV (1621–1623), canonized Philip Neri,[140] together with Ignatius Loyola, Francis Saverio, Teresa of Ávila, and Isadore of Seville. All Rome ran to St. Peter's exulting, saying in jest that the Pope had canonized "four Spaniards and a Saint."

As a Prelate Gregory had been a brother of and even Rector of the Secular Oratory of Rome, and when he became Cardinal frequented the Vallicella faithfully. In homage to Philip, "Apostle of Rome" together with Saints Peter and Paul, the tradition had begun, in 1609, that the administration of the city[141] would offer a chalice to the Chiesa Nuova annually.

On July 8, the Bull *Ex iniuncto* established the independence of the Houses. The new biography of St. Philip came out, written by Fr. Pier Giacomo Bacci.[142] Paolo Aringhi was accepted into the Congregation: he wrote the *Vite e detti de' Padri e Fratelli della Congregatione dell'Oratorio.*[143]

2. BIBLIOGRAPHY

Among the oldest biographies of St. Philip Neri, we offer these:

A. Gallonio, *Via Beati P. Philippi Nerii Florentini, Congregationis Oratorii Fundatoris, in annos digesta.* Romae, 1600; Rome, 1918.

_____., *Vita del Beato P. Filippo Neri, fiorentino…scritta e ordinata per anni.* Roma, 1601; critical edition ed. M. T. Bonadonna

Russo, Rome, 199;[144]; *The Life of St. Philip Neri*, trans. Jerome Bertram of the Oxford Oratory. Oxford: 2005.

P. G. Bacci, *Vita di San Filippo Neri fiorentino...* Rome, 1622. Successive editions, both Italian and others, number 140.

____., *Vita di San Filippo Neri...con l'aggiunta di una breve notitia di alcuni suoi compagni, per opera di* Giacomo Ricci. Rome, 1672.

D. Sonzonio, *Vita del santo Patriarca e taumaturgo Filippo Neri...*, Venezia, 1727;

____., *Vita novissima del Santo...ampliata...* Padova, 1733.

G. Marciano, *Memorie Historiche della Congregazione dell'Oratorio*, vol. 1. Naples, 1693. (This work, which is in five volumes [Naples, 1693–1702], gives a life of St. Philip in Chapter 2 of Volume 1).

Among the modern biographies:

A. Capecelatro, *Vita di san Filippo Neri.* Rome-Tournay, I, II, 1879; fourth edition 1901.

L. Ponelle and L. Bordet, *Filippo Neri e la società romana del suo tempo.* Italian translation ed. T. Casini (Florence, 1931); anastatic edition with appendix (1987); original edition in French (Paris, 1928); *St. Philip Neri and the Roman Society of His Times (1515–1595)*, trans. Ralph Francis Kerr of the London Oratory. London: Sheed and Ward, 1932.[145]

Sources and other very useful works are:

THE CANONICAL PROCESS:

G. Incisa della Rocchetta and N. Vian (ed.). *Il primo process canonico per San Filippo Neri nel Codice Vaticano Latino 3798 e in altri esemplari dell'Oratorio di Roma.* Libreria Editrice Vaticana, Città del Vaticano, I (1957); II (1958); III (1960); IV (1963).

THE MONUMENTAL HISTORIOGRAPHICAL WORK:

A. Cistellini. *San Filippo Neri: l'Oratorio e la Congregazione oratoriana. Storia e spiritualità.* 3 vol. Brescia: Morcelliana, 1989.[146]

THE CRITICAL EDITION OF THE WRITINGS OF ST. PHILIP, together with exhaustive and detailed introductory notes:

San Filippo Neri. *Gli scritti e le massime.* Ed. A. Cistellini. Brescia: Morcelliana, 1994.[147]

Among the more popular works on the life and work of San Philip, written in or translated into Italian, we suggest, in chronological order:

H. E. Schroeder. *San Filippo Neri.* Brescia: Morcelliana, 1936.

V. Magni. *San Filippo Neri.* Florence: Libreria Editrice Fiorentina, 1936.

O. Cerri. San *Filippo Neri, Aneddotico.* Rome, 1939; 2nd ed., 1986.

T. Maynard. *Il buffone di Dio.* Milan: Mondadori, 1949; 2nd ed., 1984.

G. de Libero. *Vita di San Filippo Neri Apostolo di Roma.* Grottaferrata: Tipografia Italo-Orientale, 1960.

L. Bouyer, *La musica di Dio, San Filippo Neri.* Milan: Jaca Book, 1980.[148]

G. Papasogli. *Un secolo, un uomo. Filippo Neri.* Cinisello Balsamo: Edizioni Paoline, 1989.

_____. *Filippo Neri, il santo dell'allegria.* Rome: New Compton, 1989.

P. Turks, *Filippo Neri, una gioia contagiosa.* Rome: Città Nuova, 1991; 3rd ed., 1996. [*Philip Neri: The Fire of Joy*, trans. Daniel Utrecht of the Toronto Oratory (London and New York, 1995; 2010].

A. Cistellini. *San Filippo Neri. Breve storia di una grande vita.* Florence: Ed. Memorie Oratoriane, 1996; 2nd ed., enlarged, 1998.

H. Tercic, *Filippo Neri, l'amore vince ogni paura.* Rome: Città Nuova, 2000.

Among the books in other languages we note here:

M. Trevor. *St. Philip Neri. The Apostle of Rome.* London: Macmillan Press, 1966. [Translation into Spanish (Santander, 1986).]

J. F. Bellido. *La conquista de la libertad. Vita de San Felipe Neri.* Bilbao: Desclée de Brouwer, 1998.

The personality of Fr. Philip and the spiritual way of life that he proposed are woven together so closely that most of the books delineate one as they describe the other.

Among the oldest works—and they are many and of varying degrees of usefulness—we will mention these few: *Philippus, sive de christiana laetitia*: Cardinal A. Valier, *Il dialogo della gioia cristiana.* Latin text, translation, and introduction by A. Cistellini (Brescia, 1975). This work, composed in 1591 while St. Philip was still living, was given to the Father and it was found in manuscript form among his books.

Another book, written while the Father was living but published a few months after his death, is Cardinal G. Paleotti, *De bono senectutis* (Rome, 1595). Cardinal Paleotti was closer to Fr. Philip and the circle at the Vallicella than Cardinal Vallier.

There are also:

G. Crispino, *La scuola del grande Maestro di spirito San Filippo Neri* (Venezia, 1678).

Un libro dell'Anonimo "priest of the Oratory of Venice," *Idea degli Esercizi dell'Oratorio, istuiti da San Filippo Neri* (Venice, 1742), with successive enlarged editions.

F. A. Boschis, *Discorsi sacri spieganti vari ricordi, e detti di s. Filippo Neri...* (Turin, 1744).

The "*Pregi*," a work that is very well known in the Oratorian environment, attributed to Fr. Agnelli, of the same age as and friend of Blessed S. Valfrè: *Pregi della Congregazione dell'Oratorio di San Filippo Neri, opera postuma e prima d'ora inedita d'un prete dell'Oratorio di Savigliano in Piemonte.* 2 vol. (Venice, 1825). [Translation reprinted as *The Excellences of the Congregation of the Oratory of St. Philip Neri* (Francesco Antonio Agnelli (d. 1749), and Frederick Ignatius Antrobus (1837–1903), reprinted by General Books.]

A valuable synthesis of the spirit and work of Fr. Philip are the two sermons that J. H. Newman preached at the Oratory of Birmingham on January 15 and 18, 1850: *The Mission of St. Philip*

Neri. The Second of Two Sermons Preached.... 18 January 1850, published to Pittsburgh Oratory website; contemporary with Newman's sermons is F. Faber, *The Spirit and Genius of St. Philip* (London, 1850).

Among the more recent works, we list the following in chronological order:

C. Gasbarri, *Lo spirito dell'Oratorio di San Filippo Neri.* Brescia, 1949.

G. Angilella, *Intuizione ed esperienza educative nell'apostolato di San Filippo Neri.* Pisa, 1957.

A. Mengarelli. *La Pastorale di Filippo Neri, giovane fiorentino e sacerdote romano.* Perugia, 1974.

A. Cistellini. "San Filippo Neri e la spiritualità dell'Oratorio," in *Le grandi scuole di spiritualità cristiana.* Roma, 1984.

G. Finotti. *Un modo di sentire in Cristo.* Bologna, 1983.

____. *Il carisma della Congregazione dell'Oratorio di San Filippo Neri, tra memoria e profezia.* Bologna, 1989.

J. W. Goethe. *San Filippo Neri.* Texts by Johan Wolfgang Goethe and by Giuseppe De Luca. Vicenza, 1987.

G. Lando. *Il Maestro della perfetta allegria.* Guardia Sanframondi, 1992.

G. Finotti. *San Filippo Neri. Il Profeta della gioia cristiana. Appunti di spiritualità.* Bologna, 1994.

A. Venturoli. *L'attività apostolica di San Filippo Neri.* Città del Vaticano, 1997.

____. *Il profeta della gioia; La mistica di san Filippo Neri.* Milan, 1999.

Oratorio de Albacete. *San Felipe Neri.* Barcelona, 1998.

Procura Generale, ed. *L'Oratorio di San Filippo Neri. Spiritual Path.* Verona, 1995.

The texts of many lectures and talks, published pro-manuscripto are to be found in the *Atti* of the Incontri Internazionali dell'Oratorio and in the *Memoria Congressus Generalis 2000* cited in Chapter 4; in particular, G. Carriquiry Lecour, "Promover el Oratorio como un estilo de vida en la Iglesia," in *Atti dell'Incontro Internazionale di Seville* (1992); ibid., "El Oratorio en la mision de la Iglesia al alba del Tercer Milenio," in *Memoria Congressus Generalis A. D. 2000.* The texts of the principal lectures given by Fr. Giulio Cittadini have been published in G. Cittadini, *L'Oratorio di San Filippo Neri. Origini, attualità, prospettive*, ed. Procura Generale (Rome, 2000).

3. ASTERISKS

‡ *"In his face one could see a clarity..."*

What Philip's face in his childhood was like is not known, but the memories that his mother shared with Caterina, and which she in turn passed on to Elisabetta[149] give us a no less valuable portrait of his character: the perfect obedience of the little one, when he would "stay right there" without moving, when his mother asked him to; his sweetness and good humor, which even became an occasion for jokes; his willingness to do whatever his father asked of him in adolescence: "He never did anything for which I had to scold him," except for one time when he was cross with his sister; his propriety in dressing,[150] which was expressed, as his sister remembered, in his "mantle which was very clean," in his long hair and in a little gold chain that he wore over his clothes; he was a peaceful boy, cheerful, willing to do even whatever his new mother asked of him. She loved him intensely, and suffered when he left Florence. "Filippo Buono," "Pippo Bono,"[151] "good Philip" was what they called him from that early time, and this "portrait" more than compensates for the lack of a portrait of his physical likeness.

For his adolescence, mature years, and old age, on the other hand, there are plenty of witnesses, and they agree in emphasizing the amiability that made a face which was already pleasing even more agreeable. Fr. Pier Giacomo Bacci was his second biographer and had not known Fr. Philip, since he entered the Congregation only in 1604, but he evidently heard much about Fr. Philip from others who would have had his image impressed indelibly in their minds and hearts. Fr. Bacci wrote: "Philip was of middle height, with a pale complexion and joyous expression. In his youth his features were very beautiful. He had a high and spacious forehead, not bald, however. His nose was aquiline, his eyes small and light blue, a little sunken but lively. He had a black beard, not very long, although in his last years it was completely white."[152] His "very beautiful features" the biographer mentions emerge also from the testimony of someone Philip's age, Giovanni Angelo Papio,[153] who had known Philip in Rome in the early days. Papio was also in the community for a time, and maintained a great friendship with him.[154] G. Giovenale Ancina's testimony is also important: "Father Philip is a beautiful, clean old man, all white like an ermine, his skin is sweet and virginal, and if he raises his hand against the sun, it seems transparent like alabaster." Fabrizio de' Massimi comments on this beauty, saying:[155] "The purity of Blessed Philip was such that it was visible in his face and in his eyes, which were those of a young man, and in his face you saw a clarity, in his eyes, too, that no painter has known how to portray, although many have tried."[156]

Philip's interior life shone forth in his face, his features and even in his bearing, not only from his eyes, which normally mirror the inner life. From his whole person emanated that subtle attraction which so many felt. Practical joker,[157] merry, kind, frank, simple, attentive to everyone, amiable, deep, reserved, absorbed, ecstatic…[158]: his distinctive qualities blended harmoniously into one unity. There was nothing strident in the personality of the Florentine Philip Neri: everything was harmonized by an experience of communion with God which visibly shaped his rich humanity.

In testimony given by Alessandro Illuminati,[159] among many others, we can hear this harmonious symphony: "Father Philip was loving, sweet in his conversation, with everyone, the little no less than the great, and each one who spoke to him once was desirous of speaking with him again. And when a troubled person came to him, or someone who had suffered some adversity, he sent him away consoled. He felt the afflictions of those who came to him. He was extremely humble with everyone, and was quite distressed when anyone praised him. He was respectful in giving commands and making others work, and he went about recollected and reserved and would never want anyone to suffer on his account. In food he was abstemious, eating once a day. In the morning he took a little breakfast, and in the evening two or three eggs or some salad; dairy products never and a little meat once in a while, although he didn't like it. His place was set with only a small napkin, and he didn't like to eat with others. He never wanted his door to be shut or locked, or that anyone would say "Philip is resting," or "has retired." When he was ill, he would take everything that the doctors ordered. He prayed a great deal, always alone, and never wanted to be seen. He was never idle: there was always a book or a rosary in his hand. And when someone came to talk to him of literary matters,[160] he went away satisfied. And to those to whom he gave counsel, they also went away completely satisfied."[161]

‡ *"Sì come egli era fiorentino, così haveva caro che gli altri sapessero ch'ei fusse."*[162]

Bizzarro, a word with Dantean echoes, is used by Giovanni Papini, to describe Philip in the beautiful pages of his Preface to the Italian translation of Ponnelle and Bordet's biography of Philip.[163] The term, in the pen of Papini, expresses that *fiorentinità* [Florentine character][164] which endears Philip to the whole world, and which does not at all diminish the strong *romanità* [Roman character] which also marks Philip's life. His sixty years lived uninterruptedly in the Urbe by his own personal choice certainly shaped him. Nevertheless, Papini is right: "They call him the Apostle of Rome, and he is venerated universally as a saint in all the earth, among not only Catholics but also Protestants and others. However, the fact remains that he owes his originality, his almost complete uniqueness, his physiognomy recognizable among those of all the saints in the world, to the indelible imprint of his Florentine birth. No saint has laughed and made others laugh as he did, and to no other saint except him can one apply Dante's famous definition "fiorentino spirito bizzarro."[165] In St. Francis there is serene joy at the sight of the beauty of the world, but not that natural jocularity, that love of the mocking witticism, that need to tease and to jest which in St. Philip become, by a miracle of Grace, an instrument of the apostolate, of conversion. St. Philip, in short, is a boy of Florence, more precisely, a boy from the Oltrarno,[166] who, by the supernatural intervention of the immoderate love of Christ, advanced to the heights of sanctity, while remaining in part what he was, that is, boyish, facetious, and oltrarnino."

He is also right, even more so, in suggesting that this marked Florentine component of St. Philip's can be seen only as part of a greater design: Having himself come to faith through conversion, Giovanni Papini knew what "a miracle of Grace," and "the immoderate love of Christ" mean. Because of this, he was able to grasp the essential in Philip, unlike those who simply enjoy Philip's whimsical nature.

‡ *Philip's secretum*

"Secretum meum mihi, secretum meum mihi,"[167] Fr. Philip would often say.[168] He revealed almost nothing of his inner life, or the vicissitudes of his personal life, unlike many saints, even those of his time: Ignatius of Loyola, Teresa of Ávila, Charles Borromeo, Francis de Sales, to mention a few, who wrote abundant letters and interesting autobiographies. In Philip, on the contrary, we notice almost an allergy to writing. The greater part of the letters that we have were dictated to a secretary,[169] to whom Philip merely explained the ideas he wished to have expressed. The few things that he himself wrote, perhaps personal things, he burned before he died.

That reserve is astounding in a man who made affability, love of company, of friendship, dialogue and colloquy the instruments of his apostolate. But perhaps it amazes even more when we think of Philip Neri, "the prophet of Christian joy,"[170] the apostle of a new kind of evangelization that changed the spiritual face of Rome, committed like few others to tireless activity—this Philip is above all a profoundly contemplative spirit, with a strong eremitical tendency. This last is not to be taken literally, of course, but the "solitude" of Philip, which he passionately cultivated and defended, is an interior "solitude," a love inexpressible in human words, for that *secretum* which is his profound experience of God. He loved to recite the verses of a sonnet written in imitation of Petrarch that express completely this interior richness: "Vorrei saper da te come egli è fatta / questa rete d'amor che tanti abbraccia" [I would like you to tell me of what it may be made, / this net of love which embraces so many].[171]

Santo Filippo degli opposti Amen is the title Giovanni Constantini gave to his *Mistero in quattro atti* [*St. Philip of Opposite Amens: A Mystery in Four Acts*].[172] Philip really is a man of "opposite amens," but opposite in him does not mean opposed. The *complexio oppositorum* to which Philip witnesses is the admirable synthesis of a harmonious spirituality lived out in a thoroughly Christian way. Philip's heart was inhabited in that extraordinary way by the Holy Spirit, who manifests himself in the force of an impetuous wind and incandescent fire, but also in the humble freshness of running water and the lightness and simplicity of a dove.

Enamored of intimate and solitary prayer, in the Oratory Philip lived and taught the most fraternal, communal prayer; strongly ascetic in his own penance, including corporal penance, he taught his sons to undertake spiritual mortification, which bore the imprint of joy and the serenity of play.[173] Passionate reader of books—what a library he had![174]—and wanting to know history, philosophy, theology,[175] he abandoned his studies as a young man because a Crucifix in the classroom attracted his glance and his heart so much that that he could not follow the discussions of his teachers.[176] Passionate preacher of the divine Word "qui Verbum Dei cotidianum distribuisti," says John Henry Newman in his invocations to St. Philip[177]—he was so sparing of words that he was reduced to mere phrases, or even to silence, in his last years, when emotion would not allow him to enter into a spiritual discussion in the meetings of the Oratory.[178]

"It is true," writes Fr. Cistellini,[179] "that he matured in an atmosphere of warm friendships, and that his abilities and experiences became integrated within a well-regulated community to which he gave himself totally. But even with all this, there remained in Philip a certain spirit of independence, an atavistic love of the freedom to make his own choices, a "persevering repugnance to become part of any religious order."[180] "A liking for solitude when he chose, for independence from constrictions and conventions, for the joyous freedom to be poor, undoubtedly dominate his behavior in this period, from eighteen to thirty-five years of age, between adolescence and full maturity."[181] "Nor did he ever put off these habits of mind, nor renounce them throughout his whole life, as is clear from various personal witnesses. Now however [after his ordination to the priesthood] certain attributes that one can only term flagrant contradictions begin to make themselves evident, and these remain for the length of his very long life: love of liberty and docile acceptance of order, festive joyousness in company and love for solitude; a taste for friendship and a delicate reserve, a mystical contemplative fervor and the continuous tension of the apostolate, refusal of rigid rules (taking of vows) and insistence upon obedience to the rule… Mysterious psychology of great souls, which God alone understands!"

‡ *"Ut vocantem Christum sequeretur"*

The resolution of the young Philip to abandon his studies was not determined by disinterest in those disciplines: he loved them, and in fact took every occasion that arose to discuss them. There are a number of significant testimonies in this regard, first from Antonio Gallonio: "Even though our Father's study had become continuous prayer, nevertheless when he wanted to talk about matters of theology, philosophy, or humane letters, they were as fresh in his mind as though he had studied them that very hour"[182]; then from Cardinal Girolamo Panfili: "beginning at a certain age, he was accustomed to engage in theological and philosophical arguments, in which he was quite accomplished, in order to find refreshment for his soul [from his constant mystical experiences]"[183]; and from Matteo Guerra: "I heard the Father many times in disputation with theologians and learned men, quoting many passages of Scripture, so that those same theologians and learned men and all there who were listening marveled at him."[184] What induced Philip to leave a course of study in which his lively intelligence would have assured him of success is expressed by his first biographer in a phrase that has the ring of truth: "ut vocantem Christum sequeretur."[185]

To what was Christ calling him, and where did Philip want to follow him? He apparently was not considering the priesthood, since the studies that he had abandoned would have been useful for that. Additionally, we know from Germanico Fedeli's testimony that he had such an elevated conception of the priesthood that he could not even think that he was called to it: "Out of humility he did not dare to become a priest, and he felt great an aversion to it until he was constrained by the command of his spiritual father [to do so]...and this I heard from the same blessed Father Philip, and for this reason he became a priest late."[186]

The call that Philip perceived was probably the same one that had already led him to leave San Germano, and the prospects of a comfortable life connected to his residing in the house of Romolo. This call was his total dedication to the requirements of the Gospel, lived within a powerful spiritual life. Fr. Pateri's deposition speaks of this[187]: "One may truly say that the life of blessed Philip was one continuous prayer. An infinite number of times I have heard Fr. Francesco M. Tarugi and others of the house...that he began as a youth, then left his studies in order to be able to attend to prayer. And so that he could unite himself with God better, he went away from the company of men, and went off to the Seven Churches, sometimes remaining the night under the porticoes of the churches and sometimes in the catacombs of Callistus. He never could have enough of praying and contemplating. And the sweetness he experienced in that exercise, more of angels than of men, was such that he saw to it that everyone, as much as they could, would give themselves to this prayer.... And because one cannot, down here in this life, always remain in prayer, he tried to keep his mind as much as he could united with God by ejaculatory prayers. And for this reason he continually invited and exhorted his spiritual sons to try to have God always before their eyes." There is moving testimony of a friend, Loys Ames,[188] who speaks of old memories, received as confidences also from other friends: "he was seen a number of times at night, by moonlight, on the steps of Santa Maria Maggiore and on the steps of San Pietro, saying his office, by the light of the moon."

Philip was never to give up, through his entire life, this "solitude" filled with God. G. P. Pacini observes[189]: "He knew that a day that had been too much occupied with visits and business deprived him of some interior treasure: 'Today,' he would say when evening had come, 'I have done no good; let me be alone.'[190] At night, especially in the winter, they prepared a little lamp for him, which he placed in a corner, so that its light might not shine in his eyes, and he then shut himself up in his room, where he would remain for an hour or more in the semi-darkness. When he went out into the country with a number of his spiritual sons, he loved to draw apart from them and be alone: 'I saw him' said Fabrizio de' Massimi, in his deposition, 'retire to some little copse or to some little eminence, where, seated or walking about, he set himself to prayer.'[191] And again: 'In his apartments.... there was a little staircase that led to thither [to the loggia] and very often he went up there for prayer and contemplation, and I remember how, in winter, early in the morning, he would go there by himself, dressed in a long red jacket that came down to his knees, and I was astonished when he came down again, that he was not perished with the cold. But he laughed at me and made me touch his hand, which was quite warm.'"[192]

Until the end of his life he would want to retire to high places to contemplate,[193] and at San Girolamo and at the Vallicella he had built some little rooms on the roofs[194] at considerable expense. He needed to be alone and to have glimpses of the sky.

The vocation that he felt resounding in his soul was the full encounter with that Christ of whom Philip would say at the moment he received him in viaticum: "My Christ, my love, all the world is vanity"[195]; "Whoever seeks for anything other than Christ does not know what he wants; whoever looks for anything other than Christ does not know what he asks for."[196] "May God give you the grace that you may focus entirely on his divine love," he wrote to his niece Sr. Maria Anna Trevi,[197] "and that you enter so far within the wound in his side, into the living fount of the wisdom of God who became man, that you yourself are able to annihilate your self-love and never be able to find the way out."

"What is striking in Philip is how solidly rooted he is in the 'realism of the Incarnation,'" notes Guzman Carriquiry.[198] "The divine majesty seems no longer, as in centuries past, to obscure the warmth of the holy humanity of Jesus. Beginning with Philip, this was not so, nor is it of our modern devotions.... The presence of Christ becomes a moving experience. The patristic tradition, familiarity with Holy Scripture and the witness of the martyrs and the saints open and illuminate the 'heart' to recognize and adhere to this Presence.... Philip's impressive and fundamental Eucharistic fervor is known: Church and Eucharist, totally conjoined, refer to the body of Jesus Christ, mysterious and real. Philip perceived the Face of the Lord, his real and searching presence, even in the sick, the poor, the needy. At the base of everything is Philip's conviction that the spiritual life, the journey to holiness is not founded upon some 'gnosis' for the 'initiated,' or for the 'wise' and the 'just,' but on an actual event, an encounter that is unforeseeable in the circumstances of life, accessible moreover to anyone, of any state or condition, who receives it with the marvel of a child.... This same realism makes Philip attentive to the circumstances of each person's life, since grace is incarnate in each.... What guides his whole existence and his understanding of reality is the certainty which he experienced in his encounter with Him for whom all things were made and in whom they exist and are held together in order to be recapitulated in the glory of God."

‡ *"gli astanti molto ben si accorgevano che piú tosto agebatur, quam ageret"*[199]

The young Philip's love for the Most Holy Eucharist is demonstrated above all by his intense participation in the foundation and in the life of the Confraternity of the Most Holy Trinity, which was known for Eucharistic Adoration.[200] This was essentially the purpose of the institution, which was assigned the task of assisting pilgrims only in the Jubilee Year of 1550 by the Vicar Archinto. At the end of that year, the task expanded to include assistance to convalescents, and to the poor who were released from the hospital only to fall again into illness unless they were given help. Eucharistic piety, so strongly rooted in Philip's spirituality, and linked to works of charity to the most needy members of the body of Christ, becomes a basic element of his educational proposals.

Philip received his priestly ordination at the time when the thirteenth and fourteenth sessions of the Council of Trent were defining the doctrine of the Church on the Eucharist.[201]

We do not know how much of those discussions was known to Philip, but he contributed much to the understanding of the dispositions of the Council, since he was very clear in his mind that to be a priest was to be a man of the Eucharist and a Eucharistic man. Christian art has understood this well, and has given pride of place to images of Philip clothed in priestly vestments.

Even before he was known for his brilliant intuitions about the apostolate,[202] Fr. Philip distinguished himself at the school of the "spirituals" at San Girolamo for his daily celebration of Holy Mass, in a time when this certainly was not common practice. "He celebrated every morning when he was well, and communicated every day when he was ill," says Gallonio.[203] For this reason, he could encourage priests to celebrate daily: "He would say that priests made a serious mistake when they fail to celebrate, if in fact they were able to do so. And they also erred who asked permission not to celebrate in order to have some free time for recreation. In Philip's view those who sought consolation outside were seeking their own damnation, and that whoever wants to be saved without the Savior is not well but sick, and is not wise but mad."[204]

Testimonies about Philip's love for the Eucharist celebrated and adored are numerous. G. B. Zazzara testified at the canonical Process: "Father Philip had an intense love for the Most Blessed Sacrament of the Eucharist, without which he could not live...it seemed to him that he really could not live without this sacrament"[205]; Giovanni Bernardi testified: "When he raised the sacrament, he trembled all over, and he raised himself up onto his toes: and he did this too when he communicated other persons, he would move as though he were dancing; and he himself, Fr. Philip, told me that, at the start of the Mass, he could not raise the chalice without many tears of devotion and spiritual consolation."[206]

It is for this reason that whoever assisted Fr. Philip at his Masses, which he celebrated privately in the last years of his life by concession of Pope Gregory XIV,[207] was invited by the Father to remain only until the Sanctus, as Agostino Boncompagni recalls: "The Father had us go to his Mass up to the Sanctus, when the consecration came he sent us out."[208]

His last years were distinguished by an even greater intensity of participation in the Eucharistic mystery, which was reflected in the length of the celebration, as Francesco Neri testified: "The Father usually said Mass in a room, and sent away the priest, and I think he would stay and pray for a couple of hours, and then a priest would come in and finish the Mass. And he was displeased sometimes, because it seemed to him that they came in too soon, and he would say so after the Mass. But because he was ill, the Fathers urged him to finish. And when I went in, since I was serving the Mass, I would find him all distracted and elevated in spirit."[209] Bacci remembers these moments, too, adding some details: "When he got to the Agnus Dei, those who were assisting Mass left; and the server lit a small lamp, and then extinguished the candles of the altar, and locked the windows, four double ones, and then both doors with a key.... Having thus arranged everything, he attached a small tablet outside the little chapel, on which was written: 'Silence, the Father is saying Mass.'"[210]

According to the testimony of Marcello Benci, in the Masses of St. Philip it was no rare thing to discover a real and true Eucharistic "miracle," for example the sensible conversion of the wine into blood and the species of bread into flesh: "The first time that I saw the chalice full of blood I stood there astonished; and it lasted for two years, that when he said Mass in the chapel upstairs, the chalice was first filled with wine, and at the act of communion it was blood, as I said, and I saw it a number of times while I put out the candles, and it was real blood; it was a little chalice, and he filled it with wine and consecrated it and as I said, I saw that it was real blood. I was there various times, when the Father would relate that it was real blood, and that he consumed it little by little."[211]

Bacci makes an observation in his Life of Philip that summarizes the profound reaction of those who witnessed this: "those present were very much aware that agebatur, quam ageret…"[212] Here is the secret of Fr. Philip's Masses and of his impassioned love of the Eucharist: in this total receptivity to God's action in him, rather than his own doing something. It is receiving the Mystery in the pure adhesion to the gift of Grace, in the most active and fruitful "passivity" of man.

A priestly life consummated in the reception and transmission of this gift must necessarily end by becoming strongly Eucharistic. Fr. Philip celebrated his last Mass exactly on the feast of Corpus Christi in 1595, and all the witnesses agree: "He said his last Mass with happiness, as though he were singing."[213]

Some days earlier, during a serious relapse of his illness, receiving viaticum from the hands of Cardinal Federico Borromeo, he said: "I am not worthy of it, nor have I ever been worthy; come my love"[214]: it was the final expression and flaming peak of that humility which, in his youth, had held him back from thinking of the Priesthood.

‡ *"To change the face of the eternal City"*

The Holy Spirit, which Philip received in sensible form in 1544 as a gift he had so much desired and invoked intensely, was the seal from on high on a thirty-year journey. It was also Philip's launching into an adventure that would affect the history of the Church strongly.[215] He who would never accept the qualification of "reformer" appears to be "perhaps the greatest ever," Bremond maintains, "since nobody seems ever to have worked with greater success to change the face of the eternal City."[216]

Philip lived in a historical and cultural moment that marked the beginning of the modern age, and he incarnated the Christian witness of a new age, as Fr. Faber says: "Just as the order of chivalry, the poetry, the novel and the faith of the Medieval period were gathered together and personified in St. Francis, so in St. Philip the spirit of modern times."[217]

Quite apart from any preordained project, and consistent with his mentality which was not at all systematic, he transmitted to the Church the spiritual richness which he had received as gift "at the beginning of his conversion."[218] This was a mysterious event in Philip's journey that may surprise us, knowing the style of the life of "Pippo buono," his intense spirit of contemplation, his love of God and service to the poor and to those sick in hospitals. Perhaps this "conversion" is the desire of a love of God still more intense, certainly the desire to know the direction of his vocation more clearly. "He prayed to the Holy Spirit that he would give him spirit," and he was given it, in the mysterious Pentecost of 1544, about which he spoke only at the end of his life. As a sign of that extraordinary experience, and as a gift to the Church in this time of renewal, there remained in him that "movement of the heart," of which many witnesses speak.[219] Frederick Borromeo said: "At that time the Father told me that he felt this movement that always continued," and Antonio Gallonio deposed at the Process: "I remember having heard Fr. Philip say various times that he had so much spirit when he was young that he could scarcely stand it, and because of this he would throw himself onto the ground and cry out to God: 'no more, no more, I cannot bear it.'"[220] "I understood Fr. Philip to say, in this last illness that joined him to Christ, that the palpitation that he felt, which he called 'his infirmity,' he had borne for fifty years. This was that affect of the heart that made him exult in the living God, so that he could say with the prophet: 'cor meum et caro meo exultaverunt in Deum vivum.' This same affect of the heart made him rapt in God, so much so that he would cry: 'vulneratus charitatis sum ego.' God's flame and spirit abounded so much in his heart, that it seemed almost ready to burst from his chest, being unable to contain itself within those boundaries that nature has set. For this reason some ribs near his heart were bent and broken, being raised as much as the diameter of a fist; and of this I learned many years ago; and this bowing and breaking caused him no pain or discomfort whatsoever."[221]

From the time of Philip's so-called "hermitage" he felt strongly the need to bring all whom he encountered, and all for whom he went out to look, to Christ. He did not experience this as a duty, but it was born out of an interior richness. As layman, and then as priest, the apostolate that he exercised was above all the simple one of an encounter. The authenticity of his personal relations, fruit of his beautiful humanity, but also of the ascetic practices that formed him, became the method of his evangelization. Through the warmth of friendship[222] passed the annunciation of the Word, without any elaborate discourses, in the simplicity and zest of an invitation, like the one he issued in Banchi Street to idle and lazy young men: "Now, then my friends, when are we going to start to do some good?"[223] Marcello Vitelleschi gave this testimony, and added: "he would go into Banchi Street to exhort those young men who worked in the stores to serve God."

While Philip was living these experiences of mystical contemplation and fervid apostolate, in the most evangelical simplicity,[224] he was at the same time beginning a wide-ranging and composite action of the Catholic Reform that saw Rome as its center. The early apostolic experiences of the young Florentine coincided with the first determining initiatives taken by the new Pope Paul III: the creation of the Commission of Cardinals in 1535, the *Concilium de emendanda Ecclesia* in 1537, prelude to the great Tridentine Council. The priestly ordination of Philip in 1551, and consequently the beginning of the activity of the Oratory came at the time when the Council was reopening its work, and in 1564, when the Council had just concluded, those steps were beginning that would lead to the Congregation of the Oratory, the Community of priests formed at the school of Philip.

The commitment to the salvation of souls, alive in all the pastoral and apostolic action of the Church, returned in those times to shine with renewed light. "The new concept was that the *salus animarum* was conceived as a central idea of the Church, as a principal law though not written," writes H. Jedin.[225] "The Church had learned...that it had to provide guides and doctors of souls for the Catholic people."

Philip, who even as a layman had been a "guide," with his priestly ordination began also to be the "doctor": "he sits in the confessional and his apostolic activity configures itself as a typical expression of the reforming work, a component, one might almost say, of that vast design of restoration that the church is decisively pursuing."[226]

The strong and subtle tendency of the Renaissance was to "naturalize" Grace, reducing everything to the human, without denying God, but basing everything on man. Philip Neri responded to this destructive tendency by repeating constantly, "Lord, don't trust Philip!"; "My Lord, don't expect anything but evil from me."[227] The Christian joy of which he is the "prophet" is nothing other than the happiness of the man who knows that he is the son, the child of God, held close in the embrace of the Father,[228] enriched by the new life that gushes forth from the encounter with Christ, who brings humanity to perfection. It is an adventure of happy spiritual youth not destined to come to fruition "out of this world" but in it, with the serene awareness that it is not necessary to abandon it, as Fr. Philip said to a lady who wanted to know when he had left the world.[229]

But another temptation was emerging on the scene in that historical time as a reaction to triumphant worldliness: that of angrily defying the world that refuses to encounter Christ. Philip did not know Girolamo Savonarola,[230] whose life ended at the stake in Piazza della Signoria in Florence in 1498. But the holiness of that impetuous reformer was well remembered in his family and in the Convent of San Marco.[231] Philip esteemed his holy life, his apostolic intentions which were genuine evangelical inspirations, he prayed intensely at the Minerva in Rome when the Holy Office was deliberating whether to condemn his writings, he seems to have kept in his room a portrait with a golden halo around his head—but he did not follow him. His whole apostolate is the antithesis of Savonarola's method and of his limitless harshness, which offended both the vanity and the political ambitions of the Florentine Republic. Philip and his Oratory were the expression of a soul that was exceptionally interior and of a mind that was extraordinarily open. An apostolate animated by the purest affection for each person as he was, encountered in the reality of daily life, not imagined by the light of some ideology.[232] To Fra Girolamo's eyes, Florence, the city of the arts and of festivals, had become intolerable, and he proposed to take it from paganism to the Gospel by means of the pulpit, from which he thundered apocalyptic threats. Philip chose the chair, even when the Oratory left the room at San Girolamo and the place which had given it its name, and had assumed a more organized structure. And together with his seat in the Oratory, or rather, even before this, the seat of the confessional, where with winning tenderness he received and directed, not the masses, but individuals, onto the path of conversion. For Philip "people" did not exist: there were only the "friends," and everyone could become so, and that personal rapport really was an apostolate through friendship.

"The task of our institute is to speak to the heart," said Fr. Tarugi, who was himself conquered for Christ by Philip's method of speaking to the "heart." F. De Giorgi wrote, in the introduction to a youthful text of Rosmini on the spirit of St. Philip:[233] "In his volume on Pascal, Romano Guardini speaks of the most noble tradition that Western Christianity knows, that which has its theoretical expression in the philosophy and theology of the heart. This tradition was prepared, in a sort of time of advent, by Plato; it bursts forth in Paul, is lived by Ignatius of Antioch, and developed with prodigious force in Augustine.... In the age of the Renaissance it degenerates into neo-platonic forms, forms purely metaphysical and aesthetic, but it was quickly absorbed and lived by Teresa of Ávila; reformulated by St. Frances de Sales and by the theologians of the Oratory, by Condren and by Bérulle. In the nineteenth century it is the Oratorians again who continue it: Gratry, Rosmini and above all the great Newman. To me the fundamental matrices of the profound spirituality of Rosmini are two: Philip's and Augustine's.... That spirituality can be summarized and expressed in Rosmini's own words about St. Philip: 'All of Philip's actions were interiorly serious, by their nature, since they came forth from an extraordinary mind. Outwardly, everything was light, graceful, in order that they might welcome and enamor human hearts, making them copies of themselves, of the eternal exemplar.' Philip's Oratory was fundamentally a Christian friendship."

‡ *"He only let himself be called Father"*

"Father" was the only title that Philip accepted willingly, "because this means love."[234] He was "Father" because he belonged to the group of priests at San Girolamo, who, although they were secular priests and therefore properly called "messer,"[235] used this title. To Philip it was not just a title, since he had experienced the kind fatherhood of those priests. He had chosen some as confessors and spiritual directors: Persiano Rosa, so close to Philip in his hilarious and open temperament, who had directed him toward the priesthood, after his first experiences of the Confraternity of the Most Holy Trinity. There was also Francesco Marsuppini from Arezzo, with whom Philip established cordial relations immediately, and whom he chose as confessor in 1558 at the death of Rosa. From others he had learned that the exercise of the mission of the priesthood was a commitment to authentic spiritual paternity. There were Bonsignore Cacciaguida from Siena who came late to the priesthood after various worldly adventures, an eccentric mystic far from Philip in temperament and method, but a master of the practice of frequent communion; Enrico Pietra from Piacenza, whom Philip conquered while yet a layman, who then founded a Company of secular priests for Christian doctrine, and to whose founding Philip contributed; Teseo Raspa from Piedmont, canon of the cathedral of Vercelli, who collaborated with Pietra in the work of Christian Doctrine; from Fermo, Pensabene Turchetti, of fervent temperament, like Philip in spiritual ardor but really singular and capable of ingenious and generous witticisms that had Fr. Philip teasing: "Pensabene, give us one of your witty jokes!"[236]; Costanzo Tassoni, one of Fr. Philip's first converts and very dear to him, Philip's heir in his 1562 will; Felice Figliucci, Cesare Speciani, Vittorio dell'Ancisa, whose names recur in the chapters of this book.

The name "Father" fit the priests of that House very well, they who had renewed "the spirit of the ancient Fathers of the desert," as Marangoni[237] says; the name of "Father" passes soon to the priests of Philip's own Congregation, except that he alone was "the Father," as the Provost of every Oratorian House still is today.

This paternity, which responds to a deeply felt need of man, expresses the real definition of Philip the priest in relation to his faithful. This definition is much truer than that of "the Christian Socrates" attributed to Cardinal Agostino Valier, although this is a happy definition of the method by which Philip reaches the heart of men.

The paternal love of Philip for his spiritual sons, which the witnesses of the Process document copiously, is evident in the forms of affection[238] he has for them, by the interest he demonstrates in the questions and problems of their lives,[239] by his desire to have them near and his habit of going in search of them when he hasn't seen them for a while,[240] by his continual availability.[241] But his paternity manifested itself above all in the attentive and individual care of their souls, characterized by the perspicacious observation of the gifts and the character of each[242] and by the rightful importance given to the human qualities of each person. This was markedly different from the attitude of other confessors, even the most fervent who lived at San Girolamo, Bonsignore Cacciaguerra, for example, who "exercised a veritable charism…[but men] detached themselves from Cacciaguerra, because his mysticism was not likely to endure…because to him humanity had no existence save under [its] supernatural aspect…"[243] While he cultivated souls above all, Fr. Philip never forgot the body, and always took into account the position the person occupied in society. He understood the world of the other, lived the difficulties and the anguish of the poor and the sick, the interior struggles of both the young and of adults, and let people see clearly that he was close to them, and shared their experiences.

Fr. Philip "reads in the hearts of others that which they themselves do not know how to read, and helps them to find in themselves Him who is bigger than their hearts.… He follows personally the growth of his friends and disciples, giving great value to their consciences and their freedom in a very modern way. Individuals grow in their humanity only when they encounter a witness to something larger than themselves, a paternal presence, an extraordinary presence that indicates the path by which they may grow, the interplay between liberty and responsibility, the need to take responsibility without becoming disquieted by their own limitations, their own passions and self-justifications. Philip Neri was an authentic 'teacher of souls,' in his gift of embracing the whole person, in his circumstances, and in the depths of his being."[244]

A beautiful letter which Tarugi wrote from Avignon to Marcello Vitelleschi on September 23, 1593,[245] expresses the nostalgia of a son for Fr. Philip: "even though I am so far away, I still am there [in the Oratorian family that gathered closely around Fr. Philip and in the *cappelletta di mezza scala*], by the grace of God, with faith and love for my dear Father, because I think that I have a special place in his mind…I would like to make my own the most intimate cell in the Father's heart, because I believe that there I would find Jesus.… And when the Father is joyous, and for overwhelming love his heart leaps in his breast, I would be joyous and leap up, too. And when he communicates, I would also partake of that banquet and I would satisfy my hunger. And when he puts his mouth to the chalice, I would wash and drown in that blood, a drop of which, really, is mine, since His Reverend Paternity promised me. Enjoy this happiness, which I was able to enjoy for a long time…"

"schola di santità et hilarità cristiana"

It is certainly true that Philip's *bellissime fattezze*, his beautiful features, recalled his contemporaries, are beautiful in part because of his cheerfulness and his genial nature,[246] the "hilarity" that is so often attributed to him by the witnesses in the Process, and that explains Philip's *virtú attrattiva.*

A component of his *hilarità* is that sweetness which returns again and again in the testimonies. It is expressed in a whole range of nuances, the fruit of his natural gifts but even more of virtues that he exercised with seriousness. The first was humility, which includes them all and which becomes the "program" of the aesthetic life of Philip[247]; then patience: "he was patient in many trials, in being able to put up with many things he did not like done by various persons, and he rose above infirmity so that he did not seem sick"[248]; another was his countenance, which was "always the same,"[249] never changed by his feigned irritations[250] so that he was able to laugh again immediately[251]; his gentleness which Tiberio Astalli,[252] among others, spoke of; his sobriety in everything, including food,[253] cheerfully masked by a joke: "so that I don't get fat…like messer Francesco Scarlatti."[254]

The *hilarità christiana* of which Abate Marco Antonio Maffa speaks,[255] is part of that *schola di santità* where with the Father they loved to sing that simple laud of Feo Belcari: "Giesú, Giesú, ch'ognun chiami Giesú."[256] This was fundamentally the simplicity of the Gospel, the spirit of the "little ones" to whom the kingdom of heaven belongs. Even the heretic Paleologo who met Philip various times and asked as he went to his execution of Campo de' Fiori: "Ubi est ille vir qui loquitur in simplicitate evangelii?"[257]

The pure simplicity of the Gospel, foundation of all of Philip's spirituality, renders man transparent and exalts that which is human.[258] And so, although Philip learned useful things from other proponents of the devout life, Philip Neri the Florentine was sensitive to the beauty manifested in nature and in art; he preferred the open spaces, the hills and vineyards of Rome, the villas and gardens where he led his disciples in little groups, or all together in the visit to the

Seven Churches. He loved music and singing, which restore the soul and elevate the heart to God in the meetings of the Oratory, he was attentive to the figurative arts... We know that often he remained, in the Chiesa Nuova, in the chapel of the Visitation of Mary, where he was found in ecstasy, "seated on a low chair," by Artemisia,[259] who saw Baronio for confession, but went to "kiss the hand of Fr. Philip and to receive his blessing." In that chapel Barocci's canvas was already on display.

"When in 1586 his altarpiece with the Visitation of the Virgin to St. Elizabeth ornamented the altar of a chapel of the Oratory's Chiesa Nuova, which still smelled of plaster," wrote an art critic, "you could see how Barocci's sentimental and smiling sweetness had translated wonderfully into painting the Christian joy that St. Philip was always practicing."[260] "He would stay there happily," Bacci remembered, "since he liked that image of Barocci's' very much,"[261] an image which "portrays in a late manneristic way those characteristics of essence and simplicity dear to Neri."[262]

With his "school of Christian sanctity and hilarity," Philip had rendered the spiritual life, which was thought to be difficult, and reserved only for the few, "familiar and domestic...pleasing and easy" to persons of every condition and state, uprooting the conviction that "spiritual life and exercises...can be learned and practiced only by cloistered religious, and by those few seculars who live withdrawn from the world."[263] "Philip's idea of discretion means measure, equilibrium, moderation (*mediocritas*), the 'golden and praiseworthy mean.' Agostino Manni, one of the first disciples of Philip Neri, wrote that 'the Blessed Father made us see that man's nature has been established by God in such a way that we suffer from excesses and find peace only when we reach the proper measure.' St. Philip's spiritual orientation runs along the path of normality, does not trust sublime or extraordinary attitudes but rather exalts reasonableness...makes the case for finding holiness in the everyday. Against singularity he places simplicity, which he understands as the taste for that which is essential, against complicated attitudes and the struggles of conscience he places interior transparence, spiritual infancy."[264]

THE WORDS WITH WHICH ANGELO VELLI CONCLUDED HIS TESTIMONY about the Father at the canonical process also conclude this rapid contemplation of the face of Philip: "I conclude by saying that if I had observed and reflected upon all the actions of Father Philip I would make a large book, and I believe that even then, I would say little."[265]

CHAPTER II

The Oratory

What the exercises of the Oratory are can be known only by those who practice them and do not lose the proper spirit. I dare to say that in the Church of God there is no more useful undertaking and exercise than this, for two reasons: the first because of the familiar and devout form of reasoning, the other because it is daily, with the addition in the evening of mental prayer which seasons the rest.

(*Letter of F. M. Tarugi to G. B. Bordini* [sic] *in Poland, November 13, 1588, in Archives of the Congregation in Naples 31, 629–31*)

1. BIRTH AND DEVELOPMENT OF THE ORATORY

The inventione *of the heart of Philip*

Inventione is the term in Bacci's *Vita* and in the testimony of the first Oratorians that expresses the astonishment aroused by the novelty, originality, and freshness of that early experience. But what attracted people was not so much a method or a program but the person of Fr. Philip: the simple and fervent prayer, the familiar conversation on Christian life, prayer in the spoken language instead of Latin, the joyous walks to the basilica or the Janiculum all fascinated people because Philip himself with his rich inner life gave each thing worth and meaning. Fr. Cistellini writes[1]: "We stay most willingly in the company of that singular and kindly priest, all joy and fervor, even when we are talking about things that could seem tedious… There was no predetermined composition of the Oratorian group… One of the oldest documents on the origin of the Institute emphasizes the spontaneity of its birth and its taking shape[2]: 'the origin of that place in San Girolamo which is called Oratory was accidental, in this way. It happened that many devout persons, having begun by the grace of God to frequent the most holy Sacraments and desiring to make progress every day in the ways of God, saw that this could not happen without adding to the Sacraments conversation with other persons dedicated to similar exercises; so that, fleeing from idleness and evil conversation, the causes of all sin, began every day after the noon meal to gather where, in the presence of their spiritual Father, they could together flee sin, conquer temptation, acquire the holy virtues, and do this by collation [in the form of dialogue and comparison]. The Father began from time to time to require one young man or another to give some spiritual example, from which they put together practical documents for the acquisition of Christian perfection.'"

The *inventione* was not so much in the things that Philip proposed as in the novelty that his whole person exhibited, that of an impassioned adherence to Christ encountered and loved "not as a formula, but as a Person with the certainty that this imparts: I am with you."[3] This was the reason that Pope John Paul II could assure the Oratorians of our time that the Oratorian experience and charism is valid:

> At the dawn of the third Christian millennium your meeting plans to revisit, from a primarily pastoral standpoint, the sources of the spiritual movement that traces its origin to St. Philip Neri, in order to respond faithfully to its perennial mission: to lead man to encounter Jesus Christ, "the Way, the Truth, and the Life," truly present in the Church and the "contemporary" of every person. This encounter, lived and proposed by St. Philip Neri in an original and engaging way, makes us new persons in the mystery of Grace and instills in the soul that "Christian joy" which is the "hundredfold" given by Christ to those who welcome him into their lives. To encourage a personal meeting with Christ is also the fundamental "missionary method" of the Oratory. It consists in "speaking to the

heart" of men and women in order to lead them to an experience of the divine Master that can transform lives. This is achieved especially by showing the beauty of such an encounter, which gives life its full meaning. Those who are "distant" must not be offered a theoretical proclamation, but the possibility of a truly renewed and thus joyful life.

This is the great legacy you received from your Father Philip! This pastoral way is always valid, because it belongs to the perennial Christian experience! I hope that the revisiting by your Congress of the sources of St. Philip's spirituality and work will instill in each Congregation a renewed awareness of the value and timeliness of your founder's "missionary method," and make a significant contribution to the task of the "new evangelization."[4]

Prelude

We have seen in the preceding chapter that fifteen years before his priestly ordination Philip began his apostolate with a simple invitation, quite without any institutional concerns. His words struck the members of the Caccia household, and those of the clerks at the stores on Banchi St., the poor with whom he stayed the night in St. Peter's Basilica, the members of the Confraternity of the Trinity who heard his fervent discourses during the long hours of Adoration, even during the night, in the Church of San Salvatore in Campo.

His apostolate came directly from his heart, the fruit of the intense experience that Philip was living. His words attracted and drew people because they perceived in him the presence of something great and true that completely filled his life. The way in which he established relationships made it evident that here there was true humanity, inhabited by Grace, passionate about life and about every person.

The Beginnings

This is the magnificent prelude to the Oratory which will begin, in spite of the fact that Philip never planned it, in the first years of his priestly ministry. Once he had become priest, the usual place of meeting was the Church of San Girolamo della Carità, the "empty room,"[5] as a young man of the time remembered it. Instead of his usual invitation to "do good," now he spoke the words of sacramental reconciliation, which sows the Good in the hearts of men: "Here he gave himself over to hearing confessions, which consumed the rest of his life, so much so that even in extreme old age he never neglected it... And he was so assiduous in hearing confessions, that even before dawn many who could not come later came to see him and to confess. Afterwards, he would go into the Church and remain there until the last Mass, which he usually celebrated [a little before noon], never stirring, never leaving except for urgent necessity or to do some act of charity, so that whoever might want him found him prepared."[6]

"He was kept at home, in the very heart of Christendom," writes J. H. Newman,[7] "not to evangelize, but to recover; and his instrument of conversion was not Baptism, but Penance. The Confessional was the seat and seal of his peculiar Apostolate." For his entire life, as Bordini reminds us.[8] The last day of his earthly life[9]—he died during the night—he went down into the church to hear confessions very early, and continued during the afternoon: "he received everyone with great affability, showing kindness and affection even more than usual." After supper he heard the confessions of the Fathers who had to celebrate the first Masses of the next morning, when he would no longer be on this earth.

The ministry of Reconciliation was for Fr. Philip the field of his true apostolate, for forty-four years.[10] He believed profoundly in the action of Grace, and it was this faith that brought about the marvel that the reading in the old Breviary expressed with these words: "Innumeros filios Christo peperit": he produced innumerable sons for Christ. That capacity to "attract" of which Newman speaks (Gallonio[11] and many others have used the same word) came undoubtedly from "the characteristic gifts of his personality, his singular attractiveness which drew everyone [...] his warmth, his sweetness and mildness, his constant joy and serenity, the ringing festivity with which he did everything."[12] And Confession developed quite naturally into a dialogue which became true spiritual direction. Tarugi recalls in a memorandum: "In order to provide greater assistance to souls," he wrote on October 8, 1579 to Cardinal Charles Borromeo,[13] "it is useful not to stop simply with confession, but to begin to move them continuously toward doing good while keeping them always under the repeated discipline and care of their confessors."

The fervent age of the Catholic Reform was an era of great spiritual directors, and the Oratory was born exactly from within this ministry and developed as a relationship among friends who together were linked to the sweet spiritual paternity of Fr. Philip. For this reason the precise date of the birth of the Oratory is a question that has been in dispute among the early biographers as well as more recent historians,[14] who try to define the moment in which, having grown in numbers, a certain organization began to shape that which began simply as colloquy among souls carried out in the Father's room in familiar and fervent conversation on whatever book Philip was having them read, dialogues that touched the heart and opened the mind to vocal and mental prayer. The Oratory was not born as an institution, but developed out of the spiritual direction of individual persons which, almost inadvertently, became also a familiar and community encounter.

Fr. Philip's room[15] could not contain more than eight people.[16] He had to sit on the bed to make room for more: "His devoted followers, drawn by the devotion and love they had for Philip, went during the day, after dinner, to San Girolamo, to his little narrow rooms where the blessed Father received them, sometimes giving them a little sermon on the things of God, sometimes having them read some spiritual book on which he had each one comment according to his ability. Then in the evening he went out with them to the Seven Churches and recited the penitential psalms."[17] "Sometimes in his room," Bordini recalls, "he would interrogate someone on fleeing vices and embracing the virtues; and when each one present had answered, he ended by talking to them in a familiar way, teaching them and moving their souls to follow the way of God… And after he had been a while in this delightful and fruitful conversation, we all went together, in company, for a walk to one of the churches, especially to [Santa Maria sopra] Minerva."[18] Another witness of those beginnings, Monte Zazzara, adds some details on the walk on which Philip led his young friends: "In the morning, two or three hours before daybreak, we would go to confess to him and we always found the door open…and when we had confessed, he told us that we should go and pray until the hour of Mass; and when we had heard Mass, he would send us to the hospitals of San Giovanni, San Spirito and Consolatione where we would feed those poor sick people."[19]

This is the period when Fr. Philip's priestly apostolate was beginning, a period that lasted a little more than three years, until 1554–1555, "the sweet half-light of morning," Cistellini calls it, "barely noticed by the biographers and that only glancingly, in which we may observe foreshadowings and themes of what will become, in its full development, the Oratorian invention."[20]

The Surroundings

"We were quite a few young men," recalls Monte Zazzara in the above-mentioned testimony, but we know that these young men were not youths: they belonged to the social and historical context of sixteenth-century Rome, which Cistellini describes so vividly: "One might say that Rome in that period was a vast city half depopulated: under the pontificate of Paul IV it had no more than 50,000 inhabitants. The scars left by the Sack twenty years earlier were still evident; […] a city still medieval in appearance, strangely both ancient and opulent, a great island or aggregate of islands surrounded by vast desolate areas, intersected by unhealthy marshy and wooded areas between half-buried ruins. This space, filled also with innumerable churches, basilicas, and chapels, sumptuous palaces and dilapidated hovels, teemed with a mixed population, where there were poor of every description; the less poor constituted the plebes, although they went hungry too, and above them emerged the powerful, the patrician classes and the higher clergy with their court followers and parasitical clientele. Lacking entirely in Rome was anything like an industrious and productive middle class. Apart from workers in the building industry (the only industry really active), there were a fair number of artisans, small shopkeepers, and employees of offices, banks and apothecaries. But most of the population was idle, especially the young, and these constitute two distinct groups: some had income and were well provided for, others lived as best they could, more or less decently. In the background, and ever increasing in numbers, were the wretchedly poor—peasants who had deserted the sterile land, vagabonds who arrived from various places, given to begging and to worse expedients. This was the endemic plague of Rome, nearly impossible to eradicate in any period. When one speaks of the care that Philip took of the sick in the various hospitals and of the poor for whom he sent his own to seek alms, one must remember this lamentable state of affairs, which in times of famine or plague became really terrifying."[21]

Who were the friends who attended St. Philip's gatherings at San Girolamo? "They did not belong to the lowest social classes. They came from various groups: from patricians to courtiers, artisans, and students. They were certainly not hungry, or poorly dressed... But what is most striking in the little and highly varied group of the very first friends who gathered around Philip is that they were all completely free at any hour of the day. Most of them seemed to be really idle, without work, or at least without much to do. They were people, therefore, who did not lack the necessities of life, and needed rather to occupy their time better than to earn their living."[22]

The First Friends

The first who began with Philip this experience of a profound spiritual journey were friends he had had from the time of his lay apostolate.[23] It is important to see who they are, because they are the first "sementa,"[24] and in reviewing these names we may glimpse the nature of the journey that these men made following the path trod by Fr.

Philip and the action of Grace that transforms hearts: two artisans, who were already assiduous followers of the Confraternità della Santissima Trinità: the shoemaker Tosini and a miniaturist, Vincenzo; four from the Compagnia della Grazia: Prospero Crivelli, Enrico Pietra, Teseo Raspa, Bernardino Carnaglia; at least four Florentines: Giovanni Manzoli (about the Father's age, he had known him while he still lived at the Caccia house; Philip confided to him valuable information about his earliest years in Rome, which Manzoli testified to at the Process for canonization[25]); Simone Grazzini (who said that he had known Philip when he still lived in Florence; his deposition to the Process shows him to be among the first to remain in the Father's room during the night to go on praying[26]); Ludovico Parigi (he lived on Banchi St. at the house of one Gherardo, a Fleming, who entrusted to him the responsibility of taking to the Father every day two round loaves of bread, with a little flask of wine[27]—later on he would become a lay brother in the Congregation[28]); Giovanni Animuccia (the Florentine musician, a year older than the Father, of the household of Cardinal di Santafiora; from 1555 on he was maestro of the Cappella Giulia in St. Peter's; a man of rare piety[29], he was than once an intermediary between Fr. Philip and Sr. Caterina de' Ricci; he contributed in a singular way to the rise of the musical tradition of the Oratory); the notary Gian Francesco Bucca (who belonged to the Confraternity of the Trinity; he made three depositions at the Process for canonization, witnessing to the Oratory then being born and to the fascination exercised by Fr. Philip[30]).

New Friends

To these men, in successive waves, were quickly added newcomers, thus forming Fr. Philip's circle: Francesco Vai (employed in the Banco dei Donati, and to whom Philip and his first disciples sent an interesting letter[31]); the Roman patrician Marzio Altieri (who dedicated himself entirely to works of charity, and who said that he felt himself to be in Paradise when he was in Philip's room[32]); another noble Roman, Carlo Mazzei[33]; Antonio Fornaro[34]; the miller Pietro Molinaro[35] (miller of the Borgo at San Lorenzo, cited among the "venerable servants of the Lord, who died in the odor of sanctity"[36]); two young goldsmiths, one of whom was named Sebastian; the hosier, Michele da Prato; an anonymous seller of chicory[37]; Massarini[38] (perhaps the future priest of San Giovanni dei Fiorentini, Consolini's uncle); the Florentine perfumer Monte Zazzara[39] (father of three future Fathers of the Congregation); the Frenchman Loys Amès[40] (customs guard who had been a penitent of Persiano Rosa); the Roman Bernardino Corona[41] (gentleman of the household of Cardinal Sirleto, accepted later as an honorary layman in the Congregation); Alessandro Fedeli[42] (from Ripatransone, classmate of Philip's at the University of Rome [La Sapienza], whom Philip sent among the first to San Giovanni dei Fiorentini); the innocent cashier of the Banco dei Ceuli Marcantonio Corteselli[43] (from Como, Fr. Philip's delight, and whose portrait Philip wanted after the death of his friend, saying that he had seen his soul rise to heaven); Giulio Petrucci,[44] the priest from Siena (of the household of Cardinal Ranuccio Farnese and later of the Cardinals Charles and Frederick Borromeo).

The "Courtiers"

Those who frequented Fr. Philip at San Girolamo up to 1555–1556 belonged to every social class and every state in life: "many gentlemen plus persons of low social condition plus young people"[45]; but between 1556 and 1557, in "a single round-up," says Gian Francesco Bordini,[46] Fr. Philip drew together a goodly number of young men of good rank, who had passed from a worldly life to a definitely spiritual path. For the most part they belonged to the "families" of Prelates and of Princes, men from the courts who were refined and cultured, and who found themselves exposed "to many dangers and many occasions of sin," in that "tempestuous sea where at any hour one may shipwreck," as Antoniano says. Fr. Philip had conquered them: "with the sweetness of his word, and the example of a life perfectly integrated he attracted them to himself to the point that they could not stay far from him too long, and night and day they hardly managed to separate themselves from him."[47] Cardinal Guido Ascanio Sforza of Santa Fiora echoes Bordini but ruefully when, abandoned by his dog Capriccio he says of Fr. Philip: "It wasn't enough for him that he drew human beings to himself, he wanted to attract the animals, too."[48]

The first of the "converted" was Costanzo Tassoni, like Animuccia a member of Cardinal di Santafiora's household (we have spoken above of the affection that Fr. Philip had for him and of the esteem that induced him to make Tassoni his heir in his will of 1562). Others followed him soon in the choice of a spiritual life, beginning with Gian Battista Modio, author of a rather worldly, even licentious, book dedicated to Cardinal Del Monte, with the blessing of Julius III, in which he maintained beginning with the title that "a loose woman cannot shame a man." After his conversion he gave sermons at the Oratory on the lives of the Saints, and published *I cantici del Beato Iacopone da Todi...con alcuni discorsi sopra di essi*,[49] which he dedicated to Sr. Caterina de' Ricci. Giacomo Marmitta from Parma followed, secretary of Cardinal Ricci, a man of letters and a poet. Tasso mentions him in *Amadigi*: "E il Marmitta gentil, che a Dio rivolto, / delle cure del mondo è in tutto sciolto."[50] He brought with him from the same court among others Gabriele Tana who died an exemplary death assisted by Fr. Philip,[51] the young physician from Città del Castello Antonio Fucci, who took Modi's place giving discourses on the Saints, and Gian Battista Salviati, brother of Cardinal Antonio Maria. He had given himself over to a worldly life, but with the help of his wife, Porzia de' Massimi, became an edifying example of penitence and charity. Salviati is the one who will bring Alessandro de' Medici to the Oratory. He had come to Rome at twenty-four with a delegation of Duke Cosimo I on a visit to Pius IV.[52] Together with Tassoni, in the occasion of the extraordinary Jubilee proclaimed by Paul IV in 1555, the brilliant courtier Francesco Maria Tarugi (related to the Popes Julius III, who gave him residence in the Vatican, and Marcello II, and also related to numerous Cardinals) who was at that time a member of the household of Cardinal Ranuccio Farnese in the splendid palace that rises next to San Girolamo. He will be the dearest to Fr. Philip of the priests of the future Congregation, and the Father will choose him as his successor. Cistellini reports what Cardinal Alessandro de' Medici said of himself and Philip, that "no one had ever known in his time, in a Christian republic anyone more gifted or of rarer or greater qualities"; "and that from the time he put himself into Philip's hands, he was all his and, having overcome the last obstacle, affective in nature, by a circumstance that seemed providential, from then on the Oratory was his reason for living, forever."[53] The same period marks the arrival at San Girolamo of another distinguished figure, Felice Figliucci,[54] who had been brought to God through the misfortunes of his career, and whom Fr. Philip will direct to a religious life among the Dominicans of San Marco in Florence (some letters of his exist written to Philip, in which Fra Felice give witness, all the way to the end of his life, of his gratitude to him whom he acknowledges as his spiritual father). Around 1558 two other young men enter into Philip's circle, whose names together with that of Tarugi will be written in large letters in the history of the future Congregation. Cistellini says that "the active presence of their personalities" was immediately evident "next to Fr. Philip, who molded their spirits and their wills" and that they became "the decisive element in laying the foundations of the original initiative of the Oratory."[55] These were Gian Battista Bordini [sic][56] (a Roman, but whose family was perhaps originally from Padua, twenty-two years old and a doctor of law) and Cesare Baronio[57] (from Sora, the first disciple whom Fr. Philip encouraged to enter the priesthood and whom he chose as successor in 1593. He came from Naples to Rome to further his studies, but almost immediately came to know the Father well, and began an intense spiritual journey, "like a chick under the wing of the mother hen...happy and content and totally satisfied."[58] Fr. Philip placed him in the Parravicino house as preceptor of Ottavio, the future Cardinal who was profoundly linked to the Oratorian family. He received his degree in law in 1561).

The Oratory

Thus the number of Fr. Philip's sons increased. Philip, who had already had built, at his expense, other rooms in the spaces near his own room,[59] had to think of another place for their meetings. This was especially true because the idea of a missionary project to the Indies, which his first followers had talked about, had ended with the response of the monk Ghettini.[60] To Philip it seemed clear now that the mission field was to be that in which he found himself. It was thus that he decided to ask for the space above the right-hand nave of the Church where the brothers of the Confraternity kept the grain[61]: "the blessed Father seeing the great fruit that came to souls when he had so many near him at once, especially the young...the Lord inspired the Father, after he had prayed, how he might find space for the people who grew in number every day. He felt in his heart that he could ask the Deputies of the Charity [just at that time he had been admitted as one of the Deputies of the Confraternity] if he might have a passageway over the nave of the Church of San Girolamo."[62] It was *il primo Oratorio di San Filippo Neri* (the first Oratory of St. Philip Neri), as the stone placed over the entrance reminds us: "here they would come to pray, all the spiritual sons of Fr. Philip...and the Father would come to open the door for the first to arrive...and he had a key made that he put under the door [the entrance door to the house: the door that is still there at San Girolamo, where the stairway begins, even though it is built differently now] and the one who arrived first would open and put the key back for the others, locking the door; and then they would begin to pray...."[63]

These meetings had already taken on fixed characteristics,[64] but when they moved to this place in 1558, they assumed the name "Oratory"[65] and a more organized structure.[66] A certain intimacy continued, of course, but the spontaneous dialogue was increasingly rare because of the sheer number of participants. The dialogue form never disappeared entirely, but the practice of giving sermons was consolidated: "after having read a spiritual book for half an hour, he had some sermons given, on various subjects, for example, the beauty of the virtues, the ugliness of sin, the lives of the Saints; and he had the custom of proposing some spiritual doubt [question], to which after eliciting various responses, he concluded that whole spiritual exercise himself, very spiritedly, inciting his hearers to greater awareness of themselves and of the vanity of the world and the love of God."[67] The two hours of this daily meeting were divided into four sermons, which would become classics, entrusted to some of the disciples, and later, after they were ordained the first Fathers, to the priests. Fr. Philip, with the same discretion that he gave to everything, intervened, corrected, deepened. Above all he enlivened them, and by his very presence imparted that same fervor that burned within him: "Every day he was present for all four sermons; and if, perchance, someone said something that was not very clear, he took it up immediately and clarified it, to the wonder of all present."[68]

The old intimacy of Philip's rooms, *le stanziole sue*, was no more, but the fervor was the same, and Fr. Philip when speaking about the love of God often had to stop for a moment because he was moved to tears.[69] He would be there and participate until the very end of his life, but he would gradually reduce his interventions, also because others were now able to speak.[70] The account of the last time he tried to intervene in the Oratory, six years before his death, is moving: "I remember"—said Alessandro Illuminati—"that when a father had finished speaking, the Father got up into the place when we gave sermons with great liveliness, but he burst into such weeping that he couldn't utter a word, and came down without saying anything and never went up there again."[71]

This evolution, which was obviously determined by circumstances, has prompted some in recent times to speak of the "process of clericalization" of the Oratory. Doubtless we may look back with great nostalgia to the first meetings in Philip's "bare room," and the first to feel nostalgia for it was Fr. Philip himself, especially in the last years of his life. But if the regret is for the disappearance of a system where laymen were active in preaching, that is, the appearance of a democratic system where lay and clerics were equal, it makes no sense, simply because there was never any such system in the Oratory.

The earliest documents that show how the Oratory came to be and to develop testify to this.[72] Fr. Cistellini, who analyzed these, says: "That which catches our attention immediately in this spontaneous formation of the group around Philip is the docile dependence of each one upon him who was recognized without any reservation as leader and father… His paternal authority was beyond discussion, nor was there ever any move to choose things they might undertake without his authority… 'Never was there discussion without the Father, or at least another priest being present,' says one of the early memoranda. Philip was teacher and guide, who gave direction and order: 'the Father,' therefore."[73]

What is really to be regretted with greater reason is the loss in Philip's disciples, over time, of the simplicity and the fervor that gave spirit to the preaching in the Oratory, the spirit that Cardinal Charles Borromeo described as early as 1571: "They are attentive more to moving the heart and igniting the will and affections to spiritual things than to feeding the intellect on knowledge and doctrine."[74]

In the Oratory sermons, the wise familiarity of the origins had evidently decreased, if we may judge from a letter which Talpa wrote in 1588[75] to Fr. Philip from Naples. Talpa describes one of their Oratory meetings, which gave him a special joy because it had the same spirit of the origins in San Girolamo: "Today the Father messer Francesco Maria, spoke about a book familiarly, and he was the first, and then messer Giovenale. I listened with such consolation that I could say no more, since I seemed to see the Oratory in that same equality and simplicity that there always was in San Girolamo… May the form of reasoning proper to the Oratory be preserved and be transmitted to those who will come after us, because otherwise all the good our Congregation has will be lost."

The mild-mannered and merry Fr. Gigli responded directly to Tarugi, perhaps taking dictation from Fr. Philip as often happened, "I tell you that the Father and the deputies and priests responded with joy when they heard that Your Reverence had spoken 'on the book,' in conformity with the old custom of the Oratory, when we preached in spirit and truth and in simplicity of heart, leaving room for the Holy Spirit that He might infuse His virtues into the mouth of the one who spoke, and without deep and premeditated study and turning over of pages of books and authors and scholastics... And if someone should say: the old simplicity is gone, now we think we are more refined, I certainly don't know about this.... But I can say that the fruits of that simplicity were no less than the fruits of the present.... And I do say that then there was more fire in the preaching, and the result was more conversions, more people entering religion [the Orders and the Congregations], which is rarer today. What do we need? Fire, faith, a knife. Fire to ignite the heart of him who preaches, faith that He who gave spirit then will also give it now, and a knife to cut away our will and establish us in holy obedience, which guided us for years and years, and let us pray to the Lord that it will guide us yet for years and years to come."[76]

2. THE FACE OF THE ORATORY

The scuola de li suoi spirituali[77]

With this expression, which reminds us of the *schola dominici servitii*[78] of St. Benedict or the *prima beati Francisci schola,*[79] Vincenzo Ercolani[80] described the *opera nuova* [new work] that grew up around Fr. Philip: and the term *schola Beati Patris* [school of the blessed Father], as we said earlier, will express in Gallonio and in the first Oratorians all of the richness of a spiritual journey, of a method, a "community" of men who recognized in Fr. Philip their master and guide.

From the beginning, the Oratory was not to be confused with the numerous confraternities that flourished at the same time, which normally had a precise charitable function. Rather the Oratory had an extremely clear spiritual function: it meant to lead people to "undertake to be increasingly Christian in their relationships to God in prayer and in their practice of the sacraments, and in the evangelical witness of daily life."[81]

Works of charity were certainly not lacking either in Philip's method or in the experience he gave his followers, but the Oratory presents itself "as an institution understood to offer assistance more to souls than to bodies, or rather, the practice of charity is in direct connection and depends directly upon the former."[82] Behind the idea that the spiritual journey was of first and fundamental importance lie all the "exercises" of the Oratory and the various initiatives that characterize it. Everything is illuminated by, and takes its sense from, the basic undertaking to live a Christian life, and the force of this comes from prayer, the Sacraments, and the ascetic of humility. "The Oratory is an ingenious instrument for the realization of very high ideals, which uses methods and expedients and means of an extremely wise pedagogy, in which the incomparable genius of Fr. Philip excels."[83]

The origins of the Oratory were consonant with the Reform movement, which included or even generated a variety of expressions of the Christian life, but also drew on Fr. Philip's love for the origins of Christianity. This was manifest in his devotion to the martyrs and his predilection for the catacombs and the reminders of the apostolic age found in the "Seven Churches" and in other basilicas in Rome. The Oratory thus took on, without any official proclamations and in all simplicity, the aspect of the apostolic community described by Acts: "And they devoted themselves to the apostles' teaching and fellowship, to the breaking of bread and the prayers."[84] The first Oratorians were aware of this, and referred to the early Church to describe the Oratory: "In our present time, there seemed to reappear the lovely face of the apostolic community"[85]; "that life that was lived in the primitive Church"[86]; "it consisted only in the renewal of the spirit that the Christians had in the early Church."[87]

From the early time of the meetings in San Girolamo, and then when even that place became insufficient and they had to go down into the church, the Oratory took on an increasingly definite form: there were the afternoon and the evening meetings, the meeting on Sunday morning, the walks, the visit to the Seven Churches, music and Lauds, and the visit and assistance to the poor in the hospitals.

At the center, however, there was always the listening to the Word, and the exercise of preaching, not as ends in themselves, but as in the most genuine experience of the Church, as means to induce souls to conversion of life, to the practice of prayer and to sacramental participation.[88]

The Big Oratory

This "exercise of the Word" characterized the afternoon Oratory, which was also called *Oratorio grande* [big Oratory] because of the large number of participants who by their numbers made impossible the familiar aspect of the *domestic circle* and rendered it, "heterogeneous and composite, where you didn't see only known faces."[89] The success was due to the simplicity and fervor[90] with which the divine Word was dispensed every day.[91] The joyous atmosphere was increased still further by the Lauds and the music. This afternoon Oratory, lasting above two hours, will become "the predominant and specific end and reason for being of the Congregation."[92] The first Constitutions of 1612 will dedicate the entire third chapter to this question, but we already find it amply described in the early memoranda[93] written by the very first disciples: the anonymous written apologetic datable to 1567–1570, the brief report in Tarugi's handwriting, which was prepared for a canonical visitation to the Vallicella, another one of Tarugi's addressed to Cardinal Charles Borromeo in 1579, an anonymous memorandum but attributable with certainty to Tarugi, of the same time as the previous one, a brief report of 1581 to Cardinal Vicar Savelli, Baronio's *De origine Oratorii*[94] and the pages of the *Annales*,[95] the *Instruttione per fonder la Congregatione dell'Oratorio*[96] composed by Ancina, around 1578–1580, upon the request of the Archbishop of Turin.

The Oratory began with the reading of a devout book and continued with four sermons, or *ragionamenti* [arguments] of a half hour each. The first and second, which had to deal specifically with moral asceticism, were characterized by improvisation on themes that had emerged from the reading. The Word of God was familiarly discussed in frequent references to the Sacred Scriptures,[97] but also to the incomparable riches of the Church's reflections over the centuries. These two sermons, because of their spontaneous nature, demanded a *bravura* that not everyone possessed, partly because usually the first two speakers had, so to speak, to weave a dialogue between them, taking up themes and ideas implicit in the presentations of one another. There were Fathers in the Congregation who could never have undertaken this particular exercise: Tarugi excelled at it but Talpa, for example, had no particular gifts for it. The two sermons which followed had to be well elaborated, which required a certain preparation, and dealt with the lives of the Saints and the history of the Church. In these the Word of God was seen in the life of the mystical Body of the Church alive in time.

Music and the singing of Lauds in Italian were introduced by Fr. Philip, who remembered his years at San Marco in Florence. They "crowned the edifice, always by the grace of God," Baronio said, and the meeting concluded with prayer: "all the people knelt to make common prayer for the Church, for the Pope, the Cardinals, and the Prelates, for the Christian Princes and for many other particular cases which recommended themselves," recalled Tarugi who synthesized stupendously the purpose of the gatherings: "to form a Christian man and to keep him with the help of grace continually on his guard."

The witness given by an Englishman who was in Rome between 1576 and 1589 is beautiful and significant: "Four of them at least, one after the other, during those two hours, not from the pulpit but seated on a bench only raised a little above those listening, almost as though they did not want to be distinguishable from their listeners. They gave familiar discourses, each on a different religious argument, with great variety, elegance and vivacity, but one and the same spirit moved their tongues, because they gained innumerable souls for eternal life. Nor in those circumstances did they engage in curious behavior or strike solemn poses, but each one, depending on the circumstances, chooses a passage of Sacred Scripture, on some aspect of the life of the Church, or the life and the example of some saint...encouraging the faithful to frequent Confession, or Communion, or visits to the hospitals or the prisons… On weekdays men of high spiritual or temporal office would come, but on Sundays and feast days there was a much larger attendance at this exercise.…"[98]

The Little Oratory

There was another form of Oratory which the 1612 Institutes present in the first chapter as an essential and qualifying practice of the Institute and that "will remain an integral and fundamental part of Philip's Institute…the exercises of which the Constitutions of 1612 put into an appendix."[99]

Pateri recalls the origin of that which was called *Oratorietto, Oratorio piccolo,*[100] which came to be called "Secular Oratory" only at the end of the eighteenth century: "The blessed Father, seeing that this exercise [the big Oratory] was so successful, and that every day the numbers not only of those who belonged but also outsiders increased, decided to introduce an exercise that would be extremely useful and even necessary for those who wished to live in a Christian way, and this was the prayer of the evening…"[101]

Tarugi, in the memorandum to Borromeo mentioned above, describes it in these terms: "They must, first of all, maintain an exercise of prayer every day, in a particular place in their homes, an hour daily, part vocal and part mental.… The place where they meet together, on the other hand, is to be open not only to those who are adherents of the Congregation, but to everyone who wishes to come. In addition, they see to it that many, divided into groups, go to visit and to serve in the hospitals of Rome, always taking with them a little of whatever might appeal to the sick people and be approved by the doctors."

The members of the Congregation participated in this meeting, along with the most assiduous of the big Oratory and those spiritually closest to Fr. Philip (although no one was ever excluded). Its intimate and recollected atmosphere and the place, quiet and set apart, evoked the fervent simplicity of the prayer of the small group gathered in the

Father's room. The meeting took place every evening except Saturday. Sunday morning was the time to prepare for and to receive the Sacraments, and also to visit the sick, and for a half hour of mental and a half hour of vocal prayer. This last, modeled on the *preci* [prayers] that concluded the big Oratory, also included on Monday, Wednesday and Friday the *disciplina* [scourging] in memory of the Passion of the Lord.

The Visit to the Seven Churches

Fr. Philip had begun, as we have seen, this pilgrimage of faith and of silent contemplation in his first years in Rome, in solitude and deep intimacy. It was an ancient practice, profoundly suited to Philip's spirit and tastes. When he became priest, he shared this personal experience with his disciples. The practice became a sort of "open-air Oratory," because they took their prayer and speaking of the Word of God to places that preserved the living memory of the things that they were reading and the lives of the Saints and the life of the Church.

This experience was initially solitary, even when Philip went in the company of some disciples, but it assumed unforeseen proportions when Philip proposed it as a devout and joyous alternative to the carnival, which in Rome and elsewhere tended to be pagan and dissolute.[102] The number of participants[103] was such that it had to be rigorously organized in order to preserve the spirit of pilgrimage, and the Congregation managed to keep it in an atmosphere of prayer, accompanied with songs, music, and even refreshment breaks to relieve the fatigue and tension of the spirit[104]: "a pilgrimage for the people for Holy Thursday […] a kind of long walk both festive and penitential, along a fixed and traditional itinerary: San Pietro, San Paulo fuori le mura, San Sebastiano, San Giovanni in Laterano, San Croce in Gerusalemme, San Lorenzo fuori le mura, Santa Maria Maggiore. And this revealed yet again Philip's genius in interweaving different aspects of Christian practice: the song of vanities revealed itself in a glimpse that included both enchanting landscapes and ruins of celebrated monuments, or the most suggestive memorials of Rome, both pagan and

Christian. The devotional practices harmonized well with the picnic in the open, usually at Villa Mattei, called Celimontana, during which there was 'music of voices, cornets, and flutes,' and at the end the sermon of the *putto* [a boy who would preach in a flowery style], so that 'returning home, the people thought they had been in paradise.'"[105]

The Oratory Out-of-Doors

The Visit to the Seven Churches was not the only occasion of typical meetings of the Oratory held out-of-doors. Even the musical contributions that had helped so much to create the atmosphere of the afternoon meetings gave rise to festive meetings outside of the buildings where the Oratory normally met. The Englishman whose observations we have quoted before comments on an interesting aspect of these meetings: "in the summer they get together outside, in some garden, in order to attract more easily those who might not come into a church...." These gatherings, writes Cistellini, "were certainly a pleasant novelty among the varied devotions of the period. There are some testimonials to these...in the depositions of the canonization process, but they are not uniform or detailed...a sign that the practice did not at first follow any established order like the other Oratorian exercises, and did not occur at regular intervals. It was only a prolongation of the afternoon session, after vespers [Sundays]; a gathering in some garden or large cloister, in the most pleasant spaces, on hills thick with vegetation, or green areas looking out over the panorama of the Urbe."[106]

The Oratory of the Young

Thinking about Fr. Philip, one imagines so easily the picture of him surrounded by boys, which the iconography of Philip has handed down to us. In reality, his ministry did always, from the beginnings to his old age, unfold in the world of the young, and many have testified to his preference for this age, full of promise, for this reason often difficult, and often anything but heedless and happy. "Juvenes," observed Thomas Aquinas, "parum habent de praeterito, multum de futuro: propterea multum vivunt in spe." [Little is in the past for the young, much is in the future, and hope, therefore, is what characterizes their lives.] Fr. Philip, who kept the true spirit of youth until his last day, was essentially a teacher, an educator, and what he taught was this hope, the constitutive element of the life of the young. He was a teacher and a formator because this is what adults must provide to anyone who lives that "hope" that youth displays. Those who saw Philip in action unanimously remembered the group of youth and adolescents who would come up to him, but they said, like Charles Borromeo, that "messer Filippo has a particular gift in managing the young, and they love and revere him so much that there is no sort of obedience that they will not immediately do for him."[107] The words "managing" and "obedience" are terms that do not suggest an easy and heedless intimacy; they express, rather, Philip's awareness of his mission.

It would be a historical error to think of the Oratory, with its afternoon and evening gatherings, as a meeting place for those youths who crowded around Philip and whom he led sometimes to various places of recreation around Rome. The discourses given at the Oratory, the readings that were proposed tell us immediately that these encounters were not intended for young people in their early adolescence. They imply a greater maturity and a formation that had already begun.[108] The wise pedagogy of St. Philip found even for the young boys activities that suited their ages and their needs,[109] but the Oratory in its classic form will remain what we have seen: a "school" of Christian life for adults of various ages who already have adult lives and responsibilities.

Sources and Outlines

The following section is dedicated to the Congregation which was born out of the Oratory and placed at the service of the Oratory, with its principal object the sound functioning of the Oratory.[110] It will also present the principal aspects of Oratorian spirituality and piety, in reference to the Constitutions. Here we offer a glance at the fundamental texts on which that spirituality draws: the books dear to Fr. Philip, and which he read with taste and engagement evident in his marginal annotations. He also had his disciples read these in the meetings of the Oratory and he used them in his private encounters with people who came to see him.

John Cassian's *Conferences* holds a special place among these works, a work that may well be considered "the earliest matrix of Philip's spirituality, and even of the Oratorian method."[111] "The keen psychological analyses on the behavior of man in the face of temptation, the lucid review of virtues and vices, the insistence on themes such as humility, purity of heart and of body, patience (which includes sweetness of countenance and the tranquility of the man at peace), above all the criterion of 'discretion' which informs all the work of this distinguished monk of the fifth century (the second conference develops just this theme, and one can almost hear the voice of Philip speaking)"[112]: such discussions make clear the reasons why the book was so dear to Philip. This is confirmed by the conviction that Fr. Talpa will express in his treatise on the origins of the Institute: "the spiritual life, generally taken to be a difficult thing, became so familiar and domestic that it seemed easy to every sort of person, something for which to give thanks."[113]

In addition to Cassian's *Conferences* and *Institutes*, there were other texts[114] that passed through Philip's hands and which are still kept, at least in part, in his "library": the instruction of Doroteo di Grazia, the *Vitae Patrum*, and various works of the Fathers of the Church, above all Basil, Jerome, Augustine, Gregory of Nazianzen and Gregory of Nissa, Bernard and John Climacus; letters sent by the first Jesuit missionaries from the Indies, the *Imitation of Christ*, which was the most highly recommended among the readings of the Oratory, the *Letters* and the *Dialogue of Divine Providence* by St. Catherine of Siena, the *Cantici spirituali* by Bl. Jacopone da Todi, the *Vita* of Bl. Giovanni Colombini written by Belcari, the *Stimulus divini amoris* attributed to St. Bonaventure, the *Arbor vitae crucifixae* of Umberto da Casale, the *De quatuor novissimus* of Dionysius (Denys) the

Carthusian, the *Prato* of Giovanni Mosco, the *Specchio di perfectione* by Enrico Herp, the works of Taulero, of Diego de Estella, the *Trattato dell'oratione mentale* of Francesco Arias, the works of Granata and of Serafino da Fermo.

"This cursory listing," notes Cistellini, "forbids us to place or to interpret Philip's spirituality as primarily mystical, even if there are evidently many mystical writers. There is also Philip's fervent temperament, the enthusiasms and heroic aspirations of the first group (the missionary ideal, for example, and the cult of the martyrs). But no rigid and exclusive classification is suited to Philip and his school. One proof of this is the many ascetic aspects of Oratorian conduct and practice. What has been authoritatively observed in general with respect to Italian spirituality of the period is true here: it is not speculative nor systematic nor analytical, but rather extroverted, imaginative, and both affective and voluntary, which are just those characteristic notes that distinguish straightaway the personality of Philip and his spirituality. One may, certainly, concede that Philip with his institutions constitutes a case apart (at least because of certain unusual elements deriving from his singular temperament); but it is still true that because of his wisdom and ability in fusing different methods and tendencies, he remains the person, rather the master,[115] most representative of an integrated and harmonious spirituality in all that new direction for the renewal of the Church."[116]

3. THE ORATORY TODAY

The Constitutions of the Confederation of the Oratory approved in 1989[117] begin by declaring that "'Oratory' is the name we use for a place destined for prayer. So the Oratory founded by St. Philip Neri took its name from a place of prayer." And they continue: "The Oratory is a fraternal union of the faithful who, following the lines laid down by St. Philip, aim at what he taught and did, and so become 'of one heart and one mind' (Acts 4:32; Can. 578). The Oratory was established from its very birth for familiar discourse on the Word of

God, and for mental and vocal prayer in common. By these means the Oratory fosters the contemplative spirit and love of divine things among the faithful, as in a school. As St. Philip was a sign of this love of divine things, so the Oratory manifests and pours forth similar love, in an attractive and effective way, in joyful service and simplicity of heart."[118]

In Chapter VI, which discusses the apostolate of the Congregation, some paragraphs are dedicated to that activity which is defined as the "first": "First among these is the Secular Oratory...whose erection is already contained in the foundation of the Congregation itself (Can. 677, par. 2), and indeed was the origin of the Congregation (Chap. I, 1–4)." "This Secular Oratory can have various sections, either according to different categories of persons or different categories of work, above all regarding liturgical worship, common prayer, which gave the name to the Congregation of the Oratory, religious education or culture, the catechetical apostolate, social work or the advancement of Christian joy. The statutes of the Secular Oratory and its governance are to be drawn up or approved by the General Congregation."[119]

What the Constitutions say is undoubtedly clear, as is the *Spiritual Path*[120] which dedicates the whole second chapter to the history, method, and exercises of the Oratory.

However, a question emerges, and has emerged for years in the minds of Oratorians, from the time the General Congress formulated those texts, and with greater or lesser clarity, and that is: What, today, is the Oratory?

At the time of Fr. Philip, and in Rome long after him, the Oratory was a well-defined and clearly separate entity, but it was difficult to maintain this outside of Rome. The outline of daily meetings, and the division of them into four sermons was not easily exported, and from the beginning they had to be adapted to different environments and to the needs of the places where Congregations established themselves. The spirit of the Oratory gave rise to a variety of apostolic activities which derived in some way from the Roman Oratory and which lasted in Europe generally up to the crisis of the nineteenth century. Very few Congregations managed to survive that crisis, and those that did had few members and precarious apostolates. The twentieth century was marked by upheavals even in ecclesial matters that made it even more difficult to see how the Oratory might be the specific kind of "union of the faithful" of which the Constitutions speak.

The question: "What is the Oratory today?" still has not received an unequivocal answer. Some say even today that the Oratory is not so much an institution as a "spirit," a "style," on which Oratorians are called to draw in order to shape their varied pastoral activities in the Church, responding to the needs of the time, to the diminishing number of clergy, and to the ever more urgent needs of the diocese. It would be a "spirit" which informs their work in the parishes[121] and in the various ministries that flourish in the Church.

Even though this answer is widely agreed upon, even taken for granted, the question remains. This is evident in the fact that the General Congress of 2000 felt the necessity of revisiting the charism of the Congregation in light of its origins, and of placing squarely in the center of the discussion "The Secular Oratory at the Third Millennium." And in its discussions of the "Secular Oratory" the Congress meant to refer not only to the Oratorian "spirit," but also to say that the Constitutions define the Secular Oratory as its reason for being, and that it is to be the "first among all" of the activities of the Oratory.

It was of great help in the preparations for the Congress that periodic "International Oratorian Meetings" had begun to take place, spontaneous gatherings which had sprung from within the Confederation and which were received very warmly. They are of great value for both the richness of their content and for the significance that they assumed, and they enjoyed the participation of many, both priests and laity, in Seville in September 1992 and at Oaxtepec in July 1998.

From the meeting in Seville there were the valuable papers given by I. Talleche,[122] M. T. Russo Bonadonna,[123] G. D. Felten,[124] G. Cittadini,[125] G. Carriquiry Lecour.[126] From the meeting in Oaxtepec those of M. Gonzales Leal,[127] C. Palmer, C. Romero, and V. Gutierrez,[128] A.

Holder,[129] G. D. Felten,[130] R. Herrera,[131] H. Zolaque[132] and the many talks that were given in the study groups.[133]

Even the Federation of the Congregations of Northern Italy, in preparation for the General Congress of 2000, gave thought to the Secular Oratory organically, and presented the fruit of its reflections in a document[134] with the intention of "uncovering the essential outlines of this first-born vocation, in order that all the separate components of the Oratory may come to a better understanding of what they are called to be, and in order that even today the Congregations of St. Philip may understand that they are themselves to be at the service of the Secular Oratory, the reality that gave origin to their foundation and for which they exist."[135]

The Oratory has engaged in multiple apostolic activities since the time of St. Philip. Some activities are discerned by the whole Community as a response to particular local needs, and they are carried out as a community; others arise, in the freedom proper to the sons of Philip, from the initiative of individual Fathers, but they are always undertaken by consensus of the Community. All undertakings, however, become richness for everyone because they contribute to the sense of communion which is the soul of the Oratorian family. Because of this method and this spirit, the Oratory is and remains "a brotherly union of the faithful" who journey together freely and visibly, following the path laid down by St. Philip. This specifically Oratorian method and spirit have not been lost, even though so great a part of these innovations of St. Philip have passed into the common patrimony of the pastoral ministry and apostolic work of the whole Church.

This "union of the faithful" is more present today in the new and recent Congregations than in others. He who is writing has been able to verify this new, fruitful vitality in various places and in different continents. There is in these newer Congregations a fraternal communion of priests and laity who, keeping in all simplicity their different roles, find in the common meeting for prayer, for listening, for discussion of the Word of God, and in the common participation in the Sacraments, the source of energy that allows them to witness to the faith through the varied experiences of their lives.

What one is aware of immediately here is the unity with which the members of the Congregation participate in the life of the Oratory, not just the one responsible, but everyone, in the awareness that here is the core from which every other activity is drawn.

The Secular Oratory, where it exists, is evidently not only an expression of an evangelization that is really "new," and the only one that surprises and attracts the secularized people of our time who seem indifferent to so many programs offered by the Church, but it is an indicator of the authentic vitality of the Congregation which is placed at its service.

The presentation of G. Carriquiry, undersecretary of the Pontifical Council for the Laity at the General Congress, emphasized in 2000[136] how precious for the Church in our time the experience of "this family of clergy and laypeople coming together in spirit, in truth, and in simplicity of heart," a surprising and fascinating unity which radiates out into the life of the Church and the body civic"; "the best that Philip's Oratory can offer," he said, "is to show itself capable of proposing, drawing again upon its source, its own original epiphany" which is exactly "the miracle of this family...of this surprising unity." In this two fundamental demands of the new evangelization become possible—if this is not to be reduced to "strategies, or programs, or marketing operations designed to make the product more salable." These two demands are: "to begin from the person" and "to rebuild the supporting beams of the Christian experience in ecclesial communities"; "to reconstruct the person thanks to a new experience, in a 'network' of surprising human encounters that lead one to rediscover life as a gift, in one's vocation and in one's destiny; [...] in visible communities, made of different kinds of people—all poor sinners entrusted to the mercy and to the grace of the Lord—who live in real relationships, more human ones, of surprising fraternity, miraculous gift of the unity that men cannot acquire with their own disordered powers; [...] communities free of the excessive trust that too often is put into planning schemes and bureaucracies, which so often make the Church seem to many like a place that offers only religious services and moral exhortations; [...] communities attentive not to the multiplication of initiatives or the renewal of facades, but to the sacramental and charismatic gifts, both essential to the Church, since it is they that have founded it and that renew it perennially."

In this experience so typically Oratorian, witnessed to by the history of its origins and by the work of Fr. Philip, the promotion of the dignity of the laity is not some discourse that has become arid through repetition, even less any suggestion that the laity take over some function proper to the Congregation, but rather "the grateful and joyful impulse of those who, having received and experienced the gift of faith as truth, well-being and beauty in their own lives, communicate and propose it to all those whom they meet, who are free to accept it if they so desire. This is altogether different from the life of dull ecclesiastical routine, and such people become a merciful company even for those who live far from any Christian point of view."

"Rethinking the Oratory" through its history and the reflections of those who have recently dedicated themselves to this, we can only be confirmed in the conviction that the proper apostolate, its "own," of the Congregation has its own reason for being, today as in earlier times, and that the Secular Oratory, as the specific of a "union of the faithful," responds perfectly, perhaps more than other initiatives, to the real needs of the people of our time. The Oratory will be able to carry out its work in all different ways, as it has in various times and places, thanks to its great potential for development and to its innate dynamism. It will do this by offering the experience of an authentic encounter with Christ to the people of today, who have lost the sense of "person" and who do not easily find an adequate response to the profound needs of their hearts. Such an encounter is found in the communion of a family where the person is worth more than the initiatives and in the simplicity of which they find the strong and sweet experience of the origins of Christianity: that which fascinated Baronio and made him speak of the Oratory in his Annales. When he comes to treat the early period of the Church he says: "It is by divine plan that the edifying practice of familiar conversing about the things of God and of commenting on His Word in simple sermons has been renewed in great part in our time, in Rome, according to the model of the apostolic assemblies. This has been the work of the Reverend Father Philip Neri, a Florentine, who like a fine architect has laid the foundations. It was organized in such a way that almost every day those who desired Christian perfection flocked to the Oratory."

CHAPTER III

The Congregation of the Oratory

This form and manner of life,[1] having existed more than a thousand years in the Church of God and then been discarded, has by the pleasure of His Divine Majesty been revived with the particular spirit which He gave to our blessed Father in our times, to the end that, this state being intermediate between the Religious[2] and the secular states, those who because of lesser physical and spiritual strength feel incapable of entering into the one, or fear living in the other would have no more excuse; and so that, seeing that charity has grown cold and the misery of the peoples has increased, there might not lack soldiers who would not depend upon the people but serve using their own funds, and conversing with seculars in everything except sin, they, secular priests, gaining their own salvation, would gain also that of the people.... This was judged in the Congregation to be the vision of the blessed Father, and this is the path that all must follow. Walking in harmony in the House of the Lord, *idipsum sentientes omnes,*[3] playing not only *in timpano,* but *in timpano et choro.*[4]

(*Fr. Flaminio Ricci to the Fathers at Naples, April 15, 1601, in Archives of the Congregation in Naples, 9, 1, 258*)

1. FROM THE FIRST COMMUNITY TO THE CONGREGATION

The call to priestly life, nurtured in their filial relationship with Fr. Philip, drew some of his disciples to desire to serve the Church within the spiritual "movement" which God brought into being through Philip Neri.

At San Giovanni dei Fiorentini

Fr. Philip was inclined by nature and by spiritual outlook not to plan anything and not to organize anything, but to entrust everything to the Spirit. He accepted those vocations and sent them to the national church of the Florentines, a few steps from San Girolamo. This was a church of which he now had the pastoral care, thanks to pressure from the authorities.

This was in 1564, and Fr. Philip was just recovering from a grave illness that had threatened his life, as tended to happen when a significant change was about to take place. It was the year that historians define as the first year of the post-Tridentine Church: the bull of approval of the Constitutions and of the conciliar decrees both came on January 26. Charles Borromeo became archbishop of Milan and began vigorously to make the new spiritual direction of the diocese felt. The foundation of the new Roman Seminary was announced. The reforms of the religious orders began, and plans for visits to the diocese were sent out. On November 13, the bull on the Profession of Faith was issued.

In this fervent atmosphere of renewal the Florentines in Rome had wanted St. Philip to assume the pastoral care of their church, since he was Florentine and was well known in the city for both the holiness of his life and for the fervor of his apostolate.

Fr. Philip accepted reluctantly: parish work did not suit his temperament or his vocation. In the group of priests at San Girolamo, he had even refused a stipend in order to serve the church of the Confraternity with all dedication, but with the freedom to carry out his apostolate in his own way.[5]

While accepting the new assignment, Philip remained at San Girolamo, and sent those new disciples, who would be known in the Oratorian tradition as "vetustiores," to San Giovanni dei Fiorentini: the twenty-six-year-old Cesare Baronio, the thirty-four-year-old Giovanni Francesco Bordini, whom Fr. Philip ordained as priests between May and September 1564. Shortly afterwards, two more priests, Pompeo Boccaccio and Giacomo Salort entered San

Giovanni, and between 1565 and 1566 Angello Velli, twenty-eight years old, and Francesco M. Tarugi, forty years old, also came. Almost all of them came from the study of law, and already had promising careers at court. Tarugi, in particular, was already well known for his personal giftedness and his kinship with families of Popes, in addition to his position in the court of Cardinal Farnese. The decision to entrust themselves to Fr. Philip in the Oratory was for all of them a step involving real conversion—"we became deserters, but without shame," Baronio wrote later, "and fugitives, but with honor!"[6]

While waiting for parish assignment, they all continued to participate in the activities of the Oratory of San Girolamo, where they went three times a day and where each also had his meeting with Fr. Philip. They lived in community at San Giovanni, and Fr. Philip continued to send more men, still not thinking of any particular institution. He probably was content to have a "family" of secular priests who were authentically "spiritual," living together in a rather loose structure like the Fathers at San Girolamo, subject to some general rules necessary in order to live together,[7] but bound, above all, by a strong spiritual bond with himself. To all of them, he was the *pater familias* of an ordered communion.[8]

There are letters that provide important information about the system of life adopted by Philip's community, which quickly showed the desire to take on a different form than that of the "Convitto" at San Girolamo. This community at San Giovanni wanted to reproduce, in a fervent and festive familial environment, the ideal Christian community described by the Acts of the Apostles.

Fraternal charity was the essential rule, and they lived under the guidance of Philip, undisputed head and the one and only moderator. The first rules,[9] meant to give order to the common life, came forth a few years later, when Tarugi settled definitively into the community, around 1569. He wrote them himself, "with the consensus of all" and "with good cheer, and quickly accepted by everyone."[10] The rules prescribed, among other things, that "each of those who are in the house or who will enter in the future will know Fr. Philip and will place his will into his hands…ready for every obedience…and will take this as the chief precept, quod si solum fiet sufficit." The rector of the House was named directly by Philip to whom, says the rule of the time, "belongs the right to relieve him of his post when it seems best to him. Experience has shown that this is by far the best way. Everyone is to be at peace, and never to answer back."[11]

These rules show the basic elements of the earliest community life, and prescribe the community's presence at the evening Oratory and at the Chapter of Faults, service at table by turns, reading at table and proposal of doubts, recreation, and the criteria for accepting new members. They obviously foreshadow the principal features of the future Congregation of the Oratory.

The Community was growing, and experienced some opposition from some who were suspicious of the singularity of the new manner of common life and of the Oratorian method. However, Cardinal Borromeo intervened, as their great protector, because of the esteem in which he held the Oratorians. He also began to ask for some of these to come to work with him in his great plan of reform for the Diocese of Milan.

Beginning in 1565, spiritual privileges were conceded to Philip, given first orally to Fr. Philip and his followers, and then confirmed by a papal Brief,[12] which showed clearly that the Authorities were giving benevolent attention to this presence which had as yet no official recognition. Neither did the Oratory have such recognition, having been born and having grown by the breath of the Spirit: never had Fr. Philip thought to make it into an institution.

In 1571 Pope Pius V decided to impose upon Tarugi "by virtue of obedience" the responsibility of the head of household of the House of Cardinal Bonelli, the legation of the Cardinal in Spain, France, and Portugal, which Tarugi was obliged to accept. At the same time, Baronio fell gravely ill, and these two things made the community and Fr. Philip fear for the future of the Oratory and the church. However, amidst these difficulties, new members came into the House, providing some relief. They were men who attended the Oratory assiduously, the young Tommaso Bozzi, minute in stature, called the *tantillus homo* in the early sources, cultivated and refined; Giovanni Antonio Lucci, who left the Congregation after it transferred to the church of Vallicella; the Spaniard Francesco Soto de Langa, a man of great goodness and a fine musician; and the Frenchman Niccolò Gigli, particularly beloved of Philip because of his innocent ways and spiritual depth.

About the same time, Fr. Philip accepted three others into the community against the judgment of Tarugi. All three gave good promise but they had not come from the Oratory of San Girolamo. They were all from the Marche, and belonged to an association of reformed priests and clerics which had formed in 1568 in San Severino. The best known of the three was Fr. Antonio Talpa, who later contributed so much to establishing a more regular community life. Fr. Tarugi returned from the legation in April 1572, full of interesting experiences and his meetings with famous personages, and even more fervent about reforms to be carried out beyond the walls of Rome. This renewed awareness of the urgency of the reform brought him close to Talpa, in spite of significant differences of character and sensibility. Eventually Tarugi adopted Talpa's ideas and later became one of his supporters, together with Bordini and Baronio.

The community progressed toward a more cohesive, organized form, as is shown by a document that Talpa, who was away in Gaeta, sent to Tarugi in December of 1572. Talpa included a memo asking him to forward it to the newly installed Pope Gregory XIII, "if the Father agrees." Many of the people associated with Pope Gregory were in sympathy with the circle of the Oratory.

However, the most decisive step was the resolution, taken in 1574, to construct a new building for the Oratory, near San Giovanni dei Fiorentini. Fr. Philip must have approved this, since there was nothing, even of minor importance, that was done without his approval. The decision was motivated by the inconvenience of going to San Girolamo for the daily exercises, especially now that the family had grown, and by the fact that the spaces available at the Confraternita della Carità were cramped.

Fr. Cistellini wondered in a substantial article while his major work was nearing completion: "Were those in charge aware of the full significance and the consequences of this undertaking? This did in fact seem to express the members' conviction that they constituted an autonomous and organic group that was no longer the same as the Oratory. At the same time they knew that their origins and the justification for their existence came from that. Their affective detachment from both San Girolamo and San Giovanni came from this, that the Oratorian exercises had merely been housed there.... The regulation of the community from then on moved away from the earlier paternalistic system."[13]

The Oratory was inaugurated with a sermon given by Bordini on April 15, 1574, but the difficulties which had arisen some time earlier with the Florentines, who apparently did not like the activities of the Fathers, urged even Fr. Philip, who was always reluctant to formalize things, to seek to systematize their common life so as to guarantee their autonomy.

Fr. Tarugi summarized the events of this period when he wrote in October 1579[14] to Cardinal Charles Borromeo, who was a guest for a whole day at the Vallicella: after the transfer of the Oratory to San Giovanni, "the fathers saw that their work could increase greatly if they had a better location and more members. Since it did not seem a good idea to establish their work in a church which was not theirs, they resolved in the Jubilee Year to petition Our Lord [the Pope] to provide them a place of their own. The place where they are now was given to them, and at the same time His Holiness erected the Congregation, calling it the Congregation of the Oratory of Secular Priests."

At Santa Maria in Vallicella

Thus in the heart of the Jubilee Year of 1575, while the "project" of transferring to Milan was not yet quite closed, and while there was still some possibility of uniting with the Barnabites, who had come to Rome and were given hospitality by Fr. Philip at San Girolamo, Pope

Gregory XIII issued his Bull. It bore the date of July 15 and was entitled *Copiosus in misericordia*, and in it the Pope assigned to "Filippo Neri Prete Fiorentino, e Preposito di alcuni Preti e chierici," the parish church of Santa Maria in Vallicella, and at the same time, erected "in the above-named church a Congregation of secular Priests and clerics which is to be called the Oratory." It gave the mandate "to the same Congregation and to its Rector and Priests to formulate Statutes and regulations which are reasonable and honest and not contrary to Canon Law or to the dispositions of the Council of Trent, and to alter these and to create new ones as necessity and circumstances dictate. These Statutes, once they are approved by the Holy See, must be observed as inviolable by every member of the Congregation, and freely and lawfully obeyed."[15]

Fr. Philip, "Provost of some Priests," is clearly the "founder" of the new Congregation: it is born out the womb of the Oratory, which is his work; his disciples are those who gather closely around him and who constitute that family; under his authority those steps are taken which lead to canonical recognition, but it is also evident that other Fathers collaborated with him to give shape to the Congregation.

Philip's decision to remain himself at San Girolamo, in that same little room, is eloquent witness to his special personal vocation. He saw no reason why he could not be Provost of the newly created Congregation and reside outside of it: he bore within himself an intense desire for freedom, a yearning for the infinite, which could not be contained within the boundaries of any one project.

This was the reason, certainly, beyond his sincere humility, that he never wanted to be called "founder": "I did not make this Congregation, God made it, for I never thought of founding a Congregation," as Egidio Calvelli testified at the Process, quoting the words of Fr. Philip.[16] Only in November 1583, in obedience to the Pope, and mounting a self-mocking procession,[17] he left his "nest" at San Girolamo to move to the Vallicella, which he loved, which he visited daily, and which he had insisted be large and solemn. He continued to pay the rent for that room, to which he returned often, even when in the house at the Vallicella he had managed to have refuge of his own constructed, high up, where he could retire to look at the sky.

2. THE CONSTITUTIONS

The writing of the Constitutions, prescribed by the Bull of foundation, was a slow and difficult undertaking. The slowness of it will surprise only those who do not see the extraordinary originality of the Oratorian community. It was not a problem of merely laying down rules for the common life, but of finding the juridical formulas that would express adequately an experience of community life that had arisen spontaneously, characterized by freedom of spirit and tied to the personal charism of a man whom everyone in community held to be "the living rule." And there were in the Congregation from the beginning two ideas, the vision of a community governed "more with customs than bound by laws,"[18] together with the awareness that the Institute needed a more precise system of rules.

1583

In the book of Decrees of March 1581[19] we read that: "By order of Fr. Philip it was decreed that nothing pertaining to the Congregation shall be dealt with without the participation of all the Deputies" and in May of 1582 that "the community shall meet as Congregation twice a week to discuss the Constitutions of the Congregation."[20] Prepared essentially by Talpa and Bordini, the first text of the Constitutions was reviewed by Fr. Philip who made some additions, and was put into good Latin by Bordini in 1583 with the title *Compendium Constitutionum Congregationis Oratorii.*[21] The Congregation decided that it should be summarized by Fr. Talpa in a *Summa* or *Breviatio*[22] which was approved in a meeting on November 28, 1583, one of those rare meetings in which the Father also participated. The decennial Fathers signed it; and Fr. Philip, who had confined himself just to approving it, required that everyone observe its essential points.

1588

Only with the Constitutions of 1588[23] did Fr. Philip give his explicit approval. In the Congregation of August 29, which the Father presided over in person,[24] Fr. Cistellini tells us: "to guarantee their integrity there was the authority of the Father (who himself had urged that they be approved), and the harmonious consensus of all the members.... If we wish to speak of a first Oratorian rule that was authentically Philip's, there is no doubt that it would be that of 1588."[25]

Together with the decrees issued by the Congregation from 1577 on, when it met for the first time and assigned the first responsibilities, these Constitutions were taken in hand and integrated, right after the death of Fr. Philip, in 1595–1596 by the new Provost Cesare Baronio, who was keenly aware that the charismatic authority of Fr. Philip could not perpetuate itself in the community.

1612

A definitive version of the Constitutions was finally put together between 1609 and 1612, and Paul V gave his pontifical approval on February 24, 1612 in a Brief entitled *Christifedelium quorumlibet*.[26] The editing was the work of a commission of four Fathers: Pietro Consolini, Francesco Bozzi, Giovanni Severani, and Giuliano Giustiniani, who saw their task as one of collecting and compiling all that belonged with certainty to the original norms of the common life, and validated by the tradition and experience of the community. The book of Decrees, under the dates of their meetings, documents meticulously their aim of absolute fidelity of the *Institutes* to the mind of Fr. Philip, to which Consolini gives witness in a letter of 1615: "thus they are, both because of the authority that he had to make these rules for this house in Rome, and because of the care with which this house has guarded them, not wanting to admit into them anything except what he left and what was observed for so many years while he was living." The signatures of thirty-three Fathers,[27] some twenty of whom had lived with Fr. Philip, guaranteed the exact agreement of that document with the mind of the founder. It was not easy work, since it had to take into account the various tendencies always present in Congregations, and it had to codify the system of government of "men free [from vows], who yet wished to be governed," as Fr. Giustiniani said. Fr. Flaminio Ricci,[28] Doctor of Law, who had entered the Congregation at thirty-three years old in 1578, played an important role in this process. He was one of Fr. Philip's intimates by affinity of mind and spirit, and was named in 1596 to an important office of the Community of that time, that of confessor of the House. It was he during his two three-year terms as Provost, from 1602 to 1608, who preserved the continuity in the direction of the community that Philip had wanted, and who, without ever appearing among the Fathers who were occupied in writing the Constitutions, nevertheless exercised an extremely valuable authoritative role.

1943

The *Institutes*[29] sustained both the Roman Congregation and the other Congregations erected down the centuries in the same way, until 1942, when the General Congress of the Oratory undertook the first revision,[30] updating them in conformity with the Pio-Benedictine Code of Canon Law which had been issued in 1917. The following chapter is entirely dedicated to the history of this revision, and to the organization that was born out of this Congress. Here it suffices to say that the revision undertaken by Fr. Larraona, the Apostolic Visitor, over almost ten years of consultations and careful reflection, was done with so much respect to the venerable original text, that, apart from slight changes rendered necessary by the new Code, all the modern additions and formulations were placed in a separate text entitled *Statuta Generalia*.[31]

1989

The *Constitutiones* and the *Statuta Generalia*[32] presently in force are the work of the General Congresses of 1969, 1982, and 1988, which had the aim of updating the texts of 1942 once again, in the spirit of Vatican II and in the light of the new Code of Canon Law published in 1983. They were approved by the Apostolic See in 1989.

3. THE FACE OF THE CONGREGATION OF THE ORATORY

The Foreword

The Foreword of the present Constitutions, exactly the same as that of the 1943 Foreword, reproduces a page of incomparable value, composed in all probability by Fr. Consolini, one of St. Philip's most beloved and faithful disciples. This text stood at the beginning of the *Institutes* of 1612:

> The Congregation founded by St. Philip Neri at Santa Maria in Vallicella at Rome, takes the name of ORATORY from a place dedicated to prayer, and then from the sacred exercises, especially the evening exercises, which were performed in it.[33]
>
> The Congregation of the Oratory, guided by its Holy Father Philip with the customs of daily life rather than bound by laws, had no special rule in the beginning by which the activities of its pious members might be directed.[34]
>
> For that excellent Father, accustomed to moderate with fatherly affection the spirit and the will of each of his sons in accord with the nature of each, thought it sufficed for him to see them inflamed with piety and daily becoming more fervent in evangelical contempt of earthly things, and in love for Christ. Only gradually did he gently approve and confirm, as truly springing from the Spirit of the Lord, the things he knew from daily experience would suit them and always be of benefit to them for pursuing virtue, perfection, and the honour of God.
>
> And this way of life, though differing notably from that of the existing Religious Institutes, he strongly affirmed to be most suitable to Secular priests and the Laity and conformed to the Divine will, while again and again saying that he was not the founder of the Congregation but that the Great and Almighty God had wanted it, and was its head and builder.
>
> Hence such things, which either our holy Father Philip took

> care to establish in this manner, or which after his instituting of them among the members of his Congregation were accepted as customary and then uninterruptedly observed, have been gathered together in these Constitutions so as to be understood as succinctly as possible.

Congregation and Oratory

The first element underlined in the Foreword is the *close relationship* which obtains between the Congregation and the Oratory, from which it derives its very name and without which its specific identity could not be sufficiently grasped.

It will never be possible to disown this fundamental link of the Congregation with the work first conceived by St. Philip. New expressions of the initial spirit arise out of changing circumstances, but this first work will remain always as the fundamental form of apostolate for the priests of the Oratory.

But neither is it possible, if one wishes to remain faithful to the mind of the Father, to minimize the distinction between the two: while the Oratory is made up of the laity, the Congregation, instituted by Apostolic Authority, is an association of priests whose particular vocation is to dedicate itself to the Oratory with the functions appropriate to the ministers of God: administration of the Sacraments, of Confession above all, celebration of the sacred mysteries, and proclamation of the Word of God specifically oriented to prepare the faithful to receive the Sacraments worthily.[35]

From the beginning, in fact, it was clear that the reason for the existence of the Congregation of the Oratory is the perfection of priestly life: this is testified to by its very birth from the "womb" of Fr. Philip, but it is also affirmed explicitly by the writings of the earliest Fathers.

In a letter datable to 1581–1582,[36] Fr. Tarugi affirms: "That the Congregation wants to show in everything, by leading a virtuous life, in literature, in divine worship and other exercises in preaching, readings, prayers, confession and communion, how perfectly these can be done, what the clergy should be, and particularly by living in common, with love together with concord." And the first Constitutions of 1583 attest: "This above all we are proposing: that regardless of time and place, always and everywhere we present ourselves as Ministers of God and seek that which is useful to the salvation of souls, not that which looks to our own interest or to our own tranquility"[37] with "an attitude of innocent and completely blameless priestly life."[38]

Secularity

The Foreword also emphasizes the secular character of the priests of the Congregation, which is also a fundamental characteristic, "a way of life certainly different from that of the Religious united in the existing Institutes" but equally intending to "reach sanctity and perfection in order to be pleasing to God."

Fr. Antonio Talpa in his treatise *Principles of the Congregation*, dated July 20, 1599, explains the reason for the choice of "secular" on the part of Philip and of the priests of the Oratory: "Although Philip saw some beginnings of the reform through the agency of some congregations of religious priests, which were then arising, he thought that the reform could not be born entirely out of the religious clergy. The cause therefore that moved our blessed Father and the purpose that he had in instituting this Congregation within the state and the life of secular clergy was…to insinuate the reform into the clergy by way of the same clergy, reformed."[39]

It is difficult to say whether the motivations that Fr. Talpa attributes to Fr. Philip reflect fully the Saint's intentions. He certainly never used the word "reform," even while being the greatest reformer that Rome ever had. In any case it is evident that the priestly life of Fr. Philip and of his first disciples is an authentic expression of the life of the reformed secular clergy, or to say it with an expression more familiar to the Father, of the "spiritual" secular clergy.

The secularity which the Congregation guarantees, within a family life lived in an ordered Community,[40] is not only the absence of religious vows and a particular role in the local Church,[41] but a quality, a style, that in present-day terms we might define as a spirit of empathy, sensitive to human restlessness and to the movements that run through society; an attitude of listening and of dialogue, the capacity of coming close to others and to sharing in a climate of serenity and respect. Fr. Giulio Cittadini[42] calls it: "willingness to save the world by living in it, from the inside and not from without, not benefiting from a superior position without sharing at all in its anxieties and its crises. This is what Jesus did, who was not a benefactor of humanity, but who became incarnate, was with us, at our level.... Secularity is in opposition only to clericalism, if by clericalism we mean lack of participation, extraneousness, arrogance, sense of superiority, degrading and coercive paternalism."

What Fr. Agostino Manni, writing on the nature of the Congregation,[43] defined as *moderatae vitae genus* is applicable here. It is the style of moderation that Gallonio also referred to in presenting the Oratorian life as oriented to an *auream quondam mediocritatem* and which Newman in the mid-nineteenth century will express in the image of the "gentleman," incarnation of the ordinary condition of the Oratorian priest.[44]

Respect of the Person

A third fundamental element, closely tied to the two preceding, finally, seems to us to be expressed in this description: "The most excellent Father generally directed with paternal insight the spirit and the will of his own, according to the character of each." Noteworthy is the attention to and the respect of the *individual* person, whose own character has value. The good in each is to be brought to its full potential and formed in the light of the Spirit. This requires a responsible attitude that nurtures the authentic liberty of each, so that each person's journey becomes richness for the community and respect for the creative work of God.

This attitude of Fr. Philip's explains also why the composition of the Constitutions proceeded so slowly: his style gave first priority to spiritual leadership, in the personal relationship of trust and listening, rather than to directions in written form. The rule was extremely evident from the beginning, but present in the person of the Father and in the spiritual guidance that he exercised, "repaid by seeing them lit up with piety...experiencing by degrees [*pedetemptim*] and with sweetness [*suaviter*] and ascertaining as a manifestation of the will of the Lord that which, through daily experience, he found to be congenial and useful to them, day by day, for reaching sanctity and perfection in order to be pleasing to God."

The annotation of the first rules of the Community in St. John, cited above, is significant. The rules establish that "each of those who are in the house or who will enter in the future will know Fr. Philip and will place his will into his hands...ready for every obedience... and will take this as the chief precept, *quod si solum fiet sufficit*"; and then they add: "that all will confess to the same Fr. Philip, who will resolve every problem that may arise, and everyone must obey his decision; and if His Reverence cannot deal himself, for the many things he must attend to, he will appoint a substitute, who will do everything according to his orders, communicating everything to His Reverence."[45] When Fr. Philip will no longer, because of the growth in numbers and the development of the institution, be able to form personally the members of the Congregation—with the sweetness mentioned above but also with the force capable of exacting "every obedience"—the Community will find its point of reference written into the Constitutions. But the Foreword will for centuries admonish everyone that the law [of the Community of the Oratory] will be fully lived only in the climate where the rules were born: that of profound humility and of openness to a constant interior formation.

Society of Apostolic Life

The present Constitutions present the Congregation of the Oratory as: "a Clerical society of Pontifical Right (can. 589), composed of Clerics and Laymen who live the common life without vows, according to these Constitutions, bound solely by the bond of charity. It is a Society of Apostolic Life (can. 731, par. 1), a Juridical Person, (can.

114; 741, par. 1) and a *domus sui iuris*[46] or independent house (can. 613, par. 2)" (no. 15).

The lay Brothers are now also an integral part of the Congregation. Received at the beginning as collaborators in the service of the House—but never as private servants of individual Fathers—and beloved as precious confreres of the Community, they never had the right to participate in the decisions of the Congregation, the clerical character of which was—and still is—indisputable in the light of history and of the documents.

"To the end that our clerics can more easily fulfill the responsibilities entrusted to them," the Constitutions of 1583 declare—and again in abbreviated form in 1588; in those of 1612 there is no mention of it, since it was by then normative—"let there be received into the Congregation lay brothers, who after preparation and being content in their station, will take care of temporal affairs, knowing for certain that they will never participate in the election of the Provost nor of other officials."[47]

In all the Oratorian houses there have been edifying examples of beloved lay brothers whose memory is remembered with a blessing. In the Archives of the Congregation of Naples there is preserved as a precious witness of the love of the Fathers for the lay brothers. It is a letter which Mons. Tarugi, who had been consecrated archbishop of Avignon, and was about to leave Rome to go there, wrote to Michelangelo Tozzi, one of the first who had gone with him from Rome to Naples in order to found that House: "Michelangelo, dearly beloved brother, be content with your vocation, because I would exchange mine for yours and I would be content that Our Lord [the Pope] would have me renounce my new church, and I would return to Naples as a simple priest, to die and to live what remains to me of life among you. Be of profit and serve God with joy and you will see Jesus Christ Our Lord not only in each priest but in every brother of the house, and try to overtake and to outdo all in humility, obedience, and charity, never tire of doing good, and every day begin to do this again, as though you were just then starting. Try to bring together the lost sheep and comfort and encourage the bewildered. Serve the Church in everything, do not neglect the house duties, bear yourself in a well-ordered and discreet manner, praying morning and evening, take the sleep that is necessary for you, and eat what your labors require. And believe that prayer, together with the exercise of the active life that you live, will constitute a state of virtue much more certain than that of one who hears confessions and preaches. Put your faith in Fr. Antonio [Talpa, rector of the House], and be quiet and content under his counsel, and be my procurator, obtaining many prayers for me. And remember that I love you as my dearest brother, and may God bless you and keep you holy and perfect."

The present Constitutions, breathing the new ecclesial sensibility of Vatican II, have updated the older ones in these terms: "Members in the lay state were always most dear to St. Philip Neri. According to the mind of the Church they enjoy equal rights and responsibilities with the priests in the Congregation, except for those things which depend on sacred orders. The same holds for any permanent deacons. Lay members possess a consultative voice after aggregation. Each Congregation must determine whether they can receive the active and also passive voice after the sexennium. However, in any case the formation of all the members must be so arranged that, when they have been aggregated, they are capable of bearing the burdens of rights and duties" (no. 74). That the Congregation is to remain *societas clericalis* is clear from the above cited No. 15 and in reference to the election of the Provost, who must necessarily be priest (no. 42: "no one is elected as Provost unless he is in priest's orders"): fundamental declarations which permit an exact interpretation of the term *coetus* with which the present Constitutions present the Congregation as "Oratorii Congregatio est coetus qui ab initio ad servitium Oratorii institutus fuit": "the Congregation of the Oratory is the group that was instituted from the beginning for the service of the Oratory" (no. 5).

Before defining the juridical nature of the Congregation, the Constitutions emphasize that it is "a family group living in a lawfully established house and maintaining the common life (can. 710), whose members are led more by the spirit of charity than by law. The Provost of the Oratory, who leads the way in the spirit of service diligently cultivates the spirit of charity (no. 6); in the Congregation of the Oratory familiar discourse on the Word of God, or spiritual conversation, always holds first place and from this the spirit of faith and prayer, of charity and service, is always continuously stirred up and nourished" (no. 7). And they add: "The Congregation follows the primitive Christian community in that its characteristic power consists not in the multitude of its members, but rather in mutual knowledge—whereby there may be regard for well-known faces—and in the true bond of love by which those who are of the same family may be bound together through the practice of daily customs (no. 11). The Congregation always fosters fraternal association in everything through serene peace and joy, both internal and external, by which its whole service of God and care of souls are informed, so that it may always truly be said of the sons just as of the Father: IN JOY" (no. 12).

Common Life: Family Life

Without forgetting the principal purpose of the Congregation, which is the exercise of priestly ministry, it is legitimate to see the style of life that is characteristic of the Oratorians as family communion. This is an undoubted expression of the "perfection characteristic of the Congregation of the Oratory," as Fr. Fernandez de la Cuesta says,[48] quoting Newman[49]: "Our perfection is not attained by sacrificing human affections or personal inclinations. On the contrary, reciprocal love and a love for the Oratory as the domestic hearth is one of the principal characteristics and duties and bonds of its Fathers. [....] Notwithstanding our detachment, which St. Philip held in such high esteem, he commanded us in his rule 'to bind ourselves one to the other with love,' by 'daily contact' and with the 'daily knowledge of reciprocal inclinations,' and also by the same kind of 'family tone.' Consequently each House is said to be a 'family' whose Superior is 'the Father.'"[50]

The Constitutions emphasize over and over this characteristic of the common Oratorian life, based even canonically on the equality of its members—which involves sharing life and responsibilities under a governance which is clearly collegial—and the exercise of a true charity which takes into account of what each person is, rather than of what accomplishments he might be capable of attaining. Family life requires—the Spiritual Itinerary puts it this way[51]—"that all live in the same house, eat at the same table, share with the others one's apostolic experiences, discuss together problems and difficulties, help one another reciprocally in moments of need, above all share times of common prayer, meet for the 'renewal of family life' (Chapter of Faults)."

Charity

The fundamental law of the Oratorian Community, established by Fr. Philip, is charity. The *Spiritual Path* reminds us of this, quoting Fr. Pietro Consolini and Fr. Mariano Sozzini[52]: "It is characteristic of those affiliated with the Congregation to exercise a type of charity among themselves which is more than fraternal, helping each other without caring about one's own comfort. Each one ought to practice this form of life, contenting himself above all in alleviating the burdens of his neighbor; in other words, doing everything that corresponds to true and human friendship as this is found in a place governed only by charity. And there is never too much charity…" "In order to have a good family life in the community," Fr. Sozzini suggested, "Love everyone from the heart; forgive everyone; speak well of everyone; have true sympathy for all and pray daily to God for everyone; do not speak offending words, even with the intention of being clever; beware of antipathies and moderate them with virtue; be equally wary of fondness and particular friendships—yet to esteem each other from the heart does not violate charity, and being close to those who are better is most helpful; make sure that diversity of opinion does not degenerate into factions; be charitable, joyful, peaceful, and patient during times of recreation; do not took for external works of charity if the internal ones at home are not first accomplished."

In the counsels given by the Roman Congregation to the new Congregation of San Severino we read: "Let each one remember always that this Congregation must be founded on those principles which pleased our Lord God, through the intermediary of our Father Philip, in the founding and establishing the Congregation at Rome, that is, humility and charity, to be professed in a particular way, more in actions than in words. Our blessed Father desired these to be our hair shirts and our fasts, in place of so many other exercises practiced by the Religious in God's Church."[53]

Humility

The norms that the Constitutions set, taking them from the *Institutes*[54]: "No one may accept any sort of high office," speak of a simplicity of life rooted in this virtue considered by Fr. Philip as the irreplaceable basis not only of the common life but also of the spiritual structure of each person. "Humility," writes Fr. Cistellini,[55] "helps to attain complete detachment from self, from honors and earthly goods; it preserves us from contamination of the world, and urges us on to apostolic work." "Be humble, remain lowly," St. Philip repeated constantly, inviting everyone "to rid himself of the adornment that disfigures the deep simplicity of being human."[56] This refers, obviously, to a process of growth, which occurs over time, furthered by the decisive commitment that St. Philip required. Such a commitment went contrary to the idea diffused at the time of a Saint-as-far-as-possible, meaning "Be good, if you can" [State buoni, se potete]. But the expression in Roman dialect, *State buoni*, means: "Be resolute, young men, be calm!" so that St. Philip could add: "if you are able…"; on the other hand he would say, "I want nothing more of you than that you remain joyous, and without mortal sin."[57] Nothing was more foreign to Philip's teaching than certain forms of *buonismo*[58] which has nothing to do with *il buono*[59] except a similarity of sound. Fr. Philip is a saint who is warm, joyous, and witty, capable of joking, of amusing himself and of amusing others, but *spontaneismo*[60] is foreign to him. He loved spontaneity, fled from artificiality, and chose the most amusing means to bring his disciples to make progress in virtue and to lead them to perfection, but he was rigorously even though joyously ascetic, taking on a healthy discipline of the will for himself and for his disciples.[61] "There are," St. Philip taught with respect to conquering humility, "three kinds of vainglory. The first is the Chief, and one has this when vainglory is more important than the work to be done and the work is done for the vainglory. The second is its Companion, and one has this when a man does not do the work for the sake of vainglory, but in doing the work feels complacent. The third is the Servant, and one has this when in doing the work vainglory arises, but the person immediately represses it. Be attentive at least that vainglory is not the chief thing. When it accompanies the work, it does not subtract merit from good work, but perfection consists it making it the servant."[62] Fr. Consolini affirms: "No one can say that he is a true son of Philip if he is not humble." And he shows how essential this virtue of the Oratorian is, which demands a total trust in God and produces as its fruit that peace which in vain one seeks in the proud assertion of one's own judgment: "The priests of the Oratory live in holy peace, without caring about their own opinions and judgments...obedient to the slightest sign of the Superior, depending on him with all their hearts; and if they were to give a good example externally, they must first be internally even more obedient than they appear."[63]

Mortification

Fr. Philip was the kindliest teacher of mortification, because the good humor with which he exercised it filled the rigors to which he put both himself and those under him with mirth and serenity, but he was clearly aware that "where there is no mortification, there can be no great sanctity."[64] The exercise of mortification in St. Philip, it is true, never assumed the harsh forms that no one could imitate that characterize the lives of some other Saints. He loved interior mortification more than physical mortification, although he did not reject this either: "Exterior mortifications help a great deal to acquire interior mortification." But the privileged place is still the heart: "To mortify one's passion, no matter how small, is a greater help in the spiritual life than many abstinences and fasts."[65] "If you must do excessive things," he counseled Alessandro Borla, "do them in being mild and patient, humble and charitable, because these things are good in themselves." And on the mind he said: "The whole importance of the Christian life consists in mortifying the rational [the presumption of the intellect]."[66] The awareness of human fragility, in the young, in adults and in the old, led Philip, until the last threshold of his life, to an exercise of incessant conversion: "Lord, guard yourself against me today because I will betray you and I will do all the evil in the world. Lord, keep your hand on my head today, otherwise I will apostatize. The wound in your side is great, but if you, oh my Jesus, do not keep your hand on my head, I will make it even greater."[67]

Liberty

It is in this light that we can understand, in its origin and its effects, the liberty that Philip preached, which has often been held up like a banner, without always understanding what it in fact expresses. Philip Neri carried within himself a deeply rooted yearning for that freedom which has already been mentioned. He had received it in Florence, with his mother's milk, and he always wanted to be remembered as of the "Florentine nation" [*florentinus natione*]. Those who know Dante Alighieri will understand that sense of liberty that animated the "citizens" of Florence, as opposed to those who were "subjects" of other states. He cultivated this yearning in the choices he made in his life: when he decided to leave the security of San Germano, and earlier in Rome, in the fervent experiences of his youth and his priesthood. He preserved it in his choice of that secularity that implies adherence freely given to a demanding project. He had a strong sense of the nobility of freedom, and defended it in his own Congregation when some members sought to impose narrow sets of rules. Philip Neri was a free man, fascinatingly free. But that freedom, which he lived as an ascetic form of human and spiritual maturity, does not pass automatically to those who limit themselves to admiring it. The title which a modern biographer gave to his Life of St. Philip is well-chosen: *The Conquest of Liberty*.[68] The question is exactly this. One does not acquire freedom: one conquers it. One cannot receive it even as a gift (Alessandro Manzoni denounces this political and historical illusion in the choruses of *Adelchi*[69]—no one can be liberated by someone else without having freedom rise in his own heart and paying for it by sacrifice). One disposes oneself to freedom, in a journey of liberation like the biblical journey of Exodus. Any pretense to freedom that is not rooted in this ground is either pathetic or is simply a facade concealing less noble intentions. For Philip, who undertook seriously to follow Christ, joy is essentially the discourse on the Beatitudes, and liberty belongs to that "poverty of spirit" and "purity of heart" to which Christ linked the possession of the Kingdom of God in heaven and the vision of God.

Freedom of spirit is the indispensable matrix of every expression of true liberty. The *Spiritual Path*[70] of the Oratory reminds us of this and quotes Christ's declaration: "The truth will make you free" (John 8:32), and it continues by offering this commentary by Fr. Giulio Cittadini[71]: "Freedom, a prerogative of the mature and responsible person, excludes servile submission, and the incapacity for choosing autonomously. It develops in an upright and resolute conscience, formed by daily encounters with the Word of God, in the peaceful conversations of the dialogue in the community, in fraternal teaching and correcting. This freedom cannot be confused with the anarchy and the egocentric caprice adolescents are naturally given to, nor with the defense of self-interest, which is natural for 'the old man' (*quae sua sunt quaerunt*). In the communal life of the Congregations, freedom becomes shared responsibility and glad-hearted service to one's brothers, with disinterested dedication, beyond the ordinary goings-on of daily communal life.... Only the Spirit can create in us the union of the many components of our spirituality. If the Holy Spirit does not illuminate us, the joy which distinguishes us would become mere frivolous thoughtlessness; granting secularity in concession to the world, along with licentiousness and materialism, and then freedom, too, would degenerate into anarchical dissipation."

Liberty and Obedience

Two terms that are difficult to combine. But the maturity of the Oratorian lies precisely in the ordered unity of these two fundamental realities. There is an axiom traditionally spoken in Oratorian circles: "in veritate liberi, in caritate servi, in utraque laeti"—"free in the truth, we become servants in love, and in the mature synthesis of both we experience joy." When Oratorian literature speaks of "free men," it means that while the Oratorian is not bound by vows, that same freedom itself commits us to a fidelity that is not at all optional. We must not forget, in every time and in every cultural context, that the evangelical *despicientia sui* is the first virtue in which Fr. Philip disciplined his sons seriously and of which he was a genial and imaginative teacher. From the testimony of his first disciples it is in fact clear that the Father spoke more often of obedience and humility than of love, while however always implying it. Blessed Giovenale Ancina, for example, said in recounting to his brother Matteo his own first meeting with Fr. Philip: "He saw me and he listened to me most willingly; he exhorted me to humility above everything else."[72]

Joy

Only in this climate of profound interior life is the joy of which Fr. Philip was master, or rather "prophet," as John Paul II wrote, even thinkable.[73] It was Cardinal Agostino Valier in the Dialogue, *Philippus sive de christiana laetitia* [*Philip, or Of Christian Joy*], cited above, who described in these terms that Christian joy of which Philip is the great witness: "true and intimate joy is a gift of God, the effect of a good conscience, of disdain for vain and exterior things, of contemplation of the highest truths. It is fed by meditation on death, by conversation with devout persons, by the frequent reception of the Sacraments; it is preserved by assiduous vigilance over oneself and over others, by the exercise of benevolence toward one's neighbor... It is impeded by sin; whoever is given to sin cannot even taste it; it is impeded principally by ambition and by sensuality, and also, very much, by conceit and detraction."[74]

This *Dialogue on Christian Joy*, the oldest writing that celebrates the festive personality of St. Philip and composed while he was living, is at the same time the first attempt to interpret the spirituality of Fr. Philip and of the Oratory. Cardinal Valier who composed it between August and September 1591, and set the scene in that period, puts these words into the mouth of Sivio Antoniano, another of the Father's great friends:[75] "This above all seemed to me admirable in such a man [Philip]: that he carried within him a perpetual gladness of spirit, never troubled in the least by stirrings of ambition, [notable] especially in a city like Rome. In truth this man is always joyful in the Lord; the Holy Spirit dwells within him, the Spirit whose fruit is joy, and he feeds on that celestial ambrosia as on his daily bread. Thus he always rejoices in the Lord and is held to be a distinguished master of true and authentic joy."[76]

That gift of a serene temperament and good character is therefore important (Philip was wont to say: "it is easier to guide a joyful person than a sad one on the spiritual journey," and he often said: "scruples and melancholy, get out of my house!"[77]*)*, but by itself it is not sufficient. It must feed itself constantly on the supernatural, and must undertake the arduous ascetic of humility. This alone reveals the full sense of Philip's many jokes and his humorous attitudes. He would say: "Find delight in communal life and avoid all singularity, attend to purity of heart, because the Holy Spirit dwells in innocent and simple minds, and He is the teacher of prayer, putting us in a state of continuous peace and joy, which is the foretaste of Heaven."[78]

All of these elements which characterize the "family life" of the disciples of St. Philip Neri in the Congregation of the Oratory would be enough by themselves to delineate the spiritual life of the Community, as we will see shortly. We reproduce as conclusion to these observations, the valuable summary of the *Statuta* 1943: "The Oratory of St. Philip Neri aims for, generally speaking, the sanctification of its members. According to the Constitutions and the Statutes, this sanctification must be pursued efficaciously and gently...through a worthy and holy priestly ministry; through the prescribed exercises of ascetic perfection and principally...of humility and disdain for self and for vainglory; finally, by internal and continual, almost innate, mortification, especially of one's own judgment and one's own will, and mediated by a glad interior and exterior peace, always serene in every situation, from which are molded faithful divine service, fraternal life together and ministry to souls. In this way it will always be true of the sons that which is true of our sweetest Father: IN LETIZIA!"[79]

Government of the Congregation

Only after having laid down these fundamental outlines of the nature of the Congregation, the Constitutions pass to a presentation of its juridical ordering, although at the very beginning of the chapter dedicated to governance, we are reminded that it "depends on the spirit of charity rather than on the law" (no. 24).

"The government of the Congregation and of all things which concern it rests with the General Congregation, the Deputy Congregation, and the Provost, who have ruling power over the members within the limits of their office (can. 596)" (no. 25).

The General Congregation: "All the members who have at least reached the triennium constitute the General Congregation. The triennials have a consultative vote in it, while only those who have completed the sexennium have a decisive vote" (no. 26).

"The Provost regularly summons the General Congregation so that the life of the Congregation can be reviewed with the help of all the members, at least as regards the more fundamental matters, and so that what is asked for by the brethren may be established by common counsel (can. 127)" (no. 27).

The Deputy Congregation: "The meeting of the Deputies[80] with the Provost constitutes the Deputy Congregation. The Provost will call meetings of the Deputy Congregation regularly. According to the norm of universal and proper law, nothing is to be done which concerns the government of the whole Congregation, or the election or removal of officials, without the consent or advice of the Deputy Congregation (can. 627, par. 1 and 2; *Const.*, n. 34)" (no. 30).

The Provost: "The Provost of each Congregation of the Oratory is a Major Superior of his own Congregation (can. 134, par. 1; 620)" (no. 21). "The first power in the government of the whole Congregation, and of all matters concerned with it, lies with the Provost.[81] To him alone it belongs to summon the General Congregation when necessary, and to propose matters for it to deal with, to see to the proper carrying out of what has been decided, to demand an account of what individual members have done or ought to have done who have some office of responsibility laid upon them, of whatever kind and in whatever place, and to see that everything is properly carried out. However, the Provost himself is strictly bound to summon the General Congregation and to propose matters to it in the cases prescribed by the universal law and the Constitutions especially concerning works of the apostolate undertaken by the whole Congregation. Outside these cases, even if he be not strictly bound to summon the Congregation and propose some business, let him defer to the unanimous, or nearly unanimous, wishes of the Deputies or the Congregation, and he should not go against them without a reason, sufficient in his own estimation" (no. 34). "The Provost, whom the first members of the Oratory called the Father, always conducts himself in a fraternal manner in carrying out his office (can. 618). Hence, making himself a brother among other brethren, he is to try rather to do good than to take a precedence, and to favour and promote the collegial structure and fraternal communion of the Congregation of the Oratory (can. 619)" (no. 35).

Choice and Formation of Candidates

In a family characterized by its very nature by stability[82] and in which the free exercise of obedience demands the support of a solid human and spiritual maturity, the admission and formation of candidates assumes great importance, as the *Spiritual Path* reminds us[83]: "The absence of vows or promises and the daily giving of oneself require that a disciple of St. Philip must be blessed with maturity and certain specific characteristics: one must be "born," as it were, "to the

Congregation"; and it cites a realistic consideration of John Henry Newman: "Not everyone has the gift of being able to live in community with others. Not all holy souls, and not all good secular priests are able to live in community. Perhaps there are few men capable of this."

In this regard the tradition of the Congregation is extremely rich in testimony from the beginning, when Fr. Philip was entrusted with the serious responsibility of admitting candidates. Successive regulations give careful attention to this: in proposals for the Constitutions prepared by Frs. Tarugi and Talpa in 1582,[84] four of the eight chapters are dedicated to this delicate argument. They make clear that "in addition to good health, candidates must have a number of abilities, or be disposed to acquire them, so that they may be useful to the Congregation as a whole.... Those may be admitted more readily who, in addition to the required qualities, have attended our Oratory and the Holy Sacraments of our Church for some time, whose manner of conversation is known to us and who are known to our Institute.... Those must be excluded with whom it is difficult to converse, who are unstable, who do not intend to persevere in the Congregation, those who suffer from notable mental infirmities." This became part of the Constitutions of 1583. The draft of 1588 and Baronio's notes for the Constitutions of 1595–1596 summarize these concepts which take their final form in the *Institutes* of 1612. Successive updating has resulted in the lapidary form: "Nostrae Congregationis Patres, Beati Philippi Institutoris, optimi morem secuti, nonnisi homines probatae vitae, maxime idoneos et quasi ad institutum natos recipi volunt": "The members of the Congregation, following the custom of St. Philip, wish to accept for aggregation only men of proven life, extremely suitable and, because of the family nature of the community, born, as it were, to the Congregation (can. 597, par. 1; 642)" (no. 57).

"Holy Father Philip," according to the *Merits of the Congregation of the Oratory of St. Philip Neri*, a work that has nurtured generations of Oratorians and that has had editions in various languages, "never considered persons who, however fine their other qualities might be, did not adapt themselves to the Community; he considered them incapable of reaching perfection and good only to injure others, since they desired to live according to their own tastes and whims."

The selection and formation of candidates is important for every Institute, but how important it is for the Congregation of the Oratory, is documented in a paragraph of the Letter[85] sent to all the Communities during the four hundredth anniversary of the priestly ordination of St. Philip, by the Procurator General Fr. Edward Griffith:

> The consistency of our traditions, the clear implication of the Constitutions, the democratic character of our community life, our apostolic method—in a word: our entire vocation—presupposes a certain maturity of judgment and also an evident sense of personal responsibility. To the extent that any of these qualities leave something to be desired, the essential contribution of the Oratory, its unique contribution to the life of the Mystical Body of the Church is diminished.... The entire atmosphere of Oratorian life, the open discussion, the decisions made by majority vote, the absence of rigid legislation and of severe sanctions—all of this requires from its members a delicate sense of discretion, large- and generous-mindedness and the capacity to appreciate the opinions of others, even to esteem objectively views that are different from one's own.
>
> Beyond this, all these qualities must be rooted in a strong and serious spiritual life, in solid piety and in charity. Grace perfects one's natural qualities, but it does not create them. And the qualities mentioned above are indispensable to a fruitful and undisturbed common Oratorian life. Whenever a member does not possess these requirements, that is, is not *quasi natus*, as the Constitutions say, he would not be adapted in any way to our life, nor would he find there the atmosphere suitable for his own spiritual development.
>
> What should we say, then, of communities who keep members who are ill-adapted? Democracy will give way either to anarchy or to monarchy, or at least to oligarchy. What will suffer the most from this state of affairs is the apostolate. The lack of true community life

> will make itself felt in an inability to carry out the apostolate effectively, and in the ascetic and theological culture of the community. The consequences of this: lukewarm and ineffective spiritual direction, banal homilies, little or no contribution of individual members to community efforts. The ever-creative and relevant character of the genuine Oratorian apostolate will yield its place to an "institutional" formalism without dynamism, without personal effort, and without fresh and original ideas.

The Constitutions presently in effect, after having repeated that the admission of the candidate *quasi natus* "is governed by the universal law (cann. 641–645), except for what is here laid down", says: "the following are not to be admitted: those less than eighteen and more than forty-five years old; those who suffer from serious ill-health; those who have been professed religious" (no. 58). "Before being admitted to the Congregation they will live for at least a month in the house as guests, with the consent of the Deputies, or, according to Particular Statutes, by the consent of the General Congregation, in order that they may come to know our life and more maturely deliberate their decision. During this period they are to be tested in the exercises of the common life" (no. 60). "If they make a good impression, they are to be admitted afterwards by the General Congregation, an absolute majority having been obtained in a secret ballot, and they begin the first probation (can. 597, par. 2)" (no. 61). This "first probation," which is the equivalent of the canonical year of novitiate and therefore "must include twelve months to be valid (can. 648)" (no. 62), is the beginning of specific formation which will continue for two more years (the "second probation"). The novices are entrusted "until aggregation" (no. 63) to the Father to whom the Community has given the responsibility of Master or Prefect. He, "considering in everything their spiritual growth, must form them not only in individual zeal for virtue—which zeal should find the highest place among the members of the Congregation—but also so form them that they may become adapted to the family life of the Congregation, may be imbued in mind and heart with the spirit of the Oratory and that their purpose and suitability may be properly tested, so that they become capable of living a truly fraternal community life (can. 646)" (no. 64), "so formed that they learn to love to be unknown, and that, according to the mind of St. Philip, intent on prayer and imbued with a great desire of divine wisdom, they become capable of communicating divine love and fulfilling it through giving themselves. They must make progress in contemplating the mystery of salvation, in reading and meditating on the Sacred Scriptures, in taking part in the Church's liturgy, in leading a life which is dedicated to the service of God and men, and in cultivating both human and Christian virtue (can. 652)" (no. 65).

The Constitutions end the paragraphs dedicated to this subject reminding us that "the modern renewal of the Congregation of the Oratory depends greatly on the formation of the members. Therefore the formation of the members, both religious and apostolic, doctrinal and technical, must be continued even when studies have been completed, particularly on the subject of Sacred Scripture (can. 279)" (no. 65).[86]

The Spiritual Life of the Community

The spirituality that Fr. Philip incarnates and that he transmits to his disciples and to the Congregation is highly evangelical: there is no specific practice, but the pure expression of the journey of prayer, of sacramental life, and of conversion as the Church understands it. The originality lies, if anywhere, in the intensity with which the Father lives it and proposes it, and in the simplicity that characterizes it.

Prayer

The Constitutions of 1943 place the discussion of the Oratory and of prayer in the first chapter, as the first *Institutes* had done, and declares: "prayer is to be held as the cornerstone and foundation of everything."[87] The present Constitutions confirm this fundamental approach: "In the Congregation of the Oratory familiar discourse on the Word of God, or spiritual conversation, always holds the first place and from this the spirit of faith and prayer, of charity and service, is always continuously stirred up and nourished" (no. 7). "The Congregation of the Oratory and its members, responding to the Word of God, lay great stress on mental and vocal prayer in common, as something proper and essential to the Oratory, and all the members practice it regularly, and when possible daily (can. 276; 1174, par. 1)" (no. 84). Moreover, "the members individually, with the Provost encouraging and setting the example, set aside stated times for prayer and meditation, and so following the example of St. Philip, they are united to one another by the spirit of prayer" (no. 85).

The experience of God for St. Philip is fundamentally prayer. His whole life testifies to this, from his youth spent in that fervent prayer in which he received, at the age of twenty-nine, the extraordinary effusion of the Spirit at Pentecost in 1544. His lay vocation continues for another seven years, marked by a crescendo in his rapport with God in prayer. His call to the priesthood and his ordination in 1551 do not constitute a turning away from this: he will continue to need many hours each day to "think of God." Prayer—"the best thing for man,"[88] he would say—was indispensable to him throughout his life, convinced as he was, that without it, "man is an animal without reason" and that "there is nothing that the devil fears more, or that he tries to impede more, than prayer"; "without prayer one cannot persevere on the spiritual journey"; "to pray well one must first humble oneself profoundly and to know oneself to be unworthy to stand before such majesty, and to show to God one's need and weakness, and humbled, cast oneself into God, in order that God may teach one to pray"; "wanting to pray without mortification is as though a bird would want to attempt to fly before having any feathers." Asked by a disciple if he would teach him to pray, Fr. Philip answered: "Be humble, and the Holy Spirit will teach you."

The *Spiritual Path*[89] ends its reflection on prayer by quoting the reminder which Fr. Mariano Sozzini left to his confreres when he was close to death: "As long as the Congregation of the Oratory prays, there will be a Congregation and it will keep its spirit."

Eucharist

"Because no Christian community can be built up unless it has its foundation in the celebration of the Holy Eucharist, the members of the Congregation of the Oratory hold it as the very center and unifying point of their whole life. The priests are invited to celebrate it daily so that all may share in it (*Presb. Ord.* 6.14; can. 276, par. 2.2)" (no. 86).

The Eucharistic piety which is so rooted in Fr. Philip's spirituality and strongly present in his proposal for formation, as indeed the intense fervor of the Father in the celebration of Holy Mass, are the best comment on the text of the Constitutions. We have already dedicated some space to this in the first chapter, but the general index of the Process gives apropos of this matter so many testimonials that it fills six columns.[90] That *agebatur* which, in the Life of Bacci expresses splendidly Fr. Philip's intense participation in the action of Christ made present by the Eucharistic celebration of the Church, throws much light on the mystery of the Masses of the Father, on the trembling with infinite emotion and the ecstasies which caught him even in public, even though he made himself conclude the celebration quickly. These increasing mystical phenomena induced him, later in his life, to seek peace in the solitary recollection of his little chapel, near his room, where he could allow himself to be shaped passively by the Eucharist, and where he celebrated the "long Masses of a saint," as a fine publication by the Oratory of Albacete[91] entitled a page dedicated to the argument.

The documents of the Second Vatican council and of the Magisterium afterward, like many studies of these years, offer abundant reflections on the Eucharist as *culmen et fons* of the whole Christian life. We limit ourselves here to underlining the richness of the mystery that sent Fr. Philip into ecstasies. In saying, "Do this in memory of me," the Lord opened to his faithful the possibility of entering into his "action." Jesus' discourse at the Last Supper, reported by John, allows us to understand clearly that the sacrifice that he was about to undertake, with the offering of himself, is not only the source of universal forgiveness, but the sublime gift of his own life: he calls his disciples "friends," he invites them to remain in him like the branch in the vine, to let themselves be carried, by the Spirit, to the whole and entire truth and to the joy that no one can take from their hearts. This experience of full communion is what made Fr. Philip's Masses "long," since he "felt great consolation in just holding the chalice in his hands,"[92] Federico Borromeo recalled.

Confession and Mutual Pardon

It can never be emphasized enough that the Oratory and the Congregation arose fundamentally from the ministry of Confession that Fr. Philip exercised with a dedication that has few other equals in history. Returning to this beginning, the early Constitutions prescribed that "three times a week" the members of the Congregation were to approach the Sacrament of Confession. Those of 1943 say: "at least once a week," and the present Constitutions counsel that the sacrament be *frequenter*: "According to the mind of St. Philip, the members frequently approach the Sacrament of Reconciliation, in order both to obtain the mercy of God and at the same time to be reconciled with the Church" (no. 87).

Such insistence reveals the necessity, for priests, for whom the dedication to the ministry of Reconciliation is a primary obligation, to experience abundantly in their own persons the gift of divine mercy, but also the need to progress, through this journey of purification, in the perfection to which everyone is called.

Fraternal correction is also linked to penitential discipline, regarding which the present Constitutions say: "The members, bearing in mind the Gospel so that they do not forget they are brothers in the Lord, correct themselves together according as necessity demands and charity urges. But the Deputy Congregation can commit the office of corrector to one of the members" (no. 89). Also linked to penitential discipline is the community review of life, the "Chapter of Faults," of which we read: "The members meet together at a time and in a manner laid down in the Particular Statutes, in order to consider their common life, to have spiritual discourse and correction, so that they may sincerely prove themselves according to the Gospel and the spirit of St. Philip, always being ready to reform themselves in the service of God and in the spirit of charity" (no. 88a). It is significant that in both the older *Institutes* and in the Constitutions of 1943 which repeated the earlier version verbatim there was an appeal to the *delicacy* that must characterize this important moment in family life, underlined by prescribed gestures and attitudes that impart the sense, undoubtedly, of some ancient ceremonial, but that express the spirit to which fraternal correction is to conform: "They invoke the Holy Spirit first of all with the usual prayers recited by the Provost. The priest to whom the office is entrusted (generally they take turns in assuming this office) is called to sit at the right hand of the Provost, and after a very brief exhortation in the spirit of delicacy [*in spiritu lenitatis*] he begins his task. In correcting priests and clerics, he uncovers his head; in correcting the Provost, he not only uncovers his head but rises to his feet."[93]

Devotion to the Most Blessed Virgin

Most artists have portrayed Fr. Philip in an attitude of prayer to the Virgin, often kneeling at the feet of Mary who offers him her Son, while Philip with his hands either open or crossed on his breast accepts the gift. "My sons, be devoted to Mary, be devoted. I know what I am saying."[94] He composed a chaplet with an ejaculation that summarizes fully the mystery of Mary: "Virgin Mother, Mother Virgin, pray to Jesus for me," and "he asked everyone with great love and many tears to recite this chaplet daily for love of him...because with this prayer one repeats the most beautiful titles of Mary."[95]

This fundamental Marian aspect[96] of Philip's spirituality singularly illuminates the project of true humanity that the Oratory follows. It is a humanity made new through the workings of Grace, like that of Mary of Nazareth who receives everything from the goodness of God and offers her entire person back, a concrete gift which involves her very body as a woman. "Following in the footsteps of St. Philip"—the

Constitutions say—"the Congregation exhibits and promotes a deep devotion towards the Blessed Virgin Mary, sign of the Church (can. 276, par. 2, 5)" (no. 91).

It is "by following in the footsteps of St. Philip" that Cesare Baronio—only one among the many who placed themselves in the "school of the Blessed Father"—manifests his very tender devotion to the Virgin. This can be seen in the *Annals*, the volumes of which open and close with the twelve sweet invocations and lyrical hymns that flowed from his soul. He sealed his works with the monogram *Caesar Servus Mariae*.[97] Baronio never forgot that Fr. Philip in 1572 had seized him back from death by saying to God: "Give him to me, give him up to me, I want him!"; and that in that circumstance: "turning to the most holy Madonna, he begged her insistently to obtain this grace for her son: and in so doing, the Lord consented to the prayers of the Mother of God and of the father, that I might live."[98]

Evangelical Counsels

The Congregation of the Oratory—as we have seen—includes secular priests and laity, committed to live as followers of Jesus without reservations, but also without the bond of vows, promises, or oaths.[99]

Philip in fact chose for himself and for his own the "free observance of the evangelical counsels,"[100] founded, that is, not on the commitment coming from vow, taken once for always through religious profession, but on personal choice continuously renewed by a free act of the will. The first disciples of the Father remembered that he would tell them: "Not vows, but the virtues of the vows, yes... In heaven they won't ask us if we have made vows but if we have lived the virtues of the vows." The testimony that Fr. Tarugi gave to Fr. Talpa is telling. It occurs in a document, written between 1580 and 1582, and is of great importance for the exact understanding of the principles which informed the Congregation from the beginning: "Living in a community with love together with concord... Let simplicity and the spirit of poverty and of obedience shine forth from the men of the Community so as to be undisputed at the Apostolic See. Let love and obedience toward our superiors of the Congregation be insisted upon. Let all those in the Congregation employ their talents for the love of God, according to the wishes of the superiors, without complaining. Let whatever they have be held more as belonging to the Congregation than as their own.... And in summary, that the Institute give an example, in the house and outside, of charity, humility, obedience, patience and detachment from every worldly goal and pretension, having as its goal the salvation of souls bought with the precious blood of Jesus Christ."[101]

We can hear the echo of the words of Philip, transmitted to us by Consolini: "Charity, humility. Detachment from things. Common life without singularity. My Christ, I want nothing other than you; whoever looks for anything other than God deceives himself. Speaking of spiritual things, he would close his eyes and raise his head. In a song-like voice he would always conclude: Obedience, humility!"

The absence of vows in the life of the Oratorian (Fr. Nicolò Gigli used to say: "Charity surpasses all the vows!") has nothing to do, as P. R. Mas writes,[102] with "anarchical freedom or with doing as one likes with regard to obedience; or with a convenient and egoistical permissiveness with regard to poverty; even if chastity remains the same as for those who live as celibates in the world, and those who take priestly orders. The biographers of Fr. Philip tell us how demanding he was and how he tested the obedience of his dearest disciples. Because of priestly orders and because of the gift of self to the community, there was never any doubt about the observance of chastity, confirmed by the traditional ascetic of the Oratory: its observance was illuminated by the joy of dedicating oneself to the service of things divine. With respect to poverty, he left us his personal example and demanded a prompt and generous detachment from material things. The show of poverty displeased him, and even less the lack of cleanliness, which also displeased St. Bernard, whom he would quote in this regard. Poverty and obedience had to be the incarnation of humility and love arising from the heart, fruit of interior virtues and the axis on which turns all of the familial and apostolic life. For Philip, a show of penances and extraordinary works were worth little or nothing. What mattered was the promptness of obedience, even in little things, and the willing submission of one's judgment, one's 'reason.' He rejected, however, any servile obedience and obedience exacted 'by force,' believing that if someone could not obey or murmured, he would do better to abandon the Oratory, since this was a sign that he had erred in his choice of vocation. With regard to poverty and detachment he would say that with only ten men truly detached he could change the world, and convert it to God."

Obedience

"The members show reverence and obedience to the Supreme Pontiff as their supreme head (cann. 273; 590 par. 2)" (no. 92). "Although not bound by vows, the members honour and practice obedience to the Constitutions, to the Provost, and to the General Congregation (can. 273). In what concerns public worship, the care of souls, and other works of the apostolate, they are also under the Bishop of the Diocese (can. 738, par. 1, 2, 3)" (no. 93).

The *Spiritual Path*,[103] which dedicates ample space to this, begins by quoting the author of the *Instruction for the Spiritual Exercises*,[104] who says: "obedience is the only law imposed by God for the universal ordering of things and for their conservation." And it continues: "Obedience is born from the virtue of humility, which recognizes one's own limits, of poverty and of the need for help. At times obedience is difficult, because it requires the renunciation of one's own desires and egoism."

St. Philip said that obedience is: "the true holocaust which is sacrificed to God on the altar of our hearts; it is a shortened route to arrive quickly at perfection; whoever lives an ordinary life in obedience is more praiseworthy than another who does penance at his own choosing." "He desired in his spiritual sons a willing obedience, and often said that it was not enough just to do what obedience commanded, but also that it was necessary to be obedient without complaint and to believe with certitude that what obedience required would be the best thing, the most perfect that can be found, even when it seems that the opposite should be true. He often said to his spiritual sons, and in particular to those of the house who were eager to be obedient that they should leave aside every other thing to attend to community matters, even if it were prayer itself or something else that seemed more important." Father Tarugi said time and again: "In the Congregation, even though the members are not bound with a vow of obedience, they are obligated to freely live in obedience."

It is worth remembering the admonition that Fr. Philip wrote with his own hand, one of the rare autographs of the Saint: "Because, my Fathers, I am absolutely resolved not to have in this house men who do not observe those few regulations and rules that everyone agrees can be easily followed."[105] The choice that Fr. Philip made in indicating that Tarugi was to succeed him is founded exactly on this evaluation: "for having always been obedient to me; and although once in a while in some things he has shown his disagreement, yet he quickly submitted and humbled himself, and having obeyed he is ready to govern and to command others."[106]

The virtue of obedience challenges and binds one who must obey, but it binds also the one who has the obligation of commanding. And Fr. Philip showed his originality in this, too: "He commanded little" and "he said that he who wishes to be perfectly obeyed should give but few orders."[107] "Discretion" on the part of one who has authority is merely respect for the truth. The superior's sense of responsibility must always be accompanied by humility and by the awareness of his own limits. And the others, while committing themselves to obey, remain free men, whom it would be absurd to drive to exasperation by heavy-handedness. Philip's "give few orders" keeps both commanding and obeying realistic.

Poverty

Fr. Philip, who had a great sense that property was an instrument of personal freedom, and who wrote *habeant, possideant* on the draft of the first Constitutions, administered his own small personal patrimony with detachment but shrewdness. However, he lived true evangelical poverty in the gift of both himself and his income in the service of charity. He would say that he wanted to be so poor that he would live "on a few cents,"[108] and he really did this to the point of begging for his meager food, he, who was in the secular state, and not bound by a vow of poverty. His was a poverty founded not so much on the refusal of material goods, as sometimes happens as an affectation in persons overly supplied with wealth, but as an exercise in humility and grounded in profound virtue: as when he dressed in such a way as to arouse hilarity in those who saw him put on big white shoes, which Cardinal Bonelli had given him, or a pontifical coat, a gift of Pius V. Disdain for material goods was foreign to St. Philip, because to him they were part of his serene Christian vision of the created world. It is interesting in the Pontifical document "Towards a Pastoral Approach to Culture"[109] that St. Philip Neri is likened to St. Francis of Assisi: "the light of faith clarifies the meaning of creation and the relationship between humanity and the rest of nature. St. Francis of Assisi and St. Philip Neri are symbolic witnesses of respect for nature, which comes from the fact that nature does not belong to the human race but to God, its creator." Philip's poverty, like that of Francis, is a communion with God, the Creator and Lord of all that exists. It is a filial relationship with the Provident Father, who generates a new way to possess things and to stand in relation to one's brothers and sisters through them. Philip searches for the Spirit in the use of goods, and in the Spirit he senses that everything has been given to him. The *Spiritual Path*[110] reminds us of Fr. Philip's words: "God will not fail to give you things, but be sure that when you do have things you do not lack spirit… If you go after material things and want money, I won't look after you any more, because having them without the proper caution makes men incapable of having spirit." "Give me ten detached people and with them I will have enough spirit to convert the world." He wrote to his niece, who was a nun, Anna Maria Trevi: "To acquire the love of God there is no truer and shorter way than to detach oneself from the love of things, even if they are small and inconsequential, and from the love of self, while loving the will and the service of God more than we love our own will and self-satisfaction."

Evangelical poverty is lived out in the Congregation of the Oratory as the commitment to support oneself by one's own work, as a sense of personal responsibility in the use of goods, in the proper exercise of freedom and as generous sharing of all that one possesses: "The members live on their own incomes. Those who devote themselves entirely to the Congregation and its work live on stipends from the community. Income which is acquired from external ministries is acquired by permission of the Congregation" (no. 102). "Therefore the General Congregation is to define in Particular Statutes how this income is to be divided between the Congregation and the members carrying out these external ministries" (no. 102). The members "are invited to embrace voluntary poverty, by which they will be more clearly likened to Christ (*Pres. Ord.* 17, 4; *Perfectae Carit.* 13). Hence, after freely contributing, each according to his means, a percentage to the common benefit of the Congregation, they will use what is left over from the income of each year for good purposes and not accumulate anything (cann. 282, par. 1; 741, par. 2)" (no. 104).[111]

Chastity

"The members take the greatest care to observe a perfect and perpetual continence and celibacy, which is a special gift from God (can. 277, 1, par. 1, 2). and prudently to abstain from anything which is unfitting and alien to the clerical state (cann. 285, par. 1, 3; 286; 666)," say the Constitutions (no. 94).

The *Spiritual Path*[112] reports Philip's lively teaching on this matter: "He said: 'Be attentive to purity of heart, because the Spirit dwells in innocent and simple souls. One should fear carnal temptations and flee from them even in illness, old age, and for as long as one lives, because the spirit of incontinence exempts no place, nor time, nor person." Philip often said: "The young should beware of the temptations of the flesh and the old should beware of avarice. Temptations of the flesh can be better overcome by flight than by fight." And he proposed five remedies: "Flee temptation, do not pamper the flesh, flee from idleness, pray frequently, and frequent confession and the Most Holy Eucharist." The discourse applies, obviously, to a whole way of life of which chastity is an expression. The *Spiritual Path* develops the argument in a text written by Fr. Cittadini: "Chastity is mentioned by St. Paul as being one of the fruits of the Spirit. Chastity ought to be lived as the freedom of the heart, as a total giving of oneself to the Lord; not as a rejection of a human reality that was willed by God and sanctified by Grace. Chastity is a foretaste of the Kingdom, which yearns for the fullness of love, and for making oneself available to a positive and serene intimacy; it is a spiritual richness which puts right all the possible deviations of egoism and immaturity."

Apostolic Works

Born to the service of the Oratory, which remains the "first among these" (no. 118) apostolic activities, the Congregation does not contain in itself its own purpose, as a monastery might, but its purpose lies in its apostolate to its neighbor, as it is in the Societies of Apostolic Life.

It is indispensable to remember, however, that the expression "apostolic life" cannot be reduced to merely "life dedicated to apostolic works." The very life of the Community is "apostolic," as the Code of Canon Law makes clear, and as is detailed in a valuable Document of the Holy See entitled "Fraternal Life in Community."[113] What the Acts of the Apostles say of those who were part of the first Christian community: "See how they love one another," remains the perennial invitation to tend the common life as the highest form of apostolate, and perhaps the most effective. The Constitutions note this at the beginning of the chapter dedicated to "Service, or the Apostolic Works of the Congregation": "Therefore, let the whole ministry and the fraternal communion be inspired by the example of those who "breaking bread from house to house took their meat with gladness and simplicity of heart, praising God and having favour with all the people" (Acts 2:46ff.; *Sacr. Conc.* 10; *Pres. Ord.* 5)" (no. 109).

From the point of view of fraternal life in community, the invitation of the Church to avoid undue individualism is important, since such individualism can lead to dispersion of effort and can prejudice the results of apostolic and pastoral work: "Respect of the person, recommended by the Council and by the documents which followed, have had a positive influence on community practice. At the same time, however, individualism has become widespread, to greater and lesser degrees in various parts of the world. It has taken the most diverse forms, such as the preference for one's own work…the absolute priority given to one's own personal aspirations and one's own individual journey without paying attention to others and without reference to the community.… It is necessary to remember that the apostolic mission is entrusted above all to the community."[114]

What Fr. Tomaso Bozzi, Rector of the Roman House, wrote to Fr. Tarugi, Rector of the House in Naples, on August 10, 1590, about the works of the Congregation should be of abiding interest for the Congregation of the Oratory: "Our aim is to serve God and to care for souls, not to look for the sublimity of our Institute. Therefore, it is well to do everything with deep humility, with the exercise of charity among ourselves and to dedicate ourselves to the well-being of our neighbor with good works and with interior virtues that are not apparent, because it is God who gives the growth."[115]

The Constitutions delineate the principal areas of the apostolic action of the Congregation reminding us most opportunely here, too, of the importance of the family life in Community: "The Congregation is to follow willingly the traditions of St. Philip. These traditions, however, always need to be adapted and renewed according to the mind of the Church" (no. 83) and that "attention must always be paid to the mind and spirit of our blessed Father St. Philip, as described in the original Constitutions" (no. 96).

Divine Worship

"The origin and final end of all apostolic work, and the essential ministry of the Congregation, is the Holy Eucharist" (*Const.*, no. 110).

"Divine worship is always to be celebrated in our churches so carefully, devoutly, and worthily that both due honour may be given to God and the people built up and instructed" (no. 112).

In the tenth chapter of the Constitutions of 1583, which were reviewed by Fr. Philip, there is a rich section which reflects the particular sensibility that from the very beginning has characterized the Oratorians in the celebration of the Liturgy and everything connected with it: "Among the works of our Institute we hold that divine worship is of prime importance, through which the souls of the faithful are strongly urged to piety towards God.... Therefore we exhort our Fathers, and also the sons who will come after us, to commit themselves to dedicating a vigilant and most diligent attention to this work, and never allow themselves to be distracted from it by reasons of fatigue or expense. They will further commit themselves to seeing that the sacred vessels, the vestments, and the churches themselves will shine with such decorous beauty as to urge the love of God upon those who see them. Those who stand at the altar to celebrate or to assist the celebrants are to be conscious of Him in whose presence they stand, are to think of what they are doing, are to consider the presence of the angels, and are to exercise the highest vigilance of the mind and the greatest composure of the body."[116]

Preaching

"The preaching of the Gospel must be in a familiar style and adapted to the needs of the hearers and those of the present day (cann. 762–772)" (no. 113).

The *Institutes* of 1612 dedicated all of Chapter III to preaching, in order to emphasize that this is a fundamental apostolic work. The title itself announces the nature of Oratory preaching: "The wholesome exercise of familiar sermons whether in church or in the Oratory." "Those who have been chosen for this office nourish the souls of the listeners with a kind of preaching that is truly fruitful, adapting above all the vocabulary, in an ordered way, to the understanding of the people, without empty show or vanity. They will support their teaching by the example of the Saints and by documented historical facts. In their sermons they will avoid complicated subjects, dogmas, and any arguments that belong rather to the schools than to the Oratory."[117] Fr. Tarugi's report to Cardinal Borromeo, cited above, says that the "familiarity" of the discourse must not be separated from "due dignity," but it also illuminated the purpose of the Congregation in this primary and principal exercise: "the purpose of this exercise is Christian formation, and to keep those so formed, with the help of Grace, continually built up." This is the reason that the study of sacred doctrine is recommended, as well as the study of Sacred Scripture, of the Fathers, the Councils, canon law and ecclesiastical decrees, the lives of the Saints, and the history of the Church and spiritual writings.

The *Spiritual Path* says, "We can affirm that Philip created a true school with this method in the environment of Renaissance Rome, where ecclesiastical orators competed with the pagan classics. [And there were many new and older Institutes that drew inspiration from Oratory preaching to form their members according to the preaching of the Divine Word.] The Saint taught that in order to preach, it was necessary first to pray a great deal, to give great importance to the practice of virtue, to have the proper intention while studying, and to refer frequently to examples taken from the life of the Church and of the Saints. Fr. Giuliano Giustiniani used to say that a priest of the Congregation should die upon one of these 'three pieces of wood': the predella of the altar, the confessional, or the chair of discourse."[118]

The Ministry of Confession and Spiritual Direction

"The diligent ministry of spiritual formation, through discourses on divine things and through the hearing of confessions, corresponding to the mind of St. Philip, is also proper and peculiar to the Congregation. All the members are to strengthen a truly Christian life and filial piety toward God in their neighbors, always 'being made all things to all men,' especially in caring for the poor" (no. 115).

The present writer recalls that in the General Congress of 1982, in which the Constitutions presently in force were put together, a confrere proposed to insert the expression "especially in caring for the poor—*maxime in praediligendis pauperibus*." The proposal was not made in reference to this specific area of apostolic work of the Congregation, but referring in general to the pastoral and teaching work of the Oratorians. The current placement of the expression in the context of the Sacrament of Reconciliation and spiritual direction obviously does not reflect the original meaning of the proposal. However, all Christians who recognize their sins and beg pardon for them are seeking guidance for their spiritual journeys. Placed as it presently is, the invitation to care for the poor reminds us that the apostolic work of the Oratory must not exclude anyone, exactly as St. Philip and his early disciples demonstrate: among the faithful of the Oratory we find humble artisans along with men who were illustrious for their culture and social position. St. Philip led both the one and the other along the paths of the Spirit, dedicating the hours of the day and of the night to his ministry of Reconciliation, up to his last day on earth. The sympathetic cheerfulness that the father demonstrated in the art of confession and spiritual guidance[119] derived, as always, from the sweetness with which he drew souls toward that which was good. His penitents felt that they were loved as persons, outside of their situations, and they were treated with that patience which is authentic charity. Fr. Philip was "there for them"; and the direction for their spiritual journeys which each received came not from some abstract moralistic system, but from the real encounter of one person with another, and from the communication of a gift that passes from one heart to another.

Apostolate to Youth

"The members zealously devote themselves to the apostolate of youth, which was most dear to St. Philip, in forms corresponding to the needs of the place (e.g., through a secular Oratory, college, religious instruction in schools, charitable undertakings, etc.) (cann. 795; 801)" (no. 116).

Fr. Philip undertook a large part of his apostolate among youth, even if, contrary to widespread opinion,[120] his primary work was not among young children. Adolescents certainly gathered around this kindly priest of Rome, perhaps mostly the sons of those who attended the Oratory. Among the scholars who have given attention to St. Philip's pedagogy is Filippo Marino, who in a recent book (the title in English would be: *Becoming a Child Among Children Wisely*), has demonstrated the appeal of the Father's rich personality, and his appropriateness for our own time[121]; he also provides a summary of the work of other scholars on this argument.[122] That word *wisely* in the title[123] contains all the force and all the sweetness of Philip's pedagogical method. He knew how to draw the young with healthy amusement, merrily and with wit in his words, but even more with the gift of himself, disinterested, completely available to them, capable of accepting totally the young man full of troubles, suffering from growing pains. Exactly because he did not try to make himself one of them ("The young, they burn up like straw..." he would say[124]), Philip attracted the young. They found in him not a happy companion, but a man who was young (and he remained so into his eighties) because of the richness of a harmonious life, which attracts and holds everyone.[125]

St. Charles Borromeo put it this way: "Philip has a particular gift for caring for the young and they love and revere him so much that there is nothing he could ask that they would not immediately do."

"He had an predilection for the young," says the *Spiritual Path*[126]: "Blessed are you young people, because you have time to do good." "Be merry, but do not sin." "Stay still if you can": Fr. A. Cistellini calls this "an invitation that is gentle but firm, demanding that they continue to grow in the moral and spiritual life, to learn to channel their energies toward what is good, and to trust themselves to know the good. St. Philip understood the deficiencies of human nature. Without knowing much about psychology, he came to be able to penetrate the human mind and to discover the extent to which one cannot be held responsible for so many of one's attitudes, and this explains his wide tolerance. The only line that must not be crossed is that of sin, of serious disorder. Freedom of spirit, even if chaotic or noisy, could be accepted, but not if it was disorderly or destructive. Healthy and purifying joy, which is constructive, was what he approved. As a reflection of these principles, Philip was against moroseness, isolation, obstinate silence. This describes Philip's deeply human, understanding way of dealing with people, his sweetness in approaching his neighbor, in trying to convince him, to draw him toward the ideal, to nurture within him the strength to ascend interiorly."[127]

Lay Formation

"Each Congregation is to foster the spirit of brotherhood, not only among the members but also with those outside the community, so that all Christians may help each other and undertake joint work for the good of the world. Hence, the members are also sincerely to recognize and promote the dignity of all the faithful, and their specific participation in the mission of the Church (*Lumen gentium* 32; *Presb. Ord.* 9)" (no. 117).

"St. Philip, with regard to the laity, was ahead of his time in his ideas and methods which would later be shown to be fruitful in the life of the Church," said John Paul II in his discourse to the Oratorians gathered for the General Congress in 2000. History documents this, and shows something of those ideas and methods. Fr. Cittadini summarizes them in this way[128]: Philip, who as a layman was a disciple and apostle of Christ in Rome and as a layman received his *stigmata*, never considered laymen as merely as objects of pastoral care, but always thought that they could legitimately be disciples and apostles. This esteem of the laity will remain a constant in the history of the Oratory. Witnesses to this include St. Francis de Sales, who may be considered one of the most important theorists of the spirituality of the Christian laity; John Henry Newman whose thought, tested as it was by his actions and trials, was fully accepted by the Second Vatican Council; and Cardinal Giulio Bevilaqua, who helped to demonstrate how contemporary thought and witness could be at the same time firm proclamation of the unchanging nature of the Gospel. These masters help us to enter into the spirit of the Second Vatican Council, with regard to the role of the laity in the Church and in the world; and to understand, for the promotion of the laity, the successive declarations of the Magisterium, all the way up to John Paul II's *Christifideles laici* and *Redemptoris missio.*

Parish Ministry

The Constitutions of 1943 read: "Because the good and the salvation of souls, the supreme duty of the priestly ministry, can morally require that the Congregations of the Oratory assume Parish responsibilities due to local situations and the needs of the time, these do not seem to conform to the original intention of the Oratory"[129]; the attitude of the present Constitutions is much different, codified as the following: "Parish work is truly suitable for the Congregation of the Oratory" (no. 120). An entire chapter is dedicated to the relevant juridical questions and competence.

Changed historical circumstances have undoubtedly influenced the decision of so many Congregations, reflected in the new paragraph of the Constitutions. That demanding expression "truly suitable" seems nevertheless excessive, even in relation to the needs of the present, if one keeps Oratorian history and tradition in view. Forcing ourselves to find a justification, not for taking on parish ministry in the Congregation but for the undue sureness with which this possibility is presented, we find only the evident reality that St. Philip Neri's method and the formation of the laity which he, alone in his time, carried out became to varying degrees the common patrimony of the pastoral, and therefore parish, ministry of the Church. Fr. Cistellini mentioned this in 1954: "The principles deriving from Philip's wisdom and brilliance that were incarnated four centuries ago in the Oratory, while at that time they appeared to be the remarkable discovery of St. Philip, and prerogative of his circle, have now become the common patrimony of the most elementary forms of ministry and of teaching practice."[130] It is however legitimate to observe in relation to the Institute of the Oratory what others have also observed: that Institutes which by their foundational charism and apostolic activity are intended to be very different from those of parish work are becoming increasingly identified with parishes, and this constitutes a real danger.

"To what can we attribute this situation?" asks Fr. R. Mas in an interesting article written in 1994.[131] "Principally to two errors: the Institutes have forgotten their charism, and have lacked imagination and creative fidelity to the genuine spirit of the Congregation; and the Bishops, who instead of understanding the originality and specific aim and spirituality of these communities, have seen them merely in a utilitarian light, in a time of scarcity of priests and of difficulties in placing them; or because some Bishops see this originality as just spiritual and therefore irrelevant." The topic of the article is "The Oratory and the Parish," and the author reviews the history of the parish in the life of the Church, noting that "all the Church is mission, but some parts more than others." In these situations, for example in the huge metropolises of Latin America, or in countries that are largely Protestant, the Oratory, like other Institutes, has accepted parish work but in such a way that it does not exhaust all the Institute's potential. But he warns that "the services that the Oratory has been able to render to the diocese in which it is established have been the more positive the more faithfully the sons of St. Philip have disciplined themselves to live his spirit and to conserve it in decisions and planning which are coherent with their tradition." Referring to the experience of Newman who "in founding the Oratory in England had to accept parish responsibilities," Fr. Mas says, "he always considered that mission secondary, not really part of the Oratorian apostolate, and he mentioned it in various occasions, as when he said that the Oratorians had to do things that the diocesan priests could not do, and that above all 'we must return to the formation of a Lay apostolate in connection with the Oratory.'"

External Obligations

The reference that the Constitutions make to this argument allows us to consider what the history of the Congregation witnesses to from its origins: the Secular Oratory is its specific field of apostolate, the activity termed "first among" the forms of cooperation with laity (no. 118), but this does not signify the exclusion of other forms of apostolate in which a member may exercise his ministry: "Ministries outside the Congregation can be accepted..." (no. 101). The Constitutions explain: "...if they are in accord with the Oratorian spirit and do not damage the common life and work" (no. 101); "No external offices or ecclesiastical benefices are to be accepted which could take a member away from the common life. The decision as to incompatibility with the common life is to be made by the General Congregation" (no. 100). We find one more requirement in the Constitutions, meant to safeguard the appropriateness of the choices of ministries that members may make, and how such work should be viewed: "external work is not to be accepted without the consent of the General Congregation, and remains always subordinate to the will of the same. The manner of accepting such work is to be determined in the Particular Statutes" (no. 101).

To conclude this section, in which we have tried, although perhaps inadequately, to delineate the principal features of the Congregation of the Oratory, we would like to offer yet another page that is venerable for its antiquity and clear in its content. It forms part of the discourse that Fr. Pompeo Pateri addressed to the followers of St. Philip in Naples at the conclusion of the canonical Visitation which he conducted between May 13 and June 4, 1594[132]:

> It has been an incomparable consolation, after having seen and spoken with everyone, to have discovered in you one spirit, one heart, and one will. This truly is something for which to thank and praise the majesty of God, because this is the greatest joy and greatest treasure that there can be in a Congregation. And so I rejoice with you with all the affection of my heart and together with you who are so charitable, exhorting you and praying that you may continue in this union of spirit and in this our vocation. While our vocation, it is true, is not founded upon the bond of solemn vows and similar

external things, it is founded, however, on the bond of charity, on obedience, on humility, and on the asceticism of the interior man, things that are so pleasing to the Majesty of God and are so edifying to our neighbor... One sees clearly that Our Lord [the Pope] is pleased with our Institute and our way of living, which I have heard time and again praised not only by persons of high rank and authority, but also by many religious distinguished for sanctity, doctrine, and experience...who will say in our presence and also when we are not present that our Institute and way of living is as useful to the Church of God as any other, because of the fruit that we see and hear of it... The Majesty of God has given us a most singular grace, more than to any other Congregation, because to us He has given not only the possibility of giving service to our neighbor, as the other Congregations do, but also something more: the Oratory, the continuous Word of God. It is a great thing to speak and hear the Word of God at all times... We are certain that if we will be those faithful servants that we ought to be, and if we will correspond to our vocation, not only will we be able to set Naples and Rome on fire, but all the world: because it is the same Christ who will give us that strength and that spirit that He gave to His holy Apostles.... And this is one of the things that our Reverend Father Philip most desired: to serve the Lord with joyfulness and contentment of heart.[133]

4. THE FOUNDATION OF NEW CONGREGATIONS

Some indications on this vast area of the Oratorian experience will be found in the last pages of Chapter IV dedicated to the history of the Confederation. Here we will merely reproduce the text of the document *Modus procedendi in praeparandis novis Congregationibus*, formulated by the Procurator General of the Confederation, which has the responsibility of guiding new foundations, assisting them in their formative journey, and to evaluate their soundness.

Preface

1. The spirit and the practice of the Oratory, like the Congregation of Secular Priests which took its origin from St. Philip, has always aroused an admirable interest in many groups of persons. And over four centuries in many parts of the world, new Congregations of Oratorians have been born, erected by the Holy See "ad instar Congregationis Oratorii Santa Mariae in Vallicella de Urbe." To the earliest of these the direct disciples of St. Philip transmitted valuable advice for their journey of formation.

The Confederation of the Oratory watches with joy these events which continue in our time, and it prescribes the encouragement of new Congregations in its General Statutes (no. 13; cf. also no. 17).

2. The present document has been written in consideration of the *noteworthy importance* that *the journey of formation* assumes for the Communities that are preparing to be recognized by the Holy See as Congregations of the Oratory. Remaining faithful to the norms contained in the General Statutes of the Confederation and drawing on the rich experience of those who have worked in the foundation of new Congregations, this Document intends to offer above all a clear indication of method to these Communities and a help to those responsible for preparing the new Congregations.

3. This document, prepared in Italian, approved and adopted by the Permanent Delegation July 19, 1998, and by the most Reverend Fr. Delegate to the Apostolic See, in his competence, is made public by the undersigned Procurator General in the solemnity of the Assumption of the Blessed Virgin Mary, entrusting to the maternal protection of the Holy Mother of God the journeys of formation of the new Communities, at the dawn of the third Christian Millenium.

Given at Rome, by the Seat of the Procurator General, August 15, 1998.

Chapter I: Foundations Prepared by Congregations

I. The *foundation* of a new Congregation can be prepared by an already approved Congregation, or by a Federation (with members of federated Congregations. If the members do not belong to the Oratory, the foundation will follow Chapter II of the present Document), or by members of one or more than one Congregation of the Oratory, with the written permission of the diocesan Bishop (cf. *Stat. Gen.* 13).

II. The General Statutes (nos. 14–16) establish everything concerning the preparation, as well as the life of the new Congregation after its canonical erection where the foundation has been promoted by a Congregation already erected.

III. From the beginning the Procurator General must be informed of this initiative, and everything else that he should know about the foundation. Should the case described in no. 14 arise, the procedures outlined in no. 17 must be followed, and the Procurator General must lend his help, following the prescriptions of Heading II of this Document, taking into account in every case the Oratorian formation already achieved by its members.

Chapter II: Foundations Prepared by Priests and Laity Not Belonging to the Oratory

I. The foundation of a new Congregation can be an initiative of "a group" of Priests and Laity who do not belong to one or more Congregations of the Oratory (cf. *Stat. Gen.* 17).

II. In this case, the journey to foundation and in the formation of the members are to be carried out in *two phases*:

(1) The first phase is the development and maturation of the project by those involved. The Procurator General must be contacted and adequately informed in writing of this project of foundation and of the curriculum vitae of all those who intend to begin this foundation.

In the absence or insufficiency of such contact, the Procurator General reserves the right not to approve the steps relative to the following second phase even if these have already been formalized.

We therefore invite insistently all the members of Congregations of the Oratory to maintain contact with groups interested in making a foundation, and to urge them to stay in contact with the Procurator General.

(2) The second stage begins with the written consent of the Local Ordinary who is willing to accept in his diocese the establishment of a group of Priests and Laymen who want to live the community life according the Oratorian spirit (*Stat. Gen.* 17), while the process of seeking the canonical erection of the Oratory takes place, as required by the Norms, no. 18, of the General Statutes.

III. The Bishop's document which initiates the second phase must contain: (a) the consensus described above; (b) the understanding about the incardination status of the members belonging to the diocese, once the Oratory is canonically erected; (c) the title of ordination of those members who are ordained during the preparatory stages preceding canonical erection; (d) any other matter may be useful to establish a clear relationship between the Ordinary and the Community in formation.

A copy of the Document must be given to the Procurator General.

IV. In the second phase, which is specifically "preparatory":

(1) The Community "must follow the Oratorian common life for a certain period of time" (*Stat. Gen.* 17) taking as a point of reference the Constitutions of the Confederation and the "Norms for the Common Life" which the Community itself establishes (using as guidelines the Particular Statutes of Congregations which are already erected—cf. *Const.*, 20). The minimum duration of this experience is three years, which is equivalent to the first and second probations as required by our Constitutions for the aggregation of members in a Congregation (cf. *Const.*, 63–67).

(2) The Community must maintain frequent contact with the Procurator General in order to keep him informed concerning: (a) the living of the common life, (b) any difficulties there may be in applying the Constitutions and the "Norms of the Common Life," (c) the acceptance of new members into the Community, and (d) relationships with diocesan Authorities.

It is the task of the Procurator General "to encourage the foundation, for assistance both for [its members] and for the Ordinary" (*Stat. Gen.* 17); and he is charged with witnessing to the Holy See (*Stat. Gen.* 20c) concerning the existence and the good state of the Community and whether it meets the requirements established by the General Statutes (no. 18) for canonical erection; and it is his task also to evaluate if there has been "a good example, during a certain period, both of the observance of the common life and of the carrying out of work according to the mind of Philip" (*Stat. Gen.* 18d).

(3) It is recommended that the Procurator General nominate a Delegate who is able to follow the community's path of formation closely. The Community would still always be able to turn to the Procurator General for any eventuality, who in any case is the one who must express a definitive judgment on the foundation. He may also collect, even secretly, any useful information on the foundation and on individual members of the Congregation to be erected.

(4) In order that the Procurator General may have a clear knowledge of the situation, to the end that he may help the Community achieve the conditions required by the General Statutes, the Community will present him with a written report, which may be updated as often as necessary, concerning the following points: (a) the maturation and development of the project of foundation which characterized the first phase; (b) the organization of the common life as it responds to the "Norms for the Common life": division of internal responsibilities, times of community prayer, what the community does in common, pastoral activities in common, and activities outside the community done by individual members as "external responsibilities" (cf. *Const.*, 101); (c) the Oratorian plan of formation of the community: community meetings on themes and arguments inherent to the Constitutions and to the *Spiritual Path*; personal or community reading and study on the history, tradition, and spirituality of the Oratory; opportunities to meet and know members of other Congregations of the Oratory, and also the Federation—where that exists—*which shall be consulted by the Procurator*

General with regard to the petitio canonicae erectionis[134]—and with other Communities in formation; (d) the program of formation of those members who are candidates for the Presbyterate: where they complete their studies; to whom is entrusted their priestly formation; what are the means and the times established for the Oratorian formation for those who live out of the Community, in seminaries or elsewhere; (e) the economic situation of the Community in relationship to the "means necessary for leading the common life in the future" (*Stat. Gen.* 18b) and a description of the structures adapted as habitation for the Community and used for apostolic activities.

(5) With regard to the Oratorian formation of its members and the preparation of the "Norms of Common Life," the Community is invited to take advantage of the counsel and the help of one or more Congregations or of individual Oratorians. It is of great importance that members of Communities in formation meet with Congregations already erected, and experience Oratorian life together with them.

(6) Until canonical erection is achieved, the Community may not assume the title of "Congregation of the Oratory" (cf. *Stat. Gen.* 19), but it will use a designation agreed upon with the Procurator General, which will express clearly in various languages the Oratorian nature of the institution. Thus will be avoided, both internally and externally of the Community, designations and titles that could be confused with the Congregations of the Oratory already erected. The Responsible of the Community, for the same reason, will not be called "Provost"—a title belonging to erected Congregations—but, for example, "Moderator."

V. (1) When, having evaluated attentively all the circumstances, and in agreement with the diocesan Bishop and the Procurator General, the Community decides to ask the Holy See for canonical erection of the Congregation, it delivers the following documents to the Procurator General: (a) a document, signed by all the founding members and addressed to the Holy Father. In which it requests canonical erection of the Congregation; in the same document, it also gives a brief history of the foundation and its apostolic activities; (b) authentic documents, no. 20b of the General Statutes in particular the authentic and separate testimonials of the holy Ordination of members in Holy Orders;

(2) The diocesan Bishop and the Procurator General present their testimony separately, drawn up in authentic form, to the Holy See "concerning the good state of the new Congregation, the results of its apostolic works, its true Oratorian spirit and its possession of the means necessary for continued existence" (*Stat. Gen.* 20c).

VI. (1) The new Congregation, in virtue of its canonical erection, is aggregated to the Confederation (cf. *Stat. Gen.* 10).

(2) All of the members who were signatories of the petition of canonical erection addressed to the Holy See acquire the rights of triennials beginning on the day of the canonical erection.

(3) The Most Reverend Father Delegate to the Holy See, in his function as canonical Visitator of the Oratory (cf. *Stat. Gen.* 67), by analogy to what is prescribed by *Stat. Gen.* 15 for Congregations founded by others already erected—may by a Decree concede that those who have lived at least four years of the common life become sexennials. Having evaluated the circumstances, he may decide to call elections or instead to appoint *ad tempus* a Provost, the Vicar, and the Secretary; he exercises vigilance over the beginnings of the life of the new Congregation to see that it develops in fidelity to the Constitutions.

(4) With respect to the members of other Congregations already elected, the members of the new Congregation, even if they become sexennials by the act of canonical erection, are considered "triennials" at the moment of canonical erection.

5. THE CONGREGATIONS THROUGH THE CENTURIES

The rule of absolute autonomy that characterized the life of the Congregations until 1933, the year in which the Apostolic Visitator was instituted and the Procura General began to operate in Rome, has had the result that there is no General Archive in which to find official documentation before this date.

Therefore the *Memorie Historiche* of Marciano,[135] the Archive of the Roman Congregation,[136] and some *Elenchi* [lists] widely scattered among the Houses, have assumed official value. One of these was printed in Rome in 1744, in the print shop of Pietro Rosati in Parione Street. Another, a revised edition of this, is to be found in many Archives of Congregations, for example in the Mexican Houses of Guanajuato León, founded respectively in 1794 and 1838, among the last to be born in an epoch which saw both the end of the projects of foundation, but also the death of many ancient and glorious Oratorian Communities. Among the more recent publications that carry updated lists we may cite those of Gasbarri[137] and of Addington.[138]

The sixteenth century saw some fifteen Congregations arise; the greater part saw the light in the sixteenth and seventeenth centuries, ten or so in the nineteenth century; in the twentieth century before 1933, there were very few Communities founded; beginning with this date, the renewal was visible: slowly at the start, more consistently after 1960, when a good twenty-nine Congregations received canonical recognition from the Apostolic See.

In listing the Congregations we have followed Gasbarri, updating his list to the present, but eliminating the subdivision relative to the States and their borders which he understandably conserved, from the time at which the Congregations arose.[139]

Europe

Italy: Rome (1575), San Severino (1586), Naples (1586), Fermo (1586), Camerino (1591), Palermo (1593), Fano (1598), Lanciano (1598), Brescia (1598), Cammarata (1604), L'Aquila (1607), Agnone (1608), Trapani (1608), Casale (1613), Noto (1614), Bologna (1615), Perugia (1615), Ripatransone (1615), Corleone (1616), Comiso (1617), Valguarnera (?), Fossombrone (1621), Città di Castello (1622), Padua (1624), Paternò (1628), Reggio Emilia (1629), Messina (1632),

Florence (1632), Fabriano (1632), Pesaro (1637), Urbino (1637), Spoleto (1640), Lodi (1640), Bronte (1640), Montecchio (1644), Cesena (1644), Jesi (1644), Matelica (1644), Montefiore (1645), Nocera Umbra (1645), Macerata (1645), Pirano (1645), Genoa (1646), Murazzano (1646), Gubbio (1649), Turin (1649), Fossano (1649), Udine (1650), Tursi (1652), Ferrara (1654), Ancona (1654), Chieri (1658), Ascoli (1660), Osimo (1661), Venice (1661), Recanati (1665), Pistoia (1665), Como (1668), Faenza (1670), Cingoli (1671), Savigliano (1674), Girgenti (1675), Carmagnola (1681), Sulmona (1682), Caltanisetta (1684), Castelvetrano (1685), Cento (1685), Mantova (1689), Sinigallia (1690), Demonte (1693), Norcia (1693), Sciacca (1693), Mazzara (1695), Montealboldo (1695), Asti (1696), Penne (1696), Catania (1698), Castroreale (1700), Pergola (1700), Siena (1708), Montefalco (1710), Guardia Sanframondi (1710), Alcamo (1710), Trento (1710), Cremona (1711), Verona (1713), Mondovì (1714), Orbetello (1715), Piana dei Greci (1716), Spello (1717), Gradoli (1718), Vicenza (1720), Bevagna (1725), Monreale (1725), Monteleone Cal. (1725), Crescentino (1730), San Elpidio (1735), Villafranca (1737), Cortona (1738), Lucca (?), Biella (1742), Scigliano (1744), Chioggia (1752), Acireale (1756), Assisi (1760), Giarre (1763), Treia (1825?), Civitella Roveto (1895), Cava de'Tirreni (1896), Castelletto Ticino (1957).

France: Cotignac (1592), Aix en Provence (1615), Marsiglia (?), Hyeres (?), Tolone (?), Grasse (?), Avignon (?), Drauguignan (1877), Rouen (1893), Reims (1897), Nancy (1995).

Switzerland: Thonon (1598; allora nello Stato del Duca di Savoia), Zurigo-Glattbrugg (1981).

The Netherlands: Montaigu (1620), Apremont (1620), Douai (1626), Kavelaer (1646), Braine (1712), Chievres (1713), Maastricht (1997).

Spain: Valencia (1645), Villena (1650), Madrid (1660), Soria (1670),

Granada (1671), Cadiz (1672), Barcelona (1673), Saragoza (1690), Palma de Mallorca (1690), Villa de Ezcaray (1695), Carcabuey (1695), Medina de Pomar (1695), Alcala de Henares (1696), Sevilla (1698), Cordoba (1699), Cifuentes (1700), Murcia (1700), Molina de Aragon (1700), Baeza (1702), Vich (1723), Cuenca (1738), Malaga (1742), Baeza (1760), Barcelona Gracia (1885), Tudela (1891), Porreras (1891), Soller (1891), Lugo (?), Ecija (?), Canarias (?), Albacete (1953).

POLAND: Gostyn (1655), Poznan (1671; re-founded 1999), Studzianna (1674), Biscovia (1722), Tarnow (1879), Bytow (1952), Radom (1972), Tomaszow Mazowieski (1980), Kamianna (1988).

MALTA: Senglea (1662).

PORTUGAL: Lisbona (1668), Porto (1680), Freixo (1680), Braga (1686), Visau (1688), Stremonzio (1697).

GERMANY: Aufhausen (1692), Munich (1710; re-founded 1954), Leipzig (1930), Dormund (1958), Essen (1960), Aachen (1956), Frankfurt/Main (1956), Dresden (1961), Heildelberg (1968), Frankfurt/ Oder (1971), Celle (formerly Goslar) (1991), Ilsede (1997).

AUSTRIA: Vienna (1710; re-founded 1978), Maria Lanzendorf (1991).

ENGLAND: Birmingham (1848), London (1848), Oxford (1993).

America

MEXICO: Puebla (1669), Guadalajara (1679), San Luis Potosi (1686), Oaxaca (1695), Mexico (1697), San Miguel de Allende (1712), Orizaba (1762; re-founded 1974), Queretaro (1763), Guanajuato (1775), Leon (1830), Tlalnepantla (1966), Mexico San Pablo (1973), Mexico N. Sra de la Paz (1995).

Brazil: Pernambuco (1671), Sao Paulo (1996).

Bolivia: Potosí (1668), Sucre (?), Las Lajas (?).

Cuba: La Habana (?).

Peru: Lima (1689).

Guatemala: Guatemala (1694).

Colombia: San Juan de Pasto (1830), Ipiales (1892), Santa Fe de Bogotá (1952).

United States: Rock Hill (1947), Monterey (formerly Yarnel, 1953), Pharr (formerly McAllen, 1966), Pittsburgh (1968), Brooklyn (1988), Metuchen (1998), Philadelphia (2000).

El Salvador: San Salvador (1952).

Chile: Villa Alemana (1966).

Costa Rica: San José de Costa Rica (1962).

Canada: Toronto (formerly Montreal, 1975).

Asia

India: Goa (1686), Bicciolim (?), Banda (?), Shaul (?), Oner (?).

Sri Lanka; Kandy (1700), Puttalam (1707).

Africa

South Africa: Oudtshoorn (1997).

CHAPTER IV

The Confederation of the Congregations

When the Holy See decided to unite your *Domus sui iuris* into a Confederation, it did so in order to offer you an instrument suitable to fraternal communion. In giving form and substance to this bond of charity, it turned to the great heart and clear mind of Father Arcadio Maria Larraona, who became Cardinal of the Holy Roman Church.

How much he loved the Oratory of St. Philip and how much of its essence he preserved you yourselves have demonstrated in your elaboration of your new General Statutes, approved in 1989, in substantial conformity with what he had planned.

You must love this instrument of communion that is the Confederation, and avail yourselves of all that it offers. Thus the Oratory may grow and flourish abundantly in the Holy Church of God, *circumdata varietate*, in the beautiful biblical image that your confrere the Venerable Cardinal Cesare Baronio, disciple and first successor of St. Philip, used to express the richness of gifts in the Church.
(Cardinal Eduardo Martinez Somalo, Prefect of the Congregation of Institutes of Consecrated Life and Societies of Apostolic Life, October 6, 2000)

1. HOW THE CONFEDERATION WAS BORN

While the Oratory has its clear origins in Fr. Philip's ministry, and while the Congregation, constituted for the Oratory, is also his creation, we cannot say that any form of federation of the outlying Congregations was ever in his mind. These arose outside of Rome through the initiative of priests who had come into contact with the Roman Oratory and were fascinated by the new method of evangelization, or through the initiative of certain members of the Roman Oratory itself.[1]

We have already spoken of the original intention of Fr. Philip for a priestly Community of his spiritual sons, and of his profound conviction that the Congregation was born, not from him, but by the Lord by means of Mary, Mother of all beginnings, and by the initiative of his disciples who were priests. It was his disciples rather than he, and some in special ways, who brought the Community to the papal recognition of 1575, even though that Community was born from him, and had developed in his hands. The drafting of the first rules, which he had reviewed and approved, are also due more to their initiative than to his.[2]

The apostolic desire to see the Oratory spread was certainly alive in Fr. Philip, and with the Oratory, the Congregation designed to serve it. We have a document which is significant in this respect—a letter that the Father wrote on January 13, 1580, to the Archbishop of Fermo Mons. Domenico Pinelli: "The Lord God knows that my desire and that of the whole Congregation that this Institute of the Oratory be spread, because of the fruit that we continually see coming from it. And we commit ourselves to this, since it seems to us that this is really our vocation. But up to now, considering our numbers, it has seemed to me best to be very cautious about assuming new Oratories outside of Rome, even if many have asked us, and especially the illustrious and most reverend Santa Prassede [Cardinal Charles Borromeo] and Paleotto for Milan and for Bologna. We have always been constrained to excuse ourselves, and now for the same reasons also with your Reverend Lordship and with your City, which so lovingly invites us; it grieves me that I cannot totally correspond to the faith and devotion that you have for this Congregation. But yet desiring to satisfy your desire in some way, we have thought that your very Reverend Lordship could send to Rome for a few months two of those priests who have this inclination and who seem to you to be adapted to the exercises of the Oratory; then, being present to our way of life and our practices they will, with the help of the Lord, be instructed so that they themselves will know how to commit themselves to this service, and from us they will receive every possible introduction. And I offer myself to care for them as I do for my own here. And if it would be a consolation for your Reverence and for the City that one from the Congregation would come to begin the work, I will do all that I can to gratify your desire."[3]

He would, therefore, willingly have sent priests to begin an Oratorian presence in Fermo, but was held back by the limited number of members, which was always a problem relative to the intense activity of the Oratory. The Oratory by now was structured according to an ordered succession of sermons, for which all the Fathers did not have the necessary skill or the time. Very probably he was also reluctant to change his intimate, original conviction, that the Oratory should be a family of priests gathered around himself. It would have its identity and its apostolic power not in organizing structures, but in the spiritual rapport of father and sons that had created it and continued to characterize it.

We have already seen that this rapport of close spiritual dependence on the Father did not keep some members from making foundations elsewhere and thus spreading the Congregation. Fr. Philip allowed it to happen, trusting in God and continuing his own commitment to incessant apostolic activity, which left him little time for questions of ecclesiastical organization. This did not mean that the Father was indifferent to these emerging experiences in the Oratory, only that he dealt with them quietly and, above all, allowed other Fathers to handle them.

It is clear in the texts of the Constitutions that preceded the *Institutes* of 1612 that the Houses had a centralized structure, which corresponds more to the intention of Frs. Talpa, Tarugi, Bordini, Baronio, and others, than to the Father's intimate conviction. But Fr. Philip accepted his sons' idea, and he and his first successors, beginning with the Constitutions of 1583[4] bore the title of "Padre Generale"

[Father General].[5] The title appears also in the Constitutions of 1588, which were the only ones not only reviewed but expressly approved by St. Philip. They exercised this function on some of the aggregated Houses, also by means of the official Visit of the Houses.[6] But this practice lasted for only the time when the Constitutions, following the norms of the Bull of erection of the Congregation, were being written and the outlines of the Institution were being laboriously shaped by the Father and his priest disciples.

The juridical bond among the existing Oratorian Houses which favored, especially after the death of St. Philip, fidelity to the Founder's original intention would be abolished. The new Constitutions codify this decision,[7] which Gregory XV reasserted with the Brief *Ex iniuncto Nobis* on July 8, 1622.[8]

If this is the history of the origins, how was the "Confederation" born?

The idea of the Confederation matured only in recent times, under the pressure of historical events that induced the Congregations to seek some way to unite themselves organically. However, the autonomy of each desired by their Founder was always fully respected, and all the Communities considered St. Philip their founder. The Confederation came into being about sixty years ago. Although not foreseen at the time of the origins of the Oratory, it has proved itself to be, in its half century of abundant life, the safeguard not only of Oratorian identity and the original autonomy of the Congregations, but sometimes of their very survival. Strongly desired by many and looked upon with suspicion by others, the new institution, quite apart from the historical circumstances of its founding, sunk its roots into the bond of charity that from its founding had united the Congregations of the Oratory. The Oratory had quickly been diffused into various parts of the world, which made communications among them difficult in centuries past, but they always felt themselves to be a *moral unity*. In addition, and respecting the principle "unaquaeque domus aut familia...se per se regat et moderetur,"[9] they have always interwoven spiritual relationships and various kinds of collaboration:

Oratorian culture and art stand as witnesses, as do correspondence and the mutual help among the Houses in establishing new foundations and in times of hardship. The National Archives of Spain, to cite one example, preserves the copious correspondence which the Congregations in America sent to the Mother Congregation in Rome and to the Spanish Congregations, requesting legal opinions and various counsels; the archives also contain correspondence about other matters.

The author of the *Excellences of the Congregation of the Oratory* describes this habit of mutual helpfulness in his Chapter III: "this correspondence of charity between our Congregations"; "This Excellence of charity, thus closely uniting so many priests and brother in one house, unites also, as has been said, all the Congregations of St. Philip in the closest bond of love; and although in external things there is no communication between them, nor any participation in temporal goods, as the Holy Father ruled that each house should govern itself separately...nevertheless there is such an interchange of affection between all priests of the Oratory, that, although they may never have met, they still love one another with mutual love and unfeigned charity. This most close union of charity, wrote Father Consolini to a father of another Congregation, unites all our hearts and souls to God in such a bond that it makes both one; and the difference of dispositions, the remoteness of countries, the diversity arising from nationalities unknown to us, or houses greater than our own, or subjects of greater ability, none of these things chill our mutual love.... From this charity it results that when our Lord favors a Congregation with some greater gift of holiness or renown, every other one rejoices in it as if it were its own.... We recognize all as brothers because we are all sons of the same Father, practicing the same rules and customs; and when one Congregation can serve another in any way, it does so with the utmost willingness; nor are they ever at variance, but always united in emulating each others' virtues..."[10]

2. THE CONFEDERATION TODAY

Today the Houses are united in a Confederation, "established by the Apostolic See so that the Congregations, might help each other effectively, while preserving their original autonomy."[11]

The General Statutes[12] emphasize that "the bonds of love, however, by which all the Congregations are held together in St. Philip are to be fostered the more gladly that they are freely entered into," and they suggest some possible fields of collaboration: "they can cooperate together, either in geographical groups according to nation or region, or for apostolic or cultural reasons, or because of lack of members. The Confederation encourages and assists this cooperation, because by means of it the good both of the Congregations and of the Confederation itself is easily obtained. The purposes of cooperation are as follows: (1) to encourage mutual love, so that the Congregations willingly help one another; (2) to promote studies for a better understanding of the Oratorian spirit, and for the adaptation of the Oratorian mission in the circumstances of the contemporary Church; (3) to initiate and carry out tasks in common, and to encourage new foundations; (4) to promote effective collaboration with the Confederation; (5) to achieve effective collaboration with the Delegate of the Apostolic See for the Oratory." The collaboration of the Confederation is envisioned also for the formation of candidates: "Schools for candidates can be set up, not only by individual Congregations, but also by several Congregations together in a particular region. The same is true of philosophical and theological houses and studies. The year of the first probation is to be passed in one's own Congregation, unless circumstances are seen to demand otherwise. However, both the first and second probations passed in one Congregation can be valid for membership of another, so that a probation common to several Congregations is possible, in cases where it is particularly useful. Admission to probation, even in this case, according to the Constitutions, belongs exclusively to the candidate's own Congregation (can. 647, par. 1, 2, 3)."

The Organs of the Confederation, described in the fourth Chapter of the General Statutes, include the *General Congress*, the *Permanent*

Deputation, and the *Procurator General*, and other officials responsible for some specific area, such as the *General Postulator* for the causes of the Saints and the *General Archivist*.[13]

The Congress

The General Congress of the Oratory is "a meeting of all the Congregations of St. Philip, and is to take place every six years." Those who participate with the right to vote are "the Provosts, duly elected or nominated, of every Congregation; the delegates of the Congregations, duly elected according to law, from among the members who are at least triennials; the Delegate of the Apostolic See, the Procurator General, the Postulator General, the Permanent Deputies and the Counsellors of the Delegate."

The General Statutes also set out the responsibilities assigned to the Congress: in addition to listening to and evaluating the reports of the Central Organs and of the Apostolic Delegate, the Congress must reflect "on the various ways in which the Oratorian life is led, as circumstances demand"; it must examine "the difficulties in the life of the Congregations or the Confederation," for the purpose of formulating "practical solutions"; to search for "suitable means for the encouragement of fraternal union between the Congregations." "It does not ordinarily deal with the revision of Oratorian legislation," but "if during the preparations for the Congress, business is proposed regarding the revision of legislation to be submitted to the Holy See by the Congress, then it is required that individual Congregations be informed of the matter at least one year before the Congress, and that in the Congress the proposals are to be decided by a majority of at least two thirds in a secret ballot."

The Permanent Deputation

This is a "permanent organ of the Confederation which has the office of looking after the well-being and the common good of the Confederation, in the name of the General Congress. It is composed of nine "members who represent various languages or regions," who "are equals among themselves"; "the Permanent Deputation is not strictly speaking an organ of government, but a moral body set up to advise and administer." The Permanent Deputation is entrusted with "the execution of the resolutions of the Congress which are committed to it...." It is to "to receive and examine each year the reports on the financial administration and management of the Procura, the Postulator's office, and other property of the Confederation;" in addition, "it must constantly assist the Procurator, and in grave matters it is bound to direct him...and it should collaborate with the Delegate of the Apostolic See for the common good of the Confederation."

The Procurator General

"He represents the Confederation in everything, and acts in its person." Conformably to the function of the Procurator Generals of the various religious Institutes, "he legally represents the Congregations and their members, together with the Confederation of the Oratory, when dealing with the Apostolic See and all Curial Congregations, for the negotiation of all their business." In addition, he has responsibilities that in other Institutes are assigned to different Officials: he administers the patrimony of the Confederation, and must maintain relationships with existing Congregations and those just being founded and, as the General Statutes say, "he must promote the fraternal union of the Congregations and cooperation amongst them... he must seek to restore extinct Congregations, where possible...he must take part in the foundation of new Congregations...." All of this involves, obviously, a vast gamut of fraternal contacts, and a great variety of activities.

Unlike the Delegate to the Apostolic See who represents, as his title indicates, the Apostolic Authority to the individual, confederated Congregations and the Central Organs of the Confederation, and is confirmed by the Holy See, although elected by the Congress, the Procurator General carries out his functions within the Confederation. "Inspire, not direct," the motto adopted by the Procurator General Fr. Edward Griffith (1948–1958), expresses very well the substance of the office. Fr. Arcadio M. Larraona, to whom we owe basically the institution of the Confederation, expressed it in these words: "The Procurator General represents all of the Congregations of the Oratory and the entire Institute to the Holy See. He is therefore the one who officially reports, the defender of the Constitutions, the organ of communication among all the Houses; If asked he provides counsel, enlightens, helps with difficult internal questions, intervenes to defend those whose rights are attacked by others."[14]

The Delegate of the Holy See

The General Statutes dedicate a separate chapter to the office of the Delegate, beginning with a preface explaining its institution: "The Apostolic See took to itself the power of watching directly over the Congregations because of the absolute autonomy and immunity of jurisdiction of the Congregations of the Oratory of St. Philip Neri, and the absence of a central government with a Superior General (*Decree of the Sacred Congregation for Religious*, no. 14536/58). The Apostolic See exercises this right through its Delegate."

The function of the Delegate is presented by the Statutes, in conformity with the cited Decree of institution, as that of "guardian of the common law of the Church and of the proper laws of the Oratory." He must do things in such as way "that the observance of the Constitutions and faithfulness to the spirit of the Father who gave us our law are never lacking," and he must exercise "his office within the limits of the faculties granted him (can. 305, par. 2)" including "the office of canonical Visitor of the Oratory of St. Philip." As Visitor he has both ordinary and extraordinary functions which the Statutes clearly specify.[15] He also has "three Counselors, who in law have only a consultative vote, by reason of the fact that the Delegate's power is granted by the Apostolic See."

Because he belongs to the family of St. Philip ("he must be a priest...outstanding for his learning, zeal, piety, and experience of the common life of the Oratory"), he is able to represent the Apostolic Authority, to whom the Oratory bows recognizing in the Supreme

Pontiff its own supreme Superior,[16] with a knowledge of the Oratorian tradition and an Oratorian style that will make his actions more fruitful.

3. THE STAGES OF THE JOURNEY

The road that led to the formation of the Confederation was long and marked by many difficulties. However, these difficulties served to make it advance with prudence and greater maturity. In the following historical notes we mean to reconstruct this development, presenting its various stages and remembering the men who committed themselves to this undertaking.

1893–1918

The first official step toward the *Institutum*[17] *Oratorii San Philippi Nerii* was completed by the Decree of the Sacred Congregation of Religious ex Audientia Sanctissimi of March 21, 1933, which instituted the *Visitatio Generalis Oratorii* and named on behalf of all the Oratorian Congregations an Apostolic Visitor in the person of the Claretian Fr. Arcadio Maria Larraona.[18] Meanwhile, Fr. Carlo Naldi had been named Procurator General and had begun to carry out the proper functions of his office. Fr. Naldi,[19] from the Oratory in Florence, was chosen by the Congress of Provosts in Bologna in 1932, and was named by the Apostolic See in February 1933 to be the "Procurator General of the Oratory."[20]

But the road that led to the configuration of this new bond between the Congregations had begun some decades earlier, when everyone became aware that the dramatic situation that arose in the course of the nineteenth century required a solution.

Mown down, in fact, by the policies of Napoleon, by the laws of suppression of the newly independent Italy, and by political upheavals in Latin America, the Oratorian Houses came to find themselves reduced in numbers and in grave poverty. A goodly number, although having had a glorious history, ceased to exist, while many others were close to extinction.

"With the end of the eighteenth century," writes Fr. Carlo Gasbarri,[21] "thanks to regimes that were revolutionary, Jacobin, repressive, Masonic, and anticlerical in various European countries, there began the crisis that in a few years would reduce the number of Congregations from one hundred and eighty-two to fifty-six. This is explained also, and in good part, by their juridical structure, each completely autonomous, completely isolated from one another, with scant and irregular communication among them."

Beginning in the last years of the nineteenth century,[22] there were two Oratorians in particular who took this problem to heart and worked with sincere love for the Oratory to find a solution, the Servant of God Fr. Giovanni Battista Arista[23] of the Oratory of Acireale and then Bishop of the same diocese, and the Servant of God Fr. Giulio Castelli, originally from the Oratory of Turin and founder of the Congregation of Cava de' Tirreni.[24]

The Supreme Pontiff Leo XIII supported their idea: he was very close to the Oratory from the time of his thirty-year episcopate in Perugia. Pope St. Pius X, while he was still Patriarch of Venice, expressed approval for the attempt to find a solution to the problem.[25] There were also Oratorians who were convinced that this plan was necessary, the first among whom being Cardinal Alfonso Capecelatro[26] of the Oratory of Naples, then Archbishop of Capua and Librarian of the Holy Roman Church, but there were many Oratorians who were averse, fearing the loss of the characteristic autonomy of the single Congregations.[27]

A letter of Fr. Arista to Fr. Castelli dated August 13, 1893, can be taken as the first of many steps on the long road:

> And now, since I have the fortune to find in Your Reverence such goodness of spirit, let me share with you an idea that has pursued me insistently for a long time, in order to ask you to shed some light upon it and to know whether this might be possible, or it is to be entirely rejected.

St. Philip in his Constitutions established that each House of his Congregation is independent of all the others and is recognizable by its observance of its Rules.

Now I am thinking: if one were to think to bring the Houses together in one Body, while there would remain to each all the liberty required to remain in fact independent, would this be to separate ourselves from the mind of our Holy Founder?

Let me explain more clearly. At the moment, as far as I know, the separate Houses are so detached from one another that they do not know of one another's existence. And I am supposing that even the very House of Rome, which is the cradle and center of the Institute, may not be aware of the true state of that same Institute in the various Houses that compose it.

From this arise a number of inconveniences, of which the most evident is that no House knows to whom it may turn for advice and help. Because of this, who knows how many Houses have closed, and others may be only subsisting. This much is certain. Would it not be true that at times the cooperation of a confrere might serve, with divine favor, to infuse new vigor and avoid a collapse?

This said, I am thinking: might it be possible, with the consensus of the Fathers Provost, and with the approval of the Sacred Congregation, to establish and recognize as the Central House the House of Rome, and its Provost as Superior General?

Certainly his rights would not be equal to those of the General Superiors of the Orders, since everything must be regulated *ad mentem Fundadoris*, by the mind of the Founder. This means that every Congregation could maintain its independence, supporting itself, and only in correspondence with that of Rome. The House of Rome, knowing the state of each House could, with charity and prudence, provide for all, for example inviting the members of a House with an abundance of Fathers to come to the aid of one in need.

Even if the rights of the Provost General were limited to that of a simple invitation, without the faculty of imposing anything, it would be a great advantage. With sincerity I tell you that, without doing any harm to my Congregation, I would not have a moment's hesitation in running elsewhere to help another House.

And by this means, how many new foundations might there be. When I think that in Sicily, where there were so many flourishing Houses, there is not one (I cannot yet count our own House, since we are not yet reunited in Community), oh, one feels one's heart break!

Father, with your insights strengthened by advice and by prayer, do think of what I have told you, and counting on your charity I will await your response in its time.

Fr. Giulio Castelli moved from the Oratory of Torino to the Roman Oratory in December of 1889 following a dramatic appeal to all the Oratories in the world in 1881 and repeated in the following years by the Provost of the Vallicella Fr. Scaramucci.[28] Fr. Castelli was very much aware that something had to be done, not only for the Roman Oratory, which was only one of many Congregations that found themselves in sorry conditions. Fr. Castelli had begun to work with the zeal he had already shown in Torino, so much so that he remained favorably impressed in the mind of the thirteen-year-old Eugenio Pacelli, altar boy at the Chiesa Nuova. Pacelli never forgot his old master and, having become Pope with the name of Pius XII, would say[29]: "I am happy to see introduced the Cause for the Beatification of such a worthy son of St. Philip. When he came here to Rome, I was just thirteen years old and in the Chiesa Nuova he was my master of catechism. Everyone esteemed him as a saint, and I remember him well: a tall, frail figure, completely recollected, completely humble, with his eyes lowered, like this," and joined his hands, interlacing them on his breast, in the habitual gesture of Fr. Giulio.

With immense sacrifices and a total lack of economic means, Fr. Castelli managed to set up a little Collegio for the formation of candidates for the Oratory, who would be sent to those Houses that had requested them; he had also, on the occasion of the third centenary of the death of St. Philip, assumed the responsibility of publishing a

Collectio Costitutionum et Privilegiorum Congregationis Oratorii a San Philippo Nerio fundatae,[30] with the declared intention of issuing an invitation to revitalize the Oratory and the life of the Congregations.

The idea about which Arista wrote to Fr. Castelli he also shared with another Oratorian friend, Mons. Jourdan de la Passadière,[31] who answered on March 19, 1895, declaring his full agreement with the idea expressed, and saying that he had even spoken about this, a few months earlier, on his own initiative, to the His Holiness Leo XIII: "Most Holy Father," he writes that he said, "the occasion of the centenary of St. Philip is perfect for the realization of this plan. Your Holiness would resuscitate the Congregation of St. Philip if you would deign to do for it what you have done recently for the Benedictines and the Cistercians, whose primitive organization was analogous to ours." He added: "The Holy Father was pleased with the idea, and told me that he would think about it, and he urged me to talk about this to our Most Eminent Confrere Cardinal Capecelatro who was at that time in Rome, and I did that."

Mons. de la Passadière, after having explained to Arista in a letter his idea of a President General of the Institute, an Institute in which "every House would be absolutely independent, as the Constitutions require, in its autonomy, its governance, its economic resources, the choosing and accepting of its novices," he expressed the hope that "more frequent fraternal relations among Houses, with annual or triennial reunions of the Oratorians of the same country, and with a Visitor who would be sent on occasion by the President General." He added in the letter: "Above all, and this point of view seems to me primary, each Oratory could, should it seem useful and if it were itself short of members who could teach and form its novices, send some young men of good promise for the novitiate and theological studies.... The beginnings of this holy and great work has been already established in Rome by the good and zealous Father Giulio Castelli."

On April 3, 1895, Fr. Castelli, who in addition to sharing openly Arista's worries had personal reasons for understanding his anxieties, communicated his enthusiastic praise at the "solemn gathering of

Oratorians to mount a universal reawakening," but he added: "One point only I would emphasize, which has been already said, that we must not propose to establish a head, like the General of an Order. There is no need. And in fact it would change our Institute too much and might even take away our freedom to do good..."

Pope Leo XIII, meanwhile, in order to celebrate the centenary feast, wrote a Brief full of admiration for St. Philip and his work.[32] And in the Audience of June 6 given to the Fathers present in Rome for the occasion,[33] he expressed his love for the Oratory and his ardent desire to see it rise again. He also asked all those present to come together in convocation the following day, under the presidency of Cardinal Capecelatro, in order to find a way to draw the Congregations together in a fraternal bond of active and effective charity.

The meeting, the first of this kind, arrived at some practical conclusions,[34] but its proposals did not offer material suitable for responding to the Sacred Congregation of Bishops and Religious, to whom Capecelatro reported. Nevertheless, it held out hope for those who believed that it was necessary to find some solution. Fr. Giulio Castelli, for example, wrote August 6, 1895, to the Provost of Perugia Fr. Enrico Bondi: "We confide in the Lord. A new horizon has opened for the Institute of St. Philip. The Congress held by order of the Pope has already borne fruit. Let us continue to pray, and to labor, and to plant, and to water."[35] Fr. Arista knew now that his desire coincided with that of the Vicar of Christ, and he continued his work intensely. For that reason, he took advantage of a personal trip in Italy, France, Spain, and Belgium and contacted as many Congregations as he could. The project aroused interest in many Oratorians, but there was also some perplexity.

Father Castelli left the Roman Oratory on the last day of the year 1895, exhausted by the constant opposition of two elderly confreres. He went to Cava, at the invitation of the Bishop of that Diocese. In 1899, shortly before the Beatification of the Venerable Fr. Antonio Grassi, expected in the Jubilee Year 1900, he sent a circular letter to the Provosts, inviting them to Rome for the occasion in the hope that another meeting might be possible. Immediately the Roman Provost Fr. Generoso Calenzio[36] sent out another printed circular which mocked and scorned Castelli with biting sarcasm, rejecting his initiative.

The situation of the Oratorian Houses in Italy, meanwhile, worsened to the point that the Sacred Congregation for Bishops and Religious, under the direction of Pope Leo XIII,[37] issued a decree on May 29, 1900,[38] naming Fr. Clemente Benedettucci[39] Apostolic Visitor of the Oratorian Houses, existing and extinct, in the Marches, Umbria and Emilia.

The report of the Apostolic Visitor resulted in the intervention with which Pope Leo, as a sign of his paternal love,[40] erected in Perugia by a Motu Proprio of September 30, 1900,[41] the Pontifical College of the Oratory—"ut ex eo, recte posito tirocinio, operarii prodeant digni in spem decusque Oratorii." Its Provosts were Fr. Paolo Recanatesi, of the Oratory of Osimo and Fr. Ercole Salvatori, of the Oratory of Recanati.[42]

Also in 1900, a journal entitled *San Filippo Neri: Monitore delle Congregazioni dell'Oratorio*[43] began through the initiative of Fr. Giovanni Battista Tonella of the Oratory of Biella. In that same year, a circular letter from Fr. Arista to the Provosts put forward the idea of presenting an appeal to the Holy Father asking him to intervene with his authority to unblock this stalled situation that had existed since 1895, and from which no one was in a position to move forward.

Cardinal Capecelatro, perplexed by the resistance of so many, was of a mind to postpone it, but in those days Fr. Benedettucci was urging that the appeal be presented, and wrote to Arista: "I believe that the petition should be presented quickly. In these days Fr. Recanatesi had a private audience with the Holy Father about our affairs and found him so benevolent in our regard that he was quite moved."

Dated February 8, 1901, signed by the majority of Provosts, and with the recommendations of numerous Bishops and Cardinals,[44] the appeal reached its destination. However, those opposed to any such union unleashed a battle, of which the published letters of Fr.

Calenzio (March 13, 1901) and Fr. Lais give witness.

The appeal ran aground, and even its promoters recognized that this was due once again to its weakness. Fr. Arista treated the material with the respect and prudence that a delicate subject seemed to demand, but as Fr. Recanetesi suggested, "In Rome it is necessary to present projects that are strong and well-formed, otherwise Rome does not move."

This was in fact the tenor of the response received from Cardinal Giotti, the Prefect of the Sacred Congregation of Bishops and Religious, on March 13: "From His Holiness Pope Leo XIII there has been sent to this Sacred Congregation the printed memorandum asking that there be established some bond among the various Congregations of the Oratory of St. Philip, while maintaining their respective autonomy according to the Rules of the Institute. This Sacred Congregation, while praising the reasons of all those who have signed and recommended this appeal, would like to see that they themselves, *collatis inter se consiliis*, would propose some plans or practical projects, which would translate their desires into action. We desire therefore that Your Paternity work toward this end and send the results to this Sacred Congregation, which will take them under due consideration."

Fr. Arista then decided, and was encouraged in this by friends, to present to the Dicastery information on the state of the existing Congregations—thinking that the Apostolic Authority would intervene directly. But when he asked for the necessary information from a number of Congregations, some did not answer, perhaps in the wake of the circular letters from the Roman Provost.

The Oratorians had toward Leo XIII a debt of gratitude equal to the admiration felt by the entire Church for his Pontificate.[45] After his death, the interest of the new Pontiff Pius X, elected August 4, 1903, for the Oratorian question is documented, among other things, by a letter of Fr. Recanatesi to Arista. Fr. Arista had in November 1904 accepted in obedience to the Pope the nomination as auxiliary Bishop of Acireale; he had managed in 1901, to elude the nomination to be Bishop Prelate Nullius of Santa Lucia del Mela. Fr. Recanatesi wrote: "I have been with the Holy Father, and after having spoken at length about our Congregations, I understood that he has in mind to do something to their advantage.... He ended by giving to Your Excellency and to me the responsibility of formulating a program and giving it to him" (November 21, 1904).

Since Mons. Arista had now been asked directly by the Pope, he set to work, consulting far and wide as demonstrated by his correspondence which includes material from Fathers Castelli, Colletti of the Oratory of Genova, Recanatesi, and Benedettucci. Arista was still looking for more counsel when Fr. Recanatesi[46] wrote to him on December 19, 1904: "What you write is put together with such wisdom that I would not know how to add or to take away anything... but it does not seem to me opportune to go looking here and there for consensus... Your Excellency knows only too well how many enemies there will be opposing any attempt to bring better order..." The proposal was competed, but in spite of much urging, it was presented to the Holy Father only in September 1906.[47]

Some problems internal to the Roman Curia managed to slow the progress of the proposal, if one can credit what Fr. Recanatesi wrote to Arista on August 20, 1907.

At the death of Bishop Genuardi, Mons. Arista was called to succeed him as Bishop of Acireale. His responsibilities in the Diocese had increased enormously, and left him little time for the Oratorian cause so dear to his heart.

This fell to Fr. Giuseppe Timpanaro,[48] of the Oratory of Acireale, very close to Arista in ideas and devoted to him. He had occasion in 1910 to make fraternal visits to many Italian Congregations, continuing his visits in 1912 in company with Mons. Arista and completing them in the period of his military service (1917–1918). He met with some negative reactions, but he also gathered observations from eminent Fathers who induced him to modify the 1906 project.

Fr. Castelli, too, continued to work on the question. Between 1913 and 1914, he went to see the Prefect of the Sacred Congregation of Religious, Cardinal Cagiano de Azevedo, and presented to him a project of union. Having gotten wind of this, Fr. Lais, Provost of Rome, intervened immediately with the Cardinal, but the sad condition of the House of Rome, which continued to have unresolved problems, sadly interwoven with the whole journey that led to the raising of the Institutum, provoked an Apostolic Visit to the Roman Oratory, which was then extended to the Italian Congregations. Mons. Melata was given the responsibility for this, and after two years, Abate Arcangelo Lolli, of the Lateran Canons, succeeded him. In an attempt to find a solution for the intricate questions involved, Lolli called a Congress of Provosts, set for Rome at the Apostolic See for November 20, 1918.

1918–1932

In 1918 there began the epoch of Congresses. These united the Provosts in legitimate meetings by pontifical disposition,[49] and thereby already constituted an early embryonic form of a unitary organism. At the Congress of 1918 sixteen of the nineteen Houses existing in Italy participated, and both Fr. Castelli and Mons. Arista were present. Fr. Timpanaro showed in that meeting all his dynamism and his passion, and it became clear that here was a most convinced and industrious exponent of the movement for unification. It was he who presented to Abate Lolli a memorandum describing the project, modified according to his ideas; he also gave typed copies to the participants. The Congress decided that their meetings would be triennial and concluded its work again appealing to all Congregations to send members to the House in Rome.

Fr. Calenzio had died in 1915; Fr. Lais' health was steadily worsening and in 1919 he retired to live privately. From that time there was a continual rotation of Fathers in the Roman Community.[50]

At the end of the triennium the Sacred Congregation of Religious announced another Congress with a circular of June 13, 1921. A questionnaire was included asking that proposals for the increase of members of the Oratory be sent to the Sacred Congregation; it also asked: "If, notwithstanding the changes wrought by the passage of time, the Institute of the Oratory should remain just as it has always been, or if instead one ought not to apply the prescriptions of current Canon Law to some areas."

This second Congress of the Italian Congregations took place in Rome on November 23–24 with the participation of seventeen Houses. In this meeting, in which the aging Fr. Castelli took part (Mons. Arista had died in odor of sanctity the previous year), the idea took shape to give the Houses a more unified structure by means of a Representative in Rome.

The institution of such a Representative, to whom was granted to represent the separate Houses to the Holy See, did not take away even minimally the autonomy of the single Houses, since each one had the right to deal with the Holy See regarding its own questions and by means of its own representative. The common Representative would be elected by the Congregations, and deal with questions common to all. The Congress also agreed that the Representative would take care of correspondence by letter with all the Houses, above all, whatever matters would concern the deliberations of the Congress, and also would take special care of Houses reduced to fewer than three members, and of suppressed or extinct Congregations, and would try to revive them or at least to locate their possessions.

That Representative was identified with the Provost in Rome, who at that time was Fr. Davide Viola. He did for a brief time exercise the function assigned to him by the election. In fact, he left for Trappa in 1922, right after the solemn festivities for the centenary of the canonization of St. Philip, made even more joyous by a Letter of Pope Benedict XV[51] and by solemn celebrations.[52]

Fr. Timpanaro succeeded him, and due to the scarcity of members persisting in the Roman House along with other grave problems, invoked the presence of the Apostolic Delegate. Father Abbot of St. Paul Outside the Walls, Dom Ildefonso Schuster,[53] had been named to this post on January 5, 1923.

The Apostolic Delegate deemed it appropriate to invite the Houses outside of Italy to the new Congress, celebrated from February 6–8, 1924, under his presidency.

Seventeen Italian Houses, two Spanish—Barcelona and Palma de Mallorca—two Polish, and one Mexican participated in the Congress. The office of secretary was held by two Fathers who would have a notable role in later Oratorian affairs, Paolo Caresana,[54] of the Oratory of Brescia, and Cesare Nanni,[55] of the Oratory of Bologna. The Congregation of Rome was entrusted to that of Bologna, a puzzling decision since there were very few members in Bologna. The revision of the Constitutions was entrusted to Fathers Castelli and Timpanaro. The Congress confirmed the decision of the preceding Congress with respect to the Representative of the Houses.

Pius X received those attending the Congress in an audience, spoke to them of his admiration for St. Philip, and said that he had always venerated the image of Philip's face in wax at the Biblioteca Ambrosiana. The image had been given as a gift by Neri's great spiritual son, Cardinal Federico Borromeo. Because of his intimacy with Fr. Philip, the Cardinal had had the privilege of obtaining this image on his departure for Milano.

This Congress, which closed peacefully, opened a long and sad dispute between Fr. Nanni and Fr. Timpanaro. Fr. Nanni had adopted and adapted the ancient texts of the Constitutions, those that preceded the approval of the Institute in 1612. He decided and brought about the union of some of the Houses under the Roman Congregation and exercised over them the authority of the Provost General. Fr. Timpanaro, meanwhile, continued tirelessly his work as herald of a respectful reform, in the light of the projects of Arista and of Castelli.

We will not enter into this episode, which would require considerable space to treat properly, preferring rather to refer to the published documents and to the studies that describe its development.[56]

It is only necessary to clarify, in the context of this condensed presentation, that the burning questions of this period forced the suspension of the triennial Congress which should have taken place in 1927. Just in that year, in fact, the Apostolic Delegate requested the direct intervention of the Sacred Congregations of Religious, which announced a Visit for the Roman House, entrusting the task to Schuster. The policies of Fr. Nanni were openly repudiated, and the observance of the traditional Oratorian organization was restored.

In 1928 Abbot Schuster was sent to Milano as Apostolic Administrator and the following year was named both Archbishop and Cardinal. The Holy See did not name another Apostolic Delegate.

Fr. Castelli had died on July 21, 1926. In 1931, Fr. Timpanaro took the initiative to meet with the other Italian Provosts in Cava de' Terreni. There on September 6, in the presence of Cardinal Lavitrano, former bishop of Cava and by then Archbishop of Palermo, a former penitent of Fr. Castelli, they translated the venerated remains of this Servant of God[57] to the sanctuary of Santa Maria dell'Olmo. The Fathers present at this rite had occasion to speak of the many events that had occurred after the last Congress. They renewed their commitment to see the Constitutions reviewed in the light of the new Code of Canon Law, and they gave this task again to Fr. Timpanaro, who with Fr. Castelli, had been entrusted with this charge in 1924.

Extremely active and indefatigable, Fr. Timpanaro succeeded in organizing a new Congress, set for Bologna for November 15–18, 1932, in the ancient monastery of San Vittore, property of the Bolognese Oratory. Fifteen of the nineteen Congregations participated.[58] The Secretary of the Sacred Congregation for Religious was reassuring; Fr. Bardellini was sent to Rome for this purpose, *sui placet* of the Holy See; a minute examination was conducted of the proposal for updating the Constitutions; the deliberations of 1924 regarding the Representative in Rome—now, following the terminology of the Code of 1917, called the "Procurator"—and Fr. Giulio Bevilacqua[59] was elected to this office, or Fr. Carlo Naldi in case the first did not accept; it was decided that all these decisions would be submitted to the approval of the new Congress, set for April 1934; and they finished the work at one o'clock in the morning with the signing of the verbal agreements and a memorable Eucharistic adoration, guided by Fr. Caresana. An exultant Fr. Timpanaro offers his witness to this event: "What did Fr. Caresana say to Jesus that night? What did he say to his confreres? Inspired words, never before heard! Fr. Romualdo

Barigelletti of the Oratory of Osimo, articulated it for everyone: 'I have never heard such words in my entire life, nor have I ever been present at a more evocative function.'"[60]

1933–1958

Cardinal Lavitrano sent the votes of the meeting to the Holy See and Fr. Naldi, in place of Fr. Bevilacqua who had immediately refused the position, reported the results to Mons. La Puma, secretary of the Sacred Congregation. He, in turn, sent them to Fr. Arcadio M. Larraona, instructor at the Lateran University and a qualified canonist. On April 17, 1933, Fr. Larraona was received in an audience with the Holy Father Pius XI and explained to him the matter of the Oratory. Immediately the Sacred Congregation of Religious announced a General Visitation to all the Oratorian Congregations and named Fr. Larraona as Apostolic Visitor.

On May 26 of the same year the Visitor communicated in a circular letter to all the Congregations the decision of the Holy See and the opening of the General Visitation, enclosing the Decree of the Sacred Congregation that authorized it. It listed five *Monita et Ordinationes* relative to the primary goal of the Visit which was the updating of the Constitutions which was to be done in a General Congress, during which in addition "all those questions which deal with the general well-being of the Oratory must be examined." All the Congregations were invited to send suggestions. Fr. Naldo was named secretary of the Visit on June 19, and from this moment until 1942 he would be the very close collaborator with the Father Visitor.

The new Congress, set for September 12–16, 1933, in Rome, was celebrated with the participation of around thirty Italian, Spanish, German, and English Congregations, and discussed the *Schema correctionum ac variationum quae in Constitutionibus faciendis proponuntur*, prepared by the Visitor himself. The most innovative contribution in this first phase of revision undoubtedly is Chapter IV of the revised text, which in a fuller development will make up the General Statutes. The analysis concentrated above all on the definition of the Congregation: "The Institute of St. Philip Neri, founded by him in Rome by divine inspiration, as it is believed, is a clerical society of pontifical right, made up of secular priests and clerics and of lay brothers who live a common life without vows"; "it is made up of different Houses which are called Congregations," each independent and autonomous, but "conjoined one to another by bonds, which are especially ideological and moral."[61]

There were those who looked with suspicion on this definition, in which if to the term *Institutum* were given the meaning of *Corpus institutum*, it would detract from fidelity to the mind of the Founder and to the wording of the Bull of erection of the Congregation of the Urbe and of the other Houses. There were also those who saw in the formula "Institute… made up of different Houses" the idea of Castelli, of Arista and of many others whom we have encountered in this excursus.

When the Congress closed, some remained perplexed, and others were satisfied. Many observations were sent to the Visitator on the first draft of the Constitutions which had been sent to the Congregations in the fall of 1935; these made a reordering of the work necessary, and the projected Congress of 1936 was not possible. The Spanish Civil War and the outbreak of World War II in 1939 made other postponements necessary, until the Sacred Congregation suggested that the Congress not be further put off, even though the war in Europe was fully underway.

The Congress of 1942. Convoked by the Fr. Visitator as "extraordinary…not exactly juridical, like those, that is, that are defined in the new Statutes,"[62] it was celebrated at the Vallicella from April 20–23, 1942, with the participation of around fifty Fathers.

It was opened in the rooms of Fr. Philip the evening of April 20 with a brief inaugural celebration, and the following day after the community Mass at the altar of St. Philip, the first session began with the Report of the Fr. Visitator. There followed those of Fr. Caresana on "The Oratorian Spirit and Its Characteristics" and Fr. Angilella on "The International Oratorian College Pius XII"; in the second session, after talks by the Fr. Visitator on the Constitutions and Fr. Naldi on the Procura and the Postulation. Fr. Cottinelli spoke on "The Priesthood and Oratorian life" and Fr. Timpanaro on "The Secular Oratory." In the third session, on April 23, the Visitator continued his Report on the Constitutions, Fr. Caresana spoke on "Present Conditions of the Roman Congregation"; and Frs. Mino and Meggiolaro on "Oratorian Vocations: Selection, Admission, Formation, Incardination." The fourth session was dedicated to an examination of the Constitutions and Statutes, guided by the Visitator, with responses by Fr. Bevilacqua on "Oratorian Apostolate and the Apostolate of the Oratorian," Fr. Acchiappati on "Liturgical Spirit and the Liturgical Apostolate." And finally Fr. Caresana again on "The Apostolate of the Confessional and of Spiritual Direction."

The last day, in the fifth session, after the Fr. Visitator's continuation on the Constitutions and Statutes, the talk by Fr. Cistellini on "The Apostolate of the Culture and of Teaching," and Fr. Gasbarri's on "The Oratorian Apostolate and Catholic Action," the commissions began their reports, which continued in the sixth session.

The Congress closed with an "Oratorian Evening," in the Oratory of Borromini, introduced by a discourse of Fr. Bevilacqua on "Living the Oratorian Ideal" and ending with a "Spoken Chorus" and closing remarks by Fr. Caresana.

On the basis of the *textus emendatus* of the *Constitutiones* and of the *Statuta Generalia*, previously sent to the Congregations from which many observations had come to the Visitator, the new constitutional provisions were approved. The Permanent Deputation required by the Statutes was elected, and Fr. Larraona assumed, on an interim basis, the office of the Procurator General. Fr. Naldi did not agree to be considered; he felt rather put aside, and was disappointed in the decision of the Congress to transfer the headquarters of the Procurator from the house at San Nereo, which had been decorously adapted by the Procurator General, to the uncomfortable residence of San Girolamo della Carità where Fr. Naldi had lived at the start of his mandate.

The text of the Constitutions was approved *ad experimentum*, awaiting the next Congress, which would be celebrated at the end of the war. Pius XII confirmed them in an *Audientia Sanctissimi* on April 4, 1943.

The published text was divided into two parts: the frontispiece of the first bears the title: *Constitutiones Congregationum Instituti Oratorii San Philipi Nerii, a Paulo V per Breve "Christifidelium" (24-II-161) approbatae et post diligentem Codicis Juris Canonici accommodationem, a Sacra Congregatione de Religiosis ex Audientia SS.mi (12 apr 1943) ad experimentum confirmatae*; the frontispiece of the second part reads: *Statuta Generalia Congregationum atque Instituti Oratorii San Philippi a Sacra Congregatione de Religiosis ex Audientia SS.mi (12 apr 1943) ad experimentum confirmata.*[63]

To Fr. Arcadio M. Larraona one owes the immense task of revising the Constitutions, and also the configuration of the *Institutum Oratorii*, in the form that the General Statutes present them and the Apostolic Authority sanctioned them.

Even those in the Oratory who had doubts about how positive the changes in the new Constitutions were still recognized Fr. Larraona for the dedication with which he worked and for the merit of having followed, in his work of revision, the criteria of reverential respect and constant comparison with the early *Institutes* approved by Paul V in 1612. He was greatly esteemed as a splendid priest, and Pope John XXIII would recognize him with the red hat of a Cardinal.

The opinions most critical of the *Statuti Generali* and of the nature of the new institution were particularly strong in the two English Congregations,[64] which were fearful that in the dispositions of the Statutes there might be a *novum quoddam instrumentum gubernandi*, but the great majority of the Congregations received the decisions of the Congress with the understanding that something highly positive had been brought to completion. The remedy for all the problems had certainly not been found. The Oratorian Congregations, however, were operating in times and situations, even ecclesial situations, very different from those of the origins. In the Confederation they now had at their disposal an instrument of communion that would guarantee the autonomy desired by the Founder, and that would also defend and promote Oratorian identity and life.

With a Circular Letter dated Corpus Domini 1943,[65] Fr. Larraona communicated to the Congregations the approval of the Constitutions and the General Statutes, saying that:

> [They] are exactly the text reviewed by the Congress of 1942, after incorporating the observations received from the Congregations of the different nations. Here and there we have polished, completed, and corrected a phrase or an idea to take into account observations made in the Congress. We have also included some of the reservations expressed in a letter from the English Congregations (cf. no. 108)... The Decree of approval, while it confirms in a very precise and solemn way the autonomy of the Congregations, also approves with evident satisfaction their union and confederation. This union rests on the same Constitutions and on the communion of the same spirit and the same ideals. It has as its purpose reciprocal and fraternal help. This will take care of common needs, for which the single, isolated Congregations, abandoned to themselves, are inadequate. The document of the Sacred Congregation, the approved text of the Constitutions and especially the General Statutes all employ a clear and technically precise formula, that is, *Institute of the Oratory* to indicate this union. The phrase itself is new, as is the fraternal union that it expresses, and we could say of it what Pius XI said of the Congresses of Oratorians: it is a happy innovation.
>
> The *Institute of the Oratory* in the respectful, wide, and flexible form that it has taken on will, in the mind of the Sacred Congregation, be of undoubted usefulness and will bring certain juridical advantages and moral support to all the Congregations. Approving the Statutes *ad tempus*, the Holy See, in its gracious goodness, desires that we try out the Institute, that we make a sincere, trusting, and loyal attempt to make use of its various organs, that we show ourselves willing and desirous of collaborating... This work, when

> everything is complete, will represent the fruit which has slowly matured through fifty years of anxieties and efforts and a decade of willing and constructive collaboration, prayer and effort of all the Congregations. *Of all the Congregations*, we say, but we must add a lively feeling of gratitude to those who so nobly have taken the responsibility of giving to the work the best that they could, an intelligent and sincere criticism that has enabled us to correct, polish, foresee, and provide.
>
> With the approval of the Holy See the existing institutions that have been de facto become de jure. It has been for you and for me a source of vexation that we have found ourselves these last four years in circumstances of which no one could predict the end. In order to obey the Sacred Congregation we were obliged to celebrate the Oratorian Congress without the presence of representatives of the Congregations outside of Italy. You all will remember that we *always* kept them in mind, in our deliberations, *always present*, not less present than if they had been there in person and that not one of the observations that they had sent to us from 1935 on was forgotten. We held them to be precious; every one was winnowed, discussed, yielded its profit. You all remember that, and the proceedings which are to be published will, we hope, give witness to this. Even apart from this absence from the meetings, more of form than of substance, we have had the consolation of hearing not only from you but also from the Most Reverend Commission on Constitutions, which has done so much to further the spontaneous, open, and thoroughly *Oratorian* collaboration of everyone.

The General Congress of 1948, convoked from October 4–9, ratified fully the decisions of 1942. The fifty participants included this time representatives of some of the Congregations which had not able to be present at the preceding Congress: Mexico, England, and Germany were represented. By unanimous consent, the five-year visitation of the Houses was introduced into the texts in conformity with Canon Law. The Visitator Larraona proposed for these visits that one be chosen from of an established list of designated persons, or the Procurator General, or someone designated by the Procura. The General Statutes, which had been approved provisionally (*ad experimentum*) in 1942, and to which the Congress gave now its definitive approval, never mentioned the Visitator. No one had spoken of the creation of a specific office, connected with that of the Procurator General.

The most important moment of the Congress was that of the first elections. Fr. Edward Griffith[66] of the Oratory of London received the charge of Procurator General, and Fathers Matthaeus (England), Casanovas (Spain), Manziana and Meggiolaro (Italy), Gunkel (Germany), Bustamarte (Mexico) were elected to the positions of the Permanent Deputation.

Fr. Timpanaro was elected Postulator General. In his heart and mind this Congress had a particular resonance, because he saw coming into being the "idea of Mons. Arista, who would be exulting in heaven with St. Philip and with all the Blessed of the Oratory."[67]

A remembrance of that enthusiasm remains in a painting by Giambattista Conti that portrays, below, the Congress gathered around the Seat of Pius XII, while surrounded the Apostolic Seat are the Popes who particularly worked for the good of the Oratory: Leo XIII, Pius X, Benedict XV, Pius XI. In the background, pictured in medallions, are the first Pontiffs linked to the person and to the work of St. Philip: Gregory XIII, Paul V, Gregory XV. Above, the sky is opened to reveal the Oratory in Paradise, gathered closely around Mary, "Mother and foundress"; Fr. Philip and his first disciples, St. Francis de Sales and the Blessed of the Oratory, and some Venerable Fathers who over the centuries gave luster to the Oratory. In front are Mons. Giovanni Battista Arista with Fr. Giulio Castelli, Cardinal Alfonso Capecelatro and Fr. Clemente Benedettucci with Fr. Recanatesi and others. To the side, and somewhat apart, is Cardinal John Henry Newman, founder of the Oratory in England, put there *solo per il nome* ["only for his name"], says an anonymous typescript conserved in the Archives of the Procurator General. The typescript, which comments on the representation, is in the style of Fr. Timpanaro, who probably provided the inspiration for the painting.

"*Bello e consolante*, lovely and consoling," he wrote in preparation for the Congress,[68] "to think of the work we have done, the triumphs between 1919 and 1924, and also the sorrows grieved over, the mortifications sustained, the injustices suffered, to recall everything in order to bless the Lord, and to thank him for his graces and his favors..." Timpanaro's prose, like the painting that he commissioned from Conti, reveals the temperament of the exuberant director of the theater,[69] but also the beating of the Latin heart of a man who has fought loyally for an ideal in which he strongly believed.

Peaceable but equally on fire with love for the Institute, Fr. Griffith would write at the end of his ten years of service, and sixteen years after the new institution had begun: "it is a legal transaction... it will take years for it to become spirit and life."[70]

1958–2000

The General Congress of 1958 on October 1 took note of the decision of the Apostolic Authority with a Decree on September 24, to institute a new official of the Institute, the *Visitator Oratorii San Philippi*,[71] and entrust to the Congress his election, which would be confirmed by the Holy See. The Apostolic Visitator Fr. Enrico di Santa Teresa, O.C.D. (Romolo Compagnone, bishop of Anagni), made fundamental contributions to this decision. In 1951 he had succeeded Fr. Arcadio Maria Larraona, who was involved in higher and higher offices in the Roman Curia.

The nature and responsibilities of the new official were delineated in the decree of institution which, after twenty-five years, put an end to the Apostolic Visit. Since it was a Decree of the Apostolic See, it was not open to discussion in the Congress. It had arrived unexpectedly—even the Procurator General learned of it together with the members of the Congress—it was greeted with great favor by many, who saw in it the end of the presence of a non-Oratorian in the Visit to the Congregations of the Oratory. Some, however, emphasized that the Decree established a solution without having asked the view of the Oratorians, contrary to what had happened in the long history of Oratorian affairs, and without having taken into account the proposals that Fr. Larraona had formulated.

The Congress was received in audience at Castel Gandolfo by Pope Pius XII, who by now was in the last days of his life. Fr. Edward Griffith was elected to the new office of Visitator and Fr. John Nedley of the Oratory of Rock Hill succeeded him as Procurator General. At Fr. Griffith's premature death in 1959,[72] the Apostolic See, on the suggestion of the Permanent Deputation, named as Visitator Fr. Ugo Oggè of the Oratory of Mondovì, who exercised this office until the next Congress.

In 1969 Fr. Patrizio Dalos, Provost of the Roman Oratory, presided over the General Congress,[73] which opened with a report by Fr. J. Gulden.[74] The Congress was dedicated to a new revision of the provisions of the Constitutions, with the declared intent of bringing them up-to-date in light of the Second Vatican Council. The Permanent Deputation and the Commissions which were instituted for this purpose had prepared new texts which were discussed and approved by the Congress. These texts became part of the *Constitutiones seu Institutes Oratorii San Philippi Nerii a Congressu Generali Oratoriano anni 1969 approbatae* and the *Statuta Generalia Confoederationis Congregationum Oratorii San Philippi Neri*, promulgated *ad experimentum* by the Delegate of the Apostolic See, which was the newly established designation.[75] The *Institutum* assumed from this moment the name of *Confoederatio Oratorii San Philippi Neri*, a term[76] which had appeared in the General Statutes of 1943.

The Congress elected as "Delegate of the Apostolic See" Fr. Paul Turks of the Oratory of Aachen, and confirmed Fr. John Nedley as Procurator General.[77] The Permanent Delegation was composed of Frs. P. Dalos and G. Olcese (Italy), A. Fernandez (Spain), F. Sonntag (Germany), J. Rataj (Poland), San Desain (England), E. Wahl (U.S.A.), V. Ridriquez (Latin America).

The General Congress of 1975,[78] presided over by Fr. Edward

Wahl of the Oratory of Rock Hill, was dedicated to primarily pastoral subjects. The appointment of Fr. Paul Turks as Delegate was renewed, and Fr. Walter Oddone of the Oratory of Turin was confirmed as Procurator General. He resigned, however, for reasons of health in 1978, and Fr. Luigi Romana of the Oratory of Mondovì took his place. Deputies elected were Frs. G. Angilella and L. Romana (Italy), San Alemany (Spain), W. Muschick (Germany), M. Stebart (Poland), San Dessain (England), E. Wahl (U.S.A.), M. Herrera (Latin America).

The following two General Congresses in 1982 and 1988 gave attention once again primarily to the Constitutions, in view of their definitive approval.

In 1982 the Congress, presided over by Fr. G. Cittadini, elected as Delegate to the Apostolic See Fr. Michael Napier of the London Oratory and as Procurator General Fr. Antonio Dario of the Oratory of Verona. Deputies elected were Frs. L. Romana and A. Cistellini (Italy), J. Mas Dubia (Spain), P. Fischer (Germania), M. Stebart (Poland), J. Robinson (England), J. Wahl (U.S.A.), A. Rios (Latin America).

At the Congress of 1988, presided over by Fr. P. Turks, Fr. M. Napier and Fr. A. Dario were confirmed in their respective offices and Deputies elected were Frs. L. Romana and V. Tyka (Italy), F. De Llanos (Spain), P. Turks (Germany), M. Stebart (Poland), P. Price (England), J. Hinchey (U.S.A.), A. Martinez (Latin America).

This Congress also gave definitive approval to the new texts of the Constitutions and the General Statutes. The Decree of ratification of the Sacred Congregation of Religious came on November 21, 1989, and the new texts were published under the title: *Constitutiones et Statuta Generalia Confoederationis Oratorii San Philippi Nerii.*[79]

Strong criticism about the revision carried out between 1969 and 1988 were formulated by some Oratorians, especially Fr. Antonio Cistellini.[80] Provost of Florence and illustrious historiographer of the Oratory, he held the view that the new Constitutions, modifying "arbitrarily the ancient *Proemio* [Foreword], the foundation of Oratorian spirituality," and giving to the Congregation a definition "completely contrary to the thought of the Saint and of the uninterrupted tradition," and side-stepping the *omnimoda jurisdictio* of the diocesan Bishops decreed by the Briefs of erection, had transformed the primitive identity of the Congregation.[81]

It was the raising of this last point, above all, that brought many Oratorians to react against Cistellini's thesis. Fr. Cesare Abbate, a scholar who had collaborated with Cistellini in studies and research, was decidedly contrary to this view, and demonstrated very clearly using documented historical arguments, and logical considerations[82] that the correct interpretation of *omnimoda iurisdictio* of the diocesan Bishops was that of Larraona, extremely lucid and knowledgable, set forth in nos. 24 and 25 of the General Statutes of 1943. The jurisdiction of the local Ordinary is said to be *omnimoda* in the ancient certificate of foundation *con palese amplificazione de stylo curiae*, but in no case was it understood as subjection of the Congregation to the power of the Bishops, in anything having to do with the governance and internal life of the community. It was not ever so, not even in the case—which was normal in the past—in which the Fathers of the Oratory are incardinated in the diocese. Oratorian Houses are in fact Congregations of pontifical right, and their Constitutions are approved by the Apostolic See. Their provisions constitute inviolable norms for any Ordinaries who consent to a foundation of an Oratorian House in their local Church. The jurisdiction of the Bishops which is in fact anything but *omnimoda* being bound in this respect by precise dispositions of the pontifical Authority—is exercised only in those matters in which every institution is required to obey the Bishop. It is in these that the Oratorians are called to "give to all, to the clergy and to the people, the example of the perfect obedience owed to the Ordinary."

The General Congress of 1994, over which Fr. Giulio Cittadini of the Oratory of Brescia presided, discussed and approved the text of the Directory, entitled *L'Oratorio di San Filippo Neri. Itinerario Spirituale* [*Spiritual Path*]. It also elected as Delegate to the Apostolic See Fr. Antonio Rios Chavez of the Oratory of Mexico City and as Procurator General Fr. Edoardo Aldo Cerrato of the Oratory of Biella. The Permanent Deputation was composed of Frs. P. Zanutel e C. M.

Magnano (Italy), A. Serramona (Spain), F. Fischer (Germany), M. Stebart (Poland), I. Harrison (England), D. Corrado (U.S.A.), L. M. Cano Arena (Latin America).

The Congress was celebrated from October 2–7, and marked the official beginning of the festivities in Rome of the fourth centenary of the *dies natalis* of St. Philip Neri. It began with a solemn Mass presided over in the Vallicella by Cardinal Camillo Ruini, Vicar of His Holiness in Rome. Among those who participated the Archbishop of Florence Cardinal Silvano Piovanelli. During the celebration the Cardinal Vicar gave to the Procurator General a Pontifical Letter[83] that offered the sons of St. Philip a reflection on some fundamental aspects of the experience and the teaching of the Saint. The centenary had at Rome, in the course of 1995, notable cultural and artistic events.[84] There were also religious functions, such as the tenth World Youth Day, celebrated in Rome in April. This included a powerful evening of prayer in the Paul VI Hall, with His Holiness John Paul II, centered on the figure of St. Philip Neri and with the musical play of Marco Frisina[85] *Paradiso, paradiso.* In the great vigil of Pentecost 1995, the church of Santa Maria in Vallicella was honored with yet another visit (he had been there in 1979)[86] of His Holiness who celebrated the Mass[87] on Sunday, May 28. Numerous Fathers of the Oratory who came for the occasion from various nations participated in the Mass.

There were celebrations held also in every Congregation, and these helped to reawaken general interest in Fr. Philip's spirituality, but also in the choice as a vocation of the common life of secular priests lived in the spirit of the Oratory of St. Philip.[88]

The General Congress of 2000, after so many meetings dedicated to legislative texts, turned to pastoral matters and dealt with the topic of *The Secular Oratory in the Third Millenium.* There were present more than sixty lay persons, representing Secular Oratories from many nations and by representatives from various Oration communities in formation.

Fr. Edoardo Aldo Cerrato was elected to preside over the Congress, and Fr. A. Rios and Fr. E. Cerrato were confirmed in their respective positions. The Permanent Deputation elected as Deputies for Italy Frs. V. Tyka (Rome) and M. Di Gioia (Genova), for Spain Fr. R. Munoz Perez (Seville), for Germany Fr. H. Froehlich (Heidelberg), for Poland Fr. M. Stebart (Tarnow), for England Fr. R. Byrne (Oxford), for the U.S.A. Fr. M. Drury (Monterey), and for Latin America, by the decision of the Congress which approved two Deputies for the now vast presence of Congregations in this area, Frs. Aviles Campo (Pharr) and J. A. Arturo Gonzales (Pasto).

Two fundamental presentations and various responses in the round table[89] presented the history, the prophecy, and the relevance of the Oratory.

The consideration given by the Congress to the contemporary relevance of the Oratory brought out an interesting point: in the course of the nineteenth century, which saw quite a number of Houses extinguished, only around ten were founded; in the twentieth century which saw another fair number of Houses extinguished, very few were born before 1933; beginning with this date, which marked the start of the Apostolic Visitation and the office of Procurator General, the increase is notable. Twenty-nine Congregations were erected, and the number of Houses increased from fifty-three in 1965 to seventy-four in two thousand two. In the decade 1960–1970, eight new Congregations: Essen, Germany; Dresden Germany; San José in Costa Rica; Villa Alemana, Chile; Tlalnepantla, Mexico; Pittsburgh, U.S.A.; Mac Allen—now in Pharr, U.S.A.; Heidelberg, Germany; Frankfurt/Oder, Germany (Essen and Frankfurt/Oder no longer exist). In 1970–1980, five: Radom, Poland; San Pablo, Mexico; Orizaba, Mexico; Montreal—now in Toronto, Canada; Vienna, Austria. In 1980–1990, four Congregations: Tomaszow Mazowieski, Poland; Glattburgg-Zurich, Switzerland; Brooklyn, U.S.A.; Kamianna, Poland. In 1990–2000, twelve: Maria Lazendorf, Austria; Goslar—now in Celle, Germany; Oxford, England; Nuestra Señora de la Paz, Mexico; Nancy, France; São Paolo, Brazil; Oudtshoorn, South Africa; Maastricht, Holland; Ilsede, Germany; Metuchen, U.S.A.; Poznan, Poland; Philadelphia, U.S.A.

The Congress concluded with the Eucharistic Concelebration,

presided over in Santa Maria in Vallicella by Cardinal Eduardo Martinez Somalo, Prefect of the Congregation for Institutes of Consecrated Life and Societies of Apostolic Life.[90]

The Holy Father John Paul II received the participants of the Congress in a special audience, and expressed his pleasure "at the growth that the Oratory is experiencing in various parts of the world." Making explicit reference to the institute of the Confederation he said: "Your Congregations, faithful to the autonomy desired by your holy Founder, live in a way particularly linked to the needs of your local Churches and your local areas. But for the sake of your own Communities and your own members, you must not forget the importance of the fraternal bond with the other Congregations that make up the Confederation. It is through this bond that the characteristically autonomous Houses open themselves up to the gift of active charity. This is also the way the confederated Communities find help in growing in fidelity to the Oratorian charism."[91]

With the realistic hope that Fr. Edward Griffith expressed in 1958, that "it will take years for the legal transaction to become spirit and life," we greet the sixtieth anniversary of that Congress from which the Confederation was officially born. We are grateful for the witness of fidelity and commitment that so many Oratorians have given in these years, working with courage and at times in the midst of difficulties.

CHAPTER V

On the "Path" of the Oratory: Examples of Holiness

It is not pride to desire to surpass in holiness any Saint: because the desire to be a saint is the desire to want to love and honor God above everything; and this desire, if it were possible, ought to extend into infinity because God is worthy of infinite love.

To acquire the love of God there is no truer or shorter path than to detach oneself from the love of the things of the world, even if small and of little account, and from the love of oneself, loving in ourselves more the will and the service of God than our own satisfaction.

(*From the* MAXIMS *of St. Philip Neri*)

IN THE CHURCH, *circumdata varietate* LIKE THE QUEEN whose raiment is woven with the most varied colors,[1] divine Grace has brought into being an authentic treasure of sanctity in the path traveled by many people on the "way"[2] of the Oratory. For an account of their lives, which really merits more space than we allow here, we refer to the bibliography, to which our brief profiles are correlated. There is also Fr. Gontranno Tesserin's fine book[3] which offers a concise description of many who are merely mentioned here.

The sons of St. Philip to whom a more attentive look is dedicated are those whose names are registered in the various editions—from 1890 to 1999—of the *Index et Status Causarum*,[4] but it is indispensable to add that the examples of Oratorian sanctity goes well beyond the list of these candidates for glorification: in Oratorian houses and among the faithful stories are told of men who have given witness, even in recent times, to faith, hope, charity, and the exercise of human and Christian virtues. They have given rise sometimes to apostolic work of undisputed value, and other times have simply dedicated themselves as Priests to the ordinary exercise of their ministry, or to lay witness, if they were Brothers.

Together with Fr. Philip and the Saints and Blesseds who are officially recognized, and those of whom the Church is evaluating the fame of sanctity, these men are the greatest witnesses to the validity of that *via*, that path or "way," that the Holy Spirit has traced out in the Church, and which the journey of St. Philip Neri demonstrates.

1. AMONG THOSE WHO SAW FR. PHILIP

A memorial stone, located in the presbytery of Santa Maria in Vallicella, extremely simple in its elegance and therefore according perfectly with the style of Philip, notes that two Cardinals of the Roman Church, Cesare Baronio and Fancesco Tarugi rest alongside one another in the sepulcher of the Congregation to await the resurrection. They rest there in that fraternal communion which they lived at the school of Fr. Philip: "ne corpora disiungerentur in morte quorum animi, divinis virtutibus insignes, in vita coniunctissimi fuerant."

Among the *vetustiores* who had formed the Congregation with Fr. Philip and had created its outlines, the two Cardinals undoubtedly occupy a special place and in the "school of the Blessed Father"[5] shine "resplendent for their holy virtues."

The Venerable Cesare Baronio,[6] whom Fr. Philip in 1593 wanted as his successor, and whom he loved for his great virtue although they had very different temperaments, began when he was twenty to attend the Oratory in San Girolamo della Carità.

He was born at Sora, in the Kingdom of Naples, on October 30, 1538, and came to Rome after finishing his first studies at Veroli and briefly studying law in Naples. He had left Naples and moved to Rome troubled by the prospect of war between the Spanish and the French, but also surely attracted by this *communis patria*. He lived with a classmate in Piazza del Duca, now Piazza Farnese, close to San

Girolamo, and attended the school of the great jurist Cesare Costa at the Sapienza. But he found in Fr. Philip the true teacher of his soul.

He would recount later that the first time he met Philip he was so struck by his sweet charity and holy words that he decided never to leave him. "And as soon as he had begun to take counsel from the Saint, God put such abundance of spirit into him and such indifference for the world that if Philip had not commanded him under obedience to continue his studies of the law, he would have left the world and retired into some strict life of religion in order to serve God perfectly... But the Blessed Father never would give him permission, saying that the Lord wanted something else of him."[7] On January 5, 1558, the vigil of the Epiphany of the Lord, in the Father's little room which was full of people, the Father suddenly ordered Cesare to say something about the coming feast. He had never before spoken in public, but he did well. From that moment, Philip began to nurture intensely the spiritual life of his disciple, especially his humility, and subjecting him to hard exercises in interior mortification which Baronio did with great freedom of spirit. He continued to speak at the Oratory, preferring themes of death and the afterlife. Philip, however, wanted something else: Baronio was to speak of the history of the Church. He did this for thirty years, beginning all over again every four years. On December 16, 1560, he wrote to his family his decision to take Holy Orders, and the next day was ordained subdeacon. In a letter of May 21, 1561, he announced to his father: "last evening by the grace of God I fulfilled my duty and satisfied your wish by receiving my doctorate in civil and canon law..." He neglected however to say that he had torn up his diploma and destroyed the book of poetry that he had written. He would be ordained priest on May 27, 1564, the first of the disciples of Philip, in the church of San Giovanni dei Fiorentini. He had refused the living offered him by the church in Sora. From now on his life was totally interwoven with the rise and the development of the Congregation. In April 1577 he transferred to the Vallicella with his confreres from San Giovanni: while he was giving the last sermon, a mysterious dove entered the Oratory and awaited its conclusion.

Then it flew toward the new home of the Fathers. Beginning in 1589, by a decision of the Congregation, he began the publication of the *Annales ecclesiastici*, the fruit of the meticulous study with which Fr. Cesare prepared the sermons of the Oratory, and of various other works which had been received with unanimous favor. Among these was the *Martirologio* which the Church used until the new edition of 2001—Baronio's text still forms the basis for this. While his fame as a scholar was growing, and Philip continued to subject him to trials of humility in every way possible, there grew within him the increasing intense yearning for the path of perfection. This was especially in the form of the spirit of prayer and penance, the exercise of the virtues, especially humility and charity, apostolic labors that continued despite the incessant intellectual work and various infirmities (from some he was healed miraculously by Fr. Philip, especially that of 1572 when Cesare recovered by Philip's ardent prayer: "Give him back to me, I want him!") These were accompanied by an increase in supernatural gifts for which he was much esteemed. In 1593 Fr. Philip chose him, as we have said, after Tarugi's departure for Avignon, as his successor, and in July by Baronio's express will, the Congregation held elections, and Baronio was elected unanimously as Provost. The following year, Pope Clement VII wanted to confer upon him an ecclesiastical dignity, but Baronio, throwing himself at the feet of Fr. Philip, succeeded in freeing himself from that obligation. He was, nonetheless, made confessor to the Pope, which enabled him to influence for the better the Pontiff's decisions regarding the reconciliation of Henry IV of France.

Fr. Philip was now coming to the end of his earthly life; it would be Baronio who asked the Saint for his last blessing on his family. Baronio, who had managed to refuse three times the appointment to various bishoprics, was now constrained to accept the nomination as Prothonotary Apostolic. In 1596, when he had just been reelected Provost for the second time, he had to agree to be made Cardinal in obedience to the Pope, who assigned him the presbyteral title of Santi Nereo ed Achilleo, the ancient basilica which he had chosen just because it was dilapidated and in need of restoration. He was then named Librarian of the Holy Roman Church. He lived poorly in the Vatican, and kept in a little sack the key to his room in the Vallicella, his "beloved nest" where, every fifteen days, he continued to give sermons at the Oratory. The Jubilee Year of 1600 saw him being a humble servant of the poor pilgrims, to whom he opened his house, inspiring even the highest ecclesiastical dignitaries to imitate his example. At the death of Pope Clement, he was very close to being elected Pope, but he managed to divert the twenty-eight votes he received onto his friend, and friend of Philip's, Cardinal Alessandro de Medici, who took the name Leo XI. He was, however, Pope for only a few days, as Philip had predicted. The next Conclave elected Cardinal Camillo Borghese, who took the name Paul V. Again Cesare Baronio's name had much support, and this time, too, he managed to avoid it. Sorrowful that he had to die as cardinal and with the ardent desire to return to being a simple priest, in 1606 Baronio returned to the Vallicella where he breathed his last on June 7 of the following year, with his confreres present. Thirty Cardinals participated in the ceremonies in the Church of the Congregation and an immense crowd of the faithful followed: they tore off his robes and his hair, as "is often done at the death of a great servant of God." He rests in the sepulcher of the Fathers, under the presbytery of Santa Maria in Vallicella, in the most complete humility, with no other monument save that stone on the right wall, that remembers him and his confrere, who was also Cardinal.

The Venerable Francesco Maria Tarugi,[8] the most "brilliant" of the Oratorians of the first generation—*dux verbi*, the prince of the word, as Baronio called him—was born in Montepulciano on August 25, 1525, of a noble family, related to Pontiffs. He had received in court circles a good literary and juridical formation, and demonstrated uncommon gifts in poetry and the art of oratory. Having arrived in Rome in 1555, almost by chance he met Philip Neri, and was conquered by him. He entrusted himself to Fr. Philip's spiritual care like an obedient child, and from 1565 on he attended the Oratory assiduously, deciding in 1571 to choose the priesthood. He left the court of Cardinal Farnese in order to enter the Community of priests to whom Fr. Philip had entrusted the pastoral care of the Church of San Giovanni dei Fiorentini. When he was advanced in years, he loved to say: "For the space of more than fifty years I have been a novice of blessed Philip."

He had the gift of uniting the active life to the contemplative, works of piety to the organization of the new Congregation. The first rule, which lays out the essential norms for community life, is attributed to him. He had a profound love for the Congregation, and the Congregation owes its canonical recognition in large part to Tarugi's entrance into the Curia. He never hid his aspiration to see the Congregation propagated in many places as one of the most valid instruments for the reform of the Church. He did not always share the mind of Fr. Philip, but he was always completely obedient, and he merited to be chosen, as we have seen, as his successor. His life, too, like Baronio's, is so interwoven with the history of the Congregation that it is not possible to peruse one without reference to the other.

Together with other eminent men, St. Pius V wanted him to be an assistant to his nephew, Alessandrino Cardinal Bonelli, giving him difficult assignments and important missions. In 1586 he moved to Naples, where the Oratory had begun to be organized, thanks to the support of Fr. Talpa and other Fathers of the Roman Congregation. Tarugi's incessant apostolic work won him the esteem of the clergy and of the people, who had wanted Archbishop Tarugi to be in their city; instead, in 1592 he was nominated to the seat of Avignon, where, as a very zealous shepherd and wise reformer in the spirit of the Tridentine Council, he introduced community life into his palace, and gave impetus to the spiritual life of the diocese.

Tarugi's work day was extremely dense, from dawn to dusk, a prodigious interweaving of prayer and pastoral and charitable work. His ideal of the "apostolic man" led him to spread the Tridentine reform even in Spain, in France, in Flanders, and in Germany.

Pope Clement VIII made him Cardinal on June 4, 1596, together with Baronio, and the following year transferred him to the

Archbishopric of Siena, and there, too, he worked intensely for some years.

Now old, and having recovered from a serious illness, he obtained from Paul V permission to end his days in the much-loved Vallicella, where on June 11, 1608, kissing devotedly Fr. Philip's rosary, piously he died.

Blessed Giovanni Giovenale Ancina,[9] from Piedmont, was a member of the Oratory in Rome and later in that of Naples. Born in Fossano in 1545, he came to Rome in 1574, after having completed excellent studies in Montpelier, in Padua, in Mondovi, and in Turin, where he graduated in medicine and philosophy. His great literary and musical gifts, which he cultivated all his life, were interwoven in Fr. Giovenale with a profound knowledge of theology, which he had studied in Rome through the lectures of St. Robert Bellarmine. In fact, at the examination in Rome for the episcopate, Clement VIII who was present declared that he had never heard a candidate so well prepared. In October 1578 he was accepted into the Congregation and gave himself to the apostolate with a delicate sensibility and profound example of piety. In 1586 he went to the house in Naples and undertook multiple activities, of preaching and study, and he also dedicated himself to music, poetry, and musical composition. There still remains a collection of spiritual songs and laude for three, four, five, eight, and even twelve voices entitled *Tempio armonico della B. V. Maria.* In Naples he also promoted cultural and formative events in various settings, but above all for the Neapolitan aristocracy, for which he introduced the Oratory of the Princes.

Fr. Giovenale was recalled to Rome in 1596, to his great consternation—of which his flight is witness; Pope Clement VIII made him bishop in the Ducal State of Savoy, entrusting to him the bishopric of Saluzzo, where the heretical movement was creating considerable problems. Fr. Giovenale finally accepted. He was ordained bishop at the Vallicella by Cardinal Tarugi, and entered his diocese in March 1603. His episcopate was very brief, but it was characterized by innumerable works of spiritual renewal and of charity: he began the seminary, convoked the diocesan synod for the application of the decrees of the Tridentine Council, undertook the pastoral Visitation.[10] He increased piety, participation in the Sacraments, and the cult of the Eucharist; he was indefatigable in encouraging catechesis, and reformed the life of the people and the clergy with dedication and sacrifice. He had the joy of receiving a visit from St. Francis de Sales,[11] with whom he had had correspondence, in the spirit of fraternal friendship. He greeted him, after a moving talk by the Bishop of Geneva in the Church of Carmagnola, with the words: "Vere Tu es Sal," to which de Sales, alluding to Ancina's diocese, replied: "Immo Tu es Sal et Lux, ego vere neque sal neque lux."

A suspected poisoning, possibly the work of some friars who led a dissolute life, led to his death on August 30, 1604. Leo XIII inscribed him in the list of the Blessed on February 9, 1889; his body rests in the cathedral of Saluzzo.

2. THE "GEM OF SAVOY" AND ORATORIAN GLORIES IN PIEDMONT

The Piedmontese Ancina had the experience of knowing Fr. Philip and of working in the communities at Rome and Naples which he founded. But he also transmitted the fruits of this experience to his native region, through his brief but intense episcopate. His ministry is the beginning of Oratorian spirituality in Piedmont. Thirteen Oratorian Congregations[12] arose between 1613 and the middle of the 1700s and they provided illustrious examples of holiness and apostolic dedication. They also spread throughout the Oratorian world the fame of this fertile land. The name of Blessed Sebastiano Valfrè—who was called "the fount of holy priests in eighteenth-century Turin"—alone is enough to justify the praises of the Piedmont Oratory. But following Valfrè we encounter other noble figures, for example, Fr. Felice Carpignano (1810–1888),[13] of the Turin Oratory, who was confessor of Archbishop Gastaldi and spiritual director of St. Giuseppe Benedetto Cottolengo and of numerous others who demonstrated great

Christian charity and holiness, some of whom have been raised to the dignity of the altar. Others still await their glorification. There was also Fr. Agnelli, of the Oratory of Savigliano, who did not want his name printed in that *I Pregi dell'Oratorio* on which generations of Oratorians have been formed.

St. Francis de Sales lived and worked in the Duchy of Savoy. He was founder and first Provost of the Oratory of Thonon, *Sabaudiae gemma*,[14] as Paul VI called him.

Born at Thorens on August 21, 1567, he died at Lyons, consumed by apostolic labors, on December 28, 1622, the year of the canonization of St. Philip Neri. De Sales came to know Fr. Philip through Gallonio's *Vita*, which had been sent to him by his friend Giovanni Giovenale Ancina. Inscribed among the Blessed in 1661, he was canonized in 1665, and proclaimed Doctor of the Church in 1887 by Leo XIII.

Francis de Sales received a classical and philosophical formation from the Jesuits, receiving at the same time a solid spiritual base. His father, who dreamed of a brilliant career in the law for him, sent him to the University of Padua, where Francis graduated, but also matured in his priestly vocation. Ordained on December 18, 1593, he was sent to the region of Chablais, which was dominated by Calvinism. He dedicated himself above all to preaching, choosing not the polemical method of opposing other ideas, but the method of dialogue. In order to reach many whom his preaching could not reach, he came up with the idea of having large notices put up in public places, which were composed in a very effective, easy to read style. This idea produced great results, even leading to the collapse of the Calvinist "stronghold," and in 1923 earned for St. Francis the name of patron of Catholic journalists.

At Thonon, he founded the local Congregation of the Oratory, erected by Pope Clement VIII with the Bull *Redemptoris et Salvatoris nostri* in 1598, "iuxta ritum et Institutes Congregationis Oratorii de Urbe." His contact with the world of the Oratory was not so much the person of Fr. Philip as that of some of his first disciples, whom he met in Rome in 1598–1599: Fr. Baronio, Fr. Giovanni Giovenale and Fr. Matteo Ancina, Fr. Antonio Gallonio.

Francis undertook a vast work of spiritual direction, in the deep conviction that the life of holiness is a gift of the Holy Spirit for all the faithful, both religious and lay. This made of him one of the greatest of spiritual directors.

He committed his mind and heart, time and stamina to this work, so that those with whom he dialogued experienced his sweetness, his serene optimism, and a real desire for personal encounter, which resonated strongly with the spirit and method of St. Philip Neri.[15] The innate spiritual agreement between the two is evident even in the titles of the principal works of de Sales—*Introduction to the Devout Life*, *Treatise on the Love of God*, and also in the *Letters* and the *Discourses*.

He was made Bishop of Geneva in 1602, at the same time that Ancina was named, and he continued to work with the same pastoral dedication. One of the fruits of his spiritual direction and undertaking of works of charity is the foundation, in collaboration with St. Jane de Chantal of the Order of the Visitation, which diffused the spirituality of the Sacred Heart of Jesus into all the Church. This took place particularly through Christ's Revelations to another Visitation sister, St. Margaret Mary Alacoque. The resulting spiritual movement had firm adherents in many Oratories, especially in Northern Italy.

Then there was Blessed Sebastiano Valfrè[16] who celebrated the feast of the Sacred Heart of Jesus for the first time in Italy, perhaps in the world, in Turin in 1694. It would be officially instituted only a hundred years later.[17]

He was born at Verduno, in the diocese of Alba on March 9, 1629, of a humble family. Duke Vittorio Amadeo II in 1689 wanted him to be Archbishop of Turin because of the extraordinary qualities that he had demonstrated in more than thirty years of fruitful ministry, but the modest circumstances of his family, whom he brought purposely to the Capital, allowed him to escape this high honor.

He had completed his studies at Alba, at Bra, and at Turin, living poorly and working as a scribe in order to do so, he entered the Congregation of the Oratory. This had been founded two years previously by Fr. Pier Antonio Defera, who was asked to do so by the Nuncio in Piedmont, Alessandro Crescenzi. Fr. Crescenzi was extremely devoted to St. Philip and wished to promote devotion to him and to his work. Fr. Defera, with Ottavio Cambiani, a priest of modest natural gifts but who had an intense spiritual life, had begun the Oratory in a style of evangelical simplicity. A chronicle in manuscript[18] describes their life as follows: "Their capital was the truth and their faith in God: poor in material goods but rich in devotion, they assisted at Mass in the little church [set up in a rented shop in the Blancardi house, near the church of St. Francis of Assisi] with generous hearts and great fervor of spirit."

The Community and the exercises of the Oratory found themselves in great difficulty after only a year and a half of life when, on September 11, 1650, Fr. Defera died at thirty-four years of age. He had initiated an extraordinary ministry of preaching, not only in church, but also "speaking here and there throughout the city," confessions, visits to the hospitals and the prisons, all of which brought the spirit of the Apostle of Roma to life among the people of Turin. The project would have been shipwrecked if the young subdeacon Sebastiano Valfrè, eight months after the founder's death, had not presented himself to Fr. Cambiani asking to be admitted. That Congregation was composed of only one member, had meager resources and was on the verge of closing. Sebastiano himself was poor, and was unafraid of the poverty of the institution. In fact, he saw in this the environment best adapted to an unreserved giving of himself. He loved that community with his whole being, and he dedicated himself to the most humble work. At the same time, following in Fr. Defera's footsteps, he undertook pastoral work with incredible dedication. He embraced perfectly the spirit of St. Philip and he lived it with passion for the rest of his life, until he was eighty, when he died on January 30, 1710, in his little room, filled with a scholar's papers (he had received his doctorate in 1656 in theology from the University of Turin). His room was full also of bags of clothes and foodstuffs for the poor, whom Fr. Valfrè loved and served with the devotion of the faithful servant. He was assisted in his agony as nurse by His Royal Highness the Duke of Savoy, who himself did the most humble tasks. Even this last illness gave fervent testimony to Fr. Valfrè's fidelity to his commitments: on January 24 he had preached to the nuns of Santa Croce and he took himself off immediately afterwards to the prisons to give comfort to a man condemned to die, he dashed home, to arrive in time to kneel in the church for Eucharistic Benediction, and right afterwards, in the cold of the Oratory for the community exercises. The next morning, although he was feverish, he celebrated Mass and heard many confessions, but then he had to go to bed. He spent his last days receiving continuous visits of penitents and friends, and breathed his last towards eight o'clock on January 30. His body, exposed in the church, brought all of Turin, who desired to pay their respects to that priest who for sixty years had gone through the streets and the squares teaching and alleviating every sort of poverty. He did this with the same devotion with which at Court he exercised his office of Confessor to the Royal Family. In the prisons, in the hospitals, and at the fortress and on the bastions, during the war, he infused courage and gave witness to Christian charity.

A man of intense prayer nourished by contemplation, Fr. Valfré's zealous preaching was the fruit of great intellectual preparation and fervent spiritual experience. As a young deacon, he had begun to preach the Gospel in the chapel of the Oratory in Casa Blancardi, and had continued as Prefect of the Oratory and Provost of the Congregation. He was called incessantly to convents and monasteries, to parish churches and various charitable institutes and he never refused. But the desire to preach the Word of God carried him beyond these usual places. As his first biographers recall, he had learned at the school of St. Philip the method of personal dialogue and of the Word announced very simply, in the encounter with every sort of person, on the streets and in the squares. For forty years in Piazza Carlina he gave catechism to the wine merchants and their clients, by starting to talk about something interesting to a little group, and responding to the questions of those who became involved in the discussion. The "Apostle of Catechism" exercised his mission on the boys, too: among his writings[19] is a catechetical text[20] that would serve the Church for a long time.

Such devotion to the service of proclaiming the Word might lead us to think that our Blessed had little time left for other activities. But instead he was equally an Apostle of Charity. He knew the problems and the needs above all of the poor from direct contact with them; he participated actively in all the charitable works that were flourishing in Turin. But above all, it was his personal care for the many situations of immediate need that touched the heart of the City: how often he was seen—only by the soldiers on duty making their rounds—in the streets at night carrying ragged people on his shoulders, bringing them to some place of shelter, or climbing furtively the steps of wretched houses to leave packages of foodstuffs at the doorstep. There was no category of needy folk in Turin that had not received concrete help from him.

The esteem that he enjoyed at Court, where the Duke had named him Confessor entrusting to him in particular the spiritual formation of his children,[21] gave Valfrè the opportunity to influence the social and political ideas of his charges. This has been amply studied by Giovanna Olgiati, under the direction of Paolo Brezzi of the University of Rome.[22] He was among the counselors that the Duke most listened to, and he reminded the Duke in a note that justice must precede charity. He exercised a profound influence on the society of Turin, at a time wracked by wars, by conflicts of jurisdiction, and by difficult relationships with the minority groups of Waldensians and Jews.

In the complex affairs of institutional conflict between the Savoy Court and the Apostolic See, Fr. Valfrè became aware of the absolute imperative that the diplomatic representatives of Rome be formed culturally but also in the spirit. It was he who suggested the foundation of a School of formation to prepare the diplomatic personnel of the Church. It is now the Pontifical Ecclesiastical Academy, which has not forgotten the work of him who inspired its foundation. On the occasion of his third centenary, the Academy solemnized this and remembered him with a great celebration on April 26, 2001, at the Vatican in the Basilica of St. Peter.[23]

On July 15, 1834, Gregory XVI inscribed Fr. Valfrè among the Blessed. Next to the altar where Blessed Valfrè's mortal remains rest, has been placed for long years the cathedra of catechetical teaching, from which the constant invitation of Fr. Valfrè seems still to resound: "Catechism, catechism!"

Another Apostle of Catechism in Piedmont, the Venerable Giovanni Battista Trona[24], from Mondovì, was of the same temperament as Fr. Valfrè, although they never met.

He was born in Frabosa Soprano on October 18, 1682, of an exemplary family, well-respected and very pious, but he also spent his childhood amid poverty and great privation, and saddened also by the death of his father and by serious physical weakness. The weakness was overcome by the intercession of St. Vincenzo Ferreri, but at thirteen years of age he was present at the murder of his mother. He reacted to this tragedy with great faith and by offering Christian forgiveness to the assassin, of whom he was later a benefactor.

He finished his studies privately and entered the seminary of Mondovì in 1695. Fired by a desire to spread the Gospel, he proposed to become a missionary, but was dissuaded by the Bishop who invited him to enter the local Oratorian Congregation, founded the preceding year.

Fr. Trono was prodigious in the instruction of the people and the reform of the clergy. He helped reconcile differences and alleviate the sufferings of the poor, especially during the wars fought in that period. He was a tireless preacher, going into the most remote areas of the diocese. He distinguished himself particularly in his catechetical Apostolate, and his teaching of all kinds of people, and all ages. It is commonly held that he was responsible for the drafting the valuable text known as the *Catechismo di Mons. Casati*, from the name of the bishop of Mondovì who promulgated it. The Catechism of St. Pius

X drew upon that of Fr. Trona. Among his works is also a *Trattato sulle virtù teologali* [*Treatise on the Theological Virtues*] written and explained for the people. Like St. Philip Neri, he loved the young people and dedicated himself to them. This was especially the case when in 1729 he became, for the rest of his life, the spiritual director of the Royal Schools of Mondovì.

He was a counselor to Carl Emmanuel III and to the Minister of State Marchese Ormea, whose friendship was helpful for the good of souls and for reconciling difficult social and political relationships. Even Pope Benedict XIV had great esteem for him honoring him with precious handwritten letters, as did numerous Bishops of Piedmont who found his counsels to be extremely sound.

The life of this apostle of catechism, which he spent ceaselessly in evangelizing, almost of necessity had to end on one of the three *legni* (the predella of the altar, the confessional, and the seat of discussion in the community), which tradition handed down from St. Philip held as the desirable places to end this life and go to God. Fr. Trona ended his earthly life giving catechism to boys on December 13, 1750, in the Oratorian house. He had, in fact, promoted the construction of the house, and the church, using the designs of Gallo, his personal friend. On May 15, 1927, his heroic virtues were recognized, and he was greeted with the title of Venerable.

The Venerable Pier Francesco Scarampi[25] belonged to the Roman Oratory, but he, too, was born in Piedmont, in 1596, of a noble family of Monferrato. He died in 1656 ministering to victims of the plague during the epidemic that raged all that year, contracting the illness while he was Provost of the Rome Oratory. The simple stone slab of his tomb in the floor of the church of Santi Nereo and Achilleo speaks to all who enter there of the humility and the greatness of a martyr of charity. He also undertook the work of "Apostolic Minister" of Pope Urban VIII in Ireland, which was suffering under the conflicts between the English Protestants and the faithful of Rome. He received high praise for this work, to which a document of 1646 penned by Senator Wadding testifies. Incessant work, prolonged Eucharistic

Adoration, which he celebrated also in the prayer of the Forty Hours, profuse charity and fervent preaching prepared Fr. Pier Francesco for the heroism of the gift which would consume him in Rome as he cared for those struck down by the plague.

3. ORATORIAN HOLINESS IN OTHER REGIONS OF ITALY

Piedmont shines brightly with extraordinary figures which the Congregations of the Oratory remember as a significant patrimony of all the Congregations in the countries to which they spread. It was, however, The Papal States at that time extended through much of central Italy, and the first diffusion of Houses of the Oratory occurred here. Some of the Houses arose while Philip was still living.

One of the oldest was constituted in Fermo, in the region of the Marches[26] in 1586. In that House lived Blessed Antonio Grassi,[27] the third of Philip's sons to be so named. He was raised to the dignity of the altar by Pope Leo XIII in the Jubilee Year 1900. Born in Fermo on November 13, 1592, even as a child he led a simple and austere life, characterized by sincere devotion. He received his education from the Fathers of the Oratory of his city.

He entered the Congregation on October 11, 1609, and was ordained priest on December 17, 1617. Elected Provost in 1635, he was reelected continuously until his death in 1671. He exercised the ministries of catechetical and spiritual instruction, of charity to the sick and those in prison, and in the care of children and young people. Even in Rome, where he went in 1625 as a pilgrim for the Jubilee Year, he gave splendid example of the faith and piety that would mark his whole life, nourished by prayer and mystical transports.

The most ordinary daily routines plus moments of extraordinary spiritual experiences were interwoven throughout the days of his life. The people were fascinated by that mysterious and prophetic simplicity, and were drawn to seek his counsel, especially in the confessional, where he would say, "we must have compassion, we must help, console."

He was "an angel of peace," resolving numerous rivalries, and he was called "father of the poor" for the heroic charity with which he gave away everything, even his own clothes.

Toward the Virgin he had an extremely tender devotion, manifested by his many pilgrimages on foot to the Holy House of Loreto. In this sanctuary on September 4, 1621, he remained miraculously unhurt by a bolt of lightning which, however, burnt his clothes.

The Holy Fathers Clement X and Innocent XI held him in great esteem, and well-known personages saw in him an authentic model for their lives. Among them was the Oratorian Cardinal Colloredo who organized his Cause for beatification.

Now close to the end of his life he would repeat over and over, "Oh, what a beautiful thing to die as sons of St. Philip!" Assisted spiritually by his confreres and by the Archbishop of Fermo, who never moved from his bedside during his long agony, he slept in the Lord on December 13, 1671. The fame of holiness which he enjoyed in his lifetime, spread immediately in Italy and elsewhere, particularly in Germany, where many miracles came about through his intercession. His body is venerated in Fermo, under the main altar of the Carmine church.

Our next three come, like Grassi, from the same soil of the Marches. The Servant of God Dionisio Pieragostini[28] (1584–1659) was a lay brother of the Oratory of Camerino, who, while spending his entire life carrying out the most humble tasks assigned him by the Community, was ordered by the Bishop to found the monastery of the Convertite. He started a shelter in Palazzo Belli, a sign of his intense charity toward the sick. Pope Clement X esteemed him to the point that he desired to canonize him himself.

Of an entirely different intellectual stature, but equal in sanctity of life was the Venerable Fabrizio dell'Aste[29] (1606–1655), who founded the Oratory of Forli, after having had an excellent preparation in law, and completed studies in the prestigious Universities of Bologna and Pisa. He had heard the call to follow the path of perfection and had discovered the way of life of the Oratory while he was in Rome, where he was intent on making a splendid career in the Roman Curia. His

Oratory shone for its spiritual life and life of charity, but also for the pedagogical and intellectual stamp which Fr. dell'Aste gave to it.

The ministry of spiritual direction found an exceptional exponent in the Servant of God Andrea Anibaldi[30] (1764–1845), of the Oratory of Treia. He was the director of several souls who were setting out on extraordinary paths of sanctity; in the last twenty years of his long life he was totally blind, but his inner light grew, and he became a true spiritual master of the clergy.

Among the illustrious examples of sanctity that the Oratory of Bologna gave to the Church was the Servant of God Carlo Maria Gabrielli[31] (1667–1745), of whom Pope Benedict XIV said: "In all the time that we were archbishop of Bologna we never had any other director or confessor save Father Gabrielli, a man honest and sincere, learned and prudent." Of lively intelligence and the highest cultural formation, such that he was considered to be one of the most learned men of his century in Bologna, he left a great number of written works, both published and unpublished, and he even helped to found the Accademia delle Scienze. He showed himself to be a real son of St. Philip in his devotion to preaching and to the ministry of reconciliation, where he welcomed every sort of person, touching the hearts of all with the sweetness of his ways and the holiness he exhibited.

Contemporary with Gabrielli, another member of the Oratory of Bologna, the Servant of God Ercole Maria Isolani[32] (1686–1756) gave illustrious example with his piety and his culture, which were admirably interwoven in his desire to serve God and to be of use to his neighbor. His devotion to the Saints rendered him a meticulous scholar, who found favor even with the Bollandists. Because of his intense experience of prayer, he was able to compose a monumental work entitled simply *L'Orazione*, which is preserved in manuscript in sixty-six folio volumes.

The nineteenth century saw the Oratorian presence almost extinguished in the territories of the ancient Pontifical States, because of suppressions but also because the new government of Italy confiscated properties. Nevertheless, Umbria gave us an example of an ardent preacher of the Gospel, in the person of the Servant of God Luigi Piccardini[33] (1812–1893), of the Oratory of Città del Castello. Of lively mind and a fascinating example of the practice of Christian virtues, he was chosen by illustrious figures as a counselor. He knew how to unite recollection and the life of prayer with study—he left a variety of writings—with apostolic work in different fields. He carried his preaching into the Marches, Lazio, and elsewhere in Italy but also outside of Italy where he was Apostolic Missionary. He erected the sanctuary of Canoscio to the Virgin Immaculate, where his remains rest, under the statue of Mary.

In the Duchy of Mantua there lived and died in fame of sanctity the Servant of God Paolo Baraldi[34] (1669–1740). Educated at the Oratory, he joined in 1694; for thirty-five years he was Provost. He lived out the greater part of his priestly ministry in the confessional, where he spent his days in prayer and in service to the souls who came seeking the mercy of God. The gentle charity which he showed them and the extraordinary gifts that he had received from the Lord—among those the gift of healing physical and spiritual maladies by invoking St. Philip—made people venerate him in his lifetime.

Florence gave to the Church the Venerable Pietro Bini[35] (1593–1635), founder of the local Oratory. He studied law in Pisa, and afterwards, in 1624, went to Rome where he had responsibilities at Court. In Rome he met the Oratorians; his call to the priesthood matured, and he placed himself under the spiritual care of Fr. Scipione de Rossi, of the Vallicella. Returning to Florence, he founded the Congregation with Francesco Cerretani in 1632, at the request of the Archbishop. He was a model of incessant prayer and merciful charity in welcoming the penitents who approached his confessional. Another illustrious Oratorian from Florence, Vittorio dell'Ancisa[36] (1537–1598), had come into Fr. Philip's circle, was a guest at San Girolamo della Carità, and shared his priestly ministry for a decade. One of Fr. Philip's last letters was written to him, sent from Rome on April 7, 1595.[37] He founded the Congregation of the Suore Stabilite nella Carità,[38] whose name is an echo of the *madre dello spirito* in Rome.

Another women's community in Florence inspired by the spirituality of St. Philip, the Suore di San Filippo, was co-founded by the Servant of God Ferdinando Fattoracci[39] (1770–1840), of the Florentine Oratory. He was an example of a humble life, given to silence, prayer and mortification, and fidelity to daily duty. The proof of his high spirituality is to be found in the Rules that he drafted for the new religious family, in which the most genuine Oratorian spirit shines through. We would like to express, in these pages, the most fraternal appreciation to the Suore Filippine di Firenze for the love with which they have cared for the room so loved by Fr. Philip and the first Oratory in San Girolamo della Carità. They have had the custody for the last forty years of this room, the true cradle of the whole Oratorian experience. Let us remember here, even if he belongs to the Oratory of Genoa, the founder of an analogous Institute, the Figlie di N. S. della Misericordia, Fr. Antonio M. Salata[40] (1661–1729).

Oratorian life was fervent in the Two Sicilies, also, and rich in illustrious examples of holiness. Two Oratorian Houses were the centers of diffusion and models of apostolic devotion, the House of Naples, begun in 1586 by the work of Talpa and Tarugi, and that of Palermo, founded with Fr. Philip's blessing, in 1593 by Fr. Pietro Pozzo. Fr. Pozzo entered the Oratory in Rome, and was sent for some time to the House in Naples, before returning to his native Sicily.

Among those who gave luster to the House of Naples was the Venerable P. Giovanni Tommaso Eustachio[41] (1575–1641), who entered the community in 1592. He was elected bishop of Larino in 1611 and consecrated in Rome by St. Robert Bellarmine. He was a man of great piety and great ability, and he sustained his diocese while reforming both the clergy and the ways of the people. In 1616 for reasons of health he renounced administrative work and obtained permission to re-enter his Congregation. There in all humility and dedication, he returned to the typical Oratorian apostolate of preaching and confessions. On his death, his cause for canonization was opened immediately, and publicized, while his reputation for holiness grew, and graces were attributed to his intercession.

Another member of the Congregation in Naples known for great humility was the Servant of God Giuseppe Pennasilico[42] (1805–1883). Cardinal Alfonso Capecelatro recognizes him as his master of the authentically Oratorian spiritual life and to whom an immense number of persons came for help. Prayer and constant union with God were his supports in his ardent desire for union with the passion of Christ for the redemption of the world. The Neapolitan Oratory was known in the nineteenth century as the "seminary of Bishops and of saints," and Blessed Bartolo Longo attributes this to the teaching of Father Pennasilico.

If we go back earlier in time, but still in the Kingdom of Naples, we find in the life of the Servant of God Marzio Piccirillo[43] (1598–1656), founder of the Oratory of Guardia Sanframondi, whose life exhibited numerous examples of holiness. Desiring to answer the call to the priesthood but too poor to undertake the necessary studies, he felt the impulse in 1623 to betake himself to Rome. He made contact with Father Giuliano Giustiniani who received him into the Vallicella and employed him in work having to do with the writings of Baronio. He was attracted to the spirituality of St. Philip. After his ordination he returned to Guardia, bearing with him as a precious relic a shirt of Fr. Philip's, a gift from the Community in Rome. During the epidemic of 1656, he cared for those struck down by the plague and contracted the sickness himself, thus closing a life dense with apostolic labors fed by prayer, Eucharistic adoration, and the heroic exercise of virtue.

The Oratory of Aquila also had the experience of a strong witness of evangelical perfection in two Fathers who lived in the Community at the same time, as master and disciple. They were the Servant of God Giovanni Battista Magnanti[44] (1603–1669) and the Servant of God Giovanni Andrea degli Afflitti[45] (1623–1698) who entered the Community respectively in 1631 and 1647. The first, though not serious in his youth, became a convincing preacher of penance and conversion, giving in his own person evidence of practicing what he taught. The second was a nobleman from Naples who came to Aquila to study. Fr. Magnanti received him into an exemplary Community, and gave him a profound spiritual formation which made him desire to become a priest. The epigraph composed on the occasion of the exhumation of his remains in 1727 summarizes the figure of this Servant of God: "Illustrious for his intelligence and doctrine, but more so for his innocence of life, his zeal for souls, his love for penance, his gift of prophecy, his discernment of spirits, his penetration of the secrets of the heart and other charismatic gifts."

In Sicily, the Servant of God Pietro Palazzo[46] (1576–1648) founded the Oratory of Comiso in 1622. He was a man of modest intellectual ability, which was compensated for by a crystalline faith and priestly zeal that led him to dedicate himself ceaselessly to the good of his people. Sufferings and even calumnies never stopped him. He conducted his ministry through the Confessional and catechesis. In the community he led the exercise of common reading of spiritual books that recalled the Oratorian experience of the early days. There was also the Servant of God Mariano Patanè[47] (1713–1804), who founded in 1756 the Oratory of Arcireale and was an ardent apostle to the young people. He was already a priest in 1737 and he dedicated himself to various ministries in the countryside of Arcireale. During Lent of 1753, in response to the invitation of a preacher, he gave his time and his gifts to a special care for children, beginning schools and formative activities. Inclined, from his childhood, to prayer and tender piety, he grew in the spiritual life to the point that he received charismatic gifts from the Lord, which attracted the veneration of both simple folk, and also of illustrious figures, including the King of Spain Charles III and his son Ferdinando IV.

The Oratory of Palermo had very many Fathers known for their sanctity of life and memorable apostolic works. Among them are particularly the Servant of God Marco Antonio Ribaudengo[48] (1703–1764), the Venerable Ignazio Capizzi[49] (1708–1783), and the Servant of God Giorgio Guzzetta[50] (1682–1756).

Fr. Ribaudengo, born at Trapani, although he and his family lived in Palermo from his childhood on, graduated in philosophy and theology. He entered the Congregation of the Oratory in 1727 in order to dedicate himself to prayer and study. A serious form of spiritual depression, fed by excessive scrupulosity, kept him for seven years incapable of entering into any form of ministry. When he came out of it, thanks to the patient guidance of Father Guzzetta, his priestly zeal was extraordinary and it led him to choose to minister in the prisons and the hospitals, in contact with the most wretched of people. Because of his example of fidelity to the Constitutions and to the spirit of the Oratory he was chosen for long years as the Master of novices.

Father Ignazio Capizzi, whose heroic virtues were recognized in 1858 and whom Blessed Pius IX called "the St. Philip Neri of Sicily," is one of the protagonists of the religious history of Palermo in the eighteenth century.

Born in Bronte, on the slopes of Mt. Etna, he attended the local Oratory of St. Philip attached to the church of Santa Maria della Catena. He became a priest in 1736 and spent the better part of his priestly life in Palermo. He dedicated himself to missions to the people, to the education of children, and to the ministry of reconciliation, while experiencing difficulties and lack of understanding. He lived from 1769 on at the Oratory of Olivella where, in addition to his well-known zeal, his great gifts as writer and theologian became evident. He became so much a part of the mind and heart of the people that the *cantastorie* [ballad-singers] sang of his "exploits" for a long time.

Giorgio Guzzetta was born in Piana dei Greci (today Piana degli Albanesi, seat of the Catholic eparchy of the Greek rite) April 23, 1682, into a poor family, and entered the seminary of the diocese of Monreale. This was the diocese ecclesiastically responsible for the colonies of Albanians who had fled to Sicily for political reasons in the course of the fifteenth and sixteenth centuries.

He showed an extremely lively intelligence, and after completing literary studies at the school of the Jesuits in Trapani, he took his doctorate in the flourishing seminary, arousing the admiration of Cardinal Archbishop Del Giudice, who wanted him in his court as translator of classical Greek. The prospect of a brilliant career, and the possibility of accompanying the Cardinal to Spain did not deter this priest from his call to a priestly life of simplicity and of great devotion to his apostolate. He entered the Oratory of Palermo, renouncing the Greek rite of ordination and thereby the possibility of dedicating himself with love to the cultural and religious traditions of his Albanian people. At twenty-four he was received, in 1706, and a year later ordained to the priesthood. His dowry was turned over to the Fathers of the Oratory. His choice, generous and convinced as it was, did not shield him from torments in the first years: fantasies of failure disquieted him, the impression of having made a mistake and of not being of use to anyone. But a second "conversion" awaited this young priest: he was able to give himself up completely, even his projects of doing good, and entrust himself entirely to God. Having left his wearying desert behind, horizons of preaching and the ministry of the confessional opened wide before him. His spiritual maturity and constant union with God in prayer gave abundant fruits, rendered more fruitful by the divine grace that had granted to Father Giorgio even the gift of clairvoyance in directing consciences and a very tender and strong fatherhood toward his people.

In 1716 he was finally able to think of helping his own people apostolically. The Oratory of Piana was born from his initiative, with celibate priests who dedicated themselves, living with admirable poverty as did the people, to the instruction and education to young people. In 1734 he was able to fulfill a desire he had held in his heart from his adolescence, that of founding a Greek-Albanian seminary in which future priests, who up until then had had to attend the Latin-rite seminaries in Sicily, could be instructed in the traditions and the splendor of the Byzantine cult. The Seminary was founded in Palermo: the Jesuits taught, and the Oratorians provided the spiritual formation. The fruits were many and the institution continued through the centuries. Although this community of oriental rite seemed to be a labored and heavy relic of the past, Fr. Guzzetta's intent was to entrust the Seminary with a highly relevant mission: that of working for the unity of Christians in the Near East, through an ecclesiastical organization. Fr. Guzzetta never saw the eparchy of

Piana deglli Albanesi, which was erected only in 1937, but fifty years after his death the Holy See instituted permanently a Bishop ordinary for the Greek rite in Sicily.

A man of culture and significant pedagogical experience, Fr. Guzzetta understood the importance of formation. For this reason, he supported to the institution of an Oriental branch of the Jesuits which would be able to dedicate themselves to the founding of Collegi [private schools] in the Near East and among the oriental communities then present in the Greek territories of the Venetian Republic. He knew that the same was true of those Christian communities of the East that had never separated from Rome but because they lacked the necessary means of communication, they depended upon the separated Churches of the Turkish Empire.

Worn out by a long illness that left him blind and also by his long years of labor, Fr. Giorgio died on November 21, 1756. His remains are incorrupt, and rested until 1954 in the Oratorian Church of Olivella. Now they are in the Cathedral of the Eparchy in Piana degli Albanesi, where the process of beatification is once again underway.

The Servant of God Nicolò Bijankovic[51] (1645–1730), founder of the Oratory of Spalato and bishop of Makarska, finds a brief mention here, because, although he was not Italian, he like Fr. Guzzetta, looked to the Orient to find his apostolic activity, among the faithful who were under Turkish domination. Born in Spalato from a Croation father and a Venetian mother, he came to Italy to study philosophy and theology at Loreto in order to prepare himself for the priesthood. He returned as a priest to continue for the doctorate at Macerata. He founded the Congregation of the Oratory at Spalato for the preaching of the Catholic faith, and worked there with great zeal, such that he was named Apostolic Missionary by the Holy See in 1673. He was elected Bishop of Makarska, and undertook long and tiring pastoral visits, initiating friendly relations with the Turks, and bringing the Jesuits and the Oratorians for the instruction of the secular clergy and the religious formation of the people. The greatest resistance that he encountered was from those who were not willing to change their habits, and set themselves against the Bishop, who wished to introduce into the diocese the spiritual renewal desired by the Council of Trent. He was a man given to active charity and to the spread of culture, and a wise pastor who was esteemed as a saint during his lifetime. He died in his episcopal seat and was buried with veneration in the choir of the cathedral. The documents of the canonical process celebrated in the diocese were destroyed in a fire in 1766, but his name still appeared in the index of Causes of 1988.

In Padua, from which the Oratory spread in the Veneto, in Trentino, and in Friuli, the exercises of the Oratory were introduced in 1602, thanks to the Capuchin Fr. Michelangelo. The first Oratorian Congregation arose in 1624, founded by Servant of God Antonio Maria Cortivo De Santi (1586–1650). He became a priest in 1614, and at the invitation of the Bishop dedicated himself to diffusing the Secular Oratory in the diocese. He even composed some much-appreciated ascetical works for the participants. In the Church of St. Thomas the Martyr[52] the cult of St. Philip Neri grew rapidly after the prodigious weeping of the painting of the Saint in 1632, an event which was amply documented by witnesses. After a brief parenthesis in Roveré, in Trent, and in Verona, where he also founded Oratories, Fr. Cortivo dedicated himself to Padua, in an intense apostolate. He died in 1650, in fame of holiness, and is buried in front of the high altar of his church.

Among the numerous examples of Oratorian virtue in the northeast, some of which have already been mentioned in this chapter, there are the Servants of God Giuseppe Musoco[53] (1668–1754), of the Oratory of Trent, and Luigi Perez[54] (1812–1895), of the Oratory of Verona. The first, from Vicenza, abandoned a brilliant legal career to become priest. He traveled to many cities to preach. In 1715 he entered the Congregation of Trent, which had been only recently founded, and was elected Provost. He continued his preaching ministry, and was invited ten times to the Imperial Court of Vienna. The second, born in Verona of a noble family, gave himself with admirable devotion to the poorest of his city, and radiated indefatigable priestly ministry. With the example he gave of holiness and tireless charity, Father Perez was a luminous forerunner of Servant of God Filippo Bardellini, whom we will meet shortly, among the founders of female institutes placed at the service of the very poor, and also of Servant of God Raimondo Calcagno[55] (1888–1964), of the Oratory of Chioggia. He was a shining figure of an Oratorian who spent nine years beginning in 1948, in the Oratory of Verona. Born in Chioggia into a humble family of fishermen, he completed his studies in the diocesan Seminary and entered at twenty-four the Congregation of the Oratory of Chioggia. His apostolic activity was devoted primarily to children and youth. He worked tirelessly to form them in all the spiritual and human values that give dignity to human existence: "a contemplative among the noisiness of children," Fr. Tesserin called him. He became dedicated to this work, and even diocesan seminarians and priests had recourse to him. "The world needs holy priests," he would say, "better still if they are learned, but they must be holy: there is an urgent need of this… It is this that makes us interesting to the world." And of this sanctity this Servant of God gave unforgettable examples: his Eucharistic piety, his spirit of prayer, his mortification, his tender piety toward the Virgin, and his zeal for the salvation of souls. He did all this in the school of St. Philip, and in the simplest and most ordinary way possible. For all of this, the Church is evaluating his heroic virtues. Since April 24, 1994, his venerated body rests in the church of the Oratory of Chioggia.

4. THE ORATORY AND "THE INDIES"

By its nature, the Congregation of the Oratory is not a missionary institute. Even in the places traditionally thought to be "mission" countries, the Oratorian Congregations have arisen through local initiative, through the desire of priests and laity to serve the Church in the spirit of St. Philip. Philip's own aspirations to go to "the Indies" as a missionary ended with the monk Ghettini incisive phrase "Rome is to be your Indies."

The "Western Indies," the New World, was then opening for evangelization. The Venerable Bartolomeo de Quental,[56] founder of the Oratory in Portugal,[57] was a figure of considerable importance for the spread of the Oratory in the New World. He sent Frs. João Duarte do Sacramento e João Roix Victoria to begin an Oratorian presence in Brazil.[58] That community closed in the nineteenth century. The Oratory returned to Brazil with the Congregation of Sao Paolo, founded by Italian Fathers and erected after a long period of gestation in 1996.[59]

Fr. de Quental, born in 1622 in Fenaes, an island of the Archipelago of the Azores, but at the age of seventeen he went to Evora and then to Coimbra to study. He was ordained priest at Lisbon in 1652, and became a famous preacher, chaplain and confessor at Court. Sustained by a deep spiritual life and by great zeal, he gathered lay persons around him, teaching them prayer and the need for charitable works, especially visiting hospitals and prisons. He also offered them the opportunity for healthy recreation, following the example of St. Philip Neri.

In 1668 he founded a Community of secular priests dedicated to intense prayer and to the care of souls using the means of preaching, missions, and works of charity on the model of St. Philip's Oratory. For almost two centuries the Congregation had a glorious history, even after the death of its founder, until the laws of the anticlerical governments suppressed all the Houses between 1832 and 1833.[60] The Statutes, terminated in 1670, foresaw a centralized structure for the Portuguese Oratorian Houses—at that time Freixa and Porto, in addition to the Mother House in Lisbon. Because of this, de Quental undertook contacts with the French Oratory, but these arrangements were soon abandoned. Rather it was his contact with the Roman Oratory between 1671 and 1672 that was the deciding factor. Now they could become a true Oratorian community. This was confirmed by the Brief "Ad pastoralis dignitatem" of 1671, which obliged the Community to take on the Constitutions of the Vallicella.

The Portuguese Oratory always retained singular characteristics, due to the strong imprint of the personality of Fr. Bartolomeo, *Fondateur impérieux*, as Girondon defines him.

The Venerable de Quental's name remains one of the most illustrious of the history of the Church in Portugal.[61] He lived in the most convincing humility, renouncing in the spirit of the Constitutions the many honors that were offered to him. He died in Lisbon on December 21, 1698. The examples of authentic sanctity which he left were the grounds for introducing his cause for beatification, and the Venerable de Quental is still registered in the Index of Causes.

The foundation of the first Congregation of the Oratory in Asia, in Goa, has close ties with this illustrious exponent of the Portuguese Church. When Blessed Joseph Vaz[62] saw in the Oratory the juridical and spiritual form he wanted for his work turned to Fr. de Quental to request the Constitutions and also advice on their new foundation,.

Fr. Vaz not only founded the Oratory of Goa, but also evangelized Ceylon, today Sri Lanka. His life, to paraphrase the title of a biography of him, could be synthesized in these terms: "the epic of a free man who made himself a slave in order to spread the Gospel."

In his homily for the Mass of Beatification, which was celebrated at Colombo, on January 21, 1995, Pope John Paul II said: "Considering all that Fr. Vaz did and how he did it and the circumstances in which he carried out the great work of saving an endangered Church, it is right to salute him as the greatest missionary that Asia has had." His confreres were aware of his extraordinary greatness. One of them, Fr. Saldanha, wrote to Goa on January 17, 1711, while Fr. Vaz's body was exposed to the veneration of the faithful in the Catholic church of Kandy: "On 16 January the venerable Fr. Vaz died, the Vicar General of this mission and father of missionaries. The sorrow and the desolation caused by his loss are tremendous and cannot be adequately described, for he was truly a holy priest."

Twenty years before, Fr. Joseph had slipped clandestinely into Ceylon, where the Catholic faithful were undergoing harsh persecution unleashed against them by Calvinist fanatics of the Dutch Empire. When he got there, carrying nothing and dressed like a slave and essentially as a beggar, he found no priests left. They had either been killed or expelled from the island. The churches were profaned or destroyed and the faithful dispersed, terrorized by death threats. When Fr. Vaz died, he left a mission of seventy thousand fervent Catholics, fifteen churches, four hundred chapels. This little man, with his holiness of life and his apostolic zeal, had re-established in Ceylon a Church with such deep roots that the successive storms would not be able to shake it.

He was born in India in his mother's village of Benaulim, in the territory of Goa, on April 21, 1651. His family had been Christian since the sixteenth century. Although his last name was Portuguese, his ancestors were Konkany Brahmins. It was surely the fervor of faith in his home that made his priestly vocation mature. This deep piety continued even after Fr. Vaz had left home, since all of his nephews became priests and the family line ended: "they immolated themselves for God."[63] Once he had completed his preparatory studies, Joseph moved to the University of the Jesuits in Goa for his formation in the humanities and then to the Dominican College of St. Thomas Aquinas for philosophy and theology. He was ordained in 1676. He returned to his native village and began his priestly ministry, but not for long. His example of faith and his cultural preparation drew attention; he was invited to preach in the cathedral and to dedicate himself in the city to the ministry of Confessions and of spiritual direction. Well-known figures entrusted their spiritual care to him. The missionary zeal that animated him led him to discover the sad plight of Ceylon. He would have liked to go there. The diocesan authorities sent him instead to Kanara. This was a territory of the Archdiocese of Goa, where the Holy See had erected a Vicariate Apostolic but there had arisen conflicts about matters of jurisdiction and authority. These things disturbed and compromised the lives of the Christian faithful, and the resulting scandal spread even among the pagans. Great humility was needed to reconcile the Pastors, and extraordinary dedication to inject new life into the faithful. Fr. Vaz did not lack either and when, in 1684, he left the Vicariate Apostolic, this painful situation was eased.

The ingratitude which he encountered after he returned to the city plunged him into solitude and shadow, and he strongly desired to enter some religious order. Again he had to search for a solution, since the existing orders accepted only candidates of European origin. There had been efforts to found indigenous communities, but they had failed. In Goa, with the permission of the Archbishop, three Indian priests had begun the common life at church of Holy Cross of the Miracles, on Mt. Boa Vista, and Fr. Joseph asked to join them. In time he was elected Superior, and became the real founder: he gave the Community a clear spiritual form, and also found in the Constitutions of the Oratory the juridical form that allowed them to continue. News of the Congregation of St. Philip Neri had arrived in Goa from Portugal, where the Oratory was flourishing and had a fervent missionary spirit. On January 9, 1686, a request was sent to Fr. De Quental for the Constitutions and for advice on the new foundation.

The reputation for sanctity of the priests of Boa Vista spread rapidly. Encouraged by the missionary zeal of Fr. Vaz they soon added an intense apostolate in the countryside to the ministry of their church.

Undertaking the foundation and then the canonical recognition was not easy,[64] but a Bull of Clement XI on November 26, 1706, confirmed its foundation and praised all that it was doing. In April 1709, a document, preserved in the archives of the Congregation of Rome, and signed by Frs. Giovanni da Guardia and Antonio de Attaide of the Oratory of Lisbon, declared that "in Western India, in Goa, there has been erected by Royal and Ordinary authority and confirmed by His Holiness Clement XI the Congregation of the Oratory of our Holy Father Philip Neri."

Toward the end of 1686, when the community was rich in vocations and bearing good fruit, and could get along without him, Fr. Vaz felt that the moment had come to his never-dormant call to go to the desperately abandoned Catholics in Ceylon. There were no other Asian priests willing to commit themselves personally to serve a persecuted and languishing Church. He revealed the secret of his plan only to Fr. Pascoal, whom he asked to substitute for him. He left to find a way to enter the island, accompanied only by Giovanni, a youth who dearly loved him and remained with him until the end.

Putting off his habit, he chose the garb of slaves and beggars; after some months of laborious attempts, he managed to disembark on the coast of Ceylon. Immediately he fell ill, and for some days lay at the edge of the road, with Giovanni, who also had caught the fever. He would have died had not some women given him a bit of food. Although he was afraid of being discovered, he began his search for Catholics, most of whom had exteriorly taken on Calvinistic ways and dared not expose themselves. Then Fr. Vaz did something courageous: around his neck, and hanging down his bare chest he placed a rosary, and so commenced to go begging from door to door. The Buddhists and the Hindus seemed indifferent to it, but he noticed some who looked at that sign of Catholic piety with interest. He began with one family, and when he was sure of their fidelity, he revealed his identity. That was the beginning of the re-evangelization of the island. He carried the secret exercise of his ministry out for two years in the safe village of Jaffna, celebrating Mass at night, with Confessions and spiritual conversations for those who wished. The re-flowering of the Community attracted the attention of the Dutch Authorities, and the governor, with the intention of strangling that regrowth, assigned a large bounty for anyone who gave that priest into his hands. But no one betrayed Fr. Vaz, whom they hid while the ire of the Calvinists was unleashed against the people. A number of people were martyred, and many Catholics ended their days in prison.

The little state of Kandy in the interior of the island was still officially independent and there were many Catholics who had never seen a priest. It was to this small kingdom that Fr. Vaz fled. In this kingdom, there reigned King Vilamadharma Surya. Calvinist agents warned him about the arrival of Fr. Vaz, telling the king that he was a spy for the Portuguese: the plan worked, and as soon as Fr. Vaz arrived, he was put in prison. The King of Kandy, a Buddhist, did not approve of the incarceration of this stranger, whose character was so deeply spiritual. He learned through the guards of the holiness of life of the prisoner and befriended him. He conveyed his veneration to his son, Narendrasinha. When his son succeeded him on the throne, he also venerated Fr. Vaz. Thus he was released from prison and was afforded the opportunity to preach and spread the faith in the whole kingdom, going on foot throughout the territory and reestablishing everywhere the presence of the Church.

The outbreak of a smallpox epidemic in 1697, according the testimony of the king himself, would have completely destroyed the population if it had not been for the charity and intelligence of Fr. Vaz. He established sanitary norms and organized the care of the sick in such a way as to contain the epidemic.

Fr. Vaz maintained a regular correspondence with his Oratory in Goa, and that same year, two Fathers arrived from Goa—Joseph de Meneze and Joseph Carvalho. At the death of Fr. Vaz, ten missionaries were working in that area, imbued with his spirit and prepared to pursue the work, for which he also prepared lay people, entrusting them with the care of many widely spread communities. He encouraged every village to build its own chapel. A layman named Annavi, a catechist, taught the people using manuals that Fr. Vaz, who had learned Tamil and Singale, had written in the local languages. The roots of the Church of Sri Lanka are sunk deep into the actions of these lay apostles, no less than in the action of the priests.

Brahmin by birth and by family, an ascetic who was totally poor and open to any sacrifice, Fr. Vaz showed, perhaps without realizing it, the happiest union of Oriental asceticism with Christian spirituality.

His body was worn out by incessant work and every sort of privation, and eventually he had not even the strength to move. In the night of January 15 he received the Viaticum and said to the Fathers who asked him for a last word: "Remember that one cannot easily do at the moment of death what one has neglected to do for a whole lifetime." And taking a candle in his hand, with the name of Jesus on his lips he closed his earthly pilgrimage.

The Provost of the Oratory of Goa wrote the first biography of Fr. Joseph in 1723, and in 1732 Pope Benedict XIV authorized the introduction of the canonical process of beatification. In 1753 the Oratory of Venice published in Italian *L'Apostolo di Ceylan. P. Giuseppe Vaz della Congregazione dell'Oratorio di San Filippo Neri.* Certain mostly political reasons delayed the beatification of this extraordinary missionary, even though he is venerated as a saint by all people. It was during John Paul II's visit to Sri Lanka (the first visit of a Pope to the country) that he was finally raised to the dignity of the altar.[65]

V. THE "ABSENT" FATHER OF THE SECOND VATICAN COUNCIL

This is the description given during and after the meeting of the Council of Vatican II to John Henry Newman[66] (1801-1890), founder of the Oratory in England. He was created Cardinal of the Holy Roman Church by Pope Leo XIII in 1879, in recognition of his high merit with respect to the Church. Paul VI called him a "sure guide" for all those who "are seeking clear direction and a path through the uncertainties of the modern world." Newman anticipated theological reflections and directions of thought that resounded throughout the last Ecumenical Council, so much so that many say that he is the modern "Doctor of the Church."

"On the occasion of the second centenary of the birth of the Venerable Servant of God John Henry Newman," wrote John Paul II in the Pontifical Letter commemorating the anniversary,[67] which followed those written for the anniversaries of 1979 and 1991, "I gladly join you, your Brother Bishops of England and Wales, the priests of the Birmingham Oratory and a host of voices throughout the world in praising God for the gift of the great English Cardinal and for his enduring witness."

"As Newman pondered the mysterious divine plan unfolding in his own life," continued the Pope,

> he came to a deep and abiding sense that "God has created me to do Him some definite service. He has committed some work to me which he has not committed to another. I have my mission" (*Meditations and Devotions*). How true that thought now appears as we

consider his long life and the influence which he has had beyond death. He was born at a particular time—February 21, 1801; in a particular place—London; and to a particular family—the firstborn of John Newman and Jemima Fourdrinier. But the particular mission entrusted to him by God ensures that John Henry Newman belongs to every time and place and people.

Newman was born in troubled times which knew not only political and military upheaval but also turbulence of soul. Old certitudes were shaken, and believers were faced with the threat of rationalism on the one hand and fideism on the other. Rationalism brought with it a rejection of both authority and transcendence, while fideism turned from the challenges of history and the tasks of this world to a distorted dependence upon authority and the supernatural. In such a world, Newman came eventually to a remarkable synthesis of faith and reason which were for him "like two wings on which the human spirit rises to the contemplation of the truth" (*Fides et Ratio*, Introduction; cf. ibid., 74). It was the passionate contemplation of truth which also led him to a liberating acceptance of the authority which has its roots in Christ, and to the sense of the supernatural which opens the human mind and heart to the full range of possibilities revealed in Christ. "Lead kindly light amid the encircling gloom, lead Thou me on," Newman wrote in *The Pillar of the Cloud*; and for him Christ was the light at the heart of every kind of darkness. For his tomb he chose the inscription: *Ex umbris et imaginibus in veritatem*; and it was clear at the end of his life's journey that Christ was the truth he had found.

But Newman's search was shot through with pain. Once he had come to that unshakeable sense of the mission entrusted to him by God, he declared: "Therefore, I will trust Him… If I am in sickness, my sickness may serve Him, in perplexity, my perplexity may serve Him…He does nothing in vain… He may take away my friends. He may throw me among strangers. He may make me feel desolate, make my spirits sink, hide the future from me. Still, He knows what He is about" (*Meditations and Devotions*). All these trials he knew

> in his life; but rather than diminish or destroy him they paradoxically strengthened his faith in the God who had called him, and confirmed him in the conviction that God "does nothing in vain." In the end, therefore, what shines forth in Newman is the mystery of the Lord's Cross: this was the heart of his mission, the absolute truth which he contemplated, the "kindly light" which led him on.

We have reproduced the Pontifical Letter in its entirety because it contains a profound synthesis of Newman's life and spiritual ideas. We must not neglect the fact that the newly converted Newman chose to become an Oratorian before he returned to England. He took with him the Brief of Pope Pius IX[68] which instituted the Oratory, giving Newman the faculty of propagating it in England, where the Catholic hierarchy had so recently been reestablished.

Father Newman loved the Oratory, and felt himself to be thoroughly an Oratorian. He wrote of St. Philip: "Yet there is one I more affect… / 'Tis an old man of sweet aspect, / I love him more, I more admire. / I know him by his head of snow, / His ready smile, his keen full eye, / His words which kindle as they flow, / Save he be rapt in ecstasy."[69] At the time when he was offered the cardinal's hat, his letter asking a favor of Pope Leo XIII rings with meaning: "I have lived now thirty years 'in my little nest,' in my much-loved Oratory, sheltered and happy, and would therefore entreat his Holiness not to take me from St. Philip, my Father and Patron, and to let me die where I have lived so long."[70]

Newman understood well the experience of the origins of the Oratory. He thus placed himself on the path traced out by the first disciples of Philip Neri, who were themselves called to the dignity of the cardinalate. This tradition of affectionate identification, of remaining at home instead of going to Rome, continues into the present. The latest of Cardinal Oratorians to make such a choice was Fr. Giulio Bevilacqua, of the Oratory of Brescia: he accepted the red hat at the insistence of Paul VI, but asked and obtained from the Pope the favor of continuing his parish ministry in the Oratorian community of Sant'Antonio, at the edge of Brescia.

What was it about St. Philip that fascinated John Henry Newman, and led him to choose the Oratory as the form and method of his priestly life in the Catholic Church?

Newman expressed it particularly in several splendid texts: his *Letters* on the Oratorian vocation; the sermons he preached in Birmingham on the "mission of St. Philip Neri"; some prayers, especially the beautiful *Litanies* asking the intercession of the Saint in order to obtain the graces with which he was particularly blessed.

But there was, we think, one thing that attracted Newman more than any other and that expresses a harmonious synthesis of the whole interior life of St. Philip. It is that spirit which shines forth in the first verse of the very well-known poem-prayer: "Lead, kindly light." That "kindliness" of Fr. Philip's is not only an aspect of his character, but includes the singular freedom of spirit, so dear to Newman, the love for a life of authentic community normed by laws of discretion, the respect for the gifts of each, the wise simplicity of Philip that made his joy "a thoughtful joy," in the lovely phrase of Goethe.[71]

The Cardinal died in his community in Birmingham on August 11, 1890, after having experienced and offered to the Lord so many sufferings and failures of understanding, suspicions and much opposition,[72] all rendered so much sharper by the extraordinary sensitivity of his soul.

He was brought up in the Anglican Church, and had at fifteen his first spiritual "conversion" which introduced him to the idea of the journey of evangelical perfection; he became a priest in his Church and pastor of St. Mary, and founded the Oxford Movement for the study of the Fathers of the Church and the history of ancient Christianity. He discovered in the Catholic Church the Church of Christ and decided to enter it in 1845, a step that took enormous courage. In 1847 he was ordained in Rome. His was a life lived in the light of a formed conscience, of fervent prayer, incessant study, and the apostolic proclamation of the Truth: "deep intellectual honesty, fidelity to conscience and grace, piety and priestly zeal, devotion to Christ's Church and love of her doctrine, unconditional trust in divine providence and absolute obedience to the will of God" characterize "Newman's genius," wrote John Paul II in the Letter commemorating the first centenary of Newman's elevation to the sacred office of Cardinal.[73]

> As we thank God for the gift of the Venerable John Henry Newman on the two hundredth anniversary of his birth, we pray that this sure and eloquent guide in our perplexity will also become for us in all our needs a powerful intercessor before the throne of grace. Let us pray that the time will soon come when the Church can officially and publicly proclaim the exemplary holiness of Cardinal John Henry Newman, one of the most distinguished and versatile champions of English spirituality.[74]

6. MARTYRS' CROWNS

Poland had always been faithful to Catholicism and even, down through the centuries, courageously resisted those who wanted to eliminate the Catholic identity of the Nation. The Congregations of the Oratory have been among those who experienced the trials of martyrdom. The first Oratory began in 1655 in Gostyn. The Servant of God Wawrzyniec Kusniak[75] (1788–1866) of that community gave fine examples of holiness. During the Second World War, Fr. Ferdynand Machay of the Oratory of Tarnow and Fr. Jan Mikalkowski of the Oratory of Studzianna were killed in hatred of the faith, and their names will figure among the Polish Martyrs at a future beatification.

In Spain during the terrible civil war, a goodly number of Oratorians witnessed their fidelity to the faith to the point of martyrdom: this, despite the fact that Spain was Catholic in the very title by which its kings had been known for centuries. The Congregation of Barcelona-Gracia lost Frs. Pedro Garet Vilar del Bosch, Candido Vila Maneja, Aleix Soler Llobera, Joaquim Serra Auferil, Martì Subirà Arumi,[76] killed *in odium fidei* for the sole reason that they were ministers of Christ; the Congregation of Barcelona-Barrio Gotico lost its Provost Fr. Agustì Mas Folch, Fr. Josep Serra Altarriba and the lay brothers Emil Prat, Miquel and Joaqim Bellera Morera,[77] courageous witnesses of the Gospel; and the House of Vich lost Fr. Ramòn Felius.

Among these martyrs, we reserve a special mention for Servant of God Salvio Huix Miralpeix[78] who gave witness of supreme love of Christ together with the greater part of the secular and religious clergy of Lerida, exterminated by the ferocity of the Red Terror between July and September of 1936. His beatification with various other Spanish martyrs is expected.

He was born in the diocese of Vic, in Santa Margarita di Vellors (Gerona) on December 22, 1877, into a family for whom faith in God and love for the Pope and the Church were a sacred and never-to-be-renounced patrimony. He was ordained a priest on September 19, 1903, and four years later entered the Congregation of the Oratory. For twenty years he dedicated himself to an intense apostolate of preaching, study, publishing, catechetical instruction, teaching in the diocesan seminary, and promotion of women's associations.

He was Provost of the Oratory of Vic when, in 1927, he was named Bishop of Ibiza, where he gave extraordinary stimulus to religious life. On January 29, 1935, he was transferred to the diocese of Lerida, and continued his intense apostolic work until July 21, 1936, when the perpetuators of the Red Terror besieged the bishop's palace. Mons. Huix reluctantly agreed to flee to acquaintances in order to save his collaborators. He learned that those who were hiding him were themselves in danger. On the night of July 23 he left his refuge, presented himself to the guards, and declared his identity. He was immediately placed in prison with others, with whom he shared both suffering and the hidden joys of prayer and the sacraments, up to the last distribution of the Eucharist (Viaticum). On the morning of August 5 they were all taken to the cemetery and were shot. The Bishop requested that he be killed last, so that he could impart absolution to all and could comfort each of his companions in martyrdom.

Before his arrest, he had given his bishop's crosier to an acquaintance, asking him that it be sent to the Holy Father for whom he was offering his life, assuring him of his fidelity.[79]

The fidelity of these Oratorians to the point of shedding of their blood, brings us now to the equally glorious evangelical witness to Charity, exemplified in works dedicated to the weakest among us.

7. ORATORIANS AS "WORKERS OF MERCY"

Holy Fr. Philip witnessed to the excellence of charity not only in the amiability of his relationships with others and in his zeal for the salvation of souls, but also in his work to provide for the needs of his neighbor. His visits to the poor in the hospitals and prisons of Rome and his loving assistance to pilgrims have inspired Oratorians throughout the centuries: John Paul II acknowledged this zeal in his Bull of Indiction in the Jubilee Year 2000.[80] There have been Oratorians who have had both great generosity and also the ability to organize works of charity. Such activities, however, have never been part of the Constitutions as activities specific to the Oratory. They have arisen, rather, out of the proclamation of the Gospel in the familiar style of the Oratory, for the formation of the faithful in a conscious participation in the sacramental life, and for a worthy exercise of the sacramental ministry. Other religious Congregations and lay Confraternities had already been instituted for this purpose. The works of charity in the service of the sick that Fr. Philip asked of his disciples in the Secular Oratory promoted spiritual formation in those who did them. Rather than the conviction of having to take responsibility in the face of serious social needs, the acquisition of humility was what mattered. Philip always emphasized the practical charity of concrete help in the moment of particular needs—for example, that of girls who could not marry because they had no dowry, or workers who could not make enough to live. The thought of organizing works of social assistance was far from his aims.

There have been individual Oratorians through the centuries who began charitable enterprises that enriched Oratorian history in a profound way. Fr. Carlo Mino (1878–1968) of the Oratory of Biella, founder and father of the local Little House of Divine Providence, is perhaps the most recent witness of this chapter of Oratorian history written by men who were generous and capable of undertaking such enterprises. They were driven by circumstances and propelled by the needs of the people. This was the case of St. Luigi Scrosoppi,[81] who became caught up with his brother's initiatives to help orphaned and abandoned little girls; he provided an institution to which he would otherwise probably not have thought to dedicate himself.

This Oratorian saint lived in a period that saw the extinction of a great number of Oratorian Houses in Italy, due to the laws of suppression. None of them, however, according to Cistellini,[82] closed with such a radiant sunset as the House in Udine, whose last Father was solemnly canonized in St. Peter's on June 10, 2001.

Pope John Paul II said of Fr. Luigi, in his homily of beatification on October 4, 1981: "he entered the Congregation of the Oratory and he made of it a dynamic center from which radiated spiritual life. He spent his own life entirely for souls. He had three great loves: Jesus, the Church and the Pope, and the 'little ones.' From the time he was very small, he chose Christ, and he loved him, contemplating him poor and humble in Bethlehem; a worker in Nazareth; suffering and a victim in Jerusalem and on Golgotha; present in the Eucharist. 'I want to be faithful,' he wrote, 'perfectly conformed to Him on the journey to heaven, to succeed in becoming a copy of Him.' The foundation of his many pastoral and charitable activities is a profound interiority. His day was a constant prayer: meditation, visits to the Most Blessed Sacrament, the Liturgy of the Hours, daily Stations of the Cross, rosary and finally long prayer during the night. He exemplified a luminous and effective synthesis between the active life and the contemplative life."

Pope John Paul II also recalled Fr. Luigi's motto, "act, suffer, be still," in his Brief *Pia Mater Ecclesia*, adding that: "there is no doubt that this expressed his manner of living and it accorded perfectly with his intention to live the third step of humility." John Paul II completed his very clear portrait of this saint in the homily of canonization: "sanctity is the gift that the Father communicates to us through Jesus Christ. Faith in Him is, in fact, the principle of sanctification. Through faith man enters into the order of grace; by faith he hopes to take part in the glory of God. This hope is not a vain illusion, but the sure fruit of an ascetic journey through many tribulations, faced with patience and proven virtue. This was the experience of St. Luigi Scrosoppi, throughout a life spent entirely for the love of Christ and his brothers and sisters, especially for the weak and vulnerable. 'Charity! Charity!': this exclamation rose from his heart at the moment he was leaving the world to go to Heaven. He exercised charity in an exemplary way, above all with respect to orphaned and abandoned little girls, gathering a group of teachers who began the Institute of the Suore della Divina Providenza. Charity was the secret of his long and tireless apostolate, nourished by constant contact with Christ."

Luigi Scrosoppi was born in Udine on August 4, 1804, into a household where his elder brother, Fr. Carlo Filaferro, son of their mother's earlier marriage, also lived. Luigi was entrusted to the care of Fr. Carlo and attended the church where the Oratorian Fathers still officiated, although the Community had been dissolved. Luigi grew up in the "school" of Philip Neri, and celebrated his first Mass on April 1, 1827. He began his ministry as an Oratorian in his soul, although juridically he could not be. In his exercise of the virtues and in his pastoral and charitable service the *Oratorian dimension* of Fr. Luigi emerges very clearly; this induced him, a young diocesan priest, to follow his brother when the political situation changed and it was possible to think of reconstituting the Congregation. Fr. Carlo died before this work was complete. It was Fr. Luigi who committed his energies and the material wealth of the family to the realization of this dream. In this undertaking he participated deeply, and succeeded through his tenacity in accomplishing that which Fr. Carlo had not been able to do.

The sad political and social conditions of nineteenth-century Italy led in the space of a decade to the destruction, even materially, of the Congregation that Fr. Luigi had reestablished with labors equal to the love that nourished them. But this disciple of St. Philip continued to consider himself and to sign himself *dell'Oratorio* until the end of his life, conquering with his steadfastness to the ideals of Philip the tremendous blows that that century dealt to the Oratorian Congregations. He never abandoned the habit, which he put on until his death as beloved livery, that habit which was ragged and threadbare that his daughters in Udine conserve as a precious relic of his fidelity to the Oratory and of his inexhaustible charity; and *presbyter Oratorii* was written on the tombstone of this Father, that description being so dear and natural to him. The Oratory, which he saw destroyed by the violence of an ideology that proclaimed itself liberal remained in his heart, with its patrimony of ideals intact. And more than a century after his death, it is moving to reflect on the fact that Bl. Luigi did obtain the miracle approved for his canonization on behalf of an Oratorian confrere.

There are some articles written by Fr. Antonio Cistellini and Mons. Guglielmo Biasutti[83] that would be of considerable help to anyone who would like to dedicate himself to a further research on the Oratorian character of Fr. Luigi. Such research would certainly bring to light rich veins of the Oratorian spirit, those which shaped the pastoral activity and apostolic style of Fr. Luigi, his way of creating relationships with other persons first, and becoming familiar with their problems afterwards, a method we easily recognize as St. Philip's.

"It is certainly not difficult," wrote Cistellini at the time of the beatification, "to recognize in him features, ways, approaches that are exquisitely those of Philip: the copious reports and depositions are eloquent testimonials of this. His lively direct manner, his predilection for simplicity and frankness in as many as he cared for and approached stand out in these reports, and the pure simplicity of a man who was gentle and severe at the same time, of lucid intelligence, even if not of great culture, and extremely personable. Even his jokes, pleasing and spontaneous, scattered along the days spent with his sisters, seemed formed on the incomparable model of the joyous priest of the Chiesa Nuova. And the humble ups and downs of his first daughters, at the beginning of the Institute, have the grace and the freshness of authentic little flowers of St. Philip. But it is above all in following the typical paths of his spirituality that one notices Fr. Luigi clear consonance with the program of religious life that Fr. Philip commended to his sons. To become a saint, above all; the indispensable basis, humility, and nothing can take its place. This was certainly not a singular admonition, but the way that Philip proposed and insisted upon it, and the sincerity and consistency with which Fr. Luigi took it as norm and directive for himself and for the souls of his own most certainly was singular. 'Humility,' he said in his proposals, 'in being, in speaking, in asking.' 'Humility and charity must be shown to everyone and in every work: *semper mel in ore et mel in corde*.' 'You will soon be a saint if you take yourself for nothing at all; if you yearn to be abandoned and held to be nothing; if you accept from God's hand everything that happens to you; if you desire nothing except to do the will of God.'"

There emerges from Fr. Luigi, in a convincing way, a profound unity of the contemplative spirit and the tireless exercise of charity.

Cistellini proposes here, too, a clear summation that merits further development:

> Like his fervent Fr. Philip, Fr. Luigi was a man immersed uninterruptedly in God, pervaded by a burning love for Him. The assiduous contemplation of the Trinitarian mystery and the tender devotion for the mystery of the Incarnation: the intense participation in the Passion, through which he felt himself to be "with Jesus Christ offered to the Eternal Father in sacrifice"; the celebration of the Mass (so much like those memorable Masses of his St. Philip), recollected, quiet, passionate, "like the seraphim," with prolonged silences in adoration in the humble chapel and in his Oratorian church; the care for the decorum of the temple (in this, too, following St. Philip perfectly), expressed in illuminating maxims: "Poor of house, rich in the church"; the devotion to the Virgin, warm, sweet, trusting in

> the Virgin (he was one of the promoters of the cult of the Immaculate Heart of Mary just at the time when the first Oratorian church in London was being built and dedicated to Mary under this title): these appear to be essential elements of his spirituality, the outlines of his interior life, modeled on and continually compared to that of his father and teacher, Philip Neri.
>
> And how could we not become aware of that perfect consonance in the distinctive character trait that informs all of his intense work and his undertakings: his joyous and trusting abandonment to Divine Providence? "Do everything well," he would say, "and then have great faith in God"; "suffer everything joyously"; "Do, suffer, be silent!" were his maxims, his habitual expressions, of clear derivation from St. Philip!

Anyone who would like to investigate and reflect more deeply on St. Luigi Scrosoppi's intense exercise of charity would find characteristics that show his profound adherence to the "school" of St. Philip.

Among these we wish to emphasize just one—one which, however, is basic: the relationship that he had with persons is not merely functional, having to do with their material or spiritual needs, but is above all an attention to persons in their intrinsic value, a *personal encounter* in which the person feels himself or herself to be loved for what he or she is, and feels in turn an impulse to be more authentically what he or she really is. The charity which he exercised was not merely a natural philanthropic response, but an authentic kind of morality—the modality within which the Christian should live every aspect of life. It responds to the theological virtues in that God is its source, and more than a human initiative, it flowers like the experience of a great Love received by the Christian in one's own life and communicated in the relationship with one's neighbor. Only one who has encountered Grace succeeds in establishing with others that rapport which is free, patient, active, and constructive; only this is authentic love because it respects the *whole* person.

As we have emphasized in the preceding pages of this book, Fr.

Philip is an incomparable teacher of the *full* interpersonal relationship that embraces the entire, concrete person standing before us. His "school," humbly active in the simplicity of the communities that wish to stay faithful to the entire direction of life transmitted by their Father, produces fruits of authentic holiness, in which that which is most human finds its greatest flowering.

Fr. Luigi Scrosoppi, humble follower of Philip of the Oratory of Udine, who died in his city on April 3, 1881, was a tremendous witness of this. His daughters, the Sisters of Providence, founded by him in 1845, continue this witness with their work in Europe, Latin America, Africa, and Asia. They in turn have written pages of stupendous witness to the spirit and style of their Holy Founder in the course of their history.

With a cursory glance at only the last two centuries, we find several Oratorians deserve to be remembered for their exercise of charity to the poor, including founders of women's communities. Among these, mention must be accorded to Fr. Marco Castaner y Seda[84] (1815–1878), of the Oratory of Seville, who founded the Religious Philippine Sisters, and to Fr. Francisco Garcia Tejero[85] (1852–1909), fervent restorer of the Oratory of Seville. The latter was also exceedingly concerned about the poor of his city, for whose material and spiritual needs he founded two women's Congregations: the Sisters Filipenses Hijas de Maria Dolorosa, and Misioneras de la Doctrina cristiana.

In Italy in those same years, there were notable examples of sanctity, including the Servant of God Emilio Venturini[86] (1842–1905) of the Oratory of Chioggia, who founded the "Serve di Maria Addolorata" for the education and assistance of the most needy. He was a man of profound humanistic formation, apparent in both his writings and in his relationships with the cultivated men of his era. He dedicated himself to an intense life of preaching and revitalizing Christian society. He had entered the Oratory in 1858 and in 1864 had been ordained priest. However, due to the laws of suppression the Community was dissolved in 1868, he was forced to live in his family's home.

His contact with the poorest areas of the city began in this period; in this he was assisted by a teacher, Elisa Sambo. In 1870 with her help he began the work of assistance to orphans, which would give rise to the Congregazione delle Suore. The Fathers of the Oratory re-entered their House in November 1883; Fr. Emilio was part of the restored community. By now the works he had begun were developing and required constant attention. Fr. Venturini dedicated himself to this without neglecting his apostolic activities. In his city he became one of the most illustrious examples of priestly zeal and goodness.

Following the same pattern of works of mercy, in the Oratory of Verona, lived the Servant of God Filippo Bardellini[87] (1878–1956), of whom we have spoken in a preceding chapter with respect to the Congress of Bologna of 1932. He was born in a difficult time into the working class quarter of the Filippini; here he spent his childhood and youth amidst difficulties that included the terrible flood of 1882, and that caused many families to emigrate.

The parish environment of the Congregation of the Oratory and the diocesan seminary provided him with a solid human and spiritual formation. He entered the Community in 1901, and was ordained on August 10, 1904. He lived the first years of his priesthood among the poorest classes, those of his own people and among the youth. This ministry was intensified after 1911 when he was named Rector of the church of San Pietro Incarnario.

From the beginning his ardent zeal, his fervent piety, his devotion in the development of pastoral activities were evident. He had chosen as his spiritual director the future San Giovanni Calabria, who became not only teacher and guide but also a very close friend.

With his encouragement, and with the help of his sister Elisa, Fr. Philip founded the Institute of the Poverette della Casa di Nazareth, with the intention of dedicating himself primarily to young girls, who were often abandoned. "Even those who are retarded," said Fr. Bardellini, "are persons: and as such must be respected and helped, just like others; such persons have the right to have their gifts cultivated and developed in every possible way."

The Oratorian Community, of which he was Provost for many years, allowed him the autonomy to dedicate himself to directing the work. The Institute grew rapidly, but like all of the works of God, was not immune to suffering. "Do not desire to mutilate your cross," Fr. Bardellini would say, "Do not touch your wounds impatiently. Abandon yourself to Divine Providence: everything is in the hand of God, and meanwhile expend your energies for the good of others. Sorrow is good for us for in so many ways; it also has some parts that are rich in comfort and in peace." Struck by serious illness, he moved in 1948 by agreement with his Congregation, to the central House of his Institute, at Ponton di Domegliara (Verona), where he spent his last years nearly immobilized. Through his spirit of prayer and his joyous submission to the will of God he provided a source of edification. Reciting the prayer that was dear to him, "In Te, Signore, ho sperato; non sarò confuso in eterno" [In Thee Lord have I trusted; let me not be confounded in eternity], he died on August 24, 1956. The Process for beatification was introduced, and the Congregation of Verona, as well as so many others, awaits the proclamation of the sanctity of this worthy son of the first Fr. Philip.

8. DESIRE FOR A WIDER ORATORIAN COMMUNION

In the preceding chapter we have tried to present the fundamental stages of the journey that led to the birth of the Oratorian Confederation. This brought to light the work done by the Servants of God Giovanni Battista Arista and Giulio Castelli and their essential contribution to the union of the Congregations of the Oratory into a juridical body which would protect their existence and their identity and original autonomy. Now we wish to delve into the minds and hearts of these two protagonists of the new institution, who lived their Oratorian vocation by walking steadfastly in the path of evangelical perfection. Their exemplary holiness gave them a unique presence in the tradition of the Oratory, a message that still goes even beyond the value of the Confederation which they so ardently desired. We hope with all our heart to see them raised as soon as possible to the dignity of the altar, perhaps even together, as together they lived their laborious adventure of a noble project.

The Servant of God Giovanni Battista Arista[88] was born in Palermo April 2, 1862, of Domenico, a lawyer, and Francesca Vigo, who moved to Acireale when their son was eight months old. The childhood and youth of Giambattista were spent in this city, an illustrious center of study and seat of a Congregation of the Oratory. The Congregation had felt the effects of those laws of suppression which in so many other cities in Italy made the life of the Oratorian Communities impossible. The child grew strong in will and gifted with a robust piety, because of the piety of his parents and that of the Fathers of the Oratory. The Oratorians, despite a thousand difficulties, and the fact that they were compelled to live privately, continued to exercise their ministry in the church of the Congregation, with particular attention to the education of youth in the Collegio San Michele.

Their spirituality, which was strongly Eucharistic, as well as a tender devotion to Mary Immaculate nourished Giambattista's formation and fostered his vocation to the priesthood. Ordained on June 25, 1888, and fascinated by the example of St. Philip Neri, he felt profoundly the call to reconstitute the highly deserving Congregation. On the vigil of the Saint's feast in 1895, third centenary of his death, Fr. Arista began living the common life with two Fathers and two brothers. "Finally we are united in community!", he wrote to Fr. Giulio Castelli on June 6, "How content my soul is I cannot express, and even less do I know how to express the gratitude that I feel for the Good God, and certainly for the intercession of the Madonna and of our St. Philip, *in bonum Congregationis nos congregavit*." He was elected Provost in 1896 and Director of the Collegio. With powerful gushes of new life, Fr. Arista instilled life and spirit into the Congregation by words, but above all by his example of tenacious fidelity to the duties of fraternal living. At the Processes, there were wonderful testimonies of his goodness: his heart shone with unlimited goodness;

his sweetness assuaged so many sorrows; his strength, which gave courage, sustained the steps of the newly reborn Congregation. At the same time these qualities attracted to the "school" of Fr. Arista many persons fascinated by his priestly spirit. There was nothing of his own that he did not give generously. For his confreres he built the house where the Congregation Acese still lives today, in place of the one that the law had confiscated. Nourished by the tradition of St. Philip, he beautified the church for God and for the Christian people. The field of his apostolate was primarily the youth, for whom he divided his day among the Oratory, the Collegio San Michele, and the Valle Filippina. His was an intense and paternal presence, joyous like that of Fr. Philip, and just as fruitful. "The young are my passion and my dream," he wrote in 1910, now as Bishop of Acireale. "Loving my young people I feel that I would endure greater sacrifices if it would do good for them. And the good that I would like to do for them is the true good that has its beginning in God, and is God." The young people loved him with the freshness and the filial trust of which young people are capable when they feel that an adult loves them with his whole heart.

The Bishop of Acireale, Mons. Gerlando Genuardi, certainly had no trouble seeing in the young seminarian, and later in the Oratorian Father the most distinguished figure of his diocese, and thought of him as his successor. When Pope Leo XIII named him Bishop of Sebaste with the charge of *Prelato nullius* of Santa Lucia del Mela, Fr. Arista's humility enabled him to decline the post, even though he had already received a note from the Secretary of State notifying him of his nomination. His same humility was, however, of no avail in 1904 when he was named Auxiliary Bishop of Acireale. Fr. Arista went to Rome at that time, and his prayers at the altar of St. Philip left a lasting impression on those who saw him. Fr. Timpanaro recalled having seen him in ecstasy, raised from the floor, during the celebration of Holy Mass. He continued to live humbly in the Congregation and to direct the Collegio, devoting part of his time to the service of the diocese and the Bishop. The Bishop was old and ill, and three years later, when Mons. Genuardi died, Pius IX personally wanted Fr. Arista to be the Bishop of the diocese: "I would like to be able to do as you prefer," the Pope wrote in his own hand to Mons. Arista who had begged him to think of others, "but how can I resist the manifest will of the Lord who wants you to be Bishop of Acireale?" *Omnia in caritate* is the episcopal motto chosen by Arista: it was the program he set in motion day by day amidst the enormous difficulties caused by natural disasters, by lack of understanding on the part of politicians, by problems in the Seminary, and by the infirmities that made him die of stomach cancer. "Oh, sorrow, sorrow!" he wrote in his Pastoral Letter of 1918, "Come and work in our souls; come and consume in them the perverse loves that want to extinguish the sacred flame of charity; come and establish there the reign of charity. Thus we will be pleasing to God; thus we will carry out the law of God!" "I want to stay on the cross," he would say, "my Jesus, I want to stay there. From the cross we rise, we do not descend… At any cost, on the cross." He was the Bishop of the Eucharist, and from the Eucharist he drew the strength to serve with limitless love each faithful member of his Church, whether priest or lay. He died September 27, 1920, worn out by illness and even more by a constant gift that he had expended little by little. He wanted to rest in the church of the Oratory, next to the tabernacle, the love of his life, and under the gaze of Our Lady of Purity, to whom he said, among his last words in this life: "Mia Signora e Madre mia, ricordatevi che io sono vostro" [My Lady and my Mother, remember that I am yours].

The laborious earthly pilgrimage of the Servant of God Giulio Castelli[89] ended six years after Fr. Arista's, in 1926, comforted by the gentle shade of the Olmo di Maria, at Cava de' Terreni. He shared with Fr. Arista the desire to see their Oratory, which they loved and for which they sacrificed, flower once again.

He was born in Turin, of a distinguished family, on June 27, 1846. Educated in the Oratory of St. Philip Neri, where was soon attracted to it. At the age of nineteen he entered the Congregation, where he completed his theological studies and was ordained on March 13,

1869. He was immediately occupied in catechesis, preaching and the ministry of Confessions. An unparalleled teacher, even as a cleric he was "teacher," of the young of the Congregation, and of many others who later held eminent posts in the Church and in the society.

His love for the Oratory impelled him to accept the invitation to go, in 1890, to assist the Congregation in Rome. This Congregation was declining into lamentable conditions of material poverty and lack of members following the enactment of the Italian laws of suppression, laws that extended to the entire Kingdom of Italy, as the process of national unification continued. At the tomb of Fr. Philip, in the Roman "Chiesa Nuova", Fr. Castelli carried on his tireless work of educating children and youth, at no little sacrifice to himself. He had among his altar boys the thirteen-year-old Eugenio Pacelli, who when he became Pope, always remembered his old "teacher" [*maestro*], and in an audience spoke of him with emotion as "a tall figure, frail, always recollected, completely humble with his eyes down." The Pope was very glad that the process of beatification was underway, and hoped to be the one who would proclaim his sanctity.

Because of his love for the ideals of the Oratory and his concern for the sad circumstances in which many Italian Congregations were living of necessity, and with the approval of Pope Leo XIII, Fr. Castelli planned and started a Collegio in Rome for alumni who were candidates for the Oratorian life. It was an undertaking that cost him not only immense sacrifices, but also the suffering of calumny from confreres who could not understand his zeal.

There were even worse sufferings to endure, beginning in 1895, when he was working toward a worthy and fruitful celebration of the third centenary of the death of Philip. These came from his own family and he found himself having to leave the House in Rome. He accepted the invitation of the Bishop of Cava de' Terreni who proposed that he found a new Congregation in that ancient city, the seat of a celebrated though abandoned Marian shrine.

On last day of 1895 he arrived at Cava, and with renewed dedication recommenced his apostolic mission, which had always earned him the esteem and devotion of many. An aura of holiness surrounded him wherever he went to work. The deep humility of this Servant of God made it very difficult for him to endure the fame the people accorded him; certainly this was not extraneous to his repeated decision to leave one place for another. The Congregation at Cava was canonically erected on October 16, 1900; Fr. Castelli exercised his apostolate as usual among the poor and the sick, the altar boys, the young, the priests and religious. Surrounded by the reputation of holiness and greeted as a "worker of miracles"—"miracles" resulting from his prayers—Fr. Castelli also left Cava for a while, but returned in obedience to the invitation of the Bishop and of his confreres.

He continued to grow in interior perfection throughout his life—sustained by humility, constant union with God, prayer and mortification. He radiated constant and sincere obedience to the Bishops with whom he labored, as well as his filial devotion to the Pope. He had enormous devotion to the Church, and within this burned his intense love for the Oratory.

He died at Cava de' Terreni July 21, 1926, and his body rests under the gaze of Mary, in the shrine to which he had restored splendor and vitality. By the time of the first anniversary of his death the usual informative process for the introduction of the cause for beatification had begun, and collected a very great number of useful testimonies.

In 1931, on the occasion of the translation of the body of this Servant of God from the city cemetery to the shrine, the Provosts of the Italian Congregations gathered in Olmo. There, in the shadow of Mary and Fr. Castelli, they made the important decisions that led to the birth of the Confederation of the Oratory.

That meeting of the Provosts at Cava and the devotion with which they wanted to carry the coffin of their holy confrere rendered justice to a true disciple of St. Philip Neri who by then contemplated history from heaven.

9. IN THE SECULAR ORATORY

Through more than four centuries, there have been many Saints, Blesseds, and Servants of God who in some way have been in direct contact with the apostolic activity carried out by the Congregations through the Secular Oratory. Some have already been mentioned. We limit ourselves here to citing just one whose cause for beatification has recently been introduced by the Archdiocese of Barcelona. The great Catalan architect Antoni Gaudí (1852–1926), a brother of the local Secular Oratory,[90] died following an accident on June 10 while he was on his way to the evening exercises at the Oratory. The relationship that Gaudí had with the Barcelona Oratory is recorded by P. F. Colas[91] in a brief study rich in bibliography. In particular it treats the relationship of Antoni Gaudí with Fr. Augusti Mas, his confessor and spiritual director; it also speaks of the surprising resemblance between the face of St. Philip Neri and that of Gaudí. This likeness, painted by Joan Llimona, is preserved in two precious canvases at the Oratory. Llimona was a member, like Gaudí, of the Cercle Artistic de Sant Lluc. The Oratorian Fr. Lluis Maria de Valls was spiritual director of the group. Gaudí was an eclectic genius, totally singular, who was universally known for his architectural work, and especially for the *Sagra Familia*. He was less known for his witness to the faith. He was known for being religious, but his faith went far beyond this. Cardinal Ricard M. Carles in announcing that his cause was being introduced spoke of his "high spirituality," which led him to live "until his death a highly mystical life, comparable to that of John of the Cross."[92] The Association that has been promoting his cause for beatification since 1994 is gathering testimonies. Among these, conversions to Catholicism stand out, including the very recent conversion of the Japanese sculptor Etsuro Sotto from Shintoism to Catholicism through his study of Gaudí.

CHAPTER VI

The Popes Have Said of St. Philip: From Leo XIII to John Paul II

1. POPE LEO XIII

On the occasion of the death of Pope Leo, universally mourned for the extraordinary greatness of his long Pontificate, the journal *San Filippo Neri, Monitore delle Congregazioni dell'Oratorio* [*St. Philip Neri, Guide of the Congregations of the Oratory*] wrote:

> In addition to these reasons, which make the memory of Leo XIII dear and venerable to everyone, there are others that are special to us who are sons of St. Philip. We can even make it our boast: he loved us with a very tender love and benefited and honored our Congregation. I am not speaking of certain acts of beneficence shown to us from the beginning of his Pontificate, pledges surely of his paternal affection, and first of all he deigned to raise two of our confreres to the cardinalate, John Henry Newman in 1879 and Alfonso Capecelatro in 1885, elevation that renewed the golden age of St. Philip. That age saw Baronio and Tarugi invested with the same honor, and in fact went beyond it, since in the last Consistory [1903] he named a third Oratorian to the College of Cardinals, Mons. Herrero y Espinoza de los Monteros, Archbishop of Valenza. It was the first time in the history of the Congregation that three new cardinals have been named during the same Pontificate. But his kindnesses did not stop here, but rose to a sublime level. Decreeing that the two Venerables Ancina and Grassi would be raised to the dignity of the altar, he satisfied the desire that the Oratorian Family had nurtured for a long time, seemingly in vain, and enriched it with a luster in comparison to which earthly honors are nothing. And when in 1895,

he had the opportunity of being alone with those of our confreres who had gone to Rome for the centenary festivities of St. Philip, he had extremely warm words of commendation for the renewal of the Institute, and for the Oratorians' labors and good will that had brought it about. His words then of two years later, in 1897, still echo sweetly in the hearts of those who heard them, when he manifested his will that he himself take a hand in the restoration of the Oratory.... What he had in mind was to found a Collegio in which a certain number of young men would be educated, at his expense, so that once they were priests they would revivify the dying Oratorian Congregations. The Oratory would thus be enabled to continue in the hard-working and beneficent life that it had in the preceding centuries. Nor was this only words: in 1900 he founded the Collegio in Perugia, chosen for the fine studies that flourished there, trusting for its growth in our cooperation. And that he continued to desire a general restoration was evident on June 5 and 6 of last year, when, having the opportunity to speak again of his work, he encouraged it again with expressions of tender affection. With his letter of July 2, the day before he fell ill, he announced his last offering.... His name will forever be conjoined with that of St. Philip since, as one founded the Congregation, the other desired to restore it. If he did not live to see that happen, Oh, may Heaven turn its gaze down upon it and inspire His Successor to bring to conclusion the work he began; may he inspire all the sons of St. Philip with sincere love for their Institute, uniformity of thought and feeling, in order that, conjoined by true charity, they may put into effect Philip's great ideals, and may we see, as he desired, the Oratory returned to its ancient luster of learning and sanctity.[1]

From the Brief for the Third Centenary of the Death of St. Philip

When we recall the singular virtues of St. Philip Neri, this of itself raises the mind and transports it sweetly to the love of God. Doctrine conjoined with innocence of life, ardent zeal for spreading the faith, limitless charity to the poor, all the highest virtues shone most admirably in him. From his seat of discussion in the community to the confessional, from his private discourses to his public exhortations, he worked to lead many persons along the path of virtue. In the hospitals, in the prisons, in the churches and on the streets he gave illustrious example of his apostolate. He enjoyed familiarity with the learned and the important figures of his time, but he was also moved by the love of humility to embrace the foolishness of the Cross and to despise the fallen things of this earth. He was assiduous in this, and in his charity he worked industriously among the poor who asked for alms, and the needy who thronged around the gates of St. Peter's.

The Congregation of Secular priests of the Oratory, which has acquired so much merit in the history of Christianity by following the norms of their founder, is very much dedicated to the formation of the young. This began with St. Philip, who was the first to lead the young people of Rome in devout pilgrimage, wisely organized, to the seven major basilicas of Rome. In addition, well knowing that sacred music elevates souls to piety, he had music written for the purpose, compositions which were later called oratorios. In this way, musical settings of poetry functioned to turn the minds of the faithful to virtue. He also visited the Cemeteries of the Martyrs, which were in ruins and nearly forgotten. And finally by his exhortations, he induced Cesare Baronio to write the huge set of volumes called the Annales Eccesiastici.

Who is there who does not know how much Rome owes to Philip?[2]

Motu Proprio Eximiis in Ecclesiam

For the highest merit with regard to the Church the name of Philip Neri shines, and will always shine brightly. He in fact is one of those men whom God made to emerge in the sixteenth century out of His merciful Providence. Both by their example of holy lives, and by founding fruitful and lasting Institutes, they helped zealously to heal the wounds suffered by the faith and by the practice of Christian life. Rome provided St. Philip large scope for his priestly zeal, and he worked there tirelessly until advanced old age with marvelous fruits. He certainly merited the title Apostle of Rome; and with good reason, on the occasion of the third centenary of his blessed death Rome paid him the tribute of solemn and grateful honors.

Although he embraced every form of piety and charity, St. Philip distinguished himself for his singular care for teaching the young and for forming the Clergy in the school of good example. These two things stand out as particularly felicitous in his founding the Congregation of the Priests of the Oratory. It was a place of preparation in solid virtue and doctrine, which earned for its Founder, while he was still living, the great favor of Popes, who bestowed on him various benefits and well-deserved approval. The Houses multiplied, and it is well known what an elect group of priests and what abundance of goodness have flowed from them down to our day.

Thinking of all of this, we feel sorrow in seeing the decline in number and vigor of the Oratorian sodality in many cities of Italy, because of the pernicious laws of suppression of the religious Orders. Therefore, since we have always had special benevolence for the Oratory, we have decided to give them particular attention, as we have done for other religious Orders. To this end we have purchased at our expense a rather large house in Perugia, near the Church of Father St. Philip. We have destined it for the education of chosen clerics for the Institute, so that through a good formation they may become worthy laborers. This will be to the advantage and honor of the Oratory and the good of souls, especially in this time that is not much different from that in which the Congregation arose. We trust that our intentions and efforts will meet with the desired success, with the favor of God and with the Provident care which he will exercise over the College together with Father St. Philip, and his illustrious disciple Antonio Grassi, on whom we are pleased to have conferred in solemn rites the dignity of the altar and the honors of the heavenly Blessed in this same most happy day.[3]

A Letter of Cardinal Alfonso Capecelatro

We give here a Letter of Cardinal Alfonso Capecelatro because it is closely connected with Pope Leo XIII's work for the Oratory. The letter was written *Ad omnes Praepositos Congr. Oratorii*, and is part of the Acta of the Convegno, which some improperly call the First Congress. Pope Leo desired that all the Provosts present in Rome for the third Centenary of Philip meet together under the presidency of His Eminence Capecelatro.[4]

Reverend Father and Brother most dear in the Lord,

His Holiness Leo XIII, most beloved of our Institute, in the Audience and conversation that he deigned to grant to me and to other members of the Oratory last June 4, congratulated us on the celebrations of the third Centenary of the pious death of St. Philip Neri, and hoped for great spiritual fruits from it. He then turned his heart to the Congregations of our Institute and the present situation, principally in Italy. Moved by paternal benevolence toward our Institute and knowing the intention of many of our confreres, he desired that the Fathers present in Rome in that circumstance meet and under my presidency discuss especially the criteria on the base of which the fraternal bonds among our Congregations might receive be reinvigorated. In so doing, the Rule would always be followed, especially where it establishes that each House governs itself and is never subject to any other. The High Pontiff desired also that the decisions made be communicated to all the Congregations of the Oratory, in order that they might confirm them by their own vote, and send a summary of their observations, and a record of any decision that they think might be better.

You will find included here, Reverend Father, the greater part of the Acts of this Convegno.

I ask you to respond as soon as you can, sending to me the approval and the observations of your Community. And I will present your responses and all the others to the Holy Father.

St. Philip Neri, who merited the title of the great apostle of charity, will confirm with his powerful intercession the projects of his sons, which proceed from charity and are directed toward charity.

I beg you to accept, dearest Brother, this service that I must complete, and I embrace you and all the members of the Oratory from my heart.

Given at Capua, from the Archbishop's palace, on the Feast of the Visitation of the Blessed Virgin Mary, in the year 1895.

Your most affectionate servant,
✠ Alfonso Capecelatro, Archbishop of Capua,
of the Congregation of the Oratory

There follow the Acts:

On June 5, 1895, at 9:30 am, in Rome, at No. 8 via Santa Basilica at the Sisters of the Holy Cross, where there resides His Eminence Most Reverend Alfonso Capecelatro of the Congregation of the Oratory of Naples, Priest Cardinal Capecelatro, Apostolic Librarian, Archbishop of Capua.

By the will and order of the high Pontiff Leo III there gathered all the Provosts and members of the Oratory of St. Philip Neri present in Rome in the occasion of the third anniversary of the pious death of the saint in the presence of His Eminence the Cardinal.

Those present:

1. His Eminence Cardinal Capecelatro, President;
2. Fr. Giovan Carlo Scaramucci, Provost of the Congregation of Rome;
3. Fr. Generoso Calenzio, of the same Congregation, whom His Eminence chose as Secretary;
4. Fr. Giuseppe Lais, of the Congregation of Rome;
5. Fr. Giulio Castelli, of the Congregation of Rome;
6. Fr. Vitaliano Confidati, of the Congregation of Rome;
7. Fr. Vincenzo Rossi, of the Congregation of Rome;
8. Fr. Francesco Cosma y Mundet, Provost of the Congregation of Barcellona;

9. Fr. Giov. Battista Porta, of the Congregation of Tudela in Navarra;
10. Fr. Giuseppe Auba, of the Congregation of Palma de Mallorca;
11. Fr. Giuseppe M. Bartolini, of the Congregation of Bevagna in Umbria;
12. Fr. Claudio Petiva, of the Congregation of Biella;
13. Fr. Giov. Battista Polverini, of the Congregation of Gradoli;
14. Fr. Giov. Battista Arista, of the Congregation of Acireale, delegate of the Provost;
15. Fr. Paolo Leotta, of the same Congregation;
16. Fr. Michele Savona, of the same Congregation.

After the invocation to the Holy Spirit His Eminence the Cardinal began to speak, reminding all present what had to be done to save the very life of the Institute. It was especially important that all the substantial parts of the Rule must be faithfully observed and must not, for any reason, be changed. Among these, and of particular importance, is the prescription that each House must maintain itself and depend for nothing on the other Houses of the Oratory.

This must not, however, stand in the way of the fact that the Houses are closely linked by bonds of fraternal charity, and thus they may help one another as best they can. This is especially true at this moment when a number of Houses have so few members, and other Houses are falling into the same condition.

On the basis of these considerations, the Cardinal proposed certain criteria, or paths, by means of which our Congregations, while preserving their autonomy, might regain their strength, and do this in such a way that others may not die in the future, as has so unhappily occurred in the past.

All of these elements, together with the observations made by the other Fathers, were examined and sifted and approved, everyone being of one mind.

This is what is proposed:

1. The union of privileges. Thus all the Congregations of the Institute will participate in the same privileges as the firstborn Roman Congregation.

2. The union of prayers and intercessions for deceased members. When any member dies, priest or lay, an announcement is sent to the other Congregations by means of a printed note in which the offices of the deceased and his contributions to our Institute are briefly listed. Each Congregation, as soon as it receives the announcement, will celebrate a Mass and recite at least one Rosary as intercessions of the person who has died.

3. The union of wills and of proposals. For this it is necessary that each House know the situation and the works of the other Houses of the Institute. To this end, it would be very useful if, in the letters that we are accustomed to send to one another at Christmas, for this first year if we could give an overview of our own Houses, which then would be updated every year.

4. The union of hospitality. No House ever denies one month's hospitality to any member, either gratis if the financial condition of the House permits it, or at minimum cost, to be established by the Provost of the House offering hospitality and by the Deputies.

5. The union of reciprocal help, in money, favors of various kinds, in works depending on the condition and needs of each House, just as brothers would do who recognize a common Father. Such help could extend to the sending of a brother from a numerous House to a needy House for a definite period of time. The brother who is sent retains all the rights and privileges he has in his own Congregation.

6. When a House of the Oratory must close for lack of members, a request must be sent to the Holy Father in order to obtain the patrimony of land, money, and goods. These holdings are given to another House of the same nation or province, for its temporary use, which has, in the judgment of the Holy Father, greater need of them. If the House to which they originally belonged should return to its previous state, the goods are returned to that Congregation.

7. If the church of the said Congregation is a parish church, it is necessary to ask the Ordinary of the place to nominate meanwhile an *economo curato ad nutum*, a temporary curate, which would al-

low other Congregations of the Oratory to offer a member capable of caring for the Parish.

8. The union of the cultural activity of the Congregations. Each Congregation must make known to the other Congregations all the intellectual work produced by its own members. A sample copy, at minimum price, should be offered. Sometimes it may be proposed that a work be translated into other languages.

9. It would be of no little usefulness to have from time to time a Convention, a gathering, of Oratorians in Rome, since this is the first community and the body of St. Philip is conserved there. The purpose would be to know the Founder and his Institute better, to strengthen the mutual charity among the Congregations, and also to understand the needs of each House and propose remedies for these problems.

10. The Collegio for students, erected in Rome in Via Giulia 163, is only a residence (*Pensionato*) designed to form young people in the spirit of St. Philip. Each Congregation is free, therefore, to accept these young men or not, if they wish to be aggregated to the Congregations. The Roman Congregation certainly approves this institution, and in fact looks after it, but does not assume responsibility for it and does not administer it. It is desirable that all the Oratorian Congregations help, according to their means, with this work, which is very important and will be of great usefulness to our Institute, and also is in need of a great infusion of money. These young men must participate in all of the prayers and devout practices of the Oratory at the Chiesa Nuova. They must form their minds in the virtues on the model of St. Philip. And they must follow constantly the manner of life of our Institute. If other Congregations should want to begin their own houses of formation or Oratorian seminaries following the model of the Roman *Pensionato*, they will surely do a good work and know that they are worthy of great praise.

2. POPE BENEDICT XV

Speaking of this Pope, Fr. Cesare Nanni, the Representative of the Oratorian Congregations to the Holy See said:

> We know that the immortal Pontiff Benedict XV inserted into the Code of Canon Law which he promulgated the lively desire that the secular Clergy return to the manner of life of apostolic times, and live united in communities (can. 234). He also pointed frequently to our glorious Patriarch St. Philip, as his Predecessors had done, not only as the perfect model of a priest, but the one who restored that most perfect method of priestly life.... Who does not discern in the quoted canon a clear allusion to our Institute and evidence of the papal solicitude for its conservation? Whoever reads: "consuetudo vitae communis laudando est, eaque, ubi viget, quantum fieri potest servanda," must think immediately of our Congregations.... In any case, the paternal interest of our Holy Father Benedict XV for the Oratorian Congregations is to be understood in practical, efficacious, and lasting terms. He studied deeply and admirably the nature and needs of these organisms, which Providence had so well devised. His investigating eye saw both the immense reserve of still fresh energies in these communities, and also their slow but progressive weakening, including the danger of a true disintegration.... Benedict was of a reconciling habit of mind, but also energetic. Having discerned the sickness, he quickly applied the remedy: exactly the one that others had thought of but not adequately pondered: the union, except for their characteristic autonomy, of the single Congregations.[5]

Benedict XV began the series of the Oratorian Congresses, convoked by the Apostolic See, in order that the Provosts would begin to meet to find new solutions to the persistent problems. The first in 1918 and the second in 1921 were celebrated under the Pontificate of this great Pope. We give one of his writings from the last months of his life.

Letter for the Third Centenary of the Canonization of St. Philip

The program for the celebration of the anniversary of the death of St. Philip seems to us most opportune, given as it is more to events and works to encourage and promote Christian faith and virtues on the model of St. Philip, rather than through the pomp of festivities.

We would like to hope that in this manner the mild figure of the Apostle of Rome might shine with new light. He knew how to join the most austere sanctity to detached amiability and the festive smile. We hope that above all the fervor of young people may be enlivened, that same that Philip aroused when he took them along on visits to sick in the hospitals, to the catechism of youth and workers, and to the tombs of Martyrs. In those moments when someone would hope for earthly honors for him, he would look to Heaven and respond: "Paradiso, paradiso!"[6]

3. POPE PIUS XI

Memories and personal affections, which he recalled during the Audiences which he gave to the Oratorians, linked Pope Pius XI to St. Philip. It was his decision to institute the Apostolic Visit, which became the first step toward the creation of the Institutum Oratorii. This has given him a special place in the history of the Oratory.

Letter for the Third Centenary of the Canonization of St. Philip

If for the celebrations of the third centenary of the canonization of St. Philip our immortal Predecessor Benedict XV of honored memory directed an opportune word of encouragement and praise, it is not less proper that similar sentiments of paternal satisfaction and legitimate joy should be expressed by us, transferred by divine Providence to this Cathedral of St. Peter from the seat of St. Charles and of Federico Borromeo. As both of these were linked by the most tender bonds with the Apostle of Rome, so we also come to have particular veneration for the same Apostle. Thus, no less than our lamented Pontiff, called by the Lord to solemnize this auspi-

> cious anniversary among the rejoicing angels, we are glad for this pious and happy third anniversary, and we offer congratulations not only to the Roman Committee for the program for the solemn and dignified commemoration, but also for the zeal in emphasizing the humble and great figure of the glorious Teacher and Father of the youth of Rome. In him the severe and rigorous austerity of the ascetic, and sweet, tender amiability and angelic charity were conjoined in the most admirable and almost supernatural harmony. We gladly predict, therefore, that the coming celebrations, gathering the Roman populace and especially the bold crowds of Catholic young people around the urn of the Saint, suffused with new glory and new splendor, will enjoy the efficacious intercessions of this great friend of God and of humanity. May they be a barrier to the spread of this corruption and lack of faith that the scourge of war has left as its legacy. May they be for a humanity that finds itself in such tribulations the dawn of that true and lasting peace that will rain down upon a truly and entirely Christian life.[7]

4. POPE PIUS XII

Eugenio Pacelli had a very special devotion to St. Philip from the time he was a boy, when, under the guidance of the Fathers of the Vallicella he attended the Collegio Vallecelliano, instituted for spiritual formation and preparation for liturgical service at the Chiesa Nuova. When he was a young priest he was a faithful celebrant and confessor at the Vallicella, until higher and higher offices no longer permitted him to do so. When he became Pope he showed his benevolence to the Fathers of the Oratory, and gave permission for the International Oratorian College to bear his name. He received with paternal amiability the participants at the Congresses of 1942 and 1948, and was pleased with the celebrations for the centenary of Newman's conversion, for the Pentecost of Fire of St. Philip, for the priestly consecration of the Saint, and every year he blessed the participants of the Visit to the Seven Churches, in which he sometimes participated when he was Cardinal. In the Audience of April 12, 1943 he approved the revised Constitutions and the General Statutes of the Institutum Oratorii. Between 1946 and 1953 he showed his love for the Oratory, helping the Congregation of Rome with the construction of the complex at Garbatella. In 1958, now at the end of his days, he still wanted to receive the General Congress of the Institute at Castel Gandolfo in the early days of October. He gave them the address below that follows his Letter for the fourth anniversary of Philip's "Pentecost".

Letter for the Fourth Centenary of the "Pentecost" of St. Philip

The imminent Fourth Centenary of the singular charism of charity that the Apostle of Rome was granted by God with visible dilation of his heart, brings a memory and an unexpected comfort, coming from the tender piety which we nourished from infancy for the dear St. Philip Neri. It pleased the divine Goodness to confirm in a tangible way the holiness of His servant and in particular his impetus of love for his divine Master Jesus, through his Mother Mary and for the good of souls. The solemn recognition of this new prodigy comes at an exceedingly opportune moment, when men, often Christians, have almost forgotten how this supreme love assumes in itself all of religion and all of civilization. It is therefore the sure guarantor of the happiness of the nations and of all men.

Therefore, we are present with lively satisfaction of mind to this celebration, and in spirit to this lovable Saint, the place where he lived and the witness of his admirable deeds and his seraphic love. But our thoughts go above all to the blind fury of hatred unleashed by the scourge of war. And to the intercession of Philip we ask that Rome and all men may be spared further human affliction, evil, sorrows, and pain, and that to everyone it may be granted to return as brothers under the sign of Jesus Christ, Prince of Peace.

In this sense, we renew to the Protector of our earliest infancy the expression of our affection and our gratitude....[8]

Discourse to the General Congress of the Oratory, 1958

From the time of our youth, we began to love your Institute in a particular way; and in the church which Alma Rome has entrusted to your care, we have exercised for the faithful some part of our priestly ministry.

Today, while we have the opportunity to see you here with us, and to speak to you with paternal concern, it seems to us that that ministry of singular charity is in some way renewed.

Desiring, as you yourselves desire, to encourage you to continue in the proper way your initiatives and your work, we recommend one thing to you above all. We desire that you recommit yourselves zealously to recovering, so to speak, that apostolic form of life, in which your founder St. Philip Neri was resplendent.

He most certainly can say to you from Heaven, as an exhortation, the word of the Apostle Paul: "I urge you, then, be imitators of me…and of my ways in Christ" (1 Cor. 4:16–17); "Brethren, join in imitating me, and mark those who so live as you have an example in us" (Phil. 3:17).[9]

Have a tender devotion to God, to His Most Holy Mother and all the Saints, which are renewed in prayer and meditation of celestial things; be ardent and at the same time happy and joyous; commit yourselves to the pursuit of virtue, not only for yourselves but for the sake of your neighbor, and above all for priests; do acts and works of voluntary penance to expiate your own sins and the sins of others, and to obtain divine grace for yourselves and for others; exercise Christian charity to the poor, by which both material and above all spiritual comfort will be afforded to those who live in doubt, in travail, and in anguish. All of these things, my dearest sons, which shone with such singular light in the life of your Holy Founder, are proposed today for your imitation.

You know how much our world today is in need of Christian virtues and of holiness more than anything else. You are called to commit yourselves to work, by means of the gifts you yourselves have received, so as to procure salvation for yourselves and for others.

Nothing in this undertaking will seem too arduous, if you work with the grace of God; and you will move with quick eagerness to the new projects which this age demands, but you will do this with the prudence necessary to be able to bring your holy work to happy fruition.

We recommend to your care especially the young people.

You know very well how important that apostolate was to your Founder. You know how he dedicated himself to seeing that the young people, hope of the future, were turned away from vice and sordidness, and through counsel, persuasion, and above all the example of holiness of life, they were able to maintain their Christian innocence, and moral integrity, or even if this had been wretchedly lost, they were led through penance and prayer to recover what they had lost.

Following Philip's footsteps with one mind and heart, you will labor tirelessly in this apostolate; and for this work you will offer supplications ceaselessly to God.

The Christian education of the young, that is giving them proper guidance for their souls, is such an arduous and difficult task that with reason Gregory of Nazianzen called "the art of arts, the science of sciences" (cf. Orat. II, *PG* 35:426).

At the beginning, therefore, it is necessary to implore divine help and illumination; then do everything that might bring the work to fruition, for example, giving counsel to individuals, exhortations, talks and teaching given to everyone, magazines and other publications from which emanate the sweet odor and flavor of Christian doctrine, and today especially physical activity, games, and amusements that are healthy and attract the young.

These things, my dear sons, we recommend to you insistently. We expect them out of your generous spirit of commitment, and we invoke upon you the bountiful help of divine grace.

As a pledge of our good wishes and our paternal benevolence, We gladly impart our Apostolic Blessing to you all.[10]

5. POPE JOHN PAUL II[11]

There are no documents on St. Philip written by two Pontiffs who nevertheless nourished devotion to and esteem for the Saint and his work. Pope John XXIII,[12] beatified in 2000, loved the Oratory from his youth, and knew it primarily through the figure of St. Charles Borromeo and Baronio. He studied Borromeo's report on Pastoral Visits, and Baronio's historiographical work; he wrote his thesis on Baronio's work, and took from it his Episcopal motto, "Obedience and peace," which became then the motto of his Pontificate. In the years when he was first in Rome, Mons. Angelo Roncalli became a member of the Secular Oratory. He visited the urn of St. Philip at the Vallicella the day before the conclave which elected him Pope, and he wanted to remain in recollection also at the tomb of Venerable Cesare Baronio. It had been ninety years since the last visit of a Pope, Pius IX before the historic events of 1870, when Pope John XXIII returned to the Vallicella for a brief devotional visit, May 26, 1960, to the great surprise of the Fathers, because he happened to be passing in front of the Chiesa Nuova.

The *Giornale dell'anima* carried this beautiful prayer to St. Philip, which came rising out the St. Pope John's heart: "O my good Father, without speaking you understand me. The time is approaching: where in me is that copy of yourself? Ah, that I would really understand the true principles of your mystical school for the cultivation of the spirit, and I would profit from them: humility and love. Seriousness, seriousness, blessed Philip, and holy joy, pure, and the fertile zeal for great works. Blessed Philip, help me to prepare my house; bring my frozen heart to yours which burns with love, of the Holy Spirit. *Fac ut ardeat cor meum.* Amen."

Pope Paul VI,[13] who also visited the Chiesa Nuova, in 1973, and the urn of St. Philip, on the occasion of the closing of the Octave of prayer for Christian unity, witnessed to his great love for the Oratory in his constant friendship with great figures of the Congregation of Brescia. Among these were Fr. Giulio Bevilacqua, who was made Cardinal in 1965. The Pope assigned to him the *diaconia* of San Girolamo della Carità, sending to him as a gift for his taking possession of the church a cage of canaries, a memory of the joyful simplicity of Fr. Philip; Fr. Paolo Caresana, his spiritual master from his youth, of whom Pope Paul VI wrote when he died: "The holy death of our Venerated Fr. Paolo Caresana evokes in our memory how much we ourselves owe to his spiritual assistance and to his cordial friendship"; Fr. Carlo Manziana, who was named the Bishop of Crema and to whom Paul VI spoke very affectionate words and expressions of great esteem; Fr. Ottorino Marcolini, to whom he entrusted, among other things, the construction of the neighborhood of Acila for those living in emergency housing on the outskirts of Rome, during the Holy Year 1975. The Congregation of Rome, too, received from him many signs of esteem and benevolence from Mons. Giovanni Batista Montini: he often exercised his priestly ministry at the Vallicella, and desired to celebrate there his twenty-fifth anniversary of priestly ordination. As a remembrance of this occasion he had the Sala Rossa restored, the room where so many relics of St. Philip Neri are kept.

Pope John Paul II knew the Oratory prior to his election as Pope, principally through his contacts with Polish Oratorians, most especially with Fr. Oldgier Kokocinski, a noted preacher to clergy retreats and missions for the people before he was named Provost of the Vallicella. This Pope has given various precious documents to the Oratory. Among these is the following, of particular importance, and which we offer first, a Discourse given to the entire Oratorian Family, Priests of the Congregations and Laypersons of the Secular Oratory, who were received in a special Audience on the occasion of the General Congress in the Jubilee Year 2000.

Address to the Confederation of the Oratory, October 5, 2000

Dear Oratorian Priests and Lay People!

1. I am pleased to extend a cordial welcome to each of you, participants in the General Congress of the Confederation of the Oratory of St. Philip Neri. With this visit you wanted to renew your sincere devotion to the Vicar of Christ and full adherence to his

Magisterium, in the spirit of your founder, who loved the Church with his whole being and left you his unreserved fidelity to the See of Peter as a legacy.

As I affectionately greet Fr. Antonio Rios Chavez, the Delegate to the Apostolic See, I extend my cordial wishes to each of the congregations represented here at your General Congress and express my deep gratitude to them for the good they do, delighted as I am with the Oratory's growth in various parts of the world.

2. At the recent General Congresses your confederation, established by the Apostolic See to unite the individual Congregations of the Oratory in a bond of charity and mutual help, has undertaken to revise your constitutions along the lines suggested by the Church at the Second Vatican Council. At the dawn of the third Christian millennium your meeting plans to revisit, from a primarily pastoral standpoint, the sources of the spiritual movement that traces its origin to St. Philip Neri, in order to respond faithfully to its perennial mission: to lead man to encounter Jesus Christ, "the Way, the Truth, and the Life," truly present in the Church and the "contemporary" of every person.

This encounter, lived and proposed by St. Philip Neri in an original and engaging way, makes us new persons in the mystery of Grace and instills in the soul that "Christian joy" which is the "hundredfold" given by Christ to those who welcome him into their lives. To encourage a personal meeting with Christ is also the fundamental "missionary method" of the Oratory. It consists in "speaking to the heart" of men and women in order to lead them to an experience of the divine Master that can transform lives. This is achieved especially by showing the beauty of such an encounter, which gives life its full meaning. Those who are "distant" must not be offered a theoretical proclamation, but the possibility of a truly renewed and thus joyful life.

This is the great legacy you received from your Father Philip! This pastoral way is always valid, because it belongs to the perennial Christian experience! I hope that this work of revisiting the sources of St. Philip's spirituality and work will instill in each congregation a renewed awareness of the value and timeliness of your founder's "missionary method" and make a significant contribution to the task of the "new evangelization."

3. The Oratory was born of the faith and genius of St. Philip Neri, who knew how to combine in a harmonious synthesis the charismatic dimension and full communion with the Pastors of the Church. In the Rome of his time he also met the spiritual and material needs of young people with deep wisdom, exemplifying the joyful dimension of faith to the point that he was considered "the prophet of Christian joy." From the beginning, the Oratory has been a feature of your congregation, which takes its name from it, as the Bull *Copiosus in misericordia* by which Gregory XIII established it in the Holy Year of 1575 recalls. Born with the participation of secular priests, who came from the early experience of the Oratory, and put at its service, your congregation must continue to focus its concerns on this worthy institution with its original intentions, method, and style, which are always adaptable to the needs of the times.

As the *Spiritual Path* approved at the General Congress in 1994 recalls: "The specific purpose and mission of the Congregation of the Oratory" is to bring "forth the creation and growth of authentic Christian communities, which are the light and salt of the earth."[14] These are presented in the very first articles of your Constitutions as a fraternal union of the faithful who, following in the footsteps of St. Philip Neri, set as their goal what he taught and did, thus becoming "one heart and soul" (Acts 4:32). They draw their inspiration from your Father Philip's example of simple family prayer meetings and spiritual talks with penitents and friends. In this perspective, the Oratory sees its identity in "the practice of discussing the Word of God together in a familiar way, as mental and vocal prayer, in order to foster a contemplative spirit in the faithful, as at a school, and the love of divine things."

I hope that the Oratory, by serving people with joy and simplicity of heart, will exemplify and spread this spiritual method in a more and more attractive and effective way. Thus it will be able to offer a consistent and incisive witness by fully living the fervour of its origins and offering our contemporaries an experience of fraternal life that is principally based on accepting and living the reality of supernatural communion in Christ.

"Those who want something other than Christ do not know what they want; those who ask for something other than Christ do not know what they are asking for; those who work but not for Christ do not know what they are doing." Your holy founder's words reveal the ever valid criterion for every renewal of the Christian community, which consists in returning to Jesus Christ: to his word, to his presence, to the saving action which he accomplishes in the Church's sacraments. This commitment will lead priests to give priority to the ministry of Confession and the spiritual guidance of the faithful, as is your tradition, in order to respond fully to your charism and to the Church's expectations. Thus they will help the lay people who belong to the secular Oratories to understand the essential value of being *christifideles*, in the light of St. Philip's experience: regarding the laity, he anticipated ideas and methods that would prove fruitful in the life of the Church.

4. Your Congregations, faithful to the autonomy desired by your holy Founder, live in a way particularly linked to the needs of your local Churches and your local areas. But for the sake of your own Communities and your own members, you must not forget the importance of the fraternal bond with the other Congregations that make up the Confederation. It is through this bond that the characteristically autonomous Houses open themselves up to the gift of active charity. This is also the way the confederated Communities find help in growing in fidelity to the Oratorian charism.

Let each congregation devote special care to the initial and continuing formation of individuals and communities, in order to assimilate the ideal passed on by St. Philip and re-proposed by the Constitutions, for the sake of a growing spiritual vitality and effective apostolic presence.

In particular, I urge you to be guided by these values, especially in approaching the world of youth, which is full of promise despite the difficulties, and to feel that you have been especially sent to those who are "distant" but very close to the Saviour's Heart. In this regard, you will find great help in the traditional sensitivity of Oratorians to art and culture, which are particularly suitable ways to support a significant evangelizing presence.

May the Virgin Mary, "Mother and Foundress of the Oratory," be for each of you the model who constantly inspires you to receive the gift of the Spirit with complete docility and to proclaim the joy of Christ to your brothers and sisters.

With these wishes, as I entrust you to the heavenly intercession of St. Philip Neri, I impart a special Apostolic Blessing to each of you and to the whole Confederation of the Oratory.[15]

Homily Given in Santa Maria in Vallicella, 1979

Dear brothers and sisters!

I could not fail to come to this holy place, loved by the Romans, to venerate him who was called "the Apostle of Rome," St. Philip Neri, one of the patron saints of this beloved City.

My coming here was a duty, a need of my soul, and much longed-for! In this church, where the body of St. Philip Neri rests, I extend my most cordial greeting to the Oratorian Priests, his Confreres.

But then, with particular love, I greet you, the faithful, and in you I mean to reach all the faithful of Rome, city of St. Philip, whom he so much loved and benefited, and whose vivifying and sanctifying memory is still so much present.

You know that in the period when he lived in Rome, from 1534 onward, arriving as a poor and unknown pilgrim, to 1595, the year of his blessed death, St. Philip Neri had an immense love for Rome! For Rome he lived, worked, studied, suffered, prayed, loved, died! He had Rome in his mind and heart, in his worries and his projects and institutions, in his joys and even in his sorrows! For Rome St. Philip was a man of culture and charity, of study and organization, of teaching and of prayer; for Rome he became a holy priest, a tireless confessor, and ingenious teacher and a friend to all. In particular ways he was an expert counselor and delicate director of consciences. Popes and Cardinals, Bishops and Priests, princes and politicians, religious and artists came to him. He had a heart of a father and a friend, and illustrious personages confided in him, for example the Cardinal historian Cesare Baronio and the celebrated composer Palestrina, St. Charles Borromeo and St. Ignatius of Loyola and Cardinal Federico Borromeo.

But that small, poor room of his apartment was above all the goal of an immense multitude of simple, poor people, of those who were suffering or disinherited, those marginalized by the society, young men and youth who went to him in order to find counsel, pardon, peace, and material and spiritual encouragement. The beneficent activity of St. Philip was such, and so large, that the judiciary of Rome decreed that a chalice be given every year to his church, on the day of the anniversary of his death, as a sign of their veneration and gratitude.

He lived in a dramatic century, one that was inebriated by the discoveries of human ingenuity, and by classical and pagan art, but in radical crisis caused by this change of mentality. St. Philip, a man of deep faith and priestly fervor, genial and far-sighted, gifted himself with special charisms, knew how to maintain undiminished the deposit of truth that he had received, and he transmitted it entire and pure, living every part of it and announcing it without compromise.

For this reason, his message is always relevant and we must listen and follow his example.

"From the precious mine of his teachings and anecdotes about his life, always interesting and engrossing, we can draw some perspectives that are especially relevant for today's world.

1. *The humility of intelligence.* This is the first call of St. Philip, because there is a fundamental danger in the pride of intelligence. He saw this frighteningly evident in his autonomous and rebellious century, and thus he insisted on humility in reason and on interior

penitence. Intelligence is a gift from God that makes man resemble Him, but intelligence must accept its limits. Intelligence should reach for the necessary and absolute Principle that sustains the universe. It should recognize the historical proofs that demonstrate the divinity of Jesus Christ and the divine mission of the Church. Then, it should pause as it comes up against the Mystery of God, which, being infinite, always remains obscure in its nature and workings. Intelligence must accept the law of God, which is the law of love and salvation, and abandon itself trustfully to God's project, which is eternal and therefore goes beyond any human perspectives.

St. Philip insisted on this sense of humility in the presence of God. Bringing his hand to his forehead he would say: "Holiness lies in the breadth of three fingers!"—meaning that it depended substantially on the humility of the intelligence.

2. *Christian integrity.* This is the second teaching of St. Philip, which is always valid and relevant. With Christian wisdom he knew how to draw from the principles of faith the deep reasons of his activity and of his entire life. From this logic of faith was born spontaneously a way of life marked by joy, by trust, by spontaneity, by his healthy optimism, which is not banal and insensitive foolishness; it is rather a transcendent vision of history, an eschatological vision of human reality.

From this interior joy came his extraordinary apostolic strength and his fine and proverbial humor, for which he was called "the saint of joy" and his habitation "house of joyousness."

On this way of life, which was sweet and austere, joyous and committed, he founded the Oratory, which came to be spread throughout the world, and which among its merits was that of the development of music and of sacred song.

St. Paul wrote: "Rejoice in the Lord always! Again I will say, Rejoice! Let all men know your forbearance" (Phil. 4:4–5).

Such was St. Philip: man of joy and good nature. May Heaven grant that we all posses such joy that comes from a convinced and lived Christian faith.

3. *Pedagogy of Grace.* This is a third teaching of our Saint, more than ever relevant and necessary.

St. Philip respected fully every single personality, and built his "education program" on the reality of Grace, developing it in five principal lines: coming to know and to be sensitive to every single child and young person by means of patient and affectionate listening; enlightening the mind with the truths of the faith by means of reading and meditation; Marian and Eucharistic devotion; charity toward one's neighbor; play, in its most varied forms.

The world today has an extreme need for sensitive and well-prepared teachers, who will teach young people to overcome sadness and the sense of aloneness and failure of communication that troubles so many young people and leaves them despairing.

Like St. Philip, you too, parents and teachers, teach the young people "whatever is true, whatever is honorable, whatever is just, whatever is pure, whatever is lovely, whatever is gracious…excellent…worthy of praise" (Phil. 4:8).

Dearest Faithful of Rome! We can and must learn these things from our great Saint!

He speaks to each of us: *Cor ad cor loquitur* [Heart speaks to heart], as the great Cardinal Newman, converted from Anglicanism, said. After long and meticulous historical studies and after great interior suffering, he found himself constrained by the evidence to embrace Catholicism and to enter the Church of Rome. There he came to know the life and spirituality of St. Philip, and was sufficiently enamored of his depth, balance, and discretion that he desired to become an Oratorian priest. He founded the first Oratory in England and always followed St. Philip's example, calling him "my personal Father and Patron" and in the name of St. Philip he ended his most famous work, *Apologia pro vita sua*.

For us St. Philip continues to be "Father." Let us invoke him! Let us listen to him!

One of his most lovable characteristics was his tender love for Most Holy Mary, and often he invoked *Mater gratiae* with total and filial trust. He would say, full of tenderness for the Mother of Heaven: "This reason only should suffice to keep a faithful person glad, knowing he has the Virgin Mary with God, and that she prays for him" (*Vita di San Filippo Neri, Fiorentino*, written by Fr. Pietro Giacomo Bacci).

Let us listen to St. Philip Neri, convinced that he who loved Rome so much in his lifetime will continue to protect and love her children.

And now...let us promise, each of us personally in his own surroundings and in his own responsibilities, to live the Gospel with absolute fidelity, following the footsteps of St. Philip Neri.[16]

Letter for the Fourth Centenary of the Death of St. Philip, 1995

On the anniversary of the *dies natalis* of St. Philip Neri, Florentine by origin and Roman by adoption, I am happy to address myself to all of the Members of the Confederation of the Oratory, to remember the example of sanctity of your Founder, and in order to confirm in each of you your work of faith and labor of love and steadfastness of hope (cf. 1 Thess. 1:3).

1. The lovable figure of the "Saint of joy" still holds for us today intact that irresistible fascination that he exercised on everyone who approached him in order to learn and to experience the authentic sources of Christian joy.

Looking again at the biography of St. Philip, one is surprised and fascinated by the hilarious and relaxed way by which he knew how to teach, putting himself alongside everyone with fraternal patience and openness. St. Philip is known for the way that he expressed his teaching in brief, pungent phrases: "Be at peace, if you can." "Scruples and melancholy, get out of my house!" "Be humble and lowly." "The man who does not pray is an animal without reason." And, putting his hand to his forehead, "Holiness lies in the breadth of three fingers." Behind the wit of these and so many other "sayings" one can observe the keen and realistic knowledge that he was acquiring of human nature and the dynamics of grace. In these quick and concise teachings he was translating the experience of his long life and the wisdom of a heart where the Holy Spirit was dwelling. These aphorisms have become by now a sort of patrimony of wisdom for Christian spirituality.

2. St. Philip appears in the panorama of the Roman Renaissance as the "prophet of joy," who knew how to follow Jesus closely, and still insert himself actively into the civilization of his time, singularly comparable to that of our time in so many respects.

Humanism, setting itself against what it misunderstood as medieval darkness, concentrated on man and on his astounding intellectual and practical abilities. It rediscovered a joyous, naturalistic freshness, free of qualms and inhibitions. Man was presented almost like a pagan god, and came to occupy the position of absolute protagonist of his life. There was also a kind of revision of the moral Law with the aim of seeking and guaranteeing happiness.

St. Philip understood how this freedom and the yearning for joy appealed to the society of his time, but he undertook to demonstrate its true source, which he had identified in the message of the Gospels. It is the word of Christ that shows us the authentic face of man, unveiling the features that reveal him to be a beloved son of the Father, welcomed as brother by the Incarnate Word, and sanctified by the Holy Spirit. What leads to joy and happiness are the words of the Gospel and the commands of Christ. This is the truth proclaimed by St. Philip Neri to the young people he encountered in his daily apostolic work. His announcement of this truth was dictated by the intimate experience of God that came to him primarily through prayer. He went often to pray at night in the Catacombs of St. Sebastian, not only for solitude but also to be face to face with the witnesses of faith, with the desire to interrogate them—just as the learned men of the Renaissance wove colloquies with the Classical writers of antiquity. For both, from familiar knowledge of them came imitation, then emulation.

The Holy Spirit, during the vigil of Pentecost in 1544, gave to Philip a "heart of fire," and thus it is possible to perceive in him an allegory of the great and divine transformations accomplished in us in prayer. A rich and sure program of formation for joy, he teaches us, is nourished and upheld on a harmonious constellation of choices: assiduous prayer, frequent reception of the Eucharist, the rediscovery of the great value of the sacrament of Reconciliation, familiar and daily reading of the Word of God, the fruitful exercise of fraternal charity and service, and then devotion to the Madonna, model and true cause of our joy. How could we forget, apropos of this, St. Philip's wise and efficacious admonition: "My sons, be devoted to Mary: I know what I am saying! Be devoted to Mary!"

3. Qualifying as the "saint of joy" par excellence, St. Philip must also be recognized as the "Apostle of Rome," or better, as the "reformer of the Eternal City." He became so almost by a natural evolution and maturing of the choices he made under the illumination of Grace. He was really the light and salt of Rome, according to the word of the Gospel (cf. Matt. 5:13–16). He knew how to be "light" in that civilization that was certainly splendid, but often the light was only the oblique rays of paganism that graze the surface of things. In that social context Philip was obedient to Authority, extremely devoted to the deposit of Truth, and intrepid in announcing the Christian message. Thus he became a fountain of light for all.

He did not choose the solitary life. His ministry unfolded among ordinary people, and he undertook to be "salt" for all who encountered him. Like Jesus, he knew how to identify with stagnating human misery, with those in the noble houses, and with those he met in the narrow streets of Renaissance Rome. He was, from time to time, helper in the fashion of Simon of Cyrene, critical conscience, enlightened counselor, and smiling teacher.

For just this reason, it is not so much he who adopted Rome, but Rome that adopted him. For sixty years he lived in this City, which kept growing in number of saints. If Philip met and comforted sorrowing humanity in the streets, sustaining them with the charity of a wise and kindly word, he preferred to be in the Oratory, gathered together with his young people, gatherings of his own invention. He made them encounters of joy, a place of formative growth, a center of irradiation of art.

It was in the Oratory that St. Philip, in addition to cultivating a religious language both new and traditional, committed himself to reforming and elevating art, directing it to the service of God and of the Church. He was convinced that the beautiful leads to the good, and he drew into his formative design everything that was artistic. And he himself became a patron of different forms of artistic expression, promoting initiatives capable of leading others to the true and the good.

St. Philip's contribution to sacred music was exemplary and dynamic, pushing it beyond the rather fatuous entertainment of the time to become music that would restore the spirit. Through his lively encouragement, musicians and composers began the reform that would find its highest expression in Pier Luigi da Palestrina.

4. St. Philip, a man who was lovable and generous, a chaste and humble saint, an apostle both active and contemplative—may he remain the constant model for the Members of the Congregation of the Oratory! He entrusts to all the Oratorians a program and a way of life that still preserves today its singular relevance. The so-called "quadrilateral"—humility, charity, prayer, and joy—remains always an extremely solid basis on which to build the interior structure of one's spiritual life.

If they will follow the example of their Founder, the Oratorians will continue to play a significant role in the affairs of the Church. Therefore I exhort all the sons and daughters of St. Philip to be always faithful to their Oratorian vocation. Seek Christ, adhere to Him with perseverance, and become generous sowers of joy among the youth, who are so often tempted by infidelity and discouragement.

Nurturing these hopes for you, I desire to invoke the heavenly protection of St. Philip Neri, who is so dear to me, upon the entire Oratorian Community. I greet you most cordially, trusting that the centenary celebrations become the occasion for a stimulating rediscovery of the person and the work of this most unusual witness of Christ, who can still teach so much, at this end of the century, to Christians committed to the new evangelization.

Along with these fervent good wishes, I impart a special Apostolic Benediction to the Members of the Oratorian Confederation and to all who draw upon the spirituality of the Saint of joy.[17]

Homily Given in Santa Maria in Vallicella, 1995

1. During the vigil of his passion, at the Last Supper with the Apostles in which he instituted the Eucharist, the Lord spoke the words that we read in today's Gospel: "I do not pray for these only, but also for those who believe in me through their word, that they may all be one; even as thou, Father, art in me, and I in thee, that they also may be in us, so that the world may believe that thou hast sent me" (Jn. 17:20–21).

In the imminence of the Paschal events Jesus reveals openly the mystery of his divinity, that he and the Father are one: the Father is in the Son, and the Son is in the Father, in the divine unity. Becoming man, the Son has come into the world in order to attract men, and introduce them into this unity.

"O righteous Father," says Christ, "the world has not known thee, but I have known thee; and these know that thou hast sent me. I made known to them thy name, and I will make it known, that the love with which thou hast loved me may be in them, and I in them" (Jn. 17:25–26).

This love, poured into our hearts by the Holy Spirit, has the effect of making us participants in the life of God, life that Christ has come to bring us as a gift, precisely in order that we may participate in it. This participation in the divine life is sanctifying Grace, and it is the source of human holiness. The Gospel of this present Sunday asks us to become aware of this truth.

We unite ourselves today with the Church of Rome to remember the four-hundred-year anniversary of the death of St. Philip Neri. He belongs to those ranks of elect souls whose existence has always marked the life of the Eternal City. It is thanks to their contribution that there has been built up the "patrimony of sanctity" that has accumulated through the centuries and that is now linked indissolubly with the history of Rome.

2. At the height of the Renaissance, in that period when the learned and the artists searched for inspiration in the Classics, Philip Neri, Florentine by birth but Roman by adoption, perceived in an extraordinary way the call of the origins of Christianity. The itinerary he preferred to follow was the visit to the "Seven Churches." Above all, he loved to remain in prayer at the catacombs of St. Sebastian, which had not yet been explored. How providential for us, at the eve of the Great Jubilee of the year 2000, is this testimony of his! Philip invites us to draw our inspiration from the holy places of Christian Rome in order to imbue the city with the newness of the Gospel, which will allow us to live once again that joyous renewal of life that is the power of the Saints.

A typical characteristic of Philip Neri was a kind of constant enthusiasm, always wisely balanced, which sustained him during the Jubilee of 1550, when so many people came to see him. It also enabled him to give origin to the Oratory, "his true invention" (Apostolic Letter to the Oratorians, no. 3). His personal sanctity and his love for the Lord, which he knew how to infuse into persons and works, was the fruit of the Spirit who had inflamed his heart in the singular experience of the Pentecost of 1544. He knew how to care for and nourish this divine gift every day by intense prayer, including assiduous meditation on the Word of God and heartfelt devotion to the Madonna, and culminated in the celebration of the Eucharist.

3. His humble and vivacious person, mild and courageous, modest and witty, still today evokes immediate sympathy. I gladly propose him as a model for the Christians of Rome, both lay and priests. In particular, he is an example for all who embrace the service of the Gospel in the Church, above all, those who dedicate themselves to the care of young people. I am thinking of all the priests who direct parish and diocesan youth ministries, and I am

thinking most especially of St. Philip's followers and sons of the Oratorian Family.

The Congregation of the Oratory is summoned to continue over time the originality of its charism, to found new communities for this purpose and to incarnate its spirit into the varied situations of our time.

With respect to this, there is no doubt that the legacy of St. Philip is a resource of great value for the work of the new evangelization. The Church is committed to this in Rome and in Europe. More generally, however, St. Philip's legacy is for the entire People of God, called to spread joy and trust and to walk in faith and hope, responding faithfully to the universal call to holiness.

4. In the Gospel proclaimed today, Jesus prays for the unity that his followers will derive from the mystery of the Most Holy Trinity, that is, from the communion of the Father and the Son in the Holy Spirit. He invokes this unity for all believers: first for the Apostles, then for all the generations of those who will believe in him thanks to their words (cf: Jn. 17:23). He prays therefore also for our unity, and for the unity of the ages: "I in them and thou in me, that they may become perfectly one, so that the world may know that thou hast sent me and hast loved them even as thou hast loved me" (Jn. 17:23). It is just this love that is the source of unity: the Love which, in the Trinitarian mystery of God, is the Holy Spirit, which proceeds from the Father and the Son and is the sanctifying Breath that pervades man, making him, like the eternal Son-Word, the adopted son of God. The work of adoption extends to the community of the People of God, which has become a community through the action of the Holy Spirit. We need to ponder all of this especially this Sunday, when the Church is making its immediate preparation for the Solemnity of Pentecost, and attempts to remain spiritually gathered in the Upper Room, in prayer together with Mary, the Mother of Christ (cf: Acts 1:14). The Church prays that the Holy Spirit may descend upon us in a way that is consonant with our needs, and in proportion to the mission that she has received from Christ for all times and all generations.

5. The last words of the Book of Revelation are eloquent: "Come, Lord Jesus!" (Rev. 22:20b); and in a preceding verse: "The Spirit and the Bride say, 'Come.'" (Rev 22:17). The Bride is the Church, which from the day of Pentecost in Jerusalem, throughout the generations and the centuries, lives in this same expectation. It is a creative expectation, a waiting period that constantly helps us to "renew the face of the earth." The mysterious source of this period of waiting in the Church is the Holy Spirit. And the witnesses of this waiting in history are in a special way the Saints. Was St. Philip Neri not a most singular witness in Rome to the expectation of the coming of Christ? And was he not one of those whose life renewed the patrimony of holiness that began in the history of the Church with St. Stephen, deacon, recalled in today's first reading? The martyr Stephen closed his brief existence with the words: "Behold, I see the heavens opened, and the Son of man standing at the right hand of God" (Acts 7:56). The Saints of every time, and St. Philip Neri in his epoch, lived in the vision of the "opened heavens." They are witnesses of the Son of man, who chose to enter history and to run its course, in order to become for everyone way, truth, and life (cf. Jn. 14:6).

I must add to this my great joy that this centenary of St. Philip Neri is being celebrated so solemnly in Rome, in his church, and in his parish. I have heard that this church is always full, and I see that it is also today, and that the memory of this Saint, who was so strongly Roman, is still alive.

I greet all who are present, the Cardinal Vicar, the Archbishops, Bishops, priests, religious, all the faithful and above all the Oratorian Fathers. I also greet the Authorities here present: Authorities of the Italian State, the Mayor of Rome, everyone for whom the person of St. Philip Neri is alive and is part of the spiritual and cultural patrimony of this Eternal City. I am grateful to God and to the Blessed Mother that during this month of May, a Marian month, we find the source of spiritual joy in the memory of St. Philip Neri and in the commemoration of his apostolic work, his sanctity, and his glory.

Praised be Jesus Christ![18]

Message for the Four Hundred and Fiftieth Anniversary of the Priestly Ordination of St. Philip, 2001

From Vatican City, March 27, 2001

On the occasion of the four hundred and fiftieth anniversary of the Priestly Ordination of St. Philip Neri in the church of San Tommaso in Parione, the Holy Father sends His very best wishes to the entire Oratorian Family, assuring them of his cordial participation in the solemn jubilee celebrations in various Nations. One of the purposes of these celebrations is to emphasize and to illuminate the great figure of the Prophet of Joy, who knew how to offer to his contemporaries the radiant testimony of faithfully following Christ and the Gospel. His Holiness sends his lively hope that the example of prayer and trust in God, of humility, charity, and serene optimism that your amiable Founder left as his legacy, may stimulate you to rediscover the person and the work of this most unusual Apostle of hope. St. Philip still has so much to teach humanity in the Third Millennium, especially Christians committed to the work of the New Evangelization. And upon the entire Oratorian Confederation and upon all those who continue to draw inspiration from the enduring vein of spirituality of the Apostle and co-patron of Rome, the Holy Father imparts His special Apostolic Benediction.

Cardinal Angelo Sodano,
Secretary of State to His Holiness.

6. CARDINAL EDUARDO MARTINEZ SOMALO

We would like to include among these documents also the homily that his Eminence Cardinal Eduardo Martinez Somalo, Prefect of the Congregation for Institutes of Consecrated Life and Societies of Apostolic Life, gave in Santa Maria in Vallicella at the close of the General Oratorian Congress of 2000.

I greet our dear Fr. Edoardo and I thank him for his affectionate greetings to me. I also greet Fr. Rios, whom, a short while ago, at the urn of your, of my St. Philip, I received as Delegate of the Apostolic See, designated as such by vote of your General Congress.

1. We are celebrating the Sacrifice of Christ the Redeemer in this church which saw the Eucharistic celebrations of Father Philip, and near to the place where the Father, in the last years of his life, would celebrate Holy Mass: celebrations which were intimate, ecstatic, with no limits of time, in which the priest Philip Neri encountered the Love of his life in an extraordinary way, and from which he drew the force to become himself, every day a "new creature," and because of this an extraordinarily effective evangelizer.

How can we not look to him, while the Word of God to which we have listened still resonates in our hearts?

He is here among us with his presence full of love, and speaks to us about the divine Word with the eloquence which the Saints possess: the eloquence of the life which is lived in Christ and offered, as a gift of love, to his brethren.

We scrutinize his amiable face: Philip Neri:

- *Florentine and secular priest of the Diocese of Rome*,
- *heart overflowing with the Holy Spirit* received in the Catacombs of the martyrs and Christians of the earliest age,
- *praying* not through dutiful fidelity and practices, but by a necessity of love that poured forth from every fiber of his being,
- *an apostle as simple and humble as he was incomparably effective in this Rome*, of which he would say: "whoever does good for Rome, does good for the whole world";

Philip Neri:

- *inspired with the inspiration that the Holy Spirit gives* to those who give their lives over to Him, an offering that is total, and full of trusting abandonment,
- *pervaded with an amiability* that is not only the effect of a felicitous human temperament, but charity derived from the encounter with God,
- *joyous with a joy* that "is the gift of God welling up from a good conscience, assisted by the disdain for worldly goods,

united to the contemplation of celestial things," as he said;

Philip Neri:

- *layman for thirty-six years and priest for the remaining forty-four of his life, but always Christifidelis,* impassioned disciple of that Master of whom Philip would say: "Whoever wants something other than Christ, knows not what he wants; whoever asks for something other than Christ, knows not what he asks; whoever works and not for Christ, knows not what he does."

It is he, Father Philip, the preacher who unveils for us, in this moment, the depths of the Word which the Lord Jesus spoke at the Last Supper, and which we have heard in today's Liturgy, perennially alive.

St. Philip does not give us a learned exegesis, because his way of approaching the Word of God is that of "familiar treatment," which presupposes preparation and study, but requires above all a heart and mind open to the action of the Holy Spirit, who is Light and Love, in a climate of prayer and fraternal communion with all those who are listening.

2. "I am the vine, you the branches... Remain in my love...because without me you can do nothing." That to which Jesus invites us is a relationship with Him that involves every part of us: there is no fiber of our being and of our daily existence that can "live" outside this tenacious and extremely tender vital rapport with the God made man for our salvation.

Jesus Christ is truly "the vine," outside of which "the branch dries up and dies."

He is *unique and indispensable*, as the Magisterium of the Church says in the Declaration *Domine Iesus*. This is what our Saints have discovered in their lives, which are transformed into a *fullness of humanity* just because they have welcomed into themselves the entire gift of grace that issues forth from the relationship with Christ.

The joy of which Philip Neri is a privileged witness in the Church of God—"prophet of joy" as the Holy Father greeted him in the Letter that he sent to you in the occasion of the fourth centenary of his death—is the joy of which the apostle Paul spoke in his first letter. It is *Christian joy*, not simply human happiness, joy that is born from the certitude of belonging to Christ, who saves *the entire person*, conferring upon each aspect of life a great value and significance for which it is worth while to live.

Communion with Him, lived out in the Church, *changes life*!

The "yes" of man meeting the "yes" of Christ receives as a gift "the miracle of change," which is based *not first of all* on pedagogical strategies and on human will, *but on the Mystery of Grace* received as a gift.

The long hours that Father Philip dedicated during the day and sometimes at night to receiving penitents and hearing confessions—*a preponderate part of his priestly ministry*—and his invitation to frequent, even daily, communion in an age when this practice was nearly unknown, shows us the solid, Catholic conviction that sustained the priest Philip in his pastoral action: the miracles that Grace brings about through the Sacraments are infinitely superior to the efficacy of other pastoral actions, however necessary and obligatory they may be.

Priests and lay Christians of our time find in his example a norm the roots of which are sunk deep into the very essence of Christianity, and which preserves them from the danger of making themselves into useful but inadequate "pastoral workers."

Dear brothers and sisters, Jesus Christ lives in our midst with His salvific Presence entrusted to the divine Word, embraced by the Church and living in the Sacraments.

It is this certainty that Father Philip communicates to us today, as much as when he lived down here, in a period of epoch-making changes that in so many respects remind us of those we are living today.

Jesus Christ lives in our midst in order to transform our life into the "prodigy" of a human existence we may affirm together with the Apostle: *"I live no longer; Christ lives in me."*

Jesus Christ lives in our midst *not* thanks to our approval, nor to our commitment to change various situations in our world, *but thanks to the unique and indispensable Event of his Incarnation, Passion, Death, and Resurrection.* This salvific act is perennially present, and by this act He takes on all that is human, and redeems it.

The great new innovation of history is his Presence: the Mystery of infinite Love that comes to meet man, takes on human flesh and saves the life of men.

The "new evangelization" which Fr. Philip lived in his own time and which the Church invites us today to actualize will be "new" to the extent that we remain united to the Vine, live His life-blood, and allow ourselves to become fruitful shoots, not by our own efforts, but by the fruitfulness that we draw from Christ.

3. In this life-giving relationship with Christ, communion with the Church is fundamental, since Christ does not live outside his own Body.

The fidelity and love of St. Philip and of all of our Saints for the Church!

They loved the Church, suffered for her, and worked incessantly in her service.

From this profoundly ecclesial "sensibility" Father Philip Neri drew his vision of the *lay community of the Oratory* and of the same *Congregation* which was born to serve the Oratory: *a family* in which laws and rules would not have pride of place, but rather supernatural *Charity*, which flows out from the Heart of the Father and of the Son and is infused into our hearts by the Holy Spirit.

This charity gives form and value to gestures, words, feelings, friendship, to all relationships in the Christian community and makes it a Communion capable of "astonishing" the world, which can only say: "look how they love one another."

You know, certainly, the document that in recent years has been issued by the Congregation for Institutes of Consecrated Life and Societies of Apostolic Life; it bears the title *Congregavit nos in unum Christi amor*.

It is easy to find in the reflections proposed by the Document so many elements that are consonant with the spirituality and direction of community life that St. Philip left as a precious legacy for you.

Oratorians, give the example, in the Church and in society, of Christian communities that really are witnesses of the fact that Christ changes lives. Be witnesses also of communities in which people of today, so often alone and anguished, can find the communion that makes existence joyful even in the midst of the difficulties of life.

Only those who have encountered Grace are able to establish gratuitous, patient, active, and constructive relationships with others.

Charity is not a human initiative. It is the experience of a great Love that we receive and that communicates itself through us to every other person.

We can demonstrate effectively, and not only affirm, that Christianity is the most profoundly reasonable and adequate response to the "heart" of man.

This is the great challenge that the "new evangelization" places *above all* before us believers.

St. Philip has for you a magisterium of gratuitousness that shows you the way with sureness.

He remains among you, *witness to that charity*, which is the source and the force of an authentic morality. But we must remember its source, and receive into ourselves *all* that it requires of us. Only in this way will you be able to say that you are disciples of your Holy Founder.

The *freedom* with which he shines in the history of the Church and which is an important element in Oratorian life has been delineated well in your *Spiritual Path*, in pages that are dense with teaching.

In the school of St. Philip, you know that *there is no true freedom outside of communion and obedience*. St. Philip presents this as the indispensable attitude for anyone who wishes to persevere in the vocation of the Oratory.

Within your Congregations and Secular Oratories you must live the *family relationship* that belongs to your tradition. Live it also in the bond that links the Communities and the individual members in the Confederation.

When the Holy See decided, years ago, to unite your *Domus sui iuris* into a Confederation, it did so in order to offer you an instrument suitable to fraternal communion. In giving form and substance to this bond of industrious charity, it turned to the great heart and clear mind of Father Arcadio Maria Larraona, who became Cardinal of the Holy Roman Church.

How much he loved the Oratory of St. Philip and how much of its essence he preserved you yourselves have demonstrated in your elaboration of your new General Statutes, approved in 1989, in substantial conformity with what he had planned.

You must love this instrument of communion that is the Confederation, and avail yourselves of all that it offers. Thus the Oratory may grow and flourish abundantly in the Holy Church of God, *circumdata varietate*, in the beautiful biblical image used, to express the richness of gifts in the Church, by your confrere the Venerable Cardinal Cesare Baronio, disciple and first successor of St. Philip, whose body rests in the humility and obscurity of the crypt of this church.

I would like to end this contemplation of the face of St. Philip remembering this great Oratorian who in obedience to Father Philip studied and elucidated the History of the Church over a period of years, and then published his very detailed work in the Annales.

His motto as cardinal, *Obedientia et pax*, summarizes his deepest convictions. It was the "word" that Baronio repeated daily visiting St. Peter's Basilica and kissing the feet of the Apostle, a motto that expresses his whole faith, his love for the Church of Christ, but it also expresses his soul, which was intensely dedicated to following St. Philip.

It is lovely to remember here near the venerated tomb of St. Philip and the hidden one of his great disciple, that that same motto was chosen, as the emblem of his episcopal service, by Angelo Roncalli, now Blessed John XXIII, who was one of the members of the Secular Oratory of Rome.

4. Dear people, the Holy Year of the Great Jubilee follows its course and enters into the Third Christian Millennium.

Looking to the future, the prospects and horizons of the Christian mission embrace not only the continents which still must receive the first announcement of the Gospel, but also those that must be evangelized anew.

The society and people of our time come to question believers with the voice of their problems, and their cultural and existential crisis and even the scientific discoveries of this age.

Look with trust at the harvest that is ripening!

Answer with the enthusiasm and apostolic fidelity of Father Philip to the Lord who incessantly calls to you. Like Philip Neri, open yourselves to the encounter with the men of our time and the situations in which they live, conserving faithfully and transmitting with courageous trust the Word that saves. Be convinced that it "saves" because it is not a formula or an idea, but the alive and efficacious Presence of Christ!

May the Oratory carry out with renewed fidelity its purpose: *in veritate liberi, in caritate servi, in utraque laeti.*

The Virgin Mary accompanies you in the holy journey that is your vocation. From the venerated image in this church of hers, she smiles down at her children with the tenderness with which she embraced St. Philip and with the strength with which she held up the beams of the building during the difficult moments of the construction.

We too invoke her, with the words of Father Philip, saying to her from our hearts: *Virgine Madre, Madre Virgine, pregate Gesù per noi.* Virgin Mother, Mother Virgin, pray to Jesus for us.[19]

NOTES

NOTES FOR CHAPTER I

1. G. Cittadini, *La spiritualità dell'Oratorio,* in "Atti della giornata di studio in occasione del quarto centenario della morte di S. Filippo Neri, Genova, 15 November 1995," *Quaderni Franzoniani*, X (1997), 29–36.
2. For the principal older and recent biographies, see the list at the end of the Compendium.
3. We have chosen this term because its etymology recalls the "stars" that appear in the coat of arms of the Neri family, which were taken into that of the Congregation of the Oratory. The Congregations have often woven this heraldic sign, characteristic of the legal profession, with the flaming heart of Philip—allusion to charity, the "only bond"—and with the white lilies of the angelic purity of the founding Saint.
4. For a chronology of the life and works of St. Philip, correlated with the texts of the principal sources, see also M. T. Bonadonna Russo, *Vita e opere di san Filippo Neri. Cronologia*, in *San Filippo Neri nella realtà romana del XVI secolo, Atti del Convegno di Studio in occasione del IV centenario della morte di San Filippo Neri. Rome, May 11–13, 1995*, edited by M. T. Bonadonna Russo and by N. del Re (Rome, 2000), 188–209.
5. TRANSLATOR'S NOTE: "Beautiful San Giovanni": Dante loved the Baptistery, and added "beautiful" to its name in the *Divine Comedy.*
6. Baptismal record in the Archives of the Merchants' Guild in Florence. The text is found in G. Incisa della Rocchetta, *Il primo processo canonico per San Filippo Neri nel Codice Vaticano Latino 3798 e in altri esemplari dell'Oratorio di Roma*, edited by N. Vian, 4 vv. (Città del Vaticano, 1957–1963), henceforth cited as *Process*; *Process*, III, 398–399.
7. A. Capecelatro, *La vita di S. Filippo Neri* (Rome, 1889), I, 36ff. Henceforth cited as Capecelatro. See also L. von Pastor, *Storia dei papi* (Rome, 1921), IV, 1ff.
8. A. Cistellini, "*San Filippo Neri e la sua patria,*" in *Rivista di Storia della Chiesa in Italia*, XXIII (1969), 54–119; N. Gigli and G. B. Ristori, "I Neri di Castelfranco di Sopra," in *Memorie Oratoriane*, XVII (1995), 67–84.

9. Descendent of the noble family that had produced magistrates, but was now of modest economic circumstances.
10. San Filippo Neri, *Gli scritti e le massime*, ed. A. Cistellini (Brescia, 1994), 41–47; 67–80; 99–100; 102–103. Henceforth cited as S. Filippo Neri, *Gli scritti e le massime.*
11. *Process*, III, 400–404.
12. St. Caterina de' Ricci (1523–1590). *Process*, I, 184. *Process*, I, 190, note 207, provides an undated letter of Sr. Caterina, a Dominican nun, to Fr. Philip, written probably during an illness of the Father's, since she says that she is praying that God will "*return him to health and maintain his well-being, because the Church has so much need of him.*" *Process*, IV, 269; M. T. Bonadonna Russo, "L'amicizia spirituale tra S. Caterina de' Ricci e S. Filippo Neri," in *Studi Medievali*, XXXVI (1995), 957–974.
13. St. Antonio M. Zaccaria (1502–1539). O. Premoli, *Storia dei Barnabiti nel Cinquecento* (Rome, 1913). The project of a union or even a fusion with the Barnabites was discussed at one time. Sidereus Nuncius (A. Cistellini), "I Barnabiti e San Filippo Neri," in *Memorie Oratoriane*, XVIII (1997), 87–95.
14. R. Spiazzi, "San Filippo e i Domenicani," in *Oratorium. Archivum Historicum Oratorii S. Philippi Nerii. Semestrale commentarium de rebus oratorianis, a Congregatione Oratorii de Urbe editum*, VII (1976) 1, 20–36. Henceforth cited as *Oratorium.*
15. "His father was a supporter of the venerable Savonarola..." A. Cistellini, "San Filippo Neri e Girolamo Savonarola," in *Memorie Oratoriane*, XIX (1999), 5–16.
16. *Process*, III, 177–178.
17. N. Vian, Filippo di Ser Francesco Neri nell' "anno trentuno," in *Memorie Oratoriane*, VI (1977), 3–5; *Process*, III, 42: "*Partì di firenze d'età 18*"; but I, 173: "*Partì di Firenze di diciassette anni*" (Gallonio).
18. A. Lentini, "Memorie di San Filippo Neri a Cassino e a Montecassino," in *Memorie Oratoriane*, III–IV (1981), 16–24.
19. On the duration of this stay and Romolo's economic circumstances, see A. Cistellini, *San Filippo Neri, l'Oratorio e la Congregazione oratoriana. Storia e spiritualità* (Florence, 1989), I, 20, note 9. Henceforth cited as A. Cistellini, *S. Filippo Neri.*
20. G. B. Bordini [*sic*], *Philippii Nerii religiosissimi presbyteri vitae compendium* (1596), ed. G. Incisa della Rocchetta, in *Oratorium*, VIII (1977), I, 3–23; Cistellini, *San Filippo Neri*, I, 23–24.
21. *Process*, III, 41; Cistellini, *S. Filippo Neri*, I, 22–23.
22. When he became cardinal, he did not forget that gesture, and had affection for Philip all his life. He also contributed to the expenses of the construction of the Chiesa Nuova.
23. "*Vitam complures annos eremiticam propemodum duxit*," says Gallonio (*Vita B. Philippi*, 13). See Cistellini, *S. Filippo Neri*, I, pp. 21–22; N. Vian, "Solitudine e mondo di san Filippo," in *Oratorium*, VI (1975) 1–2, 118–132.

24. Cistellini, *S. Filippo*, I, 27–30. M. T. Bonadonna Russo, “Il conversionismo devoto di S. Filippo Neri, tra eredità savonaroliane e rigori inquisitoriali,” in *Richerche per la Storia religiosa di Roma* (Rome, 1998), 10, 75–90.
25. M. Vanti, *S. Giacomo degli Incurabili di Roma nel Cinquecento* (Rome, 1938); M. T. Bonadonna Russo, “Problemi e istituzioni dell'assistenza romana nel Cinque e Seicento,” in *Studi romani*, XXXIV (1986), 230–252; C. F. Black, *Le Confraternite italiane del Cinquecento. Filantropia, carità, volontariato nell'età della Riforma e della Controriforma* (Milan, 1992).
26. St. Ignatius Loyola (1491–1556); St. Francis Saverio (1506–1552). *Monumenta historica Societatis Iesu* (Madrid, 1894–1925); (Rome, 1932ff.); P. Tacchi Venturi. *Storia della Compagnia di Gesù in Italia* (Rome, 1950–1951); H. Rahner, “Ignazio di Loyola e Filippo Neri,” in *Quaderni dell'Oratorio* (ed. Roman Oratory), 3.
27. *Process*, III, 253.
28. H. Jedin, *Storia del Concilio di Trento*, 2nd ed., 4 vols. in 5 parts (Brescia, 1973–1981); ibid., *Riforma Cattolica o Controriforma?* (Brescia, 1957); A. Borromeo, “Aspetti della riforma postridentina a Roma nell'età di san Filippo Neri,” in *San Filippo Neri nella realtà romana del XVI secolo…* (Rome, 2000), 37–67.
29. TRANSLATOR'S NOTE: “have spirit,” or “have the Spirit.”
30. *Process*, III, 424; in *Process*, IV, 299, see s. v. “Palpitazione di cuore, inarcatura delle costole, calori fisici,” Bacci-Ricci, *Vita…*, c. VI, 2; Cistellini, *San Filippo*, I, 32–33, note 63; Innocenzio Brix (A. Cistellini), “La Pentecoste filippina,” in *Memorie Oratoriane*, XVII (1995), 85–91; V. Fiocchi Nicolai, “San Filippo Neri, le catacombe di S. Sebastiano e le origini dell'archeologia cristiana,” in *San Filippo Neri nella realtà romana del XVI secolo…* (Rome, 2000), 106–130; A. Pampalone, “La ‘Pentecoste’ di san Filippo Neri. Iconografia e iconologia,” in ibid., 145–188.
31. *Process*, III, 178.
32. A. Cistellini, *San Filippo Neri. Breve storia di una grande vita* (Florence, 1998), 12.
33. S. Gaetano da Thiene (St. Cajetan) (1480–1547). *Regnum Dei. Collectanea Theatina* (Rome, 1945ff.); P. Chiminelli, *S. Gaetano Thiene, cuore della Riforma cattolica* (Vicenza, 1948); G. Lompart, *Gaetano da Thiene. Estudios sobre un riformador religioso* (Rome, 1969); A. Olivier *Los Teatinos: su carisma, su historia, su fisionomia* (Rome, 1991).
34. G. Marangoni, *Vita del servo di Dio Buonsignore Cacciaguerra…; con l'aggiunta delle vite di alcuni suoi penitenti…* (Rome, 1717), Appendice, p. 24; “Persiano Rosa,” in *L'Oratorio di san Filippo Neri* (ed. Rome Oratory), XVI (1959), 14.
35. Cistellini, *S. Filippo Neri*, I, 30–32; M. Borzacchini, “Un tipo di assistenza ai poveri nel' 500: l'Arciconfraternita della Ss. Trinità dei pellegrini e dei convalescenti,” in *Storia e Politica*, XXI (1982), 363–409. The principal source of documentation

on the events which gave rise to the Confraternity is still C. Fanucci, *Trattato di tutte l'opere pie di Roma* (Rome, 1602), pp. 266–267. For Philip's part in this see *Process*, I, 171–172, 175, 324; II, 324; III, 85, 142, 218.

36. *Process*, III, 156. On the origin of the Forty Hours see A. DeSanctis, *L'orazione delle Quarantore* (Rome, 1919); C. Cargnoni, *Le Quarantore ieri e oggi* (1986).
37. S. Camillo de Lellis (1556–1614); M. Vanti, *S. Giacomo degli Incurabili di Roma nel Cinquecento,* Rome, 1958; ibid., *San Camillo de Lellis e i suoi Ministri degli Infermi* (Rome, 1959).
38. Cistellini, *San Filippo Neri*, I, 33–45.
39. The expression is that of the Oratorian Fr. Giulio Savioli; San Giovanni Leonardi, who lived in spiritual intimacy with Fr. Philip, remembered San Girolamo as "the wellspring and origin of the spirit in Italy, and the seminary of so many men marked by sanctity and perfection of life." Cesare Speciani, Cardinal Charles Borromeo's agent in Rome, gave this evaluation: "[in San Girolamo] the spirit of the desert Fathers and of the first priests of the Church has been renewed, those who flourished in goodness and holiness"; G. L. Masetti Zannini, "San Filippo a San Girolamo della Carità," in *Oratorium*, VI (1975), 1–2, 4–28; on the church of S. Girolamo see F. Ardizzon, *S. Girolamo della Carità. Storia, arte, spiritualità per una chiesa nel cuore in Roma* (Città del Vaticano, 1987).
40. A. Cistellini, *S. Filippo*, I, 47–116.
41. N. del Re, "San Filippo Neri, rianimatore della visita delle Sette Chiese," in *San Filippo Neri nella realtà romana del XVI secolo...* (Rome, 2000), 89–103; C. Gasbarri, *La visita filippina alle Sette Chiese,* Rome, 1947; L. Pani Ermini, ed., *La visita alle "Sette Chiese"* (Rome, 2000).
42. Francesco Maria Tarugi (1525–1608). See brief profile in C. V. Bacci-Ricci, *Vita di San Filippo...con notizie di alcuni compagni* (Rome, 1672); A. Cistellini, "Appunti per la vita del cardinale Francesco Maria Tarugi," in *Memorie Oratoriane*, VI (1977), 6–12; ibid., "Il Cardinal F. M. Tarugi arcivescovo di Siena," in *Bollettino Senese di Storia Patria*, II (1943), 88–109; G. Tarugi, "Francesco M. Tarugi, 'Apostolicus Vir, omni laude praestantior,'" in *Oratorium*, VI (1975), 1–2, 65–84.
43. From Modena, of the household of Cardinal Santafiore, he was the first of the "converted," and he brought with him many others. He was very dear to Fr. Philip among his first spiritual sons. One of the books very much in use in the Oratorian meetings, Feo Belcari, *Vita del B. Giovanni Colombini...* (Rome, 1588), was dedicated to him by the publisher Salviani.
44. He was from Ripatransone and had known Philip at the Sapienza; he was one of the earliest members of the Congregation. Bacci-Ricci, *Vita di S. Filippo...con notizie di alcuni compagni* (Rome, 1672).
45. *Monumenta Historica Societatiis Jesu—Epistolae S. Francisci Xaverii*, I, 17; II,

5711ff. The reports of the Jesuit missionaries were part of the readings of the Oratory and were in the Library of St. Philip, now in the Biblioteca Vallicelliana. The first Roman editions go back to 1552, 1553; A. Alba, "San Felipe Neri y las Indias. Algunas consideraciones historicas sobre la vocaciòn de S. Felipe Neri '*ad gentes*,'" *Cuadernos de espiritualidad, Historia y Legislaciòn* (Alcalà de H., 1998), 3.

46. In the *Process*, III, 381–382, we find the circumstantial report of Tarugi who was present together with twenty or so other persons in Philip's room, the evening when, reading the letters of the missionaries, they were wondering whether that might be their vocation.
47. Cesare Baronio (1538–1607). See the brief profile in chapter V. H. Barnabei, *Vita Caesaris Baronii...* (Rome, 1651); Bacci-Ricci, *Vita di san Filippo Neri..., con notizie di alcuni suoi compagni...* (Roma, 1672); G. Calenzio, *La vita e le opere del Cardinal Cesare Baronio, della Congregazione dell'Oratorio, Bibliotecario di S. Romana Chiesa* (Rome, 1907); A. Cistellini, "I Cardinali Baronio e Tarugi nel ricordo e nel giudizio di un testimone coevo," in *L'Oratorio di San Filippo Neri* XXII (Rome, 1965), 2, 1–4; 4, 1–4; M. T. Bonadonna Russo, "Baronio oratoriano," in *Memorie Oratoriane*, XIV (1984), 23–41; Caraffa et. al., *A Cesare Baronio. Scritti vari* (Sora, 1963); M. Borrelli, *Le testimonianze baroniane dell'Oratorio di Napoli* (Naples, 1965); ibid., "Richerche sul Baronio," in *Studi Secentesche* (Florence, 1967).
48. Antonio Gallonio (1557–1605), a Roman, probably knew Fr. Philip from his infancy and when he was twenty put himself under his guidance. Gallonio dedicated himself entirely to assisting Fr. Philip in Philip's old age. When the Congregation wished to speed up the canonization of its Founder, Gallonio was entrusted with preparing the first biography. He composed other hagiological works, the first two of which became the best known, one on the Virgins of Rome and the other on the instruments used in martyrdom. Bacci-Ricci, *Via di san Filippo Neri... con la notizia di alcuni compagni...* (Rome, 1672); A. Gallonio, *Vita del Beato P. Filippo Neri, fiorentino... scritta e ordinata per anni* (Rome, 1601); critical edition edited by M. T. Bonadonna Russo (Rome, 1995), ix–xxii; Cistellini, *San Filippo Neri*, III, 1698–1700; M. Cuttano, "Il Padre Antonio Gallonio e l'agiografia cristiana nel Cinquecento," in *L'Oratorio di S. Filippo Neri*, XIX (1962), 11, 14–16; 12, 10–15.
49. Giovan Battista Bordini [*sic*] (1536–1609), Roman of modest family but refined in his manners and his carriage; he was a doctor at Law when he entered at twenty-two into Fr. Philip's circle. He was among the first whom Philip guided into the priesthood. He became Bishop of Cavaillon in 1592, then Archbishop of Avignon.
50. *Process*, III, 43–44; 143; 248.
51. N. del Re, "Il Cardinal Vicario Virgilio Rosari 'nemico' di san Filippo Neri," in

Strenna dei Romanisti, LII (1991), 155–166.

52. F. de Lorenzo, "Le patologie di san Filippo Neri. Esame clinico," in *Memorie oratoriane*, XVII (1995), 92–109.
53. G. Incisa della Rocchetta, "I testamenti di san Filippo," in *Oratorium*, IV (1973), 2, 3–11; V (1974), 1, 3–11; V (1974), 2, 65–74.
54. S. Francesco Caracciolo (1563–1608); promoter of the Eucharistic cult and precursor of perpetual adoration; he met St. Philip in Rome, and obtained from him some rooms in San Girolamo so that he might establish the first presence of his Order in Rome. In 1558 Sixtus V approved the Order of the Caraccioli, which cooperated with other Institutes in consolidating and diffusing the Catholic faith which was menaced by the Protestant reform. Agostino Adorno (Genoa 1551–Naples 1591).
55. St. Charles Borromeo (1538–1584). C. Bascape, *De vita et rebus gestis Caroli Cardinal S. Praxedis, arch. Mediolani* (Ingolstadt, 1592); G. P. Giussano, *Vita di san Carlo Borromeo* (Rome, 1610); G. Alberigo, A. Borromeo, E. Cattaneo, F. M. Ferro, D. M. Turoldo, *Il grande Borromeo tra storia e fede* (Milan, 1984).
56. Cistellini, *S. Filippo Neri*, I, pp. 132–136; C. Gasbarri, "San Filippo e San Carlo," in *L'Oratorio di S. Filippo Neri*, XXV (1968), 6, 101–107.
57. Cf. Cistellini, *S. Filippo*, I, 116–174; G. Incisa della Rocchetta, "I discepoli di San Filippo Neri a San Giovanni dei Fiorentini," in *Oratorium*, VI (1975), 1–2, 43–50.
58. A. Cistellini, "Nascita della Congregazione oratoriana," in *Oratorium*, VI (1975), 1–2, 4–28.
59. Germanico Fedeli (1548–1623), ordained priest in 1572; he will become one of the most intimate of the Father's disciples, who will give him duties of high trust. Taken from the Congregation because of duties given him by the Pope, he managed to finish his days in the Congregation. Bacci-Ricci, *Vita di san Filippo Neri...con notizie di alcuni compagni...* (Rome, 1672).
60. Ottavio Parravicino (1552–1611), Roman of a family from Como; Baronio had put him in contact with Fr. Philip. In 1584 he was elected bishop of Alexandria; consecrated in 1587 by St. Charles Borromeo, Sixtus V sent him as nuncio to Switzerland; in 1591 Pope Gregory XIV elevated him to the rank of Cardinal.
61. St. Pius V (1504–1572). Beatified in 1672 and canonized in 1712. Catena, *Vita del Papa Pio V* (Rome, 1586); G. A. Gabuzio, *De vita et rebus gestis Pii V Pont. Max.* (Rome, 1605).
62. Philip esteemed him, but did not follow him in many aspects of his pastoral practices, in particular his excessive mortifications and the enormous faith that Cacciaguerra placed in visions and mystical phenomena. Among Philip's books are found two by Cacciaguerra, *Trattato della tribolazione* (Rome, 1559), and *Trattato della comunione frequente* (Venice, 1566). G. Marangoni, *Vita del Servo di Dio il P. Bonsignore Cacciaguerra* (Rome, 1712); R. de Maio, "Bonsignore

Cacciaguerra a Napoli. Azione ed influssi di un mistico senese del Cinquecento," in *Studi di bibliografia e di storia* (Verona, 1964); N. Vian, "Pietà romana del Cinquecento: il Cenacolo di Bonsignore Cacciaguerra," in *Memorie oratoriane*, XIII (1983), 4–23.

63. Angelo Velli (1540–1622), of Palestrina. Hardly more than twenty years old, he put himself under Philip's guidance. He would be Philip's successor after Baronio. Bacci-Ricci, *Vita di san Filippo Neri...con notizie di alcuni compagni...* (Rome, 1672).

64. First of Cardinal Borromeo's household and then Cardinal d'Aragona's, he began to frequent the Oratory showing the authentic spirit of St. Philip in visiting the hospitals and prisons, which he continued all his life. Although he was not formally a member of the Community, Philip considered him among his own: Borromeo even asked Philip if he could "borrow" him for Milan, and Bl. Paolo Burali d'Arezzo, when he had become bishop of Piacenza and then archbishop and cardinal of Naples, asked Philip for him. Philip lamented Bl. Paolo's death in 1578 as a sorrow for all Christendom. Fr. Borla collaborated in Naples with S. Andrea Avellino in various charitable enterprises, and his presence in Naples was the first "seed" of Philip's Oratory there.

65. The texts of these are found in *Collectanea vetustiorum ac fundamentalium documentorum Congregationis Oratorii S. Philippi Nerii*, A. Cistellini documenta collegit et illustravit (Brescia, 1982), 77–99. Henceforth, *Collectanea*.

66. *Process*, III, 144.

67. Cistellini, *San Filippo Neri*, I, 149–153.

68. Antonio Talpa (1536–1624), from San Severino, whose acceptance by Fr. Philip left Tarugi very perplexed (cf. Cistellini, *San Filippo Neri*, I, 155–158). He was extremely important in the development of the Oratorian undertaking. Together with his brother Arsenio and with Bartolomeo Achillei, who had already experienced community life among the "*spirituali*" of San Severino, he had a significant role in the organization of the life of the Community. He brought a keen intelligence, but little human warmth. Strong-willed and capable of finding and following whatever path might be necessary to achieve his aims, Talpa represented a very different type from the mild and gentle Fr. Philip, who possessed an open and lovable spirit. He enjoyed within the House and outside considerable esteem for his undisputed virtues, and he was also esteemed by illustrious men of his time, such as St. Charles Borromeo, St. Camillus de Lellis, St. John Leonardi.

69. At the beginning he was one of the persons most meritorious in the launching of the institute. Then, because of his strange ideas, he was handed over to the Holy Office, which condemned him and incarcerated him for five years. Fr. Philip considered that he showed unorthodox tendencies in matters of faith, and was inflexible on the question of his readmission, the good offices of

Tarugi, Baronio and others notwithstanding.

70. A. Cistellini, *San Filippo Neri*, I, 152–153.
71. *Process*, I, 137; 261–262.
72. Tommaso Bozzi (1548–1610); from Gubbio, one of the most cultivated and representative of the early Oratorian community. Bacci-Ricci, *Vita di san Filippo Neri…con notizie di alcuni compagni…* (Rome, 1672); R. de Mattei, "Il primo antimachiavellico d'Italia," in *L'Oratorio di S. Filippo Neri*, XVII (1961), 11, 1–3.
73. Niccolò Gigli (1520–1591), from France. He was one of the most unusual figures from the time of the origins of the Congregation for the purity of his soul and the gentleness of his ways. The Father had great fondness and great esteem for him, and used him often as his scribe. Bacci-Ricci, *Vita di S. Filippo Neri… con notizie di alcuni compagni.*
74. Francesco Soto de Langa (1540–1619), from Ávila. He arrived in Rome in 1562 and from 1568 on he lived devotedly with the Father in San Girolamo. A man of unusual goodness, he was ordained priest in 1575 with others of the Congregation. He founded in Rome the monastery of S. Giuseppe of the Discalced Carmelites, the first monastery in Rome of St. Teresa's reform.
75. "The little prophet Animuccia who, when the meeting of the Oratory lasted a little longer, rejoiced," as Fr. Filippo Cesare Speciani recalled from Milan, in *Process*, IV, 206–207. Florentine like the Father, Animuccia met Philip in 1540 and from 1555 on played an active part in the Oratory. He was named in that year as Maestro della Cappella Giulia; Palestrina succeeded him in 1571. He died assisted by Fr. Philip. A. Gallonio, *Vita Beati Patris…*, 126; *Process*, I, 16, n. 67. G. Animuccia, *Il secondo libro delle Laudi* (Rome, 1570).
76. P. Alaleona, *Storia dell'Oratorio musicale in Italia* (Turin, 1925); A. Bertini, "La musica all'Oratorio dalle origini ad oggi," in *Quaderni dell'Oratorio*, 11; F. Monpellio, San Filippo Neri e la musica "pescatrice di anime," in *L'Oratorio di S. Filippo Neri*, XXIII (1966), 11, 163–167; 12, pp. 183–191; F. Torrefranca, "Carattere e destino dell'Oratorio musicale," in *L'Oratorio di S. Filippo Neri*, XVIII (1961), 8, 1–5; M. T. Bonadonna Russo, "Musica e devozione nell'Oratorio di S. Filippo Neri," in *Lunario Romano* (1986), 145–166.
77. St. Francesco Borgia (1510–1571) gave great impetus during his Generalate to the missions in America. His immense esteem for Fr. Philip is documented in *Process*, I. 87. According to the same document, St. Peter Canisius (1521–1597), apostle to Germany, was present at the Oratorian meetings in 1565, 1568, and 1573. In his letters, he testified to and kept a grateful remembrance of Fr. Philip and also of Baronio and Tarugi, "distinguished for their virtues and for their holy lives."
78. Conquered by the example of high spirituality of Charles Borromeo, his elector, and by the holiness of his Predecessor, Gregory began to nurture sympathies for the circle of Fr. Philip, especially through Pietro Vittrici, a pentitent of the

Father, and through Msgr. Cesare Speciani, who was very close to the Oratorian ambience. C. Speciani, *Considerationi sopra la vita di Gregorio XIII*, included in part in Pastor, IX, 906–908; M. Ciappi, *Compendio delle heroiche et gloriose attioni et santa vita di Papa Gregorio XIII* (Rome, 1596).

79. St. John Leonardi (1541–1614). S. Bongi, *Compendio cronologico della vita del B. Giovanni Leonardi* (Monza, 1908); V. Pascucci, "Lettere del Baronio a S. Giovanni Leonardi," in *L'Oratorio di S. Filippo Neri*, XXIII (1966), 3, 54–58; 4, 73–76; 5, 92–95; 6, 109–111. The Bull of Clement VIII, "Ex quo Divina maiestas," with which the Congregation was erected, will serve as the model for the canonical erection of the Oratorian congregations, or in the language of the bull: ad instar Congregationis Oratorii de Urbe: see *Collectanea*, 26–29.
80. Fabrizio Mezzabarba (d. 1586), from Pavia, not very well balanced in Fr. Philip's view, was the first real benefactor of the nascent community of Fr. Philip, and also supported the Barnabites in their foundation in Rome. The Oratorians welcomed this "very devout and blessed Congregation" (Tarugi writing to the General Superior of the Barnabites Fr. Paolo Omodei), and the Fathers found generous hospitality at San Girolamo, where they met Alessandro Sauli, who frequented the Oratory assiduously. He entered the Barnabites, and became General Superior of the Congregation at thirty-four years of age; later he was bishop of Aleria and of Pavia. He died in 1592; beatified in 1742, he was canonized in 1904. Boffitto, *Biblioteca Barnabitica*, III (Florence, 1934), 412–440; Cistellini, *San Filippo Neri*, I, 178–179.
81. Pompeo Pateri (1547–1624) was from Piovera in the diocese of Pavia. He entered the Congregation as soon as he arrived in Rome, and he was an important supporter of the Oratory. He was in demand as a spiritual director and able administrator, dear even to Popes and Cardinal Vicars of Rome, who drew upon his intelligent industriousness. In 1568 he founded a new Oratorian House in Lanciano to govern the Abbey of St. Giovanni in Venere held by the Congregation beginning in 1585. He left a little volume of Memoirs edited by M. T. Bonadonna Russo and published in *Archivio della Società Romana di Storia Patria* (1975), I–IV.
82. M. T. Bonadonna Russo, "1575: organizzazione di un giubileo," in *Strenna dei Romanisti* (1975), 371–385.
83. *Collectanea*, 10–16.
84. Cistellini, *S. Filippo Neri*, I, 174–199.
85. M. T. Bonadonna Russo, *Appunti sull'antica parrocchia vallicelliana*, in "Studi offerti a G. Incisa della Rocchetta," Rome, 1973, 89–115.
86. R. Lefevre, *Il primo architetto della Chiesa Nuova: Matteo Bartolini da Città di Castello,* in "Oratorium," IV (1973), I, 42–49; M. T. Bonadonna Russo, "Contributo alla storia della Chiesa Nuova," in *Studi Romani*, IX (1961), 4, 419–427; ibid., "I Cesi e la Congegazione dell'Oratorio," in *Archivio della Società Romana*

di Storia Patria, XCI (1970), XXII, fasc. I–IV, 102–154.

87. Pietro Perracchione was born in Chivasso in Piedmont in 1538. He was ordained in 1570. He was a guest at S. Girolamo when Fr. Philip lent him to Bartolomeo Porzio, nuncio in Germany. Msgr. Speciani wrote to Cardinal Borromeo that in S. Girolamo "he was held to be a saint."
88. Francesco Bozzi, brother of Fr. Tommaso, would become a worthy representative of the first generation at the Vallicellana. His brother Pietro did not persevere in the community, but held positions of great responsibility in the Rome government. Bacci-Ricci, *Vita di san Filippo Neri...con la notizia di alcuni compagni.*
89. Alfonso Visconti (1552–1608), Milanese patrician and relative of Cardinal Sfondrati, the future Gregory XIV. In 1575 he entered the Congregation, but later became a prelate. Clement VIII elevated him to the Cardinalate in 1599, on Cardinal Baronio's advice.
90. Agostino Manni (1548–1618). Born in the diocese of Gubbio, he came to Rome after studying law at Perugia; the doctor Angelo Vittori introduced him to Fr. Philip. He was one of the most significant exponents of the first generation of Philip's followers, above all as spiritual director, especially of the young. He wrote many of the Lauds of the Oratory and also works that illustrate the Oratorian spirituality. Bacci-Ricci, *Vita di san Filippo Neri...con la notizia di alcuni compagni...* (Rome, 1672); "Lo spirito dell'Oratorio secondo P. Manni," in *L'Oratorio di S. Filippo Neri*, XXI (1964), 2, 10–14; 5, 13–15.
91. Published in Pastor, IX, pp. 81–82; Cistellini, *San Filippo Neri*, I, 228–229. They are not given in order of seniority, although that would come to be the practice.
92. Flaminio Ricci (1548–1610), from Fermo. He came to Rome at age thirty-three with a degree in law, became a priest and had his first contacts with Fr. Philip. Reserved in temperament and extremely humble, gifted with a lucid intelligence and decisive in will, he was about to be named bishop of Teramo, at the death of his brother, but Fr. Philip obtained from the Pope permission to keep him for himself. In 1592 he was sent to Naples when Tarugi, who had been named Archbishop of Avignon, departed. He remained there until after the Father's death, although Fr. Philip wanted so much to have the consolation of seeing him. After Fr. Philip's death he became one of the chief figures of the Oratory and one of the most authoritative interpreters of the mind of Fr. Philip in the drafting of the definitive Constitutions of 1612. Especially during his term as Provost General, after Velli, 1602–1608, he strongly opposed the ideas of Fr. Talpa and those current in the Naples community. He had a clear understanding of the importance of the independence of the various Houses, and he prevented the House at Fermo, which had arisen by his initiative, from being aggregated to Rome, as had been the case with the Houses of Naples and San Severino, even though the Fathers at Fermo and some in Rome favored such a

move. Bacci-Ricci, *Vita di san Filippo Neri... con la notizia di alcuni compagni.*

93. Giovanni Giovenale Ancina (1545–1604). See the brief Profile in P. G. Bacci, *Vita di P. Giovanni Giovenale Ancina* (Rome, 1671); M. Pellegrino, *Il Beato Giovenale Ancina*, 2nd ed. rev. E. Dao (Saluzzo, 1968); "Atti del Process canonico," in *Memorie Oratoriane*, XIV (1984), 71–84; ibid., "Padre Giovenale Ancina, 'Pellegrino errante,'" in *Memorie Oratoriane*, XIII (1983), 48–63; P. Damilan, *Giovenale Ancina, musicista filippino* (Florence, 1956), with a list of his works and unpublished writings.
94. Bacci-Ricci, *Vita di san Filippo Neri... con la notizia di alcuni suoi compagni.*
95. A. Sala, *Documenti circa la vita e le gesta di S. Carlo Borromeo*, II (Milan, 1858), 170–171.
96. Cistellini, *San Filippo Neri*, I, 269–273.
97. Cistellini, *San Filippo Neri*, I, 257–258.
98. M. Borrelli, "San Filippo ed il Collegio Polacco," in *L'Oratorio di S. Filippo Neri*, XX (1963), 10, 3–6; Cistellini, *San Filippo Neri*, I, 303–305; N. Gigli (A. Cistellini), "Il quarto centenario del Collegio polacco in Roma," in *Memorie Oratoriane*, IV (1983), 10–11–12, 3ff.
99. *Collectanea*, 109–119; Cistellini, *San Filippo Neri*, I, 299–303; 315–334; ibid., "Il quarto centenario delle prime Costituzioni oratoriane ((1583–1983)," in *Memorie Oratoriane*, IV (1983), 13, 24–47.
100. *Collectanea*, 120–145.
101. *Collectanea*, 146–149; Cistellini, *San Filippo Neri*, I, 332–334.
102. *Process*, I, 202–203. The celebrated physician Angelo Vittori (*Medicae Consultationes* [Rome, 1640]) declared the death to be real; G. Lais, *Terzo centenario del miracolo di S. Filippo Neri al palazzo Massimo* (Rome, 1883); M. T. Russo Bonadonna, "Quarto centenario del miracolo di Casa Massimo," in *L'Urbe* (1983), 1–2.
103. Cistellini, *San Filippo Neri*, I, 335–339.
104. M. T. Bonadonna Russo, "Sisto V e gli Oratoriani," in *Sisto V: I. Roma e Lazio. Atti del VI Corso Internazionale di Alta Cultura, Libreria dello Stato* (Rome, 1973). Fr. Bordini dedicated to him the *Liber carminum de rebus praeclaris gentis a Sixto V P. M.* (Rome, 1588).
105. A. Cistellini, *San Filippo Neri*, I, 420–425.
106. C. Gasbarri, "La Badia di S. Giovanni in Venere," in *L'Oratorio di S. Filippo Neri*, XVIII (1961), 11, 8–12.
107. He was a penitent of Fr. Philip's at St. Girolamo. Fr. Philip directed him to the Dominicans. A. Cistellini, "Fra Alessio Figliucci e San Filippo Neri," in *Rassegna di ascetica e mistica*, I (1971).
108. This work, which was finished in 1581, brings together a large part of the pedagogical experience of Fr. Philip: "The careful analysis of the chapters shows readily methods and ideas consonant with those in use in the Oratory. There

is a pessimistic concept of human nature, redeemable by grace, present largely through the sacraments, and the application of human will in the continuous work of interior conversion. Great importance is laid on a formative atmosphere..." (G. P. Pacini, "Filippo Neri prete: note sulla pastorale filippina," in *Atti della giornata di studio in occasione del quarto centenario della morte di S. Filippo Neri*, Genoa, 15 November 1995, in *Quaderno Franzoniani*, X (1997), 37). The work is dedicated to "Reverendis Patribus Congregationis Oratorii" because, as the author says in the dedication, "quidquid est fructus ab eorum semente [everything is the fruit of their sowing]." Scholars of the pedagogy of the Counter-Reformation have recognized in this the most significant witness of the renewed commitment to teaching promoted by the Tridentine Council (L. Secco, *La pedagogia della Controriforma* [Brescia, 1973]). Silvio Antoniano (1540–1603) was a spiritual son of Fr. Philip's, really considered as a member of the nascent community: "huomo nostro, ma che non cohabita," Tarugi says of him, recalling that "dice [gives the sermon at the Oratory] ogni giovedì" (*Arch. Congr. Napoli.*, VII. 2, 27). Prelate and maestro di camera of Clement VIII, of excellent literary gifts and a fine and subtle humanist, it was he who composed the bull of absolution of Henry IV; the views of Fr. Philip and Baronio also had some weight in this matter; Pastor writes of this (*Storia dei Papi*, XI, 103): "it is the most important document ever to come forth from the papal chancery." Antoniano rests in the Chiesa Nuova, in the chapel of the Nativity.

109. Cistellini, *San Filippo Neri*, I, 353–409; 430–441; 504–527; M. Borrelli, *Le Costituzioni dell'Oratorio Napoletano* (Naples, 1968).

110. V. Saxer, "Baronio ed il Martirologio Romano," in *Antichità paleocristiane e altomedievali* (Sora, 1985).

111. S. Felice da Cantalice (1515–1587). He had predicted the pontificate of Sixtus V, exhorting him to behave himself well. The Pope opened the process for his canonization immediately. *Monumenta historica Ord. Fr. Min. Capuccinorum*, X (Rome, 1964); G. Incisa della Rocchetta, "San Filippo e San Felice da Cantalice," in *L'Oratorio di San Filippo Neri*, XXII (1965), 1, 1–6. See *Process*, IV, Index, s. v. Felice da Cantalice.

112. Federico Borromeo (1564–1631), first cousin of Cardinal Charles—not a nephew as is often said—arrived in Rome after having completed his studies in Pavia and Bologna. He was made Cardinal in 1587, ordained priest in 1593, and elected Archbishop of Milan in April 1595. A. Cistellini, "Il Cardinal Federico Borromeo, S. Filippo e la Vallicella," in *Atti della Accademia di S. Carlo*, IV (1981), 91–133.

113. Frederic's relationship with Fr. Philip and the Oratory began soon after his arrival in Rome. The first record of his Presence at the Vallicella is October 17, 1586: "Yesterday the Most Illustrious Count Federico Borromeo came at the end of the Oratory," Bordini wrote to Tarugi the following day. "He is young, his

face is like an angel's, and so are his ways. May Our Lord preserve him." From then on Borromeo would be one of those most bound by affection to Fr. Philip and to the House. In the letter he would write to Gallonio, accompanying his testimony for the *Process*, he says: "You know how much I honored this saint, you know my love for him which has increased, rather than diminished, since his death. If it were a useful thing, I would give my blood for his memory" (*Process*, III, 419–420).

114. C. Baronio, *Annales Ecclesiastici a Christo nato ad annum 1198*, 12 vols. (Rome, 1588–1607). This work, born out of the sermons on the history of the Church that Fr. Philip had asked Baronio to give, turned out to be, despite the intentions of the author, a replica of the *Ecclesiastica historia*, published in thirteen volumes by a group of Protestant scholars under the direction of Mattia Viacic (Flaccio Illirico), between 1559 and 1574. The material was divided by centuries—"Centuriae"—and so the authors were called the "Centuriators of Magdeburg"—had evident anti-Catholic and polemical intentions. They indulged in extreme one-sidedness, even though they quoted the sources. Baronio followed the same method, but showed a greater accuracy in the use of the documents. The *Annales* had enormous success, witnessed by twenty editions and dozens of partial editions, compendiums and translations. See Prof. Pincherle's comments on the work of Baronio in *L'Oratorio di S. Filippo Neri*, XXII (1965), 12, 18–19; H. Jedin, *Il Cardinale Cesare Baronio* (Brescia, 1982); A. Cistellini, "Attualità di Cesare Baronio," in *Memorie Oratoriane*," XIV (1984), 42–54; M. T. Bonadonna Russo, "*La cultura storica nella Congregazione dell'Oratorio*," in *San Filippo Neri nella realtà romana del XVI secolo*... (Rome, 2000), 69–88.

115. *Collectanea*, 155–163; Cistellini, *S. Filippo Neri*, I, 605–622.

116. *Process*, III, 269. Tarugi, at the occasion of his election, congratulated Cardinal Federico Borromeo because the new pope shines with "lively faith, ardent charity, chastity, gentleness, and justice with all the other virtues and Catholic doctrine all together" (C. Marcora, ed., "Corrispondenza del Cardinal Tarugi ad Cardinal Federico Borromeo," *Memorie storiche della diocesi di Milan*, XI (1964), 130–132).

117. Cistellini, *San Filippo Neri*, I, 671–674.

118. Pietro Consolii (d. 1643). Bacci-Ricci, *Vita di san Filippo Neri...con la notizia di alcuni compagni...* (Rome, 1672); "Alcune azzioni, detti et ammaestramenti del Nostro glorioso Padre S. Filippo Neri...riferiti dalla s. mem. del P. Pietro Consolini," *cod. Bibl. Naz. Roma, Fondo S. Francesca Romana*, XIIIff., 19–20.

119. Fr. Gigli was the first priest to be buried in the Chiesa Nuova. When he died, his heart was placed by the layman Giovan Battista Guerra next to the corpse of Gigli; the heart was not found when he was exhumed, while all the rest was in a good state of preservation. *Process*, I, 49–52.

120. S. Luigi Gonzaga (1568–1591). V. Cepari, *Vita del Bl. Luigi Gonzaga della*

Compagnia di Giesù (Rome, 1606); M. Scaduto, "L'azione di un mistico," in *La Civiltà Cattolica* (December 1968), pp. 544–545; M. Paganella, *S. Luigi Gonzaga. Un ritratto in piedi* (Milan, 1991).

121. A. Valier, *Il dialogo della gioia cristiana*, text in Latin, Italian translation and introduction by A. Cistellini (Brescia, 1975).
122. S. Giuseppe Calasanzio (1557–1648). F. Giordano, *Il Calasanzio e l'origine della scuola popolare* (Genoa, 1960); C. Vila Pala, "Calsanz y san Felipe Neri," in *Memorie Oratoriane*, III-IV (1981), 25–34.
123. Cf. Philip's letter to His Holiness and the Pope's response in S. Filippo Neri, *Gli scritti e le massime*, 110–114. Silvio Antoniano, mastro di camera, who carried these notes back and forth. See *Process*, IV, 303–304; s. v. "relationships with the Popes."
124. Cistellini, *San Filippo Neri*, II, 1011–1014; Pastor, XI, 89–103.
125. Cistellini, *San Filippo Neri*, II, 884–888.
126. Cistellini, *San Filippo Neri*, II, 917–935.
127. *Process*, I, 287.
128. F. Borromeo, *Argumenta*, Biblioteca Ambrosiana, A77, f. 67r, published in *Miscellanea adnotationum variorum*, ed. Gruppo editoriale Zaccaria (Milan, 1985), 57.
129. *Process*, II, 328.
130. *Process*, I, 66.
131. Cistellini, *San Filippo Neri*, II, 961–971.
132. A. Pedrini, "Filippo Neri e Francesco di Sales," in *Palestra del Clero*, LXVII (1967), 21, pp. 1321–1336. See St. Francis de Sales in Chapter V for a brief biography and bibliography.
133. G. Incisa della Rocchetta, "La cappella di san Filippo Neri alla Chiesa Nuova," in *Oratorium*, III (1972), 1, 46–52; ibid., "L'anticamera del Santo e la cappella privata di san Filippo. La 'sala rossa' e la cappelletta interna di san Filippo," in *Oratorium*, III (1972), 2, 74–101. "Il Santuario Filippino della Vallicella," in *Quaderni dell'Oratorio*, 2.
134. St. Philip still wears on the ring finger of his right hand the episcopal ring which Cardinal Alessandro put there as a sign of incomparable affection, when he venerated his body. The beautiful silver mask that covers the face of the Saint is the work of Tomaso Cortine, executed in 1603.
135. "La sepoltura del Baronio," in *L'Oratorio di San Filippo Neri*, XVII (1960), 10–11.
136. "P. Bérulle, generale della Compagnia dell'Oratorio di Gesù Christo, il quale, quando venne a Roma non si poteva staccare dalla chiea nostra, e disse d'aver animo di uniformarsi con l'Istituto di san Filippo, quanto comportano li cervelli di Francia, quali, dice, non durano troppo in inceptis" (Giustiniani al Binago, 26.6.1627). He had been in Rome in August of 1624, and at that time

had established very close ties at the Vallicella. A brief of 1625 conceded to the Oratory in France the same spiritual privileges as those of the Oratory at the Vallicella. "Lettera del Bérulle ai PP. di Roma," in *L'Oratorio di S. Filippo Neri*, XIX (1962), 7, 15–16. *Opera omnia di P. de bérulle, Oeuvres complètes* (Paris: Cerf, 1995ff.).

137. *Collectanea*, 209–253.
138. *Collectanea*, 63–65; 66–67.
139. Cistellini, *San Filippo Neri*, III, 2051–2053.
140. Bull of Urban VIII, *Rationi congruit*, August 6, 1623, in *Bulliarum Romanum*, Editio Taurinensis (1858), XVIII, 11–23; also in "Quaderni di Oratorium. Spirituallità e Storia filippina," *IV Centenario della morte di S. Filippo Neri* (1995), 2, 10–26, Italian translation ed. A. Venturoli, 27–44; F. Zazzara, "Diario delle onoranze a S. Filippo dalla morte alla canonizzazione," ed. G. Incisa della Rocchetta, *Quaderni dell'Oratorio*, VI (1962), 1–28; G. Incisa della Rocchetta, "A 250 anni dalla canonizzazione di san Filippo. La Chiesa Nuova nel marzo 1622," in *Oratorium*, III (1972), 1, 33–40.
141. M. T. Russo Bonadonna, "L'offerta di un calice a San Filippo," in *L'Oratorio di S. Filippo Neri*, XX (1963), 5, 10–12.
142. Pier Giacomo Bacci (1576–1656), entered the Congregation in 1604. His work remains of fundamental importance for the biography of Philip. N. VIAN, "Il P. P. G. Bacci e la sua opera agiografica," in *L'Oratorio di S. Filippo Neri*, XXII ((1965), 12, 1–2.
143. Biblioteca Vallicelliana, O.58, O .59, O.60.
144. A. Cistellini, "A proposito della Vita di S. Filippo Neri di Antonio Gallonio," in *Rivista di storia della Chiesa in Italia*, LIV (2000), 1, 1–6.
145. A. Cistellini, "I biografi filippini L. Ponnelle e L. Bordet e la loro opera," in *Memorie Oratoriane*, II (1981), 5–6–7–8, 47–68. See also G. de Libero, *Vita di san Filippo Neri, Apostolo di Roma* (Grottaferrata, 1960), 487–510.
146. "The Author, in addition to the intelligent, patient and critical rereading of the sources and the historiography regarding Philip, has sifted through and reviewed a considerable quantity of archival documents, often bringing them to light for the first time. With a commitment that has occupied the greater part of his life of scholarship, he has furnished us with an indispensable instrument for all those who will study Philip Neri in the future. There is also a rich and important bibliographical apparatus" (G. P. Pacini, "La Congregazione dei Chierici Secolari dell'Oratorio: novità, problemi, prime fondazioni," in *Quaderni Franzoniani*, X (1997), 8).
147. The oldest collection appears to be that published by Fr. Agostino Manni (Brescia, 1607). There is also: *Raccolta di vari detti e massime spirituali,* of unknown authorship, Cod. O.18 of the Biblioteca Vallicelliana; in the *Process*, II, 26–29: remembrances and testimony of Francesco Zazzara; ibid., II, 77–78: of Cardinal

P. P. Crescenzi; ibid., II, 88–89: of M. A. Maffa. The largest collection, datable to the first years of the seventeenth century, is found in a fascicle in the Archives of the Congregation in Rome, A.III.9; also: "Alcune azzioni, detti et ammaestramenti del Nostro glorioso Padre Filippo Neri...riferiti dalla s. mem. del P. Pietro Consolini," *cod. Bibl. Naz. Roma, Fondo S. Francesca Romana*, 13ff., 19–20. The following chapters will draw upon these sources, even when they are not expressly cited.

148. Review by A. Cistellini in *Memorie Oratoriane* (1981), 3–4, 55–57.
149. *Process*, III, 400–403.
150. An expression of Philip's natural delicacy, which others also remembered as characteristic of Philip as an adult and even in advanced age: see *Process*, II, 24; III, 9–10.
151. *Process*, I, 172; II, 223; III, 66 and 379; IV, 119.
152. P. G. Bacci, *Vita di S. Filippo...*, IV, VII, 2.
153. Born in Salerno the same day that Philip was born, and died in Rome, September 2, 1595, a little more than three months after Philip.
154. *Process*, II, 89 and note 1173.
155. *Process*, II, 346.
156. For the iconography of Philip, see: *Process*, IV, 333: s. v. *Ritratti* (funeral mask and form made in wax; also the oldest portraits); also L. Ponelli-Bordet, *San Filippo Neri e la società romana del suo tempo* (Florence, 1986), 68–69; G. Incisa della Rocchetta, "Contributo all'iconografia di S. Filippo Neri," *Studi in onore di A. Petrucci* (Milan-Rome, 1969), 35–38; N. Vian, "Schede bibliografiche oratoriane. Iconografia," in *Oratorium*, II (1971), 1, 19–39; ibid., "Per un'iconografia di S. Filippo Neri," in *Oratorium*, IV (1973), 2, 111–113; R. Carapelli, ed., *San Filippo Neri nell'arte, catalogo della Mostra* (Florence, 1989).
157. See *Process*, IV, 327, s. v. *"bizzarie e le burle."* Also G. de Libero, *San Filippo Neri gioca e ride* (Rome, 1962); N. Gigli (A. Cistellini), "Filippo, santo burlevole: tra musiche e danze," in *Memorie Oratoriane* (1982), 41–45.
158. One can see St. Philip with his heart inflamed in the "Pater extaticus" of Goethe's *Faust*. Goethe, who called Philip "my saint" (G. W. Goethe, *Viaggio in Italia*, 26, 5, 1787). In Act V there appear in the afterlife four solemn anachorites: Pater ecstaticus, Pater profundus, Pater seraphicus, and Doctor marianus. The verses that the poet gives to Pater ecstaticus, burning with divine love, draw marvelously the fervid Philip, transfixed by his "infirmity of love": "Joy ever searing on, / Love's ever-glowing bond, / Seething with ache the breast, / Foaming of God-lust blest. / Arrows, pierce through me, / Lances, undo me, / Bludgeons, come batter me, / Lightning come shatter me, / That dross might separate / All and evaporate, / Shine but the lasting star, / Timeless love's core." *Faust*, trans. Walter Arndt, ed. Cyrus Hamlin (New York and London: Norton Critical Edition, 1976, 2001).

159. *Process*, I, 142 and note 416.
160. TRANSLATOR'S NOTE: "Raggionarli de lettere": also any written matters, philosophy and theology, for example.
161. See *Process*, IV, 311, s. v. "Ammaestratore e confortore."
162. "Since he was Florentine, it pleased him that others knew that he was." G. B. Strozzi to Nero del Nero: 23.12.1595, in *Arch. Congr. di Roma*, A.III.51, 18, 7–66.
163. In the Florentine edition of 1986, pp. vii-xiv.
164. A. Cistellini, "Filippo Neri santo fiorentino," in *Memorie Oratoriane*, XVII (1995), 7–66.
165. TRANSLATOR'S NOTE: An eccentric Florentine spirit.
166. TRANSLATOR'S NOTE: Working class section of Florence, across the Arno river.
167. TRANSLATOR'S NOTE: My inner life is my secret.
168. *Process*, II, 22, 23, 30.
169. Those who did this service for him were primarily Fathers Tarugi, Gigli, Fedeli, sometimes Talpa, in addition to those who held the office of secretary of the Congregation. See S. Filippo Neri, *Gli scritti e le massime*, 17–20.
170. John Paul II, *Letter to the Oratorians on the Fourth Centenary of St. Philip Neri*, October 7, 1994.
171. *Process*, II, 77; N. Vian, "Un sonetto parodistico petrarchesco noto a S. Filippo Neri," in *Rivista di storia della Chiesa in Italia*, I (1947), 293–297; ibid., in *Memorie Oratoriane*, XIV (1984), 19–22.
172. G. Costantini, *San Filippo degli apposti Amen. Mistero in Quattro atti* (Vicenza, 1994).
173. This is the healthy root of all the jokes that characterized the life of Father Philip. It is impossible to understand them detached from this context of mortification. The tricks, witticisms, and jokes, of which Fr. Philip's life is full, are never ends in themselves, even if they are undoubtedly expressions of Philip's Florentine nature and temperament.
174. Cf. A. Cistellini, "I libri e la libreria di San Filippo Neri," in *Memorie oratoriane*, XVIII (1997), 7–43; N. Vian, "S. Filippo bibliofilo alla sua maniera," in G. Papini, *S. Filippo Neri fiorentino* (Vicenza, 1994), 29–31.
175. See *Process*, I, 298–299, s. v. "Studi e dottrina."
176. *Process*, I, 175 and note 484; II, 207 and note 1424: "I remember having heard from a number of persons and from Fr. Philip himself that, when he went as a young man to hear lectures on philosophy and theology, a crucifix that was in the hall where the lectures were brought him to such a state of devotion that he could not pay attention to the lesson, but found himself bursting constantly into tears."
177. John Henry Newman, *Meditations and Devotions* (London, 1914).
178. *Process*, IV, 28.
179. Cistellini, *San Filippo*, I, 33.

180. Note in Cistellini's text: *Capecelatro*, I, 20.
181. Note in Cistellini's text: N. Vian, "Solitudine e mondo di S. Filippo," in *Oratorium*, VI (1975), 118–132.
182. *Process*, I, 194.
183. *Process*, II, 112.
184. *Process*, II, 59.
185. A. Gallonio, *Vita Beati Patris*, 9. Translated as "in order to follow the call of Christ," in *The Life of St. Philip Neri*, trans. Jerome Bertram of the Oxford Oratory (San Francisco, 2005), 9.
186. *Process*, III, 266.
187. *Process*, III, 156.
188. *Process*, I, 248.
189. P. Pacini, "La congregazione dei Chierici secolari, dell'Oratorio: novità, problemi, prime fondazioni (1575–1622)," *in Quaderni Franzoniani*, X (1997), 2, 10.
190. Note in Pacini's text: Ponnelle-Bordet, *San Filippo Neri e la società romana del suo tempo*, p. 69. Translated as *St. Philip Neri and the Roman Society and His Times (1515–1595)*, trans. Ralph Frances Kerr of the London Oratory (London, 1932), 120.
191. Note in Pacini's text: ibid., p. 69 [Kerr, 120].
192. Note in Pacini's text: ibid., p. 70 [Kerr, 119–120].
193. *Process*, II, 86: "amava andare al piú alto della casa a fare oratione."
194. *Process*, III, 267–268; III, 273, note 2184; IV, 102; 189, note 198.
195. *Process*, I, 20.
196. *Process*, II, 328. See also S. Filippo Neri, *Gli scritti e le massime*, 157.
197. S. Filippo Neri, *Gli scritti e le massime*, 73.
198. G. Carriquiry Lecour, "El Oratorio en la mission de la Iglesia al alba del Tercer Milenio," paper presented at the 2000 General Congress of the Confederation of the Oratory, in *Memoria Congressus Generalis*, pro-manuscripto, ed. Procura Generale (Rome, 2000), pp. 8–10.
199. TRANSLATOR'S NOTE: "Those present were very much aware that he was being acted upon rather than acting."
200. *Process*, I, 103–104 and note 324; III, 84–86; 85 and note 1841.
201. In Philip's library there are two copies of the decrees of the Council: A. Cistellini, "I libri e la libreria di san Filippo Neri," in *Memorie oratoriane*, XVIII (1997), 31–32.
202. A. Cistellini, "Filippo Neri, prete romano," in *San Filippo Neri nella realtà romana del XVI secolo...* (Rome, 2000), 5–12.
203. A. Gallonio, *Vita del B. Padre*, p. 48. (The citations from Gallonio always refer to the critical edition ed. M. T. Bonadonna Russo [Rome, 1995].) Even as a layman, Philip was accustomed to receive communion daily. Cf. P. G. Bacci, *Vita*, II, 1, 125.

204. S. Filippo Neri, *Gli scritti e le massime*, 174.
205. *Process*, II, 103.
206. *Process*, I, 48.
207. *Process*, II, 359.
208. *Process*, I, 97.
209. *Process*, I, 116–117.
210. P. G. Bacci, *Vita*, II, I, 17.
211. *Process*, I, 126; see for the species of bread, II, 74.
212. P. G. Bacci, *Vita*, II, 1, 10.
213. *Process*, I, 66.
214. *Process*, I, 68.
215. Pius XII, in the fourth anniversary of this event, indicated the reach of this prodigious fact: "singular charism of charity by which the apostle of Rome was privileged by God with the visible dilation of his heart...a new prodigy."
216. H. Bremont, *Divertissements devant l'arche* (Paris, 1930), 88.
217. F. Faber, *The Spirit and Genius of St. Philip* (London, 1850).
218. We have testimony to this effect in the confidences which the Father made to Federico Borromeo: "Mi disse con grande humiltà che...nel principio della sua conversione pregò lo Spirito santo che gli desse spirito." ["He told me with great humility that at the beginning of his conversion he prayed to the Holy Spirit that he would give him spirit."] Cardinal F. Borromeo, "Argumenta," in *Miscellanea adnotationum variarum* (Milan, 1985), 57.
219. See *Process*, IV, 299 s. v. "Palpitazione di cuore, inarcature delle costole, calori fisici." ["Palpitations of the heart, bowing of the ribs, physical warmth."]
220. *Process*, I, 182.
221. *Process*, I, 185; see also the declaration given by the doctor A. Vettori, in *Process*, IV, 35–36: "He told me that when he was thirty he was in a state of great fervor and prayed to the Holy Spirit that he would give him a great portion of spirit: and he told me that he received so much that he had to throw himself onto the ground, and when he arose he could feel that his ribs had expanded outward and there was a sort of concussion within, which lasted as long as he lived." The autopsy verified that two ribs were detached from the cartilage and formed a swelling visible on the left side of his chest. See *Process*, IV, 299.
222. P. G. Bacci, *Vita*, I, 8, 1: "Filippo si accostava alla spicciolata, ora questo, ora quello...divenivano presto suoi amici."
223. *Process*, II, 105.
224. P. G. Bacci, *Vita*, II, 17, 26: "He fled every singularity, origin and fomenter of pride, especially spiritual pride"; ibid., III, 22, 26: "One must always walk in mortification and in holy humility."
225. H. Jedin, *Riforma Cattolica o Controriforma?* (Brescia, 1957), 35.
226. A. Cistellini, *San Filippo*, I, 18.

227. *Process*, II, 77; S. Filippo Neri, *Gli scritti e le massime*, 178–179: "Non farò mai bene, se tu non m'aiuti"; "io mi diffido di me stesso e confido in te."
228. "He took such pleasure in saying the 'Pater noster' that he was hardly able to finish it": *Process*, I, 182.
229. *Process*, IV, 72: "The lady who was ambassador to Spain asking him one day how long it had been since he had left the world, he answered that he had never left it."
230. Cistellini, "San Filippo Neri e Girolamo Savonarola," in *Memorie Oratoriane*, XIX (1999), 5–16.
231. *Process*, III, 177–178 and note 2023; IV, 23.
232. Braudrillart writes in the introduction to Ponnelle and Bordet's Life of St. Philip: "The spirit of Philip consists in putting one at ease, in not constraining, in allowing each one, within the limits of what is permissible, to manifest the originality of his own thoughts and of his character, in taking pleasure as much in diversity as in unity, in respecting the originality of souls."
233. A. Rosmini, *Lo spirito di S. Filippo Neri*, ed. F. de Giorgi (Brescia, 1996), pp. x–xi; see also G. Cristaldi, "Antonio Rosmini e San Filippo Neri," in *Memorie Oratoriane*, XVI (1993), 6–8.
234. *Process*, IV, 105.
235. The equivalent of "don" in Italian (dominus, lord, an aristocratic or feudal title) which is used still today in some of the romance languages as the title for the secular clergy.
236. TRANSLATOR'S NOTE: Wordplay: *Pensabene* = think well; *pensabenata* = well-thought, well-conceived, witty jokes.
237. G. Marangoni, *Vita del servo di Dio Bonsignore Cacciaguerra...di alcuni suoi penitenti*, 68.
238. Among others, there is the witness of Pellegrino Altobelli, *Process*, II, 288: "Each time that I meet him on the street, he always takes my face between his hands, saying to me: 'How are you and what are you doing?' And once when he met me at the palace of Cardinal Sforza and immediately came over to me, and with his usual caresses, taking my face in his hands said: 'what are you up to, St. Pellegrino?' and he went away happy..."; also typical is the gesture of pressing his penitents' heads to his breast, as Fabrizio de' Massimi, among many others, testifies, *Process*, II, 333: "I had the experience in my person, many times, when I was troubled or tempted, that he held my head close and holding it there for a bit to his breast, and I felt how his heart jumped around and he trembled all over: I was completely consoled, and I have heard the same thing from many others."
239. See, for example, *Process*, I, 273 (he frees Fabrizio Massimi from the troubles given him by his dependants); I, 153 (he alleviates the maladies of body and soul of his doctor Angelo Vittori); III, 188–190 (he helps Francesco de' Rustici

to recover a large sum of money that he had lent); I, 89 (he has Marcello Ferro withdraw in time some money that he had lent to a Bank that then fails). And there are so many other instances where he is attentive to the material situations of his sons, whom he visits and assists in every way possible: *Process*, II, 110: "where he could be of help to his spiritual sons, and to others, he would leave aside all his own affairs, and regardless of the inconvenience or discomfort... and especially in the case of sickness, would visit them often...and this same charity he showed in temporal things, in which both with counsel and with help he would succor everyone... And he was affable, pleasing, and caressed everyone...and rarely did anyone go entirely away from him, once they had encountered him..."

240. *Process*, IV, 2; letter to Angelo Vai, in S. Filippo Neri, *Gli scritti e le massime*, 28–32.
241. Among the many witnesses, we indicate: *Process*, I, 55–57; 186; 255; II, 336; IV, 188. See also in *Process*, IV, 308, s. v. "Confessore," his diligence in hearing confessions.
242. *Process*, II, 111: "Our holy Father knew, with the great prudence with which he was so highly gifted, the nature of his spiritual sons." *Process*, I, 141: "and he had great regard for the nature and entire being of each person"; IV, 61 (denies communion to Pietro Focile who went in costume); II, 66–67 (allows Marco A. Vitelleschi to go to dances); I, 296–297 (refuses to allow Tarugi permission to rise before dawn to pray); I, 354 (orders Antonio Fucci to continue to practice medicine in spite of temptations); IV, 167 (wants Andrea Fiorenzuola to leave his offices at Court); IV, 146–148 (dissuades Francesco Pucci from becoming a Capuchin); I, 188 (throws to the ground a man condemned to death but impenitent and convinces him to make his confession). There is no formula: each person is an unicum.
243. L. Ponnelle and L. Bordet, *San Filippo Neri e la società romana...*, 128 [Kerr, 179].
244. G. Carriquiry Lecour, "El Oratorio en la mision de la Iglesia al alba del Tercer Milenio," pp. 8–10.
245. *Process*, IV, 217–218.
246. "His face was jovial and very merry," Francesco Zazzara recalled: S. Filippo Neri, *Gli scritti e le massime*, 146.
247. S. Filippo Neri, *Gli scritti e le massime*, 145: "Our Holy Father would say that in order to arrive at perfection and acquire perfectly the gift of humility four things are necessary: spernere mundum, spernere nullum, spernere se ipsum, spernere se sperni."
248. *Process*, I, 239.
249. *Process*, I, 140; II, 124.
250. *Process*, I, 225–226.

251. *Process*, III, 278.
252. *Process*, III, 224.
253. *Process*, IV, 324.
254. *Process*, III, 276–77.
255. *Process*, II, 85.
256. *Process*, I, 239: "Jesus, Jesus, let everyone call for Jesus."
257. *Process*, I, 269: "Where is that man who speaks with evangelical simplicity?"
258. In Philip's positive evaluation of what is human, many authors have seen the influence of the spirit of Humanism which he breathed in both Florence and Rome. A clear summary of this argument can be found, for example, in M. Marcocchi, "Prefazione," in S. Filippo Neri, *Gli scritti e le massime*, 12–13: "The spiritual program of Neri nourished itself on faith in human nature and love for art.... It is characterized by an equilibrium in the relationship between God and man, between nature and grace. It flees gloomy, threatening attitudes, but illumines everything with merriment and joy. This attitude is influenced by Christian humanism, the theology of which holds that grace does not suppress nature, but rather heals, strengthens, perfects it."
259. Probably a Poor Clare nun of the Monastery of the Purification, named Maria Francesca. *Process*, IV, 116–117.
260. M. Battlori, P. Prodi, R. DeMaio, A. Marabottini, ed., "La regolata iconografica della Controriforma nella Roma del Cinquecento," in *Ricerche per la Storia religiosa di Roma*, II (1977), 43.
261. P. G. Bacci, *Vita*, III, 1, 5.
262. S. Barchiesi, "Cappella della Visitazione," in C. Barbieri, S. Barchiesi, and D. Ferrara, *Santa Maria in Vallicella. Chiesa Nuova* (Rome, 1995), 126–131.
263. A. Talpa, "L'Istituto della Congregazione dell'Oratorio," ed. G. Incisa della Rocchetta, in *Oratorium*, IV, (1973), 1, 5–37.
264. M. Marcocchi, "Prefazione," 8–9.
265. *Process*, I, 239.

NOTES FOR CHAPTER II

1. A. Cistellini, "L'Oratorio filippino ai suoi primordi," in *Memorie Oratoriane*, III (1982), 10–11–12, p. 8. Henceforth cited as Cistellini, "L'Oratorio filippino." This lengthy essay, which is included in the author's *San Filippo*, I, 47–116, is the fullest and most trustworthy reconstruction of the beginnings and the development of the Oratory. We shall rely on this constantly.
2. Anonymous document datable to 1567, in *Memorie Oratoriane*, new series, IX (1982), 9.
3. Cf. John Paul II, "Novo millennium ineunte," 29.

4. John Paul II, Address to the Confederation of the Oratory of St. Philip Neri, October 5, 2000, in *Osservatore Romano*, October 6, 2000.
5. *Process*, III, 387.
6. Ibid.
7. John Henry Newman, "Sermon 12: The Mission of St. Philip, Part 2," *Sermons Preached on Various Occasions* (London: Burns and Lambert, 1857), p. 274.
8. See also the testimony of A. Gallonio in *Process*, I, 186: "Once he became a confessor, he never left Rome, but was always present in the confessional in order to gain souls, and he continued in this way into his last years…and I saw him in the last day of his life, and the same evening that he died he confessed the illustrious Cardinal Cusano, even though he had heard confessions all morning."
9. Cf. P. G. Bacci, *Vita*, IV, III, 1-2-3.
10. Referring to the activity undertaken by St. Philip Neri and the Fathers of the Congregation of the Oratory, we prefer to use the term "apostolate" rather than the term "pastoral ministry" in common use today.
11. A. Gallonio, *Vita del B. Padre Filippo*, 52: "ardeva di desiderio di tirare le anime a Christo."
12. A. Cistellini, "L'Oratorio filippino," 4.
13. C. Marcora ed., "Corrispondenza tra S. Carlo e F. M. Tarugi," in *Memorie storiche della Diocesi di Milan*, XIV (1967), pp. 265–269; also in *Memorie Oratoriane*, III (1982), 9, 13–16.
14. The uncertainty has to do, obviously, with only the year: Gasbarri places it in 1551–1552: C. Gasbarri, *L'Oratorio filippino (1551–1552)* (Roma, 1957); Cistellini in 1554–1555: A. Cistellini, "L'Oratorio filippino ha quattrocento anni," in *Humanitas*, IX (1954), 12, 1107–1119; "L'Oratorio filippino," 4.
15. See the testimony regarding the first encounters: *Process*, IV, 301. S.V. "L'Oratorio."
16. *Process*, I, 28–29.
17. *Process*, III, 143.
18. *Process*, III, 387.
19. *Process*, I, 28–29.
20. A. Cistellini, "L'Oratorio filippino," 6.
21. Ibid., 6–7.
22. Ibid., 6–7.
23. Ibid., 10–12.
24. A. Gallonio, *Vita del B. Padre Filippo*, 55.
25. *Process*, I, 240–244; IV, 197, n. 629.
26. *Process*, I, 18–28.
27. *Process*, I, 20–21, n. 86.
28. Bacci-Ricci, *Vita di S. Filippo…con notizie di alcuni compagni* (Roma, 1672).
29. *Process*, IV, 206–207; I, 16, n. 67; A. Gallonio, *Vita B. Patris*, 126.

30. *Process*, I, 303–306, and n. 323; 270–271, and n. 1542; IV, 77–78. Cf. IV in the index.
31. S. Filippo Neri, *Gli scritti e le massime*, 28–32.
32. *Process*, I, 105–106 and note 329; III, 392.
33. *Process*, I, 187, note 514.
34. *Process*, I, 200, 319 and elsewhere; see IV in the index.
35. *Process*, III, 299.
36. G. M. Brocchi, *Vita de' santi e Beati fiorentini* (Florence, 1742), p. 625.
37. *Process*, IV, 113.
38. *Process*, I, 28–29.
39. *Process*, I, 28–31, and note 112; I, 373–375; II, 139–141; 273–278; 281–283.
40. *Process*, I, 244–250; II, 271–272.
41. *Process*, I, 285–287; Bacci-Ricci, *Vita di S. Filippo...con notizia di alcuni compagni* (Roma, 1672).
42. *Process*, I, 295–297; Bacci-Ricci, *Vita di S. Filippo*, cit.
43. *Process*, I, 95, and note 309; IV, 52.
44. *Process*, I, 15–17.
45. *Process*, I, 103–106.
46. G. F. Bordini, *Philippi Nerii, religiosissimi presbyteri Vitae compendium*, cit., 10.
47. Ibid.
48. *Process*, I, 52. See IV, 266: "Capriccio."
49. TRANSLATOR'S NOTE: "The Canticles (poems) of the Blessed Jacopone da Todi...with commentary."
50. TRANSLATOR'S NOTE: "And the noble Marmitta, / who turned to God, / from the cares of the world detached himself entirely."
51. Marmitta wrote a detailed account of this edifying death, published in the *Process*, IV, 173–186. See also the deposition of Marcello Ferro in *Process*, I, 84–86.
52. The atmosphere which Alessandro encountered at S. Girolamo and his contact with Fr. Philip certainly had an effect on Alessandro's decision to seek the priesthood. He returned to Rome as ambassador of the Grande Duke and became one of the most assiduous and affectionate spiritual sons of Fr. Philip. He was also one of the most important supporters of the fledgling Congregation of the Oratory. Fr. Philip loved him tenderly for his virtues, and shared with Alessandro his prediction of the brief duration of Pius' pontificate. It was in fact Cardinal Alessandro de' Medici who celebrated the first Mass in the Chiesa Nuova and consecrated it. As we said above, Fr. Philip still wears on his finger the Episcopal ring that Alessandro put there when he visited the body.
53. A. Cistellini, *L'Oratorio filippino*, 18.
54. A. Cistellini, "Fra Figliucci e San Filippo Neri," in *Rassegna di ascetica e mistica*, cit.; see the three unpublished letters of Figliucci to Fr. Philip.
55. A. Cistellini, *L'Oratorio filippina*, 25.

56. See note 47 in Ch. I.
57. See note 45 in Ch. I, and the brief profile in Ch. VI.
58. Letter of Baronio to his mother, 12.3.1562; see Calenzio, *Cesare Baronio...*, 62; G. L. Masetti Zannini, "Cesare Baronio e sua madre," in *Oratorium*, I (1979), 37.
59. P. G. Bacci, *Vita*, I, X, 6: "Crebbe di poi talmente il numero, che non essendo capace la sua stanza di tanta gente, il Santo ne prese alcune altre vicine."
60. A. Cistellini, *L'Oratorio filippino*, 19–23.
61. *Process*, III, 248.
62. *Process*, III, 143.
63. Stupendous testimonial of the simplicity of the origins, given by Simone Grazzini in *Process*, III, 43–44; 143; 248–253; 388.
64. *Process*, III, 43: "The blessed Father hosted them there, sometimes with a short sermon on the things of God, other times having them read some spiritual book, on which he would have them comment according to the capacity of each."
65. "Vere locum orationi destinatum Oratorium dicimus," begin the old Institutes of the Congregation: "we properly call Oratory a place destined for prayer. In fact, when the familiar treatment of the Word of God, which is born in the Oratory, matured and was transferred into the Church, it kept the name of Oratory, although less appropriately..." "Oratory was a generic term used from ancient times to indicate a place set aside for prayer, usually private prayer. Here, however, it refers to an institution, called Oratory by antonomasia. And we must not overlook the fact that, right in this time when new Confraternities were born and prospered in Rome (sixty-one were erected in the second half of the sixteenth century), the Oratory was never just one among the many, but stood part as a singular experience of the common life, because its participants were free, it had no statutes or lists of members: it was a spontaneous gathering, even if as time went on it had to develop ways of governing itself" (A. Cistellini, *L'Oratorio filippino*, 20–21). The Oratory also stood apart from other institutions because it had no official recognition and did not seek it. It was not conceived or configured as a confraternity. Those who came to the Oratorian exercises were not required to come regularly, as the old documents emphasize by saying that the place was not like "a little convent, since the place called Oratory was open every day and whoever wished to come or go could do so as he wished" (Can., vv. 2, 10). A draft of the regulations of the Oratory datable to 1574 is even more precise in this regard: "let it be clear, however...that all these things are voluntary, without any obligation, because this is not an institute but rather each may come and go as he likes and these regulations are made only to avoid any confusion" (B.V.O. 571, 234–235).
66. *Process*, III, 143: "The blessed Father wanted to give the exercises definite shape and he began by having Francesco Maria Tarugi and Cesare Baronio and others among his spiritual sons give sermons. He would give them help and from time

to time he would ask a question concerning that which had been said: he always put the questions to those that he knew were capable of responding and of providing edifying answers." *Process*, II, 324: "and the first who began to give talks in that place, in obedience to the blessed Philip, were Fr. Tarugi and Giovanni Battista Modio; then other laymen, Baronio, then Bordini, Ottavio Paravicino, Fr. Germanico Fedeli, Camillo and others."

67. *Process*, III, 88.
68. *Process*, III, 47.
69. *Process*, II, 85–86; III, 313.
70. *Process*, I, 274; IV, 166–167.
71. *Process*, I, 148.
72. See the documents published in "Lineamenti dell'Oratorio e della Congregation in antichi memoriali," in *Memorie Oratoriane*, new series (1982), 9, 4–29, *passim*.
73. A. Cistellini, *L'Oratorio filippino*, 9.
74. Letter to the Bishop of Padua, in the Archives of the Congregation of Rome, A. IV. 21, 104.
75. Letter of December 9, 1588. A. Cistellini, "L'annunzio della parola nel ministero oratoriano," in *Memorie Oratoriane* (1975), No. 4, 5–12.
76. In the Archives of the Congregation at Naples, XIII, 1, 157.
77. TRANSLATOR'S NOTE: The "school of his spiritual sons."
78. TRANSLATOR'S NOTE: The "school of the Lord's service."
79. TRANSLATOR'S NOTE: The "first school of blessed Francis."
80. A Dominican, he was close to Fr. Philip in Rome. When he was consecrated as bishop, he shone as one of the most sublime apostolic figures in the Church of his time.
81. A. Cistellini, *L'Oratorio filippino*, 27.
82. Ibid.
83. Ibid.
84. Acts of the Apostles 2:42, quoted from the Revised Standard Version Catholic Edition.
85. C. Baronii, *Annales Ecclesiastici*, I (Rome, 1588).
86. Letter of F. M. Tarugi to O. Mancini, Naples, June 22, 1590, in the Archives of the Congregation of Florence, Carte Mancini.
87. A. Talpa, *Instituto della Congregation dell' Oratorio*, ed. G. Incisa della Rocchetta, "Il Trattato di P. Antonio Talpa sulle origini e sul significato dell'Instituto della Congregazione dell'Oratorio," in *Oratorium*, IV (1973), 1, 3–41.
88. "The daily and familiar exercise of the Word of God," Talpa says, is an indispensable instrument "for introducing and maintaining the other two instruments, that is the participation in the Sacraments and the exercise of preaching." Talpa, *Instituto...*, cit. 8–9.

89. A. Cistellini, *L'Oratorio filippino*, 31.
90. Pateri uses a telling expression (*Process*, III, 143) to describe the preaching in the Oratory: "the blessed Father wanted his students to become accustomed to a way of speaking the Word of God that it would strike the hearts of the listeners more than their ears." "To speak the Word of God": this is perhaps the best definition of that "treat familiarly of the divine Word" that remains the indispensable charism of the Oratory; "wound the heart" with "words inflamed with spirit": this is the "style" of Oratory preaching.
91. That this happened daily was also striking and attractive, as well as the style of preaching the Word. Bacci emphasizes this, *Vita*, I, XIV, 3: "In this Oratory, Philip...was the first to introduce into Rome the daily Word of God."
92. Ibid.
93. The documents are published in *Memorie Oratoriane*, IX (1982), 4–29.
94. Published for the first time, ed. A. Bellucci in *Aevum* (December 1927), 625–633, and republished, ed. A. Cistellini, in *Memorie Oratoriane*, XVII (1995), 110–115; Italian version, ed. A. Venturoli, in *Il profeta della gioia* (Milan, 1999), 75–85.
95. *Annales*, cit., vol. 1, ad ann. 57.
96. Inserted in the papers of the canonical proceedings of Bl. Giov. Giovenale; copy in the Archives of the Congregation of Naples, XXII, 1, 406–409.
97. In the Congregation of the Oratory, as in many institutes of that time, the Scriptures were the most familiar spiritual food. The Constitutions of 1583 ask those who are destined to public preaching to be thoroughly grounded in Sacred Scripture, which they would acquire through a constant contact, "day and night" with the pages of the divine Word: "percupimus eos qui pubblicis praedicationibus destinandi erunt, Scripturae divinae paginas...diurna nocturnaque manu diligentissime pertractare" . just a glance at the writings of the first Oratorians makes evident the great wealth of information and the penetration of the Scriptures that they had acquired.
98. Gregory Martin, *Roma sancta* (1581). Italian translation by G. Incisa della Rocchetta in *Oratorium*, I (1970), 90–91. Translation into English made from the Italian.
99. A. Cistellini, *L'Oratorio filippino*, 31.
100. *Process*, I, 365.
101. *Process*, III, 143–144.
102. This organized visit began with the Carnival of 1559, according to Gallonio. Thirty-odd persons participated, since the first most devoted followers of the Oratory already were considerable in number.
103. Beginning in 1560 the Dominican novices from the Minerva joined it; then, in 1563, also Cardinal Borromeo, nephew of the Pope, who at his own expense provided refreshments for the pilgrims, taking the place of Tassoni who had

done it before; by 1565 the number of participants had reached three thousand persons.

104. Bordini describes the unfolding of this Visit: *Process*, III, 389–390.
105. A. Cistellini, *L'Oratorio filippino*, 64.
106. A. Cistellini, *L'Oratorio filippino*, 61.
107. A. C. Speciani, Roma, 31.5.1578, in Archives of the Congregation of Rome. A. IV. 21, 40.
108. "The first that the Father invited to his room were certainly young, but none less than eighteen or twenty.... Contrary to a prevailing misconception, the Oratory was always configured as an institute for adults, not for adolescents, at least not early adolescents, at the beginning and ever since." Cistellini, *L'Oratorio filippino*, 66.
109. "There has never been a lack in the Congregation of members particularly gifted in working with the young, in some way heirs to the Father's wise pedagogy, but...examination shows that the apostolate to the young will develop better elsewhere than in Rome. In the first years of the Congregation, there began at the Vallicella a group for young boys, also called 'Congregation' and under the protection of the Assumption of the Blessed Virgin Mary, and directed by a father who acted as Prefect. There remains, however, little trace of this group, perhaps because it had little importance. Toward the end of the century it became part of the Oratory of the Young (quite small, and not all young people), which participated in the practices of the Little Oratory, and finally became part of it. It was in this Oratory that new and varied activities were introduced (dramatic presentations, recreation, and devotions), just as at the beginning the presence of musicians in the Oratory contributed to the development of the Lauds..." A. Cistellini, *L'Oratorio filippino*, 67.
110. "The Institute of the Congregation is principally the exercise of the Oratory, from which this Congregation was born," says Tarugi (*Collectanea*, 105). "Great will be Fr. Philip's displeasure, clear to the end of everything, should he see some of his own disperse their talents in a variety of occupations, under pressure from persons of standing, or even from the highest authorities (the Cardinal Vicar, even the Pope himself), those whom it is difficult to oppose." A. Cistellini, *L'Oratorio fillipino*, 40.
111. A. Cistellini, *L'Oratorio filippino*, 46.
112. Ibid.
113. A. Talpa, *L'Instituto*, cit. 24.
114. A. Cistellini, *L'Oratorio filippino*, 42–44.
115. TRANSLATOR'S NOTE: maestro = teacher, master.
116. A. Cistellini, *L'Oratorio filippino*, 45.
117. For this and other texts from the Constitutions quoted in this chapter, see the following chapters dedicated to the Congregations of the Confederation.
118. *Const.*, 1–4.

119. *Const.*, 118–119.
120. Approved by the General Congress of 1994 and published by the Procurator General of the Confederation: *L'Oratorio di S. Filippo Neri. Spiritual Path* (Verona. 1995), Chapter II, nn. 35–51.
121. See in this regard the pages dedicated, in the following chapter, to the activities undertaken by the Congregations.
122. "El marco historico de un Santo," in *Atti dell'Incontro: Ponencias*, pro-manuscripto (Sevilla, 1993).
123. "San Filippo Neri: da San Girolamo alla Vallicella," in ibid.
124. "Dimension pastoral del Oratorio hoy. Tres aspectos basicos: la Palabra, el Perdon, la Comunion," in ibid.
125. "La natura dell'Oratorio nei suoi aspetti più significativi," in ibid.
126. "Promover el Oratoriocomo un estilo de vida en la Iglesia," in ibid.
127. "El Oratorio y la cultura postmoderna," in *Atti dell'Incontro*, pro-manuscripto (Oaxtepec, Mexico, 1998).
128. "Agentes profeticos del Oratorio," in ibid.
129. "La cultura postmoderna y el desafio de las sectas protestantes," in ibid.
130. "El Oratorio en la Iglesia hoy," in ibid.
131. "El Oratorio, comunidad local en el contexto de la postmodernidad," in ibid.
132. "La Parroquia oratoriana," in ibid.
133. See the Acta del Encuentro, cit.
134. Federazione Nord-Italia delle Congregazioni dell'Oratorio, *Ripensando l'Oratorio. Elementi di riflessioni sull'Oratorio Secolare* (Brescia, 1999).
135. Ibid., 5–6.
136. G. Carriquiry Lecour, "L'Oratorio en la mission de la Iglesia al alba del Tercer Milenio," in *Memoria Congressus Generalis 2000*, cit., *passim.*

NOTES FOR CHAPTER III

1. TRANSLATOR'S NOTE: The Congregation of the Oratory.
2. TRANSLATOR'S NOTE: Religious order.
3. TRANSLATOR'S NOTE: Having one mind.
4. TRANSLATOR'S NOTE: Not only playing one's own instrument, but everyone playing together.
5. Cistellini, *San Filippo Neri*, I, 184–199. TRANSLATOR'S NOTE: From the time that the Oratory began to be active around him at San Girolamo, St. Philip told the Confraternity that he was renouncing his stipend, "offerens se velle suo arbitrio servire" (Archives of San Girolamo, T. 294, June 13, 1553).
6. C. Baronio, *De origine Oratorii*, cit., 113: "sine ignominia desertores et cum honore transfugae."

7. TRANSLATOR'S NOTE: That of the common table, for example, which did not exist in San Girolamo, where each priest provided for himself, or that of other community practices.
8. Cistellini, *San Filippo Neri*, I, 184–199. TRANSLATOR'S NOTE: From the time that the Oratory began to be active around him at San Girolamo, St. Philip told the Confraternity that he was renouncing his stipend, "offerens se velle suo arbitrio servire" (Archives of San Girolamo, T. 294, June 13, 1553).
9. *Collectanea*, 87–93.
10. G. G. Bordini, *Philippi Nerii religiosissimi presbyteri...* cit., 18: "At vero Tarusius, ut vivendi religiose ritum ac formam aliquam introduceret, constitutiones quasdam, communi consensu, condendas curavit, quas alacri animo ac obviis manibus cuncti susceperunt."
11. *Collectanea*, 89; 91.
12. Brief of Pius IV, August 19, 1565: *Collectanea*, 49–50; Gregory XIII confirmed them with a Brief, March 13, 1576: *Collectanea*, 51–52.
13. A. Cistellini, "Nascita della Congregazione oratoriana," in *Oratorium* (Rome, 1975), VI, I-II, 12.
14. In "Correspondenza tra S. Carlo e F. M. Tarugi," cit.
15. *Collectanea*, 12–13: "In dicta Ecclesia unam Congregationem Presbyterorum et Clericorum Saecularium, de Oratorio nuncupandam... Auctoritate Apostolica tenore praesentium erigimus et instituimus... Eidem Congregationi illiusque Rectori, ac Presbyteris...statuta et ordinationes rationabilia, honesta ac Sacris Canonibus, et Concilio Tridentino non contraria edere, et edita reformare, limitare, et mutare, ac alia de novo condere, prout et quoties eis secundum rerum et temporum qualitates videbitur expedire, quae quidem statuta...a Sancta Sede approbari, et per singulares personas de gremio dictae Congregationis existentes inviolabiliter observari debeant, libere et licite possint et valeant."
16. "Io non ho fattto questa Congregazione, l'ha fatta Iddio, che io non ho pensato mai a far Congregazione." *Process*, I, 120, See also the testimony of Germanico Fedeli, *Process*, III, 267.
17. *Process*, III, 147; A. Gallonio, *Vita Beati Patris*, cit., 156.
18. *Collectanea*, 210: "potius moribus quam legibus."
19. Archives of the Congregation of Rome, Libro dei Decreti, Dec. 9.III.1581, I, 9.
20. Ibid., I, 20.
21. *Collectanea*, 109–119; 120–145. A. Cistellini, "Il quarto centenario delle prime Costitutioni oratoriane (1583–1983)," in *Memorie Oratoriane*, IV (1983), 13, 24–47; ibid., *San Filippo Neri*, I, 299–303; 315–334.
22. *Collectanea*, 146–149.
23. *Collectanea*, 155–163; Cistellini. *S. Filippo Neri*, I, 605–622.
24. Those present were Fathers Angello Velli, Rector; Alessandro Fedeli, Cesare Baronio, Pietro Perracchione, Pompeo Pateri, Germanico Fedeli, Nicolò Gigli,

Giulio Savioli, Francesco Soto, Tommaso Bozzi, Flaminio Ricci, Agostino Manni, G. Matteo Ancina, Fausto Roselli, Antonio Gallonio. Missing were illustrious members of the Congregation who by that time were living in Naples. Fr. Philip wanted to submit the text also to Cardinal Girolamo della Rovere, archbishop of Torino, one of the most worthy Pastors of the post-Tridentine period, who was held in great esteem at the Vallicella (elevated to Cardinal in 1585, he died during the Conclave of Clement VIII in 1592).

25. Cistellini, *San Filippo Neri*, I, 609.
26. *Collectanea*, 209–253.
27. See the list in *Collectanea*, 85.
28. A. Cistellini, "Il sodale oratoriano nella sua vita vissuta," *Memorie Oratoriane*, XIX (1999), 38–45.
29. *Institutes Congregationis Oratorii Santa Mariae in Vallicella de Urbe.* Hereafter called *Inst.* 1612.
30. *Constitutiones Congregationum Instituti Oratorii S. Philippi Nerii, a Paolo V per Breve "Christifidelium" (24.II.1612) approbatae et post diligentem Codicis Juris Canonici accomodationem, a Sacra Congregatione de Religiosis ex Audientia SS.mi (die 12 Apr. 1943) ad experimentum confirmatae.* Hereafter *Const.* 1943.
31. *Statuta Generalia Congregationum atque Instituti Oratorii S. Philippi Nerii a Sacra Congregatione de Religiosis ex Audientia SS.mi (12 Apr.) ad experimentum confirmata.* Hereafter called *Stat.* 1943.
32. *Constitutiones et Statuta Generalia Confoederationis Oratorii S. Philippi Nerii*, approved by the Apostolic See with a Decree of the Congregation for Religious on November 21, 1989. Hereafter cited as *Const.* or *Stat.* The original Latin text to which the reader is referred will be quoted only in translation for reasons of space.
33. Introduction to the new text, absent in the original.
34. *Inst.* 1612: "nullam *ad religiosorum hominum consuetudinem* propriam sibi regulam habuit": it had no rule of its own *in the way that the religious have.* The original text does not say that there were no rules, but only that the norms by which the Community regulated itself were not like those of the religious. Even before the *corpus* of laws required by the Bull *Copiosus* was written, the Father guided the Community himself, personally, and as the Foreword makes clear, he himself saw to it that certain obligatory norms were established ("ea quae ipse Pater condenda curavit"). These were the familiar usages which had governed the Community in S. Giovanni dei Fiorentini, which, together with successive texts, made up the text of the *Institutes.* The Bull of erection said that such regulations could be modified, rewritten and subjected to further examination, but only until such time as they were approved by the Apostolic See. After this ratification, as the Foreword says, they must be observed perpetually.

35. The erection of the Congregation respects the request of Fr. Philip and his followers to attend "circa missarum et aliorum divinorum officiorum in eadem ecclesia celebrationem et verbi Dei populo inibi interessenti praedicationem, aliaque salutaria monita ad salutem animarum christifidelium procurandam" [the celebration of the Mass and of the other divine offices of the same church and the preaching of the Word of God to the people who come, and of other useful discourses to the end of procuring the salvation of souls of the faithful]. See the Bull *Copiosus in misericordia*, in *Collectanea*, 11.
36. In *Memorie Oratoriane*, I (1974), suppl. to nn. 1, 3–4.
37. *Collectanea*, 121: "Illiud nobis in primis propositum est ut, nullo locorum vel temporum habita ratione, omnibus semper et ubique nos Dei ministros exhibeamus, quae aliorum salutis non nostrae commoditatis aut quietis sint inquiramus."
38. Ibid.: "sacerdotum innocens atque omni reprehensione carens conversatio et vita."
39. G. Incisa della Rocchetta, ed., "Il Trattato di P. Antonio Talpa sulle origini," in *Oratorium*, IV (1973), 1, 6.
40. Fr. F. Ricci observed that "this form and manner of life…has by the pleasure of His Divine Majesty been revived with the particular spirit which He gave to our blessed Father in our times, to the end that, this state being intermediate between the Religious and the secular state, those who because of lesser physical and spiritual strength feel incapable of entering into the one, or fear living in the other would have no more excuse." Letter to the Fathers of Naples, April 15, 1601, now found in *Memorie Oratoriane*, XIX (1999), 42. The reference is to the Rule of Aquisgrana of 816, which instituted a form of the common life for secular clergy. See in Cistellini, *S. Filippo Neri*, I, 193–199, a synthetic presentation of the forms of the common life of the secular clergy over the centuries.
41. *Const.* 122: "The Congregation, because of its particular nature, cherishes a special love for the local church and its own city"; *Const.* 70: "The custom of some Congregations can be maintained by which their clerics are incardinated into the Diocese…." A. Cistellini, "La Congregazione dell'Oratorio e la Chiesa particolare," in *Memorie Oratoriane*, new series (1980), nn. 1–2, 8–62.
42. G. Cittadini, *L'Oratorio di S. Filippo Neri. Origini, attualità, prospettive*, cit. 37.
43. A. Manni, "Primordia, mores et pia quaedam exercitia Congregationis Oratorii de Urbe," in A. Cistellini, *Il sodale oratoriano…*, cit., 42.
44. J. H. Newman, *The Oratorian* (Dublin, 1856).
45. *Collectanea*, 89.
46. *"As it has been handed down, this must always be the fundamental law of the Institute: that every house or family, which is admitted to the Institute by adopting its style of life, rules and governs itself with full autonomy, in the same manner as existing Congregations of the Oratory"* (*Const.*, 13).

47. *Collectanea*, 130–131: "*Quo vero commodius clerici nostri muneribus sibi creditis defungi possint, recipientur in Congregatione laici qui, post praeparationem, sua sorte contenti, temporalium rerum et negotiorum curam administrabunt, nec ullam circa praepositorum caeterorumque magistratuum electionem partem sibi ullo unquam tempore concedendam certe sciant.*"
48. Fr. Fernandez de la cuesta, "Carisma institucional de la Congregacion del Oratorio de S. Felipe Neri," in *Isidorianum* (Centro de Estudios teologicos de Sevilla, 1998), VII, 14, 604–607.
49. J. H. Newman, "Lettere sulla vocazione dei Filippini," *Quaderno dell'Oratorio* (Roma, 1959), I.
50. The term "perfection" in reference to the Congregation of the Oratory obviously has a different meaning than it has for the Institutes of consecrated life. The Societies for apostolic life are defined thus in Code of Canon Law, canon 731, par 1: "Societies of apostolic life resemble institutes of consecrated life; their members, without religious vows, pursue the apostolic purpose proper to their society and, leading a life in common as brothers or sisters according to their proper manner of life, strive for the perfection of charity through the observance of the constitutions." Par. 2: "Among these are societies in which members assume the evangelical counsels by some bond defined in the constitutions." John Paul II in his Apostolic Exhortation *Vita consecrata* (1996), par. 11, declared: "Also worthy of special mention are societies of apostolic life or of common life, composed of men or women. These pursue, each in its own particular way, a specific apostolic or missionary end. In many of them an explicit commitment to the evangelical counsels is made through sacred bonds officially recognized by the church. Even in this case, however, the specific nature of their consecration distinguishes them from religious institutes and secular institutes. The specific identity of this form of life is to be preserved and promoted; in recent centuries it has produced many fruits of holiness and of the apostolate, especially in the field of charity and in the spread of the Gospel in the missions." The General Statutes of 1943, no. 6, make it very clear: "The members do not take either public or private vows, or oaths or any form of promises, but are bound to their Congregations by the bond of charity freely given, out of spontaneous free will." The present Constitutions say: "The Congregation of the Oratory was founded with only one bond, that of mutual charity, and was not bound by any vow, oath, promise or bond of this kind. It is held together solely by this bond of charity" (no. 9). The *animus permanendi* is the intention of stability founded upon "a free will" (see no. 10).

   F. Carlesimo, "La Congregazione dell'Oratorio è istituto di perfezione," in *Oratorium*, IV (1973) 2, 101–110; C. Abbate, "La Congregazione dell'Oratorio: Istituto di Perfezione?" in *Memorie Oratoriane*, I (1974), 5–14; G. Sessa, "Alcune note su "Perfezione" e Vita Filippina," in *Oratorium*, V (1974), 2, 102–106.

51. *Spiritual Path*, 59.
52. *Spiritual Path*, 67, 93.
53. *Spiritual Path*, 91.
54. "Dignitatis ullas nemo posit accipere, nisi iubeat Pontifex": *Inst.* 1612, ch. VIII; *Const.*, 99.
55. A. Cistellini, "S. Filippo Neri e la spiritualità dell'Oratorio," in *Le grandi scuole di spiritualità cristiana* (Rome, 1984), 505.
56. *Spiritual Path*, 101.
57. S. Filippo Neri, *Gli scritti e le massime*, 148.
58. TRANSLATOR'S NOTE: "Good-natured," the pretense of goodness.
59. TRANSLATOR'S NOTE: The good, goodness.
60. TRANSLATOR'S NOTE: Flippancy masquerading as spontaneity.
61. Cf. N. Vian, "Tra gli uomini di Dio: San Filippo moralista," in *Memorie Oratoriane*, V–VIII (1981), 4–13.
62. S. filippo Neri, *Gli scritti e le massime*, 169.
63. Cf. *Spiritual Path*, 103.
64. *Spiritual Path*, 104.
65. S. Filippo Neri, *Gli scritti e le massime*, 173; *If God Be with Us: The Maxims of St. Philip Neri*, ed. F. W. Faber (Gracewing, 1994), maxim for January 31, p. 15.
66. S. Filippo Neri, *Gli scritti e le massime*, 143; 152.
67. S. Filippo Neri, *Gli scritti e le massime*, 173.
68. J. F. Bellido *La conquista de la libertad. Vida de San Felipe Neri* (Bilbao, 1998).
69. TRANSLATOR'S NOTE: *Adelchi* is a historical play written between 1820 and 1822 and set in the time of the last of the Lombard kings, who subjugated northern Italy from the sixth to the eighth centuries. The yearnings of the indigenous people and the heroism of an obscure deacon, known to Manzoni from chronicles of the time, helped to bring about the Lombard defeat at the hands of Charlemagne. The play was part of the political and literary stirrings that led to Italian independence from Austria and Spain.
70. *Spiritual Path*, 106–110.
71. Now in G. Cittadini, *L'Oratorio di S. Filippo Neri. Origini, attualità, prospettive*, cit., 42–43.
72. *Process*, II, 308–310.
73. See in Chapter 6 the *Pontifical Letter on the Occasion of the IV Centenary of the Death of St. Philip Neri.*
74. Cardinal A. Valier, *Il Dialogo della gioia cristiana*, cit., 103–105.
75. He had come into the sphere of the Father's influence at San Girolamo at the same time as Tarugi, Baronio, Bordini and others.
76. Cardinal A. Valier, *Il dialogo della gioia cristiana*, cit., 10–11.
77. S. Filippo Neri, *Gli scritti e le massime*, 155.
78. *Spiritual Path*, 115.

79. *Statuta Generalia* 1943, I, par. II.7: "Oratorium S. Philippi Nerii ut finem generalem, sodalium suorum sanctificationem persequitur. Haec sodalium sanctificatio, ad normam Constitutionum et Statutorum, efficaciter ac suaviter obtineri debet...per dignum et sanctum ministerium sacerdotale;" "per asceticae perfectionis praescripta exercitia, praesertim vero...humilitatis et sui ipsius vanaeque gloriae despectus; et denique internae, speciatim iudicii et propriae voluntatis, iugis et velut connaturalis mortificationis...per serenam semper atque in omnibus internam externamque pacem et laetitiam qua integrum divinum servitium, fraterna conversatio et animarum ministeria informentur, ita ut de filiis sicut et de dulcissimo Patre perpetuo verum sit: IN LAETITIA!"
80. Elected triennially "from among those who have reached the sexennium in the Congregation." *Const.*, 49.
81. He is elected triennially from among the priests who have spent ten years in the Congregation and have reached at least thirty-five years of age. *Const.*, 42.
82. "The members give themselves with a free will to the Congregation, with the intention of remaining in it until death" (*Const.*, 10).
83. *Spiritual Path*, 70–76.
84. *Collectanea*, 115–119.
85. E. Griffith, *Lettera Fraterna*, Rome, May 23, 1951, reproduced in its entirety in the *Lettera fraterna* of the Procurator General, March 16, 2001, addressed to the Congregations in the Occasion of the 450th Anniversary of the Priestly Ordination of St. Philip Neri.
86. The Federation of Oratorian Congregations of Northern Italy has issued a document entitled *Ratio formationis Oratorii* (Verona, 1996). The document draws on the Constitutions and on recent Documents of the Magisterium that offer a wealth of information on the human, spiritual and priestly formation of candidates. It has been translated into Spanish and published by Alcalà de Henares, 1998.
87. *Const.* 1943, I, 1: "oratio omnium aliorum in Instituto S. Philippi cardo habenda est ac fondamentum."
88. For this and other quotations, cf: S. Filippo Neri, *Gli scritti e le massime,* passim.
89. *Spiritual Path*, 129–130.
90. *Process*, IV, 305–308, s. v. "how he celebrates the Mass and how he takes communion."
91. Oratorio de Albacete, *San Felipe Neri. La figura, el espiritu y la obra del fundador del Oratorio* (Balcelona, 1998), 45–49.
92. *Process*, III, 422.
93. *Inst.* 1612, Ch. VIII; *Const.* 1943, 121–122.
94. *Spiritual Path*, 15, 136.
95. Ibid.
96. Cf. A. Venturolia, *San Filippo Neri. Vita, contesto storico e dimensione mariana* (Casale Monferrato, 1988).

97. A. Cistellini, "Cesare Baronio 'Servo di Maria,'" in *Memorie Oratoriane*, XVIII (1997), 59–82.
98. *Process*, I, 137.
99. What the *Stat. Gen.* 1943, note 6, say is very clear: "The members do not take either public or private vows, or oaths or any form of promises, but are bound to their Congregations by the bond of charity freely given, out of spontaneous free will." The present Constitutions affirm: "The Congregation of the Oratory was founded with only one bond, that of mutual charity, and was not bound by any vow, oath, promise or bond of this kind. It is held together solely by this bond of charity (Const. no. 9)." The "animus permamendi" is the intention of stability founded upon "free will" (See Const. no. 10).
100. *Stat. Gen.* 1943, 7.
101. In "Memorie Oratoriane," I (1974), suppl. to Nos. 1, 3.
102. MAS R., *Significado de la "vida apostolica" y del Oratoriano,* in "Isidorianum," Centro de Estudios teologicos de Sevilla, 7 (1998), 14, 586.
103. *Spiritual Path*, 121–126.
104. Published in Biella, 1875.
105. S. Filippo Neri, *Gli scritti e le massime*, 115. The original is at the Vallicella.
106. S. Filippo Neri, *Gli scritti e le massime*, 108.
107. S. Filippo Neri, *Gli scritti e le massime*, 153; translation in *If God Be with Us: The Maxims of St. Philip Neri*, ed. F. W. Faber, maxim for January 11, p. 12.
108. "Con un giulio," *Process*, I, 257; 264.
109. Pontifical Council for Culture, May 23, 1999, p. 11.
110. *Spiritual Path*, 116–118.
111. ABBATE C., *Congregazione e membri di Congregazione "in temporalibus." In margine alle Costituzioni del 1970,* in "Memorie Oratoriane," 9 (1982), 30–47.
112. *Spiritual Path*, 120.
113. Code of Canon Law, Can. 731; Congregation for the Institutes of Consecrated Life and the Societies for Apostolic Life, *Fraternal Life in Community* (Rome, February 2, 1994).
114. *Fraternal Life in Community*, 39–41.
115. In *Memorie Oratoriane*, V–VIII (1981), 46.
116. *Collectanea*, 138: "Inter alia instituti nostri opera non minimum locum divino cultui tribuendum censemus; eo etenim fidelium animi ad Dei pietatem vel maxime polliciunctur et luce clarius constat, ecclesiastica munia, quibus Deum in sacrificio celebrando ac divinis laudibus persolvendis publice colimus, si rite, si graviter, si attente, si denique expleantur caelestem illam angelorum hierarchiam in terris referre solere. Quamobrem etiam atque patres nostros ac filios, qui nobis successuri sunt, hortamur in Domino ut huic rei vigilem ac diligentissimam operam navare contendant, nec ullo vel labore vel sumptu, quominus egregie praestentur, deterreri velint. Studebunt itaque ut et vasa et vestes sacrae

et ipsa templa et arae sit niteant, sic ornentur, ut intuentium animus nedum oculos, ad Dei amorem impellere possint. Ipsi vero, qui altaribus vel celebraturi vel administraturi adsistent, videant coram quo stent, perpendant quid agant, praesentium angelorum excubias praesentes considerent, ac propterea summa animi vigilantia, summa corporis disciplina ac compostione utantur."

117. *Inst.* 1612, III.
118. *Spiritual Path*, 138–139.
119. G. Finotti, ed., *Il Maestro parla al cuore. La direzione spirituale in S. Filippo Neri* (Brescia, 1997).
120. See the reduction of Fr. Philip to a teacher of children in Luigi Magni's film *State buoni se potete* (1983). The film is pleasing in many ways: it captures Philip's depth of soul, and tells the story of his life, especially of his life-long struggle with the devil who tries to snatch souls away from him. While the vision of the film is secular, like all of Magni's films, and omits much that is essential to understanding Philip, it is sympathetic to the most genuine expressions of Christianity.
121. F. Marino, *Farsi fanciullo con i fanciulli sapientemente* (Reggio Calabria, 1994).
122. See G. Angilella, *Intuizione ed esperienza educative nell'apostolato di S. Filippo Neri* (Pisa, 1957).
123. The title is taken from the epigraph that E. Bonghi composed about the Janiculum in Rome: "All'ombra di questa quercia / Torquato Tasso / vicino ai sospirati allori ed alla morte / ripensava silenzioso / le miserie sue tutte e Filippo Neri / tra liete grida si faceva coi fanciulli fanciullo / sapientemente" [In the shade of this oak / Torquato Tasso / close to the longed-for laurels and to death / reflected in silence on all of his miseries and Philip Neri / amid happy shouts became a child among children / wisely]. In the last Mass that Fr. Philip celebrated, we know that the Saint remembered in a very special way the great, tragic poet who was dying at S. Onofrio on the Janiculum. Philip Neri and Torquato Tasso are perhaps the most significant representatives of two ways of thinking and believing present in the Tridentine age: the inner harmony of a serene faith, sustained by a trusting abandonment to God, and the gloomy closing up of oneself in an unresolved tension between the eternal and the temporal.
124. G. Fedeli to Tarugi, August 31, 1590, in the Archives of the Congregation in Naples: "The Father has told me to add that the fervor of the young burns up like straw."
125. A. Pedrini, "Don Bosco e San Filippo Neri," in Finotti, *Il maestro parla al cuore*, 229–259.
126. *Spiritual Path*, 114. See also S. Filippo Neri, *Gli scritti e le massime*, 154.
127. A. Cistellini, "S. Filippo Neri e la spiritualità dell'Oratorio," 513–514.
128. Cf. G. Cittadini, "La natura dell'Oratorio nei suoi aspetti più significativi," 58–61.

129. *Stat. Gen.* 1943, II, 30: "Quia suprema lex ministerii sacerdotalis, bonum scilicet et salus animarum, pro temporum et locorum adiunctis exigere moraliter possunt ut Congregationes Instituti Oratorii paroecias, etsi primaevae ipsius institutioni certo minus ipsae viderentur respondere, admittrere debeant...."
130. A. Cistellini, "L'Oratorio ha quattrocento anni," in *Humanitas*, IX (1954), 12.
131. R. Mas, "El Oratorio y la Parroquia in 'Laus'" (Albacete, November 1994), 133–139. Now also in Oratorio de Albacete, *San Felipe Neri, La figura, el espiritu y la obra del Fundador del Oratorio* (Barcelona, 1998), 142–149.
132. See note 6 in Chapter IV.
133. Original in the Archives of the Congregation of Roma (Q. I., 6), published in *Memorie Oratoriane*, I, suppl. no. 2 (March 1975), 2.
134. This phrase was inserted after the General Congress of 2000, after close examination.
135. G. Marciano, *Memorie Historiche della Congregazione dell'Oratorio*, 5 vos. (Naples, 1693–1702).
136. Cf. C. Gasbarri, *L'Oratorio Romano dal Conquecento al Novecento* (Rome, 1962), 7–12; A. A. Corbo, ed., "L'Archivio della Congregazione dell'Oratorio di Roma e Archivio della Abazia di San Giovanni in Venere. Inventario," *Quaderni della Rassegna degli Archivi di Stato*, XXVII; G. Morello and F. Dante, eds., "Inventario dell'Archivio della Congregazione di Roma," *Ricerche per la storia religiosa di Roma* (Ed. di Storia e Letteratura, 1978), II, 275–362.
137. C. Gasbarri. *Lo spirito dell'Oratorio di S, Filippo Neri* (Brescia, 1949), 184–187; ibid., *L'Oratorio Romano* (Rome, 1963).
138. C. Addington, *The Idea of the Oratory* (London, 1966).
139. The Congregations presently existing are given in boldface, with the date of canonical erection of each, or for the oldest, the date of foundation. For the four continents in which Congregations were or are present, the order in which the Nations are given is relative to the antiquity of the first Oratorian foundation.

NOTES FOR CHAPTER IV

1. For example, the attempt to make a foundation in Milan, which lasted for some years, and to which Fr. Philip himself sent members. Cf. the Chronological Compendium at the beginning of this volume. Also the House of S. Severino in the Marches (1579), of Fermo (1583), of Naples (beginning in 1585), the Roman Community of S. Giovanni dei Fiorentini.
2. See the letter of Fr. Germanico Fedeli to Tarugi, December 5, 1586, in the Archives of the Congregation of Naples, 166: "Reverend Father Philip has asked me to write to you...that the chapters be observed which were composed more by you [Tarugi and Talpa] than by the rest of the Congregation."

3. S. Filippo Neri, *Gli scritti e le massime*, 52–53.
4. *Compendium Constitutionum Congregationis Oratorii*, synthesized, by decision of the Congregation, by Fr. Talpa in a *Summa* or *Breviatio*, approved in the meeting of November 28, 1583, one of the rare meetings in which Fr. Philip participated, and signed by the decennial Fathers. *Collectanea*, 146–149.
5. In the assembly of the Congregation of June 17, 1587, as it is seen in the Book of Decrees, with Fr. Philip's full approval, the question was proposed and voted upon: "Do you approve that the Reverend Father Philip, our Provost General be confirmed as our Provost and as perpetual Father General?" On June 20, in the same Book of Decrees, there is the following notation: "The Reverend Father Provost General and the four Deputies have elected the Reverend Fr. Angelo Velli rector of the House [Of Rome]" and June 28 following "the Rev. Fr. Francesco Maria Tarugi is reaffirmed as the Rector of Naples...the Rector of San Giovanni dei Fiorentini, that is, Fr. Alessandro Fedeli, is reaffirmed for the following three years...." Fr. Philip in the dispositions that he signed in February 1585 affirms: "my intention and desire and will is that when it will please the Lord our God to call me to himself, my sons in the Congregation will elect as Provost General in my place Fr. Francesco M. Tarugi, at present Rector, whom I judge able to govern..." (S. Filippo Neri, *Gli scritti e le massime*, 108).
6. The first Visit was decided upon by the Provost General Fr. Cesare Baronio, with his Document of April 22, 1594: "we have decided to send to the Houses of our Congregation Fr. Pompeo Pateri...and we have given him instructions that, on our authority, he is to carry out inquiries and visits while he is with you..."
7. Cistellini, *S. Filippo Neri*, III, 1933–2034.
8. *Collectanea*, 73–74.
9. *Inst.* 1612, ch. IV.
10. *Excellences...* [*Pregi...*], cit. I.
11. *Statuta Generalia Confoederationis Oratorii S. Philippi Nerii* (Romae, 1989), Ch. 1, No. 2. The Statutes were originally prepared and approved in Latin. For reasons of space, only the English translation is given. Henceforth, *Stat. Gen.*
12. All the citations in this paragraph are taken from *Stat. Gen., passim.*
13. The office of the General Archivist was instituted by the Congress of 2000.
14. A. M. Larraona, *Circolare ai Rev.mi Padri Prepositi e a tutti gli altri RR. Padri Chierici e Fratelli dell'Instituto dell'Oratorio di S. Filippo Neri,* Rome, April 21, 1935. Pasqua di Risurrezione, hectographed, in Archivium Procurae Generalis (Arch. Pr. Gen.): "Visit res Aplici—Larraona."
15. *Stat. Gen.*, V. 74, 75, 76.
16. *Const.*, 92.
17. The term "Confederation" would become official only in 1969.
18. B. Frison, "Cardinal Larraona," *Instituto Teologico de la Vida Religiosa* (Madrid, 1979); C. Abbate, "Il Cardinal Arcadio Larraona e l'Istituto dell'Oratorio," in

In Aevum, XXXI (November–December 1953); "L'Istituto dell'Oratorio ed il Cardinal Larraona," in *L'Oratorio di san Filippo*, XVII (1960), 9, 3.

19. Fr. Carlo Andrea Naldi (1892–1957) was from Florence. He entered the Florentine Oratory and was ordained there to the priesthood in 1905; he was an example of piety, and was faithful to the common tasks of the Oratory. He dedicated himself untiringly to the ministry of preaching. He showed nobility of feeling and manners, and entered easily into both the aristocratic and the bourgeois circles of society in Florence and elsewhere, which helped him promote many charitable endeavors. During the period of his office as Procurator, he spent half of each month in Rome, carrying out his duties. The site of the Procura was for a short time at San Girolamo della Carita, and then in the house annexed to the church of Sts. Nereo and Achilleo.
20. A. Cistellini, "Di rivisione in rivisione," in *Memorie Oratoriane*, II (1981), new series, 5–8, 72; ibid., "Intorno all'indole della Congregazione dell'Oratorio," in *Memorie Oratoriane*, XV (June 1992), 75ff. The author makes reference to Fr. Naldi's *Diario*, and quotes from it.
21. C. Gasbarri, *L'Oratorio Romano dal Cinquecento al Novecento* (Rome, 1963), 205.
22. But earlier, in 1847, during J. H. Newman's stay in Rome, the Provost of the Roman Oratory Fr. Carlo Rossi was eagerly promoting a moral union among the Houses, "so as to have more force and influence"; the newly converted Newman, who was in residence in S. Croce and receiving an Oratorian formation, would have none of it (M. Trevor, *Newman* [1962], 418–419).
23. Giovanni Battista Arista (Palermo 1863–Acireale 1920). The diocesan Process of beatification was celebrated between 1946–57, the Cause for Beatification was introduced to the S. Congregazione dei Riti in 1969. G. Cristaldi, *Il cuore di un vescovo* (Rome, 1950). IACEN, *Canonizationis Servi Dei Ioannis B. Arista. Positio super virtutibus* (Rome, 1992).
24. Giulio Castelli (Torino 1846–Cava de' Tirreni 1926). The diocesan informative process began in 1927, and ended November 20, 1941, when the cause for beatification was introduced to the S. Congregazione dei Riti. F. M. Mazza, *Il servo di Dio P. Giulio Castelli* (Badia di Cava, 1950). Caven. Tyrr. *Beatificat. et Canonizat. Servi Dei Julii Castelli. Positio super introductione Causae* (Rome, 1953).
25. The autograph of the Patriarch's text is conserved in the Procurator General's offices, exposed to view.
26. Alfonso Capecelatro of the Dukes of Castelpagano (1824–1912). He entered the Oratory of Naples in 1840 and was ordained priest in 1847. Provost for many years, he became Archbishop of Capua in 1880; Leo XIII named him Cardinal in 1885. He was named Librarian of the Holy Roman Church in 1893. A man of great fame, he wrote works of history, sociology, hagiography, politics. In the

Conclave of 1903, there was some probability that he would become Pope. C. Mola, *Vita del Cardinal Alfonso Capecelatro* (Naples, 1913); F. de Feo, "Alfonso Capecelatro, oratoriano, cardinale, scrittore," *Memorie Oratoriane*, XIV (1984), 55–70; A. Russo, "Convegno Nazionale di Studi su "Alfonso Capecelatro," in *Memorie Oratoriane*, XIV (1984), 86–89.

27. G. Timpanaro, "S. E. Mons. Giambatista Arista, il filippino di oggi dai vasti orizzonti," in *In Aevum*, XX (1948), suppl. to no. 5; A. Cistellini, "Intorno all'indole," 55–107.
28. Giovan Carlo Scaramucci (1821–1897), Roman; Provost from 1878 until his death, he sustained the Congregation in extremely difficult situations produced by grave external causes. Cf. C. Gasbarri. *L'Oratorio Romano*, 125–131.
29. Audience of December 18, granted to the Bishop of Cava Mons. Marchesani—who witnessed to this—and a group of Oratorian Fathers.
30. Brixiae. Typographia et Bibl. Queriniana, 1895.
31. After his aspirancy in the Roman Oratory, he began in 1870 an Oratorian Community in the south of France, at Draguignon (Var), suppressed by the State in 1880, and he collaborated in the foundation of other Communities at Rouen (1893) and Rheims (1895, approved in 1897, which lasted until 1905); thereafter he became auxiliary bishop of Grenoble, and later of Lyons.
32. The celebrations were solemn, in Rome and in many other Congregations, some of whom prepared fine publications for the occasion. The text of the Brief is to be found in Chapter VI.
33. *Osservatore Romano*, June 6, 1895.
34. See the Acts and the Letter of Cardinal Capecelatro which accompanies them (Ar. Pr. Gen. Archivium Historicum) in Chapter VI.
35. Autograph of the letter given to the Procura and exhibited there, with other historical documents.
36. Generoso Calenzio (Naples 1836–Rome 1915); he entered the Vallicella in 1873 and became Prefect of the Library of the Vallicella and Writer of the Vatican Library; he left some works on various subjects. Lively and quite pugnacious, after years of violent disagreements with his confrere Fr. Lais, he was reduced to living alone and ill in a house near the Vallicella.
37. Pope Leo's love for the Oratory manifested itself in many ways. For this reason the commemorative painting of the 1948 Congress shows him with arms stretched out toward the sons of St. Philip, holding and protecting them while he blesses them with an ample gesture.
38. See the text in *San Filippo Neri. Monitore delle Congregazioni dell'Oratorio*, II (1901), 4, 109–110.
39. Clemente Benedettucci (1850–1949), graduated in law at Rome and entered the Oratory of Recanati which ended with his death. He left many erudite writings and a rich bibliography, which is now open to scholars. Cf. C. Fini, *Clemente*

Benedettucci oratoriano (Ancona, 1991); R. Adorante, ed., *La vita e l'opera di P. Clemente Benedettucci* (Recanati, 2000).

40. Cf. "Leone XIII. Suo Pontificato, suoi rapporti con la Congregazione dell'Oratorio," in *S. Filippo Neri. Monitore*, IV (1903), 4, 91–96.
41. In *San Filippo Neri. Monitore*, II (1901), 4, pp. 111–116; see the "Regolamento del Collegio," in ibid., 117–122. Text in Chapter VI.
42. The institution did not last long. In 1907, on the advice of the Fathers of Perugia, with the consent of Pius X and with Fr. Benedettucci as intermediary, the Leonine College was transferred to Rome to the rectory of S. Tommaso in Parione, but in 1910, to the lively regret of the Pope, it was definitively closed. It had to await the pontificate of Pius XII, another great Pontiff linked to the Oratory, before an international college was reopened at Rome, named for the Pope himself. This also, however, had a short life.
43. The journal, first a monthly and then from 1905 published three times a year, published its first issue in May 1900 and lasted until 1907. It was typographically very dignified and rich in arguments. It contained a section entitled "Cronache filippine," intended to create links among the various Communities. In the very first issue (I, 1, 3), the editorial declared the intention of the journal: "to unite in just one heart and one mind the various Congregations, some of which are newly founded, and others reestablished, in order to ignite in everyone that charity which is the solid bond that draws the Congregations together." In the September issue we find a letter of Fr. Arista: "I bless the Lord who has inspired you with the idea of undertaking such a work, which could smooth the way for this union that we desire." The journal was received with praise of many Italian and some English, Spanish, and French Congregations; in the issue of February 1902 (III, 2, 48) the intention was repeated: "What is the intent of this journal? To make known even more the Congregations of the Oratory which, with unstinting sacrifice and work, have worked so hard in the Church in the course of three centuries. We wish to sustain the Congregations, spread them, and further cordial relationships among them." We do not find this journal, published in Biella, cited in Cistellini's extensive examination of the laborious path to union of the Congregations (*Intorno all'indole*), but it seems to us a strong testimony of the desire for a closer communion that animated many Oratorians of the time, impoverished as they were by a lack of means and of members, but not resigned to dying out in a lethal isolation.
44. "Precedenti storici del Movimento Federativo Oratoriano," in *L'Oratorio di S. Filippo Neri*, XVII (1960), 11, 11–12.
45. "Sollecitudine del Sommo Pontefice Leone XIII per I figli di S. Filippo," in *San Filippo Neri, Monitore* (Biella), II (1901), 4, 106–108.
46. The article by Recanatesi which was published in the above-cited journal is interesting. It is discreet but clear in its observations about the struggles of those

years: P. Recanatesi, "Due parole ai lettori, in *San Filippo, Monitore*, Quaderno 31 (1905), 1–6.

47. *Schema d'unione fra le Case della Congregazione Filippina in Italia* (Acireale, Tip. Umberto, 1906), I.
48. Giuseppe Timpanaro (1888–1953). He possessed a vivacious temperament and a lively Oratorian spirit and began many activities, all designed to bring to life the cult of St. Philip and to renew the vitality of the Oratory. In 1931 he reestablished the Congregation in Palermo, which however is now extinct.
49. See, for example, "Lettera della S. Congregazione dei Religiosi," June 13, 1921, in Arch. Pr. Gen.-Congressus Generales: "In conformity with what has been established in the Congress of the Provosts of the Congregations of the Oratory of Italy in November 1918, this Sacred Congregation reminds all the Congregations of Italy of the obligation of sending their Superiors or other representative with full powers..."
50. Fr. Gaetano Meneghini (1882–1937), from Vicenza. He was asked to come to Rome by the Sacred Congregation of Religious which named him Provost in 1919; he renounced it in 1920. Fr. Isacco Meggiolaro (1889–1966), from Vicenza. He returned to his community after receiving his doctorate at the Gregorian. Fr. Luigi Botton (1888–1975), also from Vicenza. He remained in the Roman Congregation until his death, leaving an imperishable memory of his goodness, his wisdom and his apostolic dedication. Fr. Giuseppe Timpanaro (1888–1953), who arrived in Rome in 1921. Fr. David Viola (1873–1958), of the Oratory of Biella, named Provost in 1921, shortly after he arrived in the Community.
51. Text in Chapter VI.
52. After the identification of the remains of the Saint (for which see R. Cappio, "La ricognizione del corpo di S. Filippo Neri," in *L'Oratorio di S. Filippo*, XVIII (1961), 9, 8–10; 19, 8–10), the urn was carried through the streets of Rome, in a procession that was an authentic triumph.
53. Alfredo Ildefonso Schuster (1880–1954), beatified in 1985. T. Leccisotti, *Il Cardinal Schuster*, 2 vols. (Milan, 1969); A. Majo, *La personalità spirituale del Cardinal A. I. Schuster* (Milan, 1980).
54. Paolo Caresana (1882–1973), from Vigevano. He entered the Oratory of Brescia in 1912, motivated by the memory of the apostle of youth Fr. Antonio Cottinelli and right after the young Giulio Bevilacqua. Provost in 1928, he had a notable part, next to Fr. Gemelli and Armida Barelli, in the spread of the Gioventù Femminile of Catholic Action, of whom he was Vice-Assistente Centrale. From 1934 to 1958 he worked tirelessly in Rome, at the Vallicella, making the Congregation flourish again. He was confessor to Giovanni B. Montini (Paul VI) who had a very tender affection for him, witnessed also by his epistolary: P. Caresana and G. B. Montini, *Lettere, 1915–1973*, ed. X. Toscani (Rome: Ed. Studium, 1998), Quaderni dell'Istituto Paolo VI.

55. Cesare Nanni (1890–1977); he had entered the Oratory only a few years earlier when he was invited to Rome when he was not yet forty, to be Provost of the Congregation.
56. G. Timpanaro, *La mia permanenza nella Congregazione di Roma* (pro-manuscripto) (Stab. Tip. Galatea, Acireale, 1925); ibid., *Perchè lasciai Roma—Le Costituzioni riformate dal P. Nanni* (ibid., 1926); Anonimo (ma C. Nanni), "La fisionomia della Congregazione dell'Oratorio dagli atti e dalla pratica dei primi tempi, extract from the journal *San Filippo Neri*, III (1932), 42. Fr. Nanni condensed his thought also in various articles published in the *Corriere d'Italia* between 1928 and 1931; in *San Filippo Neri*, from the issue of May–June 1930 to 1933; and in *Constitutiones et Regulae* (Forlì, 1925).
57. The homily was given in that occasion by Fr. Ettore Ricci (1866–1946), distinguished Provost of the Oratory of Perugia, a pious and highly cultivated priest, whom the Church of Perugia numbers among its illustrious sons. E. Ricci, *Per il Servo di Dio P. Giulio Castelli* (Tip. Di Mauro, Cava, 1934).
58. It is a reason for comfort, among so many sorrowful events, to remember *at least* some of the Fathers present, men who made the Oratory famous by the illustrious virtues of their lives, including some who died in the odor of sanctity and whose process for beatification is underway: Fr. Paolo Caresana, Brescia; the Servant of God Fr. Filippo Bardellini, Verona; Fr. Carlo Mino, Biella; the Servant of God Fr. Raimondo Calcagno, Chioggia; Fr. Vincenzo Salsano, Cava (once the boy who ran up to Fr. Castelli, when he arrived at the station at Cava, and never left him again, entering himself the Oratory at Cava).
59. Giulio Bevilacqua (1881–1965), one of the great Oratorians of the Congregation of Brescia and of the whole Institute; Paul VI, to whom he was tied by reciprocal profound esteem and friendly feeling, created him Cardinal in 1965. A man of wide culture and courageous pastoral initiative, he left a profound footprint on the spiritual and cultural life of the Italian Church. A. Fappani, *Giulio Bevilacqua il Cardinale Parrocco* (Brescia: Queriniana, 1979). J. Guitton, "San Filippo Neri e il Cardinal Bevilacqua," in *L'Oratorio di S. Filippo Neri*, XXII (1965), 7, 8–10; C. Doc, ed., *Scritti e discorsi sul Cardinal Giulio Bevilacqua nel 25° della sua morte (1965–1990)* (Brescia, 1900).
60. G. Timpanaro, *Mons. Arista*, 108.
61. "Institutionum S. Philippi Nerii, ab ipso divina inspiratione, ut pie creditur, in Urbe conditum, est societas clericalis iuris pontificii sacerdotum clericorumque saecularium atque fratrum laicorum in communi viventium absque votes"; "diversis Domibus quae Congregationes nuncupantur constat," "vinculis praecipue moralibus inter se coniuncta."
62. "extraordinarius…non proprie iuridicus, illis scilicet aequiparandus qui in novis Statutis definiuntur." Letter of convocation in Arch. Pr. Gen., Congressus Generales, 1942.

63. See the extensive commentary in C. Abbate, *Costituzioni e Statuti Generali*, Italian version, notes and appendices (Acireale, 1956).
64. Cf. A. Cistellini, "Intorno all'indole," 88.
65. Arch. Pr. Gen., Visit res Aplici Larraona.
66. Edward Griffith (1899–1559), convert to the Catholic faith from Anglicism. A. Cistellini, "Intorno all indole," 93: "An amiable man of good culture, welcomed by everybody, and available to everyone, he dedicated himself totally and uninterruptedly to bring about what had been decided at the Congress and to make the new Institute function.... He lasted a decade in this position, and the judgment of what had been accomplished he mapped out in a long report of eighty-three folios, which was sent to all the Congregations before the Congress of 1958." He was also the first Visitator elected by the Congress after the decree of the Holy See that instituted this office.
67. G. Timpanaro, *Mons. Arista*, 111.
68. Ibid.
69. Cistellini, "Intorno all'indole," 75.
70. *Lettera fraterna del Procuratore Generale sulla vita oratoriana e le attività della Procura 1948–1958.*
71. *Decretum S. Congregationis de Religiosis*, 14536–58: "I. Sedes Apstolica iterum agnoscit et confirmat, secundum voluntatem Fundatoris, absolutam autonomiam et iurisdictionis immunitatem Congregationum Oratorii S. Philippi, in quo non datur ut quis praesit quo Moderator Generalis, facultatibus vi Constitutionum praeditus quoad regimen internum singularum Congregationum. 2. Cum regiminis centralizati directi Institutes desint. Sedes Apostolica potestatem sibi assumit invigilandi immediate Congregationibus eo consilio, ut observatio Constitutionum et fidelitas erga spiritum Legiferi Patris numquam non vigeant. Hoc vero ius per suum Delegatum exercet, nominee VISITATORIS ORATORII S. PHILIPPI appellatum. 3. Visitator Oratorii a Congressu eligittur et a Sede Apostolica confirmatur." [The Apostolic See recognizes again and confirms, according to the will of the Founder the absolute autonomy and immunity of jurisdiction of the Congregations of the Oratory of St. Philip Neri. This means that there is no one who functions like a Superior General who would have, under the Constitutions, authority regarding the internal governance of the Congregations. 2. Because there is no centralized authority, the Apostolic See assumes the power of vigilance directly on the Congregations with the intent that the observance of the Constitutions and the fidelity to the spirit of the Father Legislator never lessen. It exercises this right by means of a Delegate called the VISITATOR OF THE ORATORY OF ST. PHILIP NERI. 3. The Visitator is elected by the Congress and confirmed by the Apostolic See.]
72. C. Abbate, "Il P. Edoardo Griffith, primo Procuratore Generale dell'Instituto dell'Oratorio e primo Visitatore," in *In Aevum* (May–June 1960), 75–86; "In

memoriam di P. Griffith," in *L'Oratorio di San Filippo Neri*, XVI (1960), 9, p. 7; "Fr. Edward Griffith," in *The Oratory Parish Magazine* (London, 1959), 7. Fr. Griffith died in Italy, and desired to the buried in the tomb of the Fathers in Mondovì.

73. Chronicle of the Congress in *Oratorium*, I (1970), 1, 62–63.
74. J. Gulden, "Zeitgemasse Erneuerung im Oratorium des hl. Philipp Neri," in *Oratorium*, I (1970), 5–20; with translation into Italian of the principal parts. See the ample analysis of the report which Fr. Cistellini makes with incontrovertible historical arguments: A. Cistellini, "Quale Oratorio? Quale Congregatione?" in *Memorie Oratoriane*, I, suppl., no. 2 (March 1975), 3–19: "Rereading this report, my thought went to a letter of Fr. Antonio Gallonio to Fr. Antonio Talpa of 30 January 1598, which revealed one of those disagreements about the authentic interpretation of the spirit of the blessed Father Philip: "Many people say many things, that could be in conformity with the will of our Saint, and they deceive themselves, because it is not so, but rather they conform to their own will… I remember saying in Congregation one time that many made our Saint into what they want, as the shoemaker makes what he wants out of the leather" (ACN., XVI, 23)."
75. *Stat. Gen.*, "Appendix de Delegato Sedis Apostolicae…" (A3): "Delegatus Sedis Apostolicae munus Visitatoris canonici Oratorii S. Philippi haber" [the Delegate of the Holy See has the responsibility of canonical Visitator of the Oratory of St. Philip].
76. *Stat. Gen.*, par. 3: Auctoritate Apostolica confoederatio quaedam…ad normam horum Statuorum, creata fuit quae *Institutum Oratorii S. Philippi Nerii* iure denominatur."
77. He resigned in 1971, and the Permanent Deputation called Fr. Walter Oddone to substitute for him.
78. Chronicle of the Congress in *Oratorium*, VII (1976), 1, 67–69. Themes discussed: the daily preaching of the Word of God; prayer, the common life of the Oratory; cocations and formation; the Oratory and the diocese.
79. On the Constitutions approved ad experimentum in the Congress of 1969, on which those presently in force are modeled, see: T. Glover, *The Juridical Nature of the Oratory and Oratorians Today* (Rome, 1973); F. Carlesimo, *Natura juridical della Congregazione dell'Oratorio nella sua storica evoluzione.* Pars dissertationis ad lauream in Facultate Iuris Canonici apud Pont. Univ. S. Thomae in Urbe. S. Nicola La Strada (1992); P. Turks, "The Origins of the 1969 Constitutions," in *Oratorium*, II (1971), 2, 88–94.
80. Antonio Cistellini (Esine 1905–Florence 1999). M. T. Bonadonna Russo, "L'Opera storica di P. Antonio Cistellini," in *Rivista di Storia della Chiesa in Italia*, LIV (2000), 1, 7–11. In the commemorative issue dedicated to Fr. Cistellini by the publisher La Scuola—*Memorie Oratoriane*, XX (2000)—there are a biographical profile and a *Bibliografia degli scritti*, edited by E. Bini, with various articles

in memoriam, among which: I. Mezzadri, "La lezione di p. Antonio Cistellini," pp. 33–45; G. Scanzi, "Storia, 'necessità' dell'assoluto," pp. 47–49; in the same issue Nello Vian (1907–2000) is commemorated also, another valiant scholar of Oratorian history, to whom the Oratory expresses its appreciation. The issue ends with a valuable index of the twenty "Quaderni" [issues, booklets] of the *Memorie Oratoriane.*

81. A. Cistellini, "Revisione, Rinnovazione, Deformazione," in *Memorie Oratoriane,* III (May 1975), 8–16; ibid., "Di revisione in revisione," in *Memorie Oratoriane,* III (May 1975); ibid., "Intorno all'indole," 93–112; C. Abbate, "In margine alle Costituzioni del 1970," in *Memorie Oratoriane,* III (1975), 5–7.
82. C. Abbate, "Mons. G. B. Arista e la Confederazione dell'Oratorio," in *Accademia di Scienze e Lettere e Belle Arti degli Zelanti dei Dafnici, Memorie e rendiconti,* IV, 2 (Acireale, 1992), 387–400.
83. *L'Osservatore Romano,* October 19, 1994. Text is found in Chapter VI.
84. Catalogs of the Exhibitions in Rome: Palazzo Venezia, May 1995–January 1996, *La regola e la fama. S. Filippo Neri e l'arte* (Milan, Electa, 1995); Biblioteca Vallicelliana, May 24–September 30, 1995, *Messer Filippo Neri, Santo. L'Apostolo di Roma* (Rome: De Luca, 1995).
85. M. Frisina, *Paradiso, paradiso* (Rome, 1995). The centenary year produced other theatrical texts: A. Fantacci, *Fiorentino anche in Paradiso. Commedia in tre atti,* ed. Sisters of St. Philip Neri (Florence, n.d.); M. Pavan, *Filippo Neri, Santo "giovane"* (Vicenza, 1995); G. Costantini, *San Filippo dagli opposti amen. Mistero in Quattro atti* (Vicenza, 1995).
86. *L'Osservatore Romano,* May 27, 1979. Text of the homily in Chapter VI.
87. *L'Osservatore Romano,* May 29–30, 1995. Text of the homily in Chapter VI.
88. For the preceding centenaries of the birth of St. Philip, see: C. Gasbarri, "I tre centenari del 'dies natalis' di San Filippo," in *L'Oratorio di S. Filippo Neri,* XXV (1968), 1, 4–11; 2, 23–30.
89. M. T. Bonadonna Russo, *L'Oratorio di s. Filippo Neri*; G. Carriquiry Lecour, *El Oratorio en la mision de la Iglesia al alba del Tercer Milenio*; F. de Llanos Pena, *El Oratorio que somos, el Oratorio que imaginamos.* The texts were distributed by the Procurator General, along with other material, in the *Memoria Congressus Generalis A. D. 2000.*
90. Text of the homily in Chapter VI.
91. *L'Osservatore Romano,* October 6, 2000. The text of the discourse is in Chapter VI.

NOTES FOR CHAPTER V

1. The image is taken from Ps. 44:19, and was placed by Baronio at the head of his revision of the Constitutions (1595–1596). He derived it from the *Apologia*

which St. Bernard wrote in defense of his Order and sent to Guglielmo di S. Thierry.

2. *Const. Avvertenze* (B): "This, then, is the way which St. Philip wanted his disciples to follow, in complete freedom, so that there should be that progress in virtue and pious emulation of the perfect, upon which perseverance in the Congregation depends."
3. G. Tesserin, *Sulle orme di San Filippo Neri. Santi di ieri e di oggi* (Taglio di Po, 1994).
4. Congregatio de Causis Sanctorum, *Index ac Status Causarum* (Città del Vaticano, 1999). This edition reports the following Venerable and Servants of God who belonged to the Oratory of St. Philip Neri: Ven Cesare Baronio (1538–1607); Ven. Bartolomeo de Quental (1622–1698), founder of the Oratory in Portugal and its colonies; Ven. Giovanni Battista Trona (1682–1750) of the Oratory di Mondovi; Ven. Ignazio Capizzi (1708–1783) of the Oratory di Palermo; Servant of God Marco Antonio Ribaudengo (1703–1764) of the Oratory di Palermo; Blessed John Henry Newman (1801–1890), founder of the Oratory in England; Servant of God Emilio Venturini (1842–1905) of the Oratory di Chioggia; Servant of God Giovanni Battista Arista (1862–1920) of the Oratory di Acireale; Servant of God Giulio Castelli (1846–1926) of the Oratory of Cava de' Tirreni; Servant of God Filippo Bardellini (1878–1956) of the Oratory of Verona; Raimondo Calcagno (1888–1964) of the Oratory of Chioggia. The 1988 Index added: Servant of God Salvio Huix Miralpeix [see section 7] (1877–1936) whose beatification is expected with a group of Spanish martyrs of 1936; Servant of God Nicolò Bijankovic (1645–1730) of the Oratory of Spolato. The Index of 1975 reviewed the cause of Servant of God Ludovico Filippo Neri Alfaro (1709–1776) of the Oratory of Mexico City.
5. A. Gallonio, *Vita Beati Patris,* cit., 68.
6. He received the title of Venerable from Benedict XIV in 1745. Apart from the bibliography already cited in notes 45 and 112 of the first chapter, see Postulazione della Causa, ed., *Il Ven. Sv. di Dio Cesare Baronio, prete Cardinale… Compendio della vita e cenni sulle virtù* (Rome, 1956).
7. Cf. P. Vannutelli, *Vita di Cesare Baronio, estratta dagli scritti del P. Generoso Calenzio* (Rome, 1938).
8. Bibliography cited in note 40 of Chapter I.
9. Bibliography cited in note 91 of Chapter I.
10. E. Balbis [*sic*] and E. Dao, "Le visite pastorali del B. G. Giovenale Ancina alla Diocesi di Saluzzo," in *Bollettino della società per gli Studi storici, archeologici e artistici della Provincia di Cuneo*, 83 (September 2, 1980); M. F. Mellano, "Alcuni documenti sull'episcopato di G. G. Ancina," in *Bollettino della società per gli Studi storici, archeologici e artistici della provincia di Cuneo*, 73 (September 2, 1975).

11. N. Gigli (A. Cistellini), "Francesco de Sales e Govenale Ancina," in *Memorie Oratoriane*, IV (1984), 14, pp. 71–83.
12. After that of Thonon, in the Chablese, Duchy of Savoy, founded by St. Francis de Sales in 1598, there were in the principate of Piedmont the Congregations of Casale (1613), Murazzano (1646), Turin (1649), Fossano (1649), Chieri (1658), Savigliano (1674), Carmagnola (1681), Demont (1693), Asti (1696), Mondovi (1704), Crescentino (1730), Villafranca (1737), Biella (1742).
13. D. Franchetti, *Vita del venerando P. Felice Carpignano della Congregazione dell'Oratorio di Turin* (Alba-Rome, 1927); see also, *Miscellanea di studi*, su Francesco Faà di Bruno (Turin: Bottega d'Erasmo, 1977).
14. Pope Paul VI, Epistola Apostolica "*Sabaudiae gemma*," for the fourth centenary of his birth, 1967.
15. A. Pedrini "Filippo Neri e Francesco di Sales, in *Palestra del Clero*, LXVII (1967), 21, pp. 1321–1336.
16. Anonimo, *Vita del Ven. Valfrè*, ms. 1745, in the Archives of the Oratory of Turin; G. Calleri, *Vita del Bl. Sebastiano Valfrè* (Turin, 1834); P. Capello, *Vita del Bl. Sebastiano Valfrè* (Turin, 1872); N. Cuniberti, *La sorgente dei preti santi* (Turin, 1960); C. Fava, *Vita e tempi del Bl. Sebastiano Valfrè* (Turin, 1984); A. Dordoni, *Un maestro di spirito nel Piemonte tra Sei e Settecento. Il padre Sebastiano Valfrè, dell'Oratorio di Turin* (Milan, 1992). This work is valuable also for the extensive bibliography on all aspects of the life of Blessed Valfrè.
17. G. Tonello, *Un Paray-le Monial italiano dimenticato* (Turin, n.d.). He gave other talks on the Sacred Heart at the Visitation in 1695, 1698, and 1704: Archives of the Monastero della Visitazione, *Annali del Monastero*.
18. Cf. P. Cappello, *Vita*, I, p. 24.
19. In A. Dordone, *Un maestro di spirito*, pp. 153–166, there is a rich bibliography on the writings of St. Valfrè. Even though a complete list of his writings does not yet exist, this list enumerates among his manuscripts thirteen volumes of sermons and many letters, treatises, talks, collections of memoires, repertories on morality. Most of his published works were published posthumously.
20. *Compendio della Dottrina cristiana per facilitare la pratica d'insegnarla e d'impararla. Dialogo tra Maestro e Scolaro* (Turin, 1769). It was published also in a special issue of *Il B. Sebastiano Valfrè. Bollettino di informazione per la causa di canonizzazione* (Turin, 1980); and in an Appendix to C. Fava, *Vita e tempi*, pp. 317–344.
21. The Princesses Maria Adelaide (who married Luigi Duke of Borgogna) and Maria Luisa (who married King Philip V of Spain) continued even after their marriages to keep in contact with the Father who had taught them; the epistolary correspondence, which reveals their delicacy of their souls, and the profound formation that they had received, and Fr. Valfrè's responses are authentic jewels of spiritual direction.

22. G. Olgiati, *Il Beato Sebastiano Valfrè, d. O. Sua azione sociale e politica* (Turin, 1966).
23. *L'Osservatore Romano*, April 27 and 28, 2001.
24. G. M. Giaccone, *Vita del Ven. Servo di Dio Giovanni Battista Trona* (Mondovì, 1902); *Il Ven. G. B. Trona, apostolo del catechismo, Dissertazione* (Mondovì, 1910).
25. Benedict XIV conferred on him the title of Venerable. For the bibliography, see P. Aringhi, *Memorie historiche del Ven. Servo di Dio P. F. Scarampi* (Rome, 1744).
26. *La Congregazione dell'Oratorio di S. Filippo Neri. Atti del Convegno*, Fano, October 14–15, 1994, (Fiesole, 1996); M. Canti, "Lineamenti per una ricerca sulla Congregazione dei Padri dell'Oratorio di S. Filippo Neri nelle Marche," in *La Congregazione*; F. Mariano, *Le chiese filippine nelle Marche. Arte ed archittetura* (Fiesole, 1996).
27. C. Antici, *Vita del B. P. Antonio Grassi, della Congregazione dell'Oratorio di Fermo* (Rome, 1900).
28. G. Marciano, *Memorie historiche* (Naples, 1698).
29. M. Vallicelli, *Fabrizio dell'Aste e l'Oratorio di Forli* (Imola, 1990).
30. T. Curtii, *Commentarium de Andrea Anibaldi* (Macerata, 1890); ibid., *Il servo di Dio P. Andrea Anibaldi, preposito dell'Oratorio di Treia* (Rome, n.d.).
31. G. B. Melloni, *Breve ragguaglio della vita del servo di Dio Carlo Maria Gabrielli prete dell'Oratorio di Bologna* (Bologna, 1749); G. Gazzoli, *Cenni storici della chiesa della Madonna di Galliera e di Padri Filippini* (Bologna, n.d.).
32. C. Barbieri, *Memorie della vita e delle virtù del servo di Dio Ercole M. G. Isolani, prete della Congregazione dell'Oratorio di Bologna* (Venice, 1711).
33. A. Gianini, *P, Luigi Piccardini* (Selci Umbro, 1955); E. Cifferi, *Luigi Piccardini e il suo tempo* (Città del Castello, 1993).
34. *Vita del Servo di Dio Padre Paolo Baraldi, prete dell'Oratorio di Mantova* (Mantua, 1765).
35. G. Marciano, *Memorie historiche*, IV; A. Cistellini, "I primordi dell'Oratorio filippino di Firenze," in *Archivio Storico Italiano* (Florence, 1968); ibid., "Una pagina di stroai religiosa a Firenze nel secolo XVII," in *Archivio Storico* (Florence, 1967).
36. G. Marangoni, *Vita del servo di Dio Buonsignore Cacciaguerra, con l'aggiunta*, appendix, 52–62; A. Cistellini, "San Filippo Neri e la sua patria," in *Rivista di Storia della Chiesa in Italia*, XXIII (1969), pp. 97–101; G. Aranci, *Vittorio dell'Ancisa, un prete fiorentino del Cinquecento* (Florence, 1977).
37. S. Filippo Neri, *Gli scritti e le massime*, pp. 101–102.
38. Suore Stabilite nella Carità, *Vittotio dell'Ancisa e la Carità. Storia del Convento "La Carità" dal 1588 al 1817* (Florence, 1995).
39. G. Gioberti, *Elogio fatto al V. P. Ferdinando Fattoracci* (Florence, 1840), manuscript; C. Mezzasalma, ed., *Un germoglio oratoriano nella Firenze del Settecento* (Florence, 1994).

40. *Cenni storici sul Fondatore e sull'opera delle Figlie di N. S. della Misericordia*, typescript (n.d.). S. Rossi, "Antonio M. Salata, fondatore delle Figlie di N. S. della Misericordia," *Quaderni Franzoniani*, X (1997), 2, 219–236.
41. G. Marciano, *Memorie historiche*, II: *Orazione funebre in morte del P. G. T. Eustachio* (Naples, 1642).
42. A. Capecelatro, *Commemorazione di un Padre Filippino morto in fama di santità nel 1883* (Rome, 1993); B. Longo, *Storia del Santuario di Pompei* (Pompei, 1981).
43. F. Montanino, *Discorso commemorativo del P. Marzio Piccirillo* (Guardia Sanframondi, 1957), ds.; G. Lando, *Sulla scia del Neri* (Guardia Sanframondi, 1980).
44. G. Marciano, *Memorie historiche*, III.
45. G. Laderchi, *Vita del Ven. Servo di Dio G. Andrea degli Afflitti* (Rome, 1729).
46. T. Blundo, *Vita e virtù del P. Pietro Palazzo* (1770; new edition re-edited and annotated with the addition of mss. and unpublished documents by F. Staganelli: Ragusa, 2001).
47. G. di Mauro Riggio, *Memorie historiche sopra la vita del servo di Dio Mariano Patanè* (Naples, 1845; new edition with preface by Giuseppe Cistaldi: Acireale, 1991).
48. G. Martorana, *Vita del Servo di Dio Marco Antonio Ribaudengo, prete della Congregazione dell'Oratorio di Palermo, cavata dal Processo ordinario informativo* (Palermo, 1796).
49. F. Currenti, *Il fulgore della santità. Vita di Ignazio Capizzi* (Rome, 1989); ibid., *Un santo per oggi. Ignazio Capizzi* (Rome, 1993).
50. G. D'Angelo, *Vita del servo di Dio P. Giorgio Guzzetta. Greco-albanese della Piana* (Palermo, 1798), R. Petrotta, *Breve compendio della vita del servo di Dio p. Giorgio Gazzetta* (Piana degli Albanesi, 1956); G. Costantini, *Cenni della vita e delle opere di P. Giorgio Guzzetta* (Palermo, 2000).
51. M. Mikulic, *De vita et gestis Nicolai Bijankovic episcopi makarskensis* (Rome, 1964).
52. G. Beltrame, *Storia e arte in S. Tommaso M.* (Padua, 1966).
53. D. de Paoli, *Vita del servo di Dio P. Giuseppe Musoco, prete dell'Oratorio di S. Filippo Neri di Trento* (Trent, 1780).
54. M. Grancelli, *P. Luigi Perez* (Verona, 1908).
55. A. Bonivento, *Lasciateli giocare. P. Raimondo Calcagno sul filo dei ricordi* (Chioggia, 1989).
56. G. Marciano, *Memorie historiche*; *Lettera da P. Bartolomeo de Quental à la Congregation de l'Oratorio de Braga*, lecture, introduction and notes by J. Girodon (Paris, 1973), in *Oratorium*, V (1974), 1, 57-60.
57. J. Girodon, "Les origins de l'Oratoire del Portugal," in *Bulletins des etudes portugais*, XXVIII–XXIX (1967-1968).
58. E. de Lima, *A Congregação do Oratorio en Brasil* (Petropolis, 1980).

59. In connection with this, it is important to the present author to remember the figure of a young confrere in the Oratory of Biella, Fr. Maurizio Vanini, He died on March 26, 1993, in a tragic car accident in Caxias do Maranhao, leaving behind the lively memory of his goodness and his pastoral zeal. He was occupied temporarily in assisting in the Brazilian mission of the church in Biella. C. Massa, ed., *Dio sta in quel sorriso* (Biella, 1994).
60. C. Gasbarri, "Vicende e glorie dell'Oratorio in Portogallo," in *L'Oratorio di S. Filippo Neri*, XVII (1960), 7, 6-7.
61. Fortunato de Almeida, et al., *Historia da Igreja em Portugal* (Coimbra, 1912), in 4 vols., vol. 3.
62. S. G. Perera, *The Oratorian Mission in Ceylon. Historical Documents Relating to the Life and Labours of the Ven Fr. Joseph Vaz, His Companions and Successors*, trans. from the original Portuguese (Colombo, Ceylon, 1936-1937); ibid., *Life of the Ven. Fr. Joseph Vaz, Apostle of Ceylon* (Galle, 1942); "Souvenir do Tricentenario do Ven. Pe. Joseph Vaz," in *Mensario de Propaganda*, XXIII (1951), 10.
63. C. Papali, "Un apostolo delle Missioni. P. Giuseppe Vaz," *Quaderni dell'Oratorio*, 5.
64. M. da Costa Nunez, *Documentacao para a historia da Congregacao do Oratorio de Sta Cruz dos Milagres da Clero natural de Goa* (Lisbon: Centro de Estudios Historicos Ultramarinos, 1996). C. Gasbarri, "Documenti sulla storia dell'Oratorio indiano," in *L'Oratorio di S. Filippo Neri*, XXIV (1967), 3, pp. 41-44.
65. TRANSLATOR'S NOTE: Pope Francis canonized St. Joseph Vaz in Sri Lanka on January 14, 2015.
66 J. Morale Marin, *John Henry Newman, La vita*, ed. L. Orbetello (Milan, 1998); P. Murray, *Newman the Oratorian* (Dublin, 1968); A. Cistellini, "Intorno alla vocazione filippina di J. H. Newman," in *Memorie Oratoriane*, XVI (1993), 20-43. For the enormous bibliography of Newman's works and about Newman, see L. Callegari, *Newman, La fede e le sue ragioni* (Milan, 2001), pp. 187-196.
67. John Paul II, Letter to the Very Reverend Archbishop of Birmingham, January 21, 2001.
68. Pope Pius IX, Brief *Magna Nobis semper*, November 26, 1847, in *Collectanea*, 41–44.
69. TRANSLATOR'S NOTE: "St. Philip in Himself," No. 165, in the *Newman Reader*, online, the National Institute for Newman Studies, 2007.
70. TRANSLATOR'S NOTE: C. S. Dessain and Thomas Gornall, S.J., *The Letters and Diaries of John Henry Newman* (Oxford, 1976), Vol. XXIX, February 3, 1879, p. 19.
71. See *Viaggio in Italia*, Naples, May 26, 1787.
72. J. H. Newman, *Apologia pro vita sua*. The book ends in the name of St. Philip.
73. John Paul II, Letter to the Most Reverend Archbishop of Birmingham, April 7, 1979.

74. TRANSLATOR'S NOTE: John Henry Newman was beatified by Pope Benedict XVI on September 19, 2010, and canonized by Pope Francis on October 13, 2019.
75. H. Jaromin, *Il nostro passato* (Tarnow, 1968), typescript.
76. F. Colas i Periro, *L'Oratorio de Sant Felip Neri de Gracia* (Barcelona, 1996), pp. 93–121.
77. C. J. de la Plana, *L'Oratori de Sant Felip Neri de Barcelona i el seu patrimoni artistic i monumental* (Monserrat, 1978), p. 300.
78. N. Tibau Duran, *El Excmo y Rvdmo P. Salvio Huix Miralpeix, C.O. Apuntes biograficos* (Lerida, 1948); "Msgr. Salvio Huix y Miralpeix," in *L'Oratorio di san Filippo Neri*, VII (Rome, 1962); A. Montero Moreno, *Historia de la persecutiòn religiosa en Espagna (1936–1939)* (Madrid, 1961).
79. TRANSLATOR'S NOTE: Pope Francis beatified Bl. Salvio Huix Miralpeix on October 13, 2013.
80. *Incarnationis Mysterium*, 5: "St. Philip Neri demonstrates this in an exemplary way. At the time of the Jubilee Year 1550, he began what came to be called 'Roman charity,' as a tangible sign of welcome to the pilgrims."
81. L. Tinti, *Memorie di P. Luigi Scrosoppi, d. O.* (Udine, 1897); G. Biasutti, *P. Luigi Scrosoppi dell'Oratorio di S. Filippo Neri, fondatore delle Suore della Provvidenza* (Udine, 1979); M. Papasogli Zalum and G. Papasogli, *Per i piu poveri* (Udine, 1980), rev. ed.; *S. Luigi Scrosoppi, prete per i piu poveri* (Udine, 2001).
82. A. Cistellini, "P. Luigi Scrosoppi, beato filippino," in *Memorie Oratoriane*, new series, II (1981), 5–8, 14–22.
83. A. Cistellini, "P. Luigi Scrosoppi"; G. Biasutti, "Il Preposito della rinata Congregazione," in *Memorie Oratoriane*, new series, II (1981), 5–8, 23–40.
84. A. Barrios Moneo, *Dos hermanos: un carisma, una esperanza* (Madrid, 1992).
85. F. Garcia Tejero, *Autobiografia* (Seville, 1979).
86. There is a copious bibliography in P. Barcariolo, *Un uomo tra le calli. P. Emilio Venturini, fondatore delle Serve di Maria Addolorata* (Chioggia, 1900).
87. L. Silvestrelli, *Don Scarpassa: Meditazione su P. Filippo Bardellini* (Verona, 1981); G. Cappelletti, *Padre Filippo Bardellini, servo degli ultimi* (Cinisello Balsamo, 1986).
88. Bibliography given in note 23 of Chapter IV.
89. For the bibliography, see note 24 of Chapter V.
90. A. Serramona, ed., *Sant Felip Neri i Antoni Gaudi. La image de S. Felip Neri al temple de la Sgda Familia,* Vida Oratoriana, II epoca, yextos i documents, 8, 2000, 23–26; J. Bada, "Context historic d'Antoni Gaudi," ibid., 15–20; J. Riera, "Sant Felip Neri i Antoni Gaudi," ibid., 45–46; D. Vidal, "Felip i Gaudi," ibid., 63–64.
91. F. Colas, "Breu ressenya de la presencia de l'arquitecte Antoni Gaudi a l'Oratori de Sant Felip Neri de Barcelona," ibid., 23–26.
92. See also "Carta dominical del Cardenal Ricard M. Carles," ibid., 67–68.

NOTES FOR CHAPTER VI

1. IV, 4, pp. 93–95. The article is unsigned, but from internal evidence, one may deduce that it was written by Fr. Paolo Recanatesi.
2. TRANSLATOR'S NOTE: From the *Brief* for the Third Centenary of the death of St. Philip Neri, May 5, 1895. Original document in Latin; the present translation was made from Bishop Cerrato's Italian translation.
3. Motu Proprio *Eximiis in Ecclesiam*, September 30, 1900. Translation as in note 2.
4. In Arch. Pr. Gen.: Archivium Historicum. Translation as in note 2.
5. Address of Fr. Cesare Nanni to the Provosts, in *San Filippo Neri*, IV (1924), 6, pp. 1–2.
6. From the Letter to His Eminence Prince don Camillo Francesco Massimo, of the Secular Oratory of Rome, President of the Committee for the Celebration of the Third Centenary of the Canonization of St. Philip Neri, November 24, 1921.
7. From the Letter to the Most Excellent Prince Don Camillo Francesco Massimo, of the Secular Oratory of Rome. President of the Committee for the Celebrations of the Third Centenary of the Canonization of St. Philip Neri, March 8, 1922.
8. From the Letter to Fr. Paolo Caresana, Provost of the Oratory of Rome, in the Fourth Centenary of the "Pentecost" of St. Philip, May 25, 1944.
9. TRANSLATOR'S NOTE: Scripture passages are taken from the Revised Standard Version of the Bible, Catholic Edition.
10. Address to the General Congress of October 1–4, 1958, ad usum Congregationum Oratorii. Original text in Latin: *"Inde a juvenilibus annis,"* in Ar. Pr. Gen. English translation prepared from Fr. Cerrato's translation into Italian.
11. TRANSLATOR'S NOTE: Pope Francis canonized Pope John Paul II on April 27, 2014, Divine Mercy Sunday.
12. TRANSLATOR'S NOTE: Pope Francis canonized Pope John XXIII on April 27, 2014, Divine Mercy Sunday.
13. TRANSLATOR'S NOTE: Pope Francis canonized Pope Paul VI on October 14, 2018.
14. TRANSLATOR'S NOTE: *Spiritual Path*, 56.
15. Address to the General Congress of the Confederation of the Oratory, October 5, 2000.
16. Homily given in the church of Santa Maria in Vallicella, May 26, 1979.
17. Pontifical Letter for the Fourth Centenary of the death of St. Philip Neri, October 7, 1994.
18. Homily for the Fourth Centenary of the Death of St. Philip Neri, May 28, 1995.
19. Homily given in Santa Maria in Vallicella, October 6, 2000.

CLUNY MEDIA

Designed by Fiona Cecile Clarke, the Cluny Media *logo*
depicts a monk at work in the scriptorium,
with a cat sitting at his feet.

The monk represents our mission to emulate
the invaluable contributions of the monks
of Cluny in preserving the libraries of the West,
our strivings to know and love the truth.

The cat at the monk's feet is Pangur Bán, from the
eponymous Irish poem of the 9th century.
The anonymous poet compares his scholarly
pursuit of truth with the cat's happy hunting of mice.
The depiction of Pangur Bán is an homage to the work
of the monks of Irish monasteries and a sign
of the joy we at Cluny take in our trade.

"Messe ocus Pangur Bán,
cechtar nathar fria saindan:
bíth a menmasam fri scilgg,
mu memna céin im saincheirdd."

Printed in Great Britain
by Amazon

35544815R00192